THE LIFE
AND
TIMES OF
CHAUCER

THE LIFE
AND
TIMES OF
CHAUCER

JOHN GARDNER

ORNAMENTS BY
J. WOLF

BARNES
&NOBLE
BOOKS
NEW YORK

FOR JOAN,

JOEL, AND LUCY

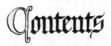 Contents

Acknowledgments

ix

INTRODUCTION

3

ONE: CHAUCER'S ANCESTRY AND SOME REMARKS
ON FOURTEENTH-CENTURY ENGLISH HISTORY

21

TWO: CHAUCER'S YOUTH AND EARLY EDUCATION—LIFE
AND THE SPECTER OF DEATH
ON THE RINGING ISLE (C. 1340–1357)

52

THREE: CHAUCER AS YOUNG COURTIER, SOLDIER,
AND, IN SOME SENSE, LOVER (1357–1360)

90

FOUR: CHAUCER'S FURTHER EDUCATION,
A SUMMARY OF SOME FOURTEENTH-CENTURY IDEAS
OF GREAT IMPORTANCE TO CHAUCER, AND THE POET'S MARRIAGE
TO PHILIPPA ROET—SPECULATIONS
AND SCURRILOUS GOSSIP (1360–1367)

127

FIVE: SIGNIFICANT MOMENTS AND INFLUENCES:
PEDRO THE CRUEL, TWO DEATHS, THAT SHAMELESS
WOMAN AND WANTON HARLOT ALICE PERRERS,
AND ITALIAN ARTISTIC HUMANISM (1367–1373)

168

SIX: CHAUCER'S ADVENTURES AS CELEBRATED POET,

CIVIL SERVANT, AND DIPLOMAT IN THE DECLINING YEARS OF

KING EDWARD III (1374–1377), WITH SOME REMARKS ON

CHAUCER'S HONESTY AND COMMENTS ON HIS ART

204

SEVEN: LIFE DURING THE MINORITY OF RICHARD II—

THE PEASANTS' REVOLT AND ITS AFTERMATH (1377–C. 1385),

WITH MORE SCURRILOUS GOSSIP

228

EIGHT: THE RISE OF GLOUCESTER,

AND CHAUCER'S FORTUNES AS A ROYALIST IN EVIL TIMES

(C. 1385–1389)

263

NINE: THE DEATHS OF GLOUCESTER, JOHN OF GAUNT,

AND THE HERO OF THIS BOOK

286

APPENDIX: THE PRONUNCIATION

OF CHAUCER'S MIDDLE ENGLISH

315

Notes

319

Index follows page 328

Acknowledgments

I have been helped by innumerable people on this book, including all of my Chaucer students over the past twenty years and various university friends and colleagues, especially Donald Howard and Russell Peck, who read versions of this manuscript and helped me avoid many errors. Southern Illinois University at Carbondale has given me grants and time off, year after year, for work on this project, and helped provide research and secretarial assistance, especially Sandra McKimmey, whose long hours helping me on this and other books are beyond the appreciation of words. I also owe thanks to Alan Cohn, Humanities Librarian at Southern Illinois, who has helped me locate and get hold of books and articles I could not have gotten without him; and to E. L. Epstein, who has for ten years patiently listened to my ideas and has sometimes published some of them for me in his magazine Language and Style. *And I thank the Houghton Mifflin Company for permission to quote from F. N. Robinson's second edition of* The Works of Geoffrey Chaucer. *(I have sometimes simplified Robinson's punctuation and spelling, and I've added aids to pronunciation and the interpretation of hard words.) Above all, in a way, I owe thanks to my former teacher John C. McGalliard, in whose Chaucer class, long ago, all this started.*

THE LIFE
AND
TIMES OF
CHAUCER

Introduction

NO POET IN THE WHOLE English literary tradition, not even Shakespeare, is more appealing, either as a man or as an artist, than Geoffrey Chaucer, or more worthy of biography; and no biography, it seems at first glance, should be easier to write. Despite the complexity of the philosophical systems and social mores that shaped his thought, Chaucer's general way of looking at things seems clear as an English April day; and since he worked for the government, which kept elaborate records, we have numerous facts to pin his life to. Yet telling his story proves more difficult than one might think. In his poetry, Chaucer does not talk about himself, except jokingly and trivially. He nowhere tells us in explicit fashion what he thought about particular acquaintances, or even how he felt when his wife died. And the official facts of Chaucer's life, numerous as they are, are frequently lures toward befuddlement, not so much because the poet and his times are mysterious—though they are, and especially so for Americans, to whom the English gentry's titles are as confusing as the names in *War and Peace*—as because, like the missing parts of old frescoes, the vital connections—that is, Chaucer's private feelings and the emotional pressures that gave shape to his age —are for the most part lost utterly, vanished from the world like smoke. However one may pore over the hints and clues in the official records of the fourteenth century, the traditional conjectures about Chaucer's life nearly all remain conjectures and the facts mere facts.

That should hardly surprise us. We can barely understand ourselves, these days; barely piece together our own biographies, though for those we have something like complete information. Since nothing remains of that once wise and gentle, much loved old man (as all his contemporaries were quick to agree)—or nothing but some dry and confusing records, some beautiful, ironic, and ambiguous poetry, two or three pictures, and some bones whose measurements inform us that, if they're really Chaucer's, he was five foot six (about average at the time)—we have no choice but to make up Chaucer's life as if his story were a novel, by the play of fancy on the lost world's dust and scrapings. So Chaucer himself made up

3

the classical age, dressed up young Troilus in crusader's armor and decorated legendary Theseus' Athens with battlemented towers, wide jousting
grounds, and sunny English gardens. This does not mean, of course,
that a biographer has license to be cavalier about historical detail, or ex-
clude possible interpretations of the facts out of preference for others
that make livelier fiction. But while I try in this book to be careful about
facts, my purpose is not academic history, but rather something between
that and poetic celebration of things unchangeable. Human history, it
seems to me, never repeats itself and can never be recaptured; but human
emotions endure like granite, for instance the lust of old men for young
girls, or the imprisoned wife's restlessness, or the anger of the scorned
homosexual—Chaucer's subjects. The age-old human emotions live on
and on, generation after generation, and the best poets feel them or spy
them out in others and cunningly transfix them; and wondering about
that, wondering about when and where the poet perhaps experienced
the emotion he describes—since no one will ever know the answer for
sure—is as much the business of the novelist as that of the historian.
For all the history I include in this book, I am no historian but a novelist
and poet, a literary disciple come centuries late. I include mere moments
of historical background, dull lightning flashes that reveal in frozen
gesture events whose development—in comparison to the story of any
single human life—were as lumbering and awesome as the shifting of
continents on Earth's vast skin. I make no pretense of explaining or even
connecting such movements. I mean only to convey my own impression
of how they affect, subtly yet profoundly, one's subjective image of the
hero of this book.

What kind of man was Geoffrey Chaucer? One begins on the answer
with easy confidence, but almost immediately one finds oneself faltering,
hunting through the poetry in increasing dismay, and beginning to
equivocate, to bluff.

What Bach and Beethoven are to music, Chaucer and Shakespeare are
to English poetry. For all the calm of his familiar portrait, Shakespeare
was a towering Romantic genius, a man who, like Beethoven, seemed
to know everything about human emotion and to flinch from none of it,
building plays not out of dramatic theory but by the impetus inherent in
conflicting passions, a poet willing to take any aesthetic risk. Chaucer,
on the other hand, was a sort of medieval, well-tempered Bach (Bach
himself was, at least on occasion, an inkpot thrower), an artist-philoso-
pher more tranquil and abstract, more conservative and formal than any
poet of the Renaissance. Though a "difficult" poet, he presented himself

as a naïve and merry storyteller, an avoider of the dark spots in human experience, a sedulous and tactful entertainer of princes. Though a devastating mimic when he turned his acquaintances into characters in poems, he remained, even at his most satiric, a devoted servant and celebrator of the orderly, God-filled universe revealed in the *Goldberg Variations.*

The comparison is oversimple, of course. In certain moods Shakespeare was more "classical," so to speak, than Bach—in the conservative, perfectly shaped *Tempest,* for instance. But what appeals to us most powerfully in Shakespeare's plays is the unexpected flight, the glimpse of darkness when Hamlet rambles or Lear rages, the leap into dazzling disquisition on Queen Mab, the Fool's moment of surreal precision, the gentle, stabilizing loblogic of some well-meaning dunce—in short, the cross-hatch of madness, stupidity, anguish, and confusion that frames and foregrounds those white bolts of sanity that strike when Shakespeare's characters lay out, simply and beautifully, how it is. And in the same way Chaucer, whose painstaking technique, endless revision, and concern about form would make him, if nothing else did, a model of the classical impulse, was in certain moods as personal, as original, and in his own mild way as eager to shock, as was Beethoven. As Beethoven attacked rococo music, emancipating musicians and their art from "the princely rabble," as he called them, so Chaucer more gently mocked and brought to ruin, or at times transmuted, those empty, artificial poetic forms so popular in his day with the lesser French and Italian poets—dream visions, stories of love-saints, and so on—forms aimed less at truth and beauty, before Chaucer took hold of them, than at amusing the courtly genteel. What came before Chaucer, in France especially (discounting one masterpiece, the *Roman de la Rose*) was wine-sippers' poetry, the poetry of house arrest, that is, verse entertainment designed to help people in remote castles get through the long evening—people in some cases not free to do much else except hear poetry, being prisoners in their own houses or some other great man's, as was King John of France after his capture by the Black Prince, or mad Isabella of England soon after her affair with Roger Mortimer. What Chaucer introduced was poetry freed of its courtly trappings, freed of philosophical narrowness, and freed of preciousness and deadly sobriety. Again like Beethoven, Chaucer occasionally inclined toward heretical positions—though he was never a man to seize any position with the revolutionary zeal of, say, John Wyclif or, worse, Wat Tyler. And, like Beethoven, or like Shakespeare, Chaucer took great delight in the outrageous and obscene pun, the practical joke, the devastating portrait.

But Geoffrey Chaucer was, for all that, no lover of windy crags and tors, no passionate, daemonic individualist. He was concerned about improving the social order. He understood and to some extent sympathized with the oppressed—including, especially, women. But his approach to the evils of his time was not protest or diatribe, the approach of his poetic contemporary, William Langland, in *Piers Plowman*. Chaucer settled for prayer and for the gentle prod of comedy or, at most, mild satire. However inaccurate in some details, the image of Geoffrey Chaucer largely at peace with the world, dabbling in poetry when not too busy at the customshouse, or in Genoa or Paris on business for the king, or sitting in parliament, or attending to his family, his religious devotions, his country place in Kent—the image of Chaucer as portly courtier dashing off little experiments in form, serenely fathering English poetry with two plump fingers of his left hand closed on a wineglass stem, his emotions as tranquil as the heavenly spheres he and Plato believed in, as Bach would later—is in general outline the image the poet himself liked to foster, for instance in his numerous delightful self-portraits and asides. One thinks, for example, of the comic passage in the *House of Fame*, where the golden eagle bearing poor terrified "Geffrey" heavenward says of him, tolerantly disparaging, that he writes only love stories he's found in old books, knowing not even the gossip about

> thy verray neyghëborës
> That duellen almost at thy dorës,   [*dwell*]
> Thou herist neyther that ne this;
> For when thy labour doon al ys,
> And hast mad allë thy rekenyngës,   [*reckonings (at the*
> In stede of reste and newë thyngës,   *customs office)*]
> Thou goost hom to thy hous anoon,
> And, also domb as any stoon,
> Thou sittest at another book
> Tyl fully daswed ys thy look. . . .   [*dazed*]

Chaucer was, of course, a serious poet; as dedicated a comic poet as has ever lived. The more we learn about his way of working—and lately scholars have been learning a good deal about Chaucer's technique—the more clearly we see just how serious he was about his "craft so long to lernë." But Chaucer's artistic seriousness was tempered, self-effacing, like everything else about the man. Like Shakespeare, he wrote as much for the pit as for the gallery, as much for the young as for sly old philosophers. This is why his poetry has, like Shakespeare's, immediate appeal, once the stumbling block of his language is removed. At the same time, precisely because Chaucer's poetry works on many levels, repaying reading after reading, one discovers that the better one knows this poetry, the more difficulty one encounters in trying to explain what it "means" or, indeed, what kind of man Chaucer was.

Every well-educated English speaker has, or at any rate thinks he has, a fair intuitive understanding of Shakespeare, both the man and at least some of the better known plays. A few years ago one might have claimed that the same held for Chaucer. But for all the lilt of Chaucer's verse, for all the clarity of his poetic voice, our picture of the man has recently become cloudy, defeatured by contradiction, some scholars finding him one kind of person, and some another, the various camps all armed to the teeth with facts. Essentially the problem is that readers were for a long time fooled by the poet's seeming openness and have now become wary, suspicious, willing to believe anything about that being who seemed once such a harmless, lovable elf.

Unostentatious, fond of hiding the layered complexity of his poetic structures—fond, as all master craftsmen are, of making the enormously difficult seem simple, the laboriously achieved seem obvious and all-of-a-piece as a pudding—Chaucer managed to trick most of his critics since the sixteenth century into thinking his poetry and character as naïve as they seemed. Poems as tortuously reasoned and meticulously crafted as John Donne's, but much longer than Donne's, he gave the appearance of flowing from his inkhorn as lightly and merrily as water from a spring. And the result of his deceptive simplicity has been that, except for ill-grounded Victorian searchings for amorous scandal or political intrigue, most readers, from the late sixteenth century until the early twentieth, no more felt inclined to ask what deeper possibilities lay hidden in the purling of Chaucer's verse than they would ask the shadow of a trout the time of day.

That now has changed; or, to put it in a way more favorable to earlier Chaucerian scholars, centuries of text collecting, collating and editing, philological study, and historical research have put us in a position to see that Chaucer was considerably more learned, more firmly committed in his philosophy and religion, and in some respects sterner in his judgment of man's follies, than we formerly supposed. In the past quarter century, Chaucer's manipulation of rhetorical devices, symbols, and various kinds of allusion, his sexual, religious, and mathematical punning, his poetic use of alchemy, physics, and dream psychology, have made his poetry a scholar's gold mine—which is to say, an endless source of mostly dreary but occasionally distinguished scholarly books and articles. With not many exceptions this activity has been specialized (the Advent tradition in patristic exegesis and scholastic thought, and its relevance to Chaucer's House of Fame), too elaborate and, in the usual case, too pedantic, too stuffed with snippets of Latin and the dry agonals of schismatic popes, to be accessible or useful to the non-specialist. But the picture of Chaucer which seems to be emerging—the sketch I will try to give color in this book—is among the most interesting discoveries being made by literary scholars of this century.

Most of what earlier scholars believed about Chaucer's personality remains true and obvious, undisputed except by the lunatic fringe. He was gentle, sensible; a shrewd and for the most part compassionate observer of humanity; as sane a man as ever walked in England. But he was doing far more with those queer dream-vision poems, tales, and lyrics than anybody guessed; and at least since publication of the complete *Life-Records* in 1966, it has come to be understood that in his daily life he was doing rather more, and in some cases rather different, things than his earlier biographers imagined. Not that recently discovered information has drastically changed the basic outlines of Chaucer's biography as it has been understood for the past fifty years. The insights and new interpretations which have come, one by one, from those who have sifted and resifted the facts, have for the most part simply confirmed older theories, filled out the picture, corrected small errors or, here and there, made old puzzles more confusing. But if few new tidings of Chaucer's whereabouts, honors, or expenses have been brought to light, our picture of everything around him has changed—his friends and patrons, his familiar landscape, his milieu. More and more, social, literary, and political historians are revising their ideas about the fourteenth century. King Richard II, once regularly viewed as England's silliest king (as Shakespeare pictured him), has lately been held up as one of the period's more imaginative monarchs, a man of clear vision and intelligent policy, doomed partly by forces beyond his control and partly by his character as an obstinate idealist in an age of wolves. (The wolves, too, have begun to be rehabilitated.) New historical research has revised our understanding of the economics of farm and city life; the role of the so-called but in fact nonexistent "party of Gaunt" (Chaucer's friend, patron, and brother-in-law, John of Gaunt) in the struggle of king and parliament; the precise effects of the plagues and riots which repeatedly battered medieval England; and the larger significance of trade agreements and treaties of the kind Geoffrey Chaucer himself, as an ambassador to France and Italy, helped to frame.

Oddly enough, despite these revisions of once standard opinion, despite the changed picture, the added information, no one has so far tried piecing together an accurate, complete biography reflecting our new knowledge. For one of England's two finest poets, we have, at the present time—discounting pleasant, outdated books—only books for specialists, for the most part studies of the poetry in isolation from the

poet's life and times. One can easily understand why biographical study
has grown unfashionable, of course. Almost nothing in Chaucer's poetry
is occasional; in fact, we can rarely be certain of a given poem's date of
composition. Nevertheless, knowing what kind of man he was, the kinds
of friends he had, and the kind of world he lived in should help us understand why he fashioned his poetry as he did.

And so I have gathered the available scholarly materials in a heap,
to make a stab at sorting them and finding out how much it is possible to
say, or rather make up, about the character of Chaucer: how he lived and
died, how he wrote poetry, how we might best read it. By available materials I mean of course a veritable Alp of writings, on fourteenth-century
history in general and on Chaucer in particular, to say nothing of the
period's philosophy, rhetorical theory, economics, and so forth. I've attempted no more here than to convey a more or less accurate impression.
My idea has been to sketch the poet in the illumination of his time, place,
and station—his history and the character of the courts he worked for—
and to suggest some of the finer details, the tics, opinions, and customary
worries, and, more important, Chaucer's greatness and goodness, by brief
and general comment on his work. The portrait which emerges will be
recognized at once as partly personal, that is, biased, not strictly a com-
posite made of other people's notions of the man and his work, although
I've read everything I could get hold of and have incorporated into my
speculations on Chaucer's life and art all that I've been able to make fit
with a manlike, imaginatively fused image, a color portrait without
noticeable extra ears or chopped-off fingers. I've tried to be judicious and
relatively objective, accepting suggestions, struggling to suppress my own
predispositions; but my work must inevitably have to some degree the
failing I see in other people's books, wherein the portrait of the poet
comes out oddly like a picture of the biographer.

I might acknowledge here one conscious bias. Although I've tried to
accommodate others' opinions, a few I've resisted, namely, those which
begin by insisting on Chaucer's medievalness and then so narrowly de-
fine medievalness as to rule out all that's most visible in the poems, such
as the humor. By a sort of scholarly sleight-of-hand, wherein the ideas of
men like St. Augustine, nine centuries before Chaucer, become the ruling
opinions of the fourteenth century, it has been made to appear in a few
recent studies—now generally rejected—that Chaucer was not, as most
people have imagined, a humane and genially comic poet. It has been
shown, rightly, that he frequently makes use of Christian symbolism, biblical allusion, and patterns of detail which establish something like extended allegory. Such features, misunderstood, can suggest the puritanical
arthritis of John Bunyan, or Jonathan Swift's ironic Christian leer. In

their historical context, the Middle Ages, they can be made to suggest doctrinal rigidity, contempt for the world: St. Augustine's scorn of his libertine days, revealed in his *Confessions,* or the Anglo-Saxon Alcuin's disapproval of the pagan Virgil he was forever quoting. Presented with this darker view of Chaucer, we are asked to abandon the complex poems for simple, rather righteous theories.

Balanced literary criticism, balanced understanding of anything, is based, as we know when we stop to think, on juxtaposition and exclusion, the principle in the old story of the man who, when asked, "How's your wife?" responded, "Compared to what?" Chaucer was Christian, but not as intensely so as, for example, St. Peter. He was interested in the theory of monarchy, but not as intensely so as Richard II. A certain kind of Christianity—a certain style in the manipulation of symbol and allusion—was a part of the general literary style of Chaucer's age. Many things in Chaucer's poetry reflect that style; some do not. To understand what Chaucer means—to understand his attitude toward his partly traditional, partly original subject matter—the critic must determine what elements of the poetry are part of the general medieval style: what Chaucer has in common with the man who wrote *Sir Gawain and the Green Knight* or the man who wrote *Piers Plowman,* what things belong to Chaucer's personal style, and what relationship obtains between the two. Most Chaucerians agree that once one has separated what T. S. Eliot would call "tradition" from "individual talent" in Chaucer's work, Chaucer stands out among his poetic contemporaries as remarkably original.

Though no defense is really needed for the standard view of Chaucer's originality, it is worthwhile asking, here at the start of this assay at reconstruction, where exactly Chaucer stood in relation to his poetic contemporaries, that is, what Chaucer's individuality consisted of. The answer, of course, is that he was an original poet in any number of ways—among others his characteristic choice of themes, his taste in subject matter, his preference for particular earlier writers (poets, philosophers, religious thinkers), and his attitudes toward, say, women and money. But when we compare Chaucer's choices with those commonly made by his fellow English poets, certain features do, I think, stand out, and perhaps the most significant, though not the first we notice, is this: In nearly everything he wrote, Chaucer worried one basic philosophical question, *the nature and spiritual effect of love.* Chaucer wrote, of course, during one of the world's great moments for love poetry; but his handling of love is nevertheless one of the essential ingredients in his uniqueness.

Chaucer's basic subject has sometimes been identified—too loosely, as we'll see—with what has been described as the central theme of all medieval literature, "What is the proper use of 'the World'?", a theme as old, by one formulation, as Homer's *Iliad,* but a theme especially urgent in the Christian Middle Ages, when "the World" was both profoundly appealing and suspect, standing out—as it did not for Homer— in dramatic contrast to the promised ultimate haven of the soul. The theme is one Chaucer cannot help having thought about, strolling beside the Thames, his hands behind his back, his round head thrown forward, large eyes staring groundward with the expression of a man "fully dazed"—a plump, conservatively dressed public official with slightly flushed cheeks, slowly heading home from his customshouse office to his handsome mansion above Aldgate in the London city wall. He was perhaps still musing on the problem of the World in his house late that night, frowning in his medieval spectacles (Roger Bacon's invention, half a century before)—the children all in bed, Philippa across the dim, shuttered room from him, fashioning small neeedlepoint flowers of vermilion and gold.

Stroking his beard, reading by fluttering candlelight his copy of Macrobius's *Commentary on the Dream of Scipio,* he must have turned over the problem's complexities, its numerous, never quite satisfactory solutions, from *carpe diem* to Macrobius and St. Paul. It was the central issue in the Christian's earthly trial, but more important, in a way, it was at the heart of most of the serious poetry Chaucer knew, the poetry against which he measured his artistic progress. (For all his humor, for all his faith, Chaucer was something of a worrier. Worry is one of the regular features of his comic self-portraits. He worries himself sleepless in the *Book of the Duchess,* worries frantically, in the *House of Fame,* that the eagle carrying him to visions may drop him; he wrings his hands in anguish, worrying about his characters in *Troilus and Criseyde,* and worries, as a pilgrim in the *Canterbury Tales,* that Our Host, Harry Bailey, may again interrupt him. Jokes, certainly, but like his jokes about his stoutness, they probably have some basis in fact. As this biography will show, Chaucer had, from time to time, more than a little to worry about.) The question must have vexed him, and like all vexing questions, it was personal, finally. He worked hard, lived by rule, as if heaven might be watching, while that great, thieving lout, his associate Nick Brembre . . . All very well to say, with eyes rolled skyward, as he'd written not long since in the *Parliament of Birds,* "ourë present worldës lyvës spacë/Nis but a maner deth, what wey we tracë. . . ." But ah, the seductive, sly-eyed World was not so easily dismissed in these days of Ricardian opulence—radiant entertainments, crimson-bannered spires. All the poets agreed.

He'd no doubt recognized that standard theme, the siren-appeal of the things of this world, in provincial court performances of the anonymous alliterative *Morte Arthure* in the days of King Edward III.[1] Chaucer had been younger then, just beginning as a poet, and the sharp-eyed old Westerner's thudding native meter—his *"rum, ram, ruf* by lettre," as Chaucer's Parson would describe it in the *Canterbury Tales*—had had, for Chaucer, no particular appeal. All the same, it was a stirring piece of poetry in its way, and a bold piece of criticism, even though in a dialect most of the audience had trouble understanding. The old Westerner was interested in nationalism, politics, war—particularly the great war of Edward III in France—and he was troubled about the queer intertanglement of good and evil in affairs of state, especially the insidious relationship of princely glory and overweening pride. He'd set to verse the legend of King Arthur's war with the Roman Emperor Lucius, a transparent allegory of Edward's war, and by imagistic and dramatic means he'd shown the degree to which Arthur was simultaneously majestic and monstrous. Wealth and power, the glories of this world, and overweening pride, were near of kin. So far so good. But there the old man of the West had reached his limit. To resolve the ambiguity in Arthur's nature (or that of any great king), the poet had applied like hopeful phlebotomies the standard legal, philosophical, and religious opinions handed down to him: a warlike king without a clearly valid claim, whatever his seeming chivalry, is a criminal aggressor; trust in Fortune leads to the failure of one's hopes; man should seek to do the will of God. Chaucer knew, listening in the audience—his hands folded, his eyes half-closed— that none of this had in fact much to do with King Edward's situation, and what proved King Arthur a monster in the poem, his killing and ravaging, had already occurred, and been noted by his victims, long before he'd overreached his claim, turned to trust in Fortune, or forgotten his Christian vassalage. Though the poem had a fine swashbuckling swing and a moral that would be pleasing to King Edward's successor, pacific King Richard—though the poem was, indeed, beside any English poem since Anglo-Saxon times a transcendent work of art—the real dramatic issue, the interpenetration of evil and good, was one the poet's mind was too loyal to old doctrines to penetrate. He delighted in war, in such lordly feats as those of the king's illustrious son in the magnificent black armor, le Prince d'Angleterre, although the poet also knew, and wouldn't pretend he didn't, that war wrecks convents and orphans little children. What could one do with such a paradox except copy it down and advise *contemptus mundi*?

Chaucer had seen early that he could do better than that. Pride of position, delight in the world, was a dangerous business—as he would write later, in his punning poem "Truth," "the wrastling for this world axeth [asketh] a fall"—but there was more to it than that.

Other of Chaucer's contemporaries, the authors of the *Parliament of the Three Ages* and *Winner and Waster* (the *Morte Arthure*-poet's apparent disciples—although the dating of these poems has proved somewhat uncertain), worked related thematic material with more or less the same intense concern and something of the same inability to pierce the mystery. Life is splendid, life is ghastly; man should hoard, man should spend. In the introduction to the *Parliament,* a poaching expedition is offered as (apparently) an emblem of the usual concupiscent (as opposed to ascetic) human life: it's hard and it's thrilling and when they finally catch you doing it they hang you. To all this world's blandishments, in each of these poems, the answer is doctrine, humility, faith, though at the end of the *Parliament* the poet has made his peace with the grove—the green world of nature. Like the alliterative *Morte Arthure,* the poems have undeniable charm and beauty, and the contempt of the world they advise is not harsh; yet their vision, Chaucer would know (if in fact he ever heard them), was limited. Their authors were able to love God and nature, including nature's law of creation and destruction, gathering and spending (that is, "winning" and "wasting"); but the heart of man was an embarrassment.

Though Long Will Langland might not look it, raw-boned and pock-marked, ranting at country and small-town humanity in a long black coat (Chaucer avoided him as he would the plague, but he kept track of his work, kept track of his readings in baronial courts and followed, with distaste, the cancerous proliferation of copies of his poem), Langland was a man able to penetrate doctrine's inadequacy and also the world's, and hunt for an adjustment. What seems true in theory, like what seems to be true when you're having a dream, may prove crooked, ill-considered when you try to apply it to the real world where things wax and wane and, in many cases, bite. In *Piers Plowman* Langland had presented this conflict of ideal and real, now looking at the world and observing its desperately struggling virtues, its chaos and stupidity, now dozing and visioning solutions which, when he'd awaken again, would prove skewbald. His subject matter—like Chaucer's own—was "Everything": poverty in the villages, the church calendar, unjust taxation, disease, corruption in King Richard's court, the seven deadly sins, the wickedness of friars, England's changing weather. . . . But what matters here is this: Langland saw behind the question, saw that the world changes (in Langland's poem, "Lady Meed," Reward, can be harmful or valuable, depending), so that truth in man must be a quality of mind and heart, a quality only apprehensible in terms of some model character, for instance, a faithful English plowman like Piers, or for instance Christ (in Langland's vision, the two turn out to be the same). It is true enough that, as Chaucer once mentioned in conversation with John of Gaunt (unfortunately no record of the conversation survives), Langland's plodding, sometimes staggering verse treats the subject of "the proper use of 'the World' "; but Langland was no mere repeater of old saws, centuries-old doctrine. Langland had boldly rejected the stance of helplessly thrown up hands, the stance of the saintly in thirteenth-century paintings; had impatiently dismissed the whole cringing business of Should-I-take-pleasure-in-the-world-or-not? ("Avoid luxury, avoid causing people needless pain, don't be fooled by a Papal pardon, and finish your soup," was Langland's advice.) What Langland offered was a positive program, a way of adjusting the ideal and the real in the spirit of Truth. "Brothers, I have shown you Piers," says Will Langland, banging his stick. "Now behave like Piers." (Chaucer grinned, glancing up past his shoulder at his elongated shadow on the wall. Except for the tone, the banging stick, he and Langland were closer than it was pleasant for a gentleman to admit.)

Somewhere up around York, where Edward III had gotten married, or perhaps in nearby Lancashire, lived Chaucer's greatest English rival, the man known today as the *Gawain*-poet. Recent evidence suggests that he was a priest named John of Massey, brother to the muralist Hugo of Massey, who may have done the illustrations in the poet's manuscript; "Hugo de" appears on one of the pictures, which are muralist in style, and other biographical details seem to fit.[2] Chaucer and John Massey—if that was his name—may have known each other. One of the poems commonly attributed to Massey, *St. Erkenwald,* shows a knowledge of London, and Chaucer probably visited Yorkshire, where several of his friends had country estates, on numerous occasions. Chaucer may have had Massey's most famous poem in mind when he alluded, in the *Canterbury Tales,* to "Gawayn, with his olde curteisyë," and he may have been thinking of Massey's *Pearl* at several points in the *Book of the Duchess.* If the two poets did in fact know each other, or know each other's work, they surely felt some affinity. Massey was a consummate gentleman, had a wit to rival Chaucer's own, and knew as well as Chaucer how to capture in English verse the spicy essence of an English seductress. More to the point, though not more important, he knew about "the World."

In his four linked poems, *Pearl, Purity, Patience,* and *Sir Gawain and the Green Knight,* Massey presents a tour-de-force treatment of two common medieval themes: *purity* (God's nature and the complementary state of a child or saint who goes to heaven directly, never having sinned) and *patience* (God's tolerance and the complementary state of a repentant sinner loyally serving God and awaiting his pardon). No poet in the whole tradition of English literature has written more lush and lyrical descriptions of the natural world and the courtly world of tapestries, jewels, beautiful ladies and handsome knights, music, cuisine, and chivalric ritual. Here sits the sweet, seductive World at her fairest; here, if anywhere, we ought to face the great question, "What is the proper use of 'the World'?" But we don't. True, Massey now and then shows his heritage. He mentions, in *Purity,* that a man and wife should not make love with the lights on; it might lead to defilement, more sex than love. But such moments in the poetry are notable because of their rarity. The real problems, the *plot* problems, are these: In *Pearl* a devout and decent Christian has a dream in which he meets the ghost of his daughter, and, though he knows better, he cannot help loving her more than he loves God. In *Purity,* a vivid and inventive retelling of Old Testament stories, some men revel in filth, sinning against purity, and others struggle with doubt, sinning against patience, while the best precariously and bravely behave as nobly as they can. In *Patience,* Jonah's story, the hero fumes because God reconsiders his plan to wreck Nineveh, making Jonah look silly after all his dire prophesies, until Jonah comes to see that God, if ruled not by patience but by self-regard and embarrassment, would have wrecked the whole universe long ago. And in *Sir Gawain and the Green Knight* a perfect courtier betrays his principles not for love of wealth or power or sex but in stark fear of losing his life. For John Massey as for William Langland (and Plato, for that matter), it is assumed that men want pleasure, not pain, that life's great aches as a rule come not from wanting still more jewels, still more mistresses or lovers, another heaping plate of breast of swan, but from the loss of dear children, from humiliation in company, from doubt that God is watching, and fear of facing Death without a penknife. Trading his Christian and chivalric codes for a green piece of cloth with a spell on it (he hopes), Sir Gawain commits, technically, a sin of pride. But that is a harsh way of stating the morality of the poem. Gawain's real sin is mere humanness, the ardent, sad wish to live, not die, which God and one's fellow human beings can forgive. When Gawain returns to Arthur's court, tells of his "shame" and shows the green cloth he now wears as a reminder, the court laughs merrily, glad that he survived, and insists on putting on green cloths exactly like Sir Gawain's. A version of the motto of the Order of the Garter is appended to this supremely genteel, supremely tolerant poem. And fittingly so. In the same spirit King Edward, picking up from the floor a lady's garter—his mistress, but a lady of inestimable worth—said in French, that being his primary language, "Evil to him who thinks evil of this," and the high-minded Order was founded.

There is a faint possibility that in King Richard II's court, for a time at least, the favorite poet was not Chaucer but a man named John Gower, "moral Gower," as Chaucer called him in his last-minute dedication of *Troilus and Criseyde*—and, despite one's hopes, Chaucer was probably not scoffing. Gower wrote in Latin, French, and English—the English book strongly influenced by Chaucer and full of borrowed lines (but fair is fair: Chaucer stole back a hundred times). Gower's best poem is the Latin *Vox Clamantis,* the first third of which presents a clear-eyed description, considering the day, of the Peasants' Revolt of 1381, though the poem most often read is, naturally, the English *Confessio Amantis.* Gower is a hard man to talk about briefly, but this much may be said "in generall," as Gower is always saying: John Gower had the keenest, most orderly of minds, one firmly entrenched in Augustinian attitudes, and also a brilliant eye for detail, as the *Vox Clamantis* shows, though unfortunately an eye he did not value.

Gower's *Confessio Amantis* is the confession of a lover to his love-priest, an interminable confession which, since time has been suspended, allows the love-priest to tell the lover, and sometimes the lover to tell the priest, exemplary stories on the virtues and vices of the love religion. Thus among other things the poem is, like the *Canterbury Tales* or Boccaccio's *Decameron,* a story collection with a dramatic frame. As a piece dealing with the love religion—that is, the courtly lover's seriocomic parody of Christian devotion, wherein he "worships" his lady, "prays" for her "saving grace," and so on—the poem may be set beside several poems of Chaucer's, notably the *Book of the Duchess* and *Troilus and Criseyde.* Though critics have not always noticed the fact, neither the priest nor the lover in Gower's poem is very smart. Retelling old stories familiar to the audience, Gower subtly alters details, here exaggerating a trifle, here pretending to have missed his own point, deftly, urbanely revealing for his audience the confusion and ultimate childishness of both priest and lover and, indeed, of all people passionately caught up in love. The poetic result is a delightful court entertainment (though one clocked to self-destruct with the passing of the sophisticated court which occasioned it), a literary trick in which mooning knights and ladies of the court, and all those too stupid to get the literary jokes, are harmlessly ridiculed, while people sufficiently religious, philosophical, and well bred to discern the irony are slyly congratulated. Gentle and compassionate as he was by nature, we may nevertheless be sure Geoffrey Chaucer was not the last to smile.

Gower's ostensible subject is love, and like Chaucer's (and like Augustine's, nearly ten centuries earlier), his handling of that subject sets up an identification between the Lady and the World. As a courtly lover, out of his wits over another man's wife, may crave more of his lady than he has any right to, so carnal, dim-spirited man may want more of "the World" than Providence allows him. What is the proper use of the world? "Keep aloof," says moral Gower, "shake hands with it lightly, as if absentmindedly; never squeeze." Which is to say, Gower's subject is not love at all; love is his springboard to doctrine. As in his earlier poems, the *Mirour de l'Omme* and *Vox Clamantis,* his interest is in surveying the virtues and vices of the world and giving good counsel. This is a program not to be scorned; but also it is a program not to be confused with Geoffrey Chaucer's.

Chaucer was, not ostensibly but actually, a love poet. Anyone can, at certain times of his life, adopt Gower's broad, thoroughly adult and philosophical view of love. Young Troilus adopts it; but the invisible arrow strikes, his chest fills with that sharp, not imaginary pain, half agony, half unspeakable joy, that we've all experienced, and he has no choice but to take his religion and philosophy head on. So it goes in nearly all of Chaucer's poetry. He tells no swashbuckling tales of King Arthur (only the Wife of Bath's little comic love story), presents no grand surveys of man like Langland's, or like Gower's in the *Mirour* or *Vox Clamantis.* He writes of happy and unhappy lovers, seducers, loyal husbands, a distraught widower, a vindictive homosexual, and, repeatedly, of the diligent and sober-minded philosopher of· love, hunting for certainty in a world where there are no certainties, himself. When he writes on other things—the tricks of crooked friars and summoners, the trials of a saint, the troubles of the rich and poor, or the conflict of lords and vassals—love philosophy, in Boethius's extended sense (on which more later), is invariably the key.

So the question must be: What was Chaucer's position on love? Did he believe, like Augustine centuries earlier, that love must either be charitable in the old sense—selfless, compassionate, and helpful—or else carnal, that is, piggish? Or did he incline to the persuasion, like Plato, that love of a woman, or of an emerald ring, or of anything else, has in it the potential to lead to a nobler and higher love? To say that his attitude was strictly Augustinian is to say that Chaucer was a "medieval" poet according to the hard-nosed notion of the Middle Ages largely invented by the Renaissance. To say that he inclined (more than Augustine) toward Platonism, that he found ways of rationalizing a fundamental love of life—fine houses, beautiful women, devoted friends—is to identify Chaucer with that aspect of the Middle Ages which came into full or at any rate self-conscious flower in the Renaissance and which we tend to call "modern." Not that Chaucer had to be either an Augustinian or a Platonist (a false opposition in any case). Most men, including men of genius, are not doctrinal. Most of humanity, including the wise, simply muddle through, suspending judgments, making tentative assertions, hopefully snatching what will serve for the moment, groping emotion by emotion toward the grave. That was especially true in the late four-teenth century, after William Ockham had severed the knot tying science to religion. The orderly universe set forth in Aquinas's thirteenth-century *Summa Theologica* had in large part given way, at least in England, under the pressure of the approximately coeval ideas of Robert Grosseteste and Roger Bacon, who had discovered through optics that nothing is certain except what we know by revelation in the Bible—and even here there were some efforts at historical criticism. This early version of the uncertainty principle was an idea of shocking importance in its time, and one that became still more important as it became more familiar in the fourteenth century. Brought down to Chaucer's day by Oxford philosophers who'd been students of Bacon (some of them probably Chaucer's friends), it would be an idea at the nervous center of every-thing Chaucer wrote. It was partly his deep sense of the uncertainty of things (not including the love and mercy of God) that enabled Chaucer to take harsh old doctrines with a grain of salt and to affirm the world, celebrate love, in a way a man less well informed on contemporary sci-ence and philosophy—John Gower, for example—could not do.

Thus we find that the intuitively satisfying traditional view of Chaucer, which describes him not as a grim satirist who felt contempt for things worldly but as a genial and sympathetic humorist, a "servant of lovers," as he calls himself in the *Troilus*—a man amused by and in love with the world, though occasionally critical—is still, at least in general, the right view. It fits with the history of Chaucer's life and the character of the society in which he moved, and it fits the poems. In Roger Bacon's terms—"experience" (scientific experiment or direct observation) versus "authority"—Chaucer's first commitment was to life, although he had also a healthy regard for authority, which is to say, literally, that in treacherous times he kept his head. And the traditional view fits, too, with the abundant evidence that the tendency of medieval thought with which Chaucer was most closely aligned emotionally was that form of Christian Neoplatonism represented by, for instance, Boethius, Ma-crobius, and St. Bonaventura, who (like Plato) saw the world as a ladder for ascending toward God (with the help of prayer, Bonaventura would say). He was a man comfortable in his relations with both worlds, this one and the next, though no one knew better how hard it is to keep the proper balance.[3]

He had a critical eye, as all his poetry proves. No fault in man or woman or poem could escape him. But he was more amused than judgmental. He enjoyed his green medieval world and all its citizens, enjoyed even execrable poetry, which in his last years he parodied—ironically celebrated—again and again. Others might scoff at the doggerel that delighted the cruder English magnates, but Chaucer saw hilarious potential in those jingling idiotic rhythms and cockeyed rhymes, so that for all his reputation as a "serious" poet he could joyfully write—

> *List*eth, *lord*ës, in *good* en*tent*,
> And *I* wol *tell*ë *verrayment*   [*truly*]
> Of *myrthe* and *of* so*lás,*
> *Al* of a *knyght* was *fair* and *gent*   [*genteel*]
> In *bat*aille *and* in *tourney*ment,
> His *nam*ë *was sir*ë Tho*pas*!

In a dark, troubled age, as it seems to us, he was a comfortable optimist, serene, full of faith. For all his delight in irony—and all his poetry has a touch of that—he affirmed this life, to say nothing of the next, from the bottom of his capacious heart. Joy—satisfaction without a trace of sentimental simple-mindedness—is still the effect of Chaucer's poetry and of Chaucer's personality as it emerges from the poems. It is not the simple faith of a credulous man in a credulous age: no poet has ever written better on the baffling complexity of things. But for all the foggy shiftings of the heart and mind, for all the obscurity of God's huge plan, to Chaucer life was a magnificent affair, though sadly transient; and when we read him now, six centuries later, we are instantly persuaded.

In this introduction I've said very little that's at all specific about what the reader will encounter in the progress of this book. As I've mentioned, I speak now and then about particular moments in fourteenth-century English history. Chaucer, as a diplomat and favored court poet, was very much involved with the history of his time and directly affected by its twists and turns. Even events in which he may not have been personally involved can sometimes shed light on his character and art. As for my version of Chaucer's life, my aim has not been startling originality but completeness, accuracy, and a measure of novelistic vividness; that is, I've tried to make the story interesting and—following the best authorities—to avoid the standard misconceptions. It has sometimes been suggested that Chaucer's origins were humble; that Chaucer was not very happily married; that in his latter years he was sickly and unable to work well at poetry; that he was profligate and in the end died poor, or even—

as early biographers like William Godwin believed—in prison. Probably some of this can never be resolved to anyone's satisfaction, but my version of the story—tentative here and there, and usually derivative—is that none of it is true. Chaucer was born rich, relatively speaking, and by diligence, legal ability, intelligence, and the extraordinary charm befitting an ambassador to Italy (on one occasion there to borrow money for the king), he grew steadily richer all his life, or at any rate rich on paper, since it was not always easy, in Chaucer's day, to collect what the government owed you. However his marriage to Philippa Roet may have come about—an interesting business which I examine at some length—he was happily married and fond of his children, and devoted, too, to his long-time friend, now brother-in-law, Gaunt. At least until very near the end, he was a healthy, vigorous man, a political conservative fearful of the peasantry—because of all he had to lose and for other reasons—and distrustful of the rising power of Commons, even when he sat as a member of that body. He was not only in some loose sense a royalist, or member of the king's party; he was a man who, even without John of Gaunt's protection, was willing to risk close partisan involvement with Richard II despite the threat of the magnates who opposed him. He spent the last years of his life putting his affairs in order, dabbling in law, running errands for the king, and, whenever he had time and found himself in the mood, recasting and polishing the whole body of his poetry, many parts of which he left in disarray at his death, with endings excised or never completed and great swatches out of place, never to be put right. He died of old age. (He was fifty-nine or sixty, but not our modern sixty. At sixty-five that former warhorse Edward III was doddering and senile.)

My examination of Chaucer's life inevitably turns now and then to the poetry, the reason for our interest in the wise and gentle public servant; but this book is not meant to be a critical study of Chaucer's art. Sometimes the poetry illuminates Chaucer's life; sometimes—more often than present-day critics generally acknowledge—the poetry directly comments on people, events, and notions his original audience recognized. But for the most part I avoid discussion of the poetry, hoping I may write of that in the detail it deserves another time. I quote in Middle English, but Chaucer's language is less difficult than one might think. (For help with the poet's antique tongue, see the Appendix.)

"And now"—to borrow a phrase from one of the first great modern Chaucerians, F. J. Furnivall, who borrowed it from Rabelais—"to our muttons."

One: Chaucer's Ancestry and Some Remarks on Fourteenth-Century English History

GEOFFREY CHAUCER WAS BORN AROUND 1340, possibly early in 1341, and possibly a little earlier than 1340. Other years have been suggested, from 1328, the year offered by the Elizabethan commentator Speght and uncritically accepted for centuries, to 1346; but Professor George Williams' analysis of the evidence has settled the matter beyond reasonable doubt.[1]

Chaucer's father, John Chaucer, was born around 1312 or '13 and died in 1366. He was "a citizen of London," as he was proud to say, a rich and influential vintner—which is roughly the fourteenth-century equivalent of the modern large brewer in Ireland or England, though John Chaucer was not by any means a personage up to the enormous wealth and power of, say, the Busch family of St. Louis or the greater beermeisters of Germany, men more nearly comparable with fourteenth-century barons. He was a master craftsman, a guildsman, which, in the case of a vintner, is not like saying a member of a trade union but more like saying a senior professor in a major university (fourteenth-century professors were in fact "masters" of the craft of knowledge) or, better yet, a senior partner in a large, politically oriented law firm discreetly on the take. The trouble with comparisons of this kind, of course, is that nothing comparable to our huge companies, universities, and law firms, our vast government bureaucracies or our sprawling cities existed in the Middle Ages. There were far fewer people in the world at that time. The members of King Edward's entire government staff could have at least nodding acquaintance. Even in a fairly large city like London—a mere town by comparison to modern London, though swarming with people packed together in small apartments like chickens in market crates—most people lived out their lives in neighborhoods, tannery workers associating primarily with tannery workers (and the hawkers or stallkeepers who sold them their fruit and vegetables, their pots and pans and the makings for their brooms), wine people associating mostly with wine people, rich men associating mostly with the rich men who attended the same parties or lodged next door, safe in the more comfortable sections of their specialized business districts, in great, sober houses to which the successful, with their servants and apprentices, fled from the noise, stink, and crowding of the poor and, worse, from the violence of such scoundrels as one met "in the suburbës of a toun," as Chaucer would write in the Prologue to the *Canon's Yeoman's Tale,*

> Lurkynge in hernës and in lanës blyndë,   [*corners*]
> Whereas thisë robbours and thisë theves by kyndë   [*by nature*]
> Holden hir pryvee fereful residencë,
> As they that dar nat shewen hir presencë.

To make clear how small and open the world of Chaucer was, J. M. Manly wrote in 1926,

> The area of England itself is smaller than we Americans readily conceive. Exclusive of Wales and Scotland, it is slightly smaller than Alabama, Arkansas, or North Carolina; including Wales but not Scotland, it is slightly larger than Michigan, but smaller than Florida or Georgia. The total population of England in Chaucer's day and for more than a hundred years thereafter was not over two and a half millions. . . .[2]

The city of London itself had only about 40,000 people, which is to say it was just slightly larger than Muskogee, Oklahoma (by 1970 census figures). It was not, as it is now, a great sprawling city with miles of cheap housing and vast stretches of factory surrounding an elegant, arched and pillared core. It was a walled city of colorful parks and gardens, with easy access to rivers and fields, a city that smelled of hay and horse manure—far nobler smells than any our cities afford now. Though medieval London houses burned wood, and trash collection was a problem, the city nevertheless was, as William Morris would later describe it, at least relatively "small and white and clean."

This Londoner John Chaucer was wealthy enough, thanks partly to his wife, to have diversified financial interests. He owned property scattered here and there throughout London and at least as far away as Ipswich, including one London house suitable only for a person of well-above-average means, the stone and timber house on narrow, heavily shaded Thames Street in the posh end of the Vintry Ward (near the present Strand) overlooking the river and the orchards beyond—the house he bequeathed to his son Geoffrey.[3] When John Chaucer first occupied this house is impossible to say. The first record of his connection with the place is from July 25, 1345, when he was summoned to answer the prioress of Chestnut Convent, from whom he held the house in fief, for his failure to pay the past two years' rent (not rent in the modern sense but in the sense, rather, of feudal tribute). He apparently settled the account and kept the house until the time of his death, when it went to his wife Agnes and eventually, no doubt when Agnes died, to Geoffrey, who released it in 1381 to one Henry Herbury, a rich and influential vintner who'd been living in the house, apparently, under arrangement with Geoffrey Chaucer's mother and stepfather, Bartholomew Attechapel.

So we must modify the traditional picture of young Jeff Chaucer in the family pub among unwashed, polyglot sailors—a poetic fancy of early biographers, though doubted by William Godwin—re-presented in gilt and alabaster by F. J. Furnivall, who wrote, introducing some of Chaucer's *Life-Records:*

> We have him as a boy at his father's wine-shop or tavern in narrow Thames St, chatting, no doubt, with English and foreign seamen, with citizens who came for their wine, helping to fill their pots, perhaps—a natty, handy lad, but full of quiet fun—messing, I dare say, in Walbrook, that bounded his father's place; fishing in the Thames, I should think; out on May-day for sweet-scented boughs to dress his father's tavern-pole. At school—St. Paul's Cathedral perchance—sharing in all the games and larks that Fitzstephen so well describes some 200 years before; seeing all the grand shows that went on in Smithfield and London streets; well up in his classes, I'll be bound; the boy the father of the man in this, that he loved his bookës well. Then he goes to serve Prince Lionel's wife as page, and gets his dress of short cloak, pair of red and black breeches, and shoes, with 3s. 6d. for necessaries. . . .[4]

The picture may have some truth in it—Chaucer's father may have had, among other things, one or more wine shops, and even the most dignified fourteenth-century establishments could be lively places, as noisy and full of merriment as a modern English pub near closing time; but we may as reasonably conjure up a picture of young Jeff Chaucer the rich boy in his father's calm house, a child to a large extent cared for by servants and privately tutored, since, almost certainly, his parents were sufficiently concerned about his prospects to give him an expensive education, perhaps in specific preparation for service at court. It is unlikely that he was ever a humble "page" to the countess of Ulster, Prince Lionel's wife (at any rate, there's no evidence that he was, as Professor Williams has shown),[5] though he did serve her court in some capacity; and, as for the record on his clothes and spending money, rightly understood it suggests no particularly humble position but fairly decent rank. To all this we will return. For the moment the point is that Chaucer's origin was far from lowly.

The family background is a little uncertain except that it was, by

John Chaucer's father's day, solidly though newly middle class insofar as such terms have any meaning in a world of lords and vassals, guild masters and journeymen, freemen and serfs. It was a family engaged, at least tangentially, in more financial ventures than one, and ferociously, litigiously, devoted to making its mark—or pound, or shilling. Part of the evidence of the family's social standing is the variety of names to which Chaucer's grandfather answered in courts of law.

Surnames could be haphazard things in the Middle Ages, given to a man by virtue of his place of origin (as in the case of John of *Gaunt,* Anglo-Norman for "Ghent," his birthplace), or by virtue of his father's name (Williamson, son of William), or his trade (Wat Tyler, that is, tile-maker, or, some think, somewhat mysteriously, tailor), or even— notably in the case of kings but sometimes also in the case of commoners —given by virtue of his character or reputation (Pedro the Cruel). As a man changed locations, trades, or habits, his name changed with him. Geoffrey Chaucer's grandfather Robert's family, which had London connections but mainly lived in Ipswich, was known as "le Taverner"—the poet's great-grandfather was Andrew le Taverner—which means some of them were tavern-keepers, guildsmen of, loosely, the lower middle class. Tavern-keepers were by law distinct from vintners, the one a retailer, the other a socially elevated wholesaler; but the family that acquired a string of taverns might profitably turn to vintry, with its control of retail outlets. In London, the poet's grandfather, Robert Chaucer, lived on Cordwainer Street ("Shoemaker" or "Leatherworker" Street) in the better section of the leather district, and was known as Robert le Saddler and also as Robert Chaucer (French *chaussier,* "hose-maker" or "shoemaker"). Both the location and the surnames have suggested to some that he may have been a master craftsman in leatherwork.[6] But the more likely explanation is that Cordwainer Street was a fashionable address that might naturally have appealed to a man rising in the wine business and not engaged in leatherwork at all—as on other grounds we know he probably was not. He also appears as Robert of Dennington (as his father, Geoffrey's great-grandfather, appears as Andrew of Dennington),* which suggests that he was born, once lived in, or owned property in Dennington (in Suffolk); and, finally, he appears as Robert Malyn, that is, apparently, Robert of Greater Lynn, as Robert of Ipswich, and as Robert Malin le Chaucer—whatever that may mean. He did, we know, have relatives in all these places.[7]

---

* That is, "de Dennington." Since medieval English usage was inconsistent and can be confusing, I anglicize *de* to *of* throughout and at times drop the *of* as later generations of these families would do. I retain *de* in direct quotations and some names of Frenchmen, e.g., Guichard d'Angle.

What seems likely is that, the family having thrived in the tavern business, Robert became a London vintner. He strengthened his position by marriage to a woman of means, who had, possibly, vintry connections, since the marriage of convenience was the rule for his class, as for peasants and kings, and since his wife, though married earlier to a pepperer by the name of John Heyroun (Heron), would be married after Robert Chaucer's death to another vintner, a man who was perhaps Robert's first cousin, Richard. That she was well-to-do seems certain: Mary Chaucer, the poet's grandmother, came from the substantial Ipswich family of Westhales (or Westhalls). In the country, it should be mentioned, even women of the highest class could be bought and sold like cattle, but not so in the cities. There a woman could legally own property, even run her own business. Thus Chaucer's grandmother's choice of husbands suggests that she had something in the way of property or position that was useful to vintners—in fact, to at least two in a row. Robert Chaucer increased his wealth through the wine import business, becoming notable enough to be named as deputy to the king's butler in 1308 and 1310, and as a collector of the king's customs—a powerful position, profitable even if a man were burdened, as most collectors apparently were not, by moral scruple.

There are other proofs of the family's standing. After Robert Chaucer's death, between 1312 and 1315, his wife Mary (Geoffrey's grandmother) took as her husband Richard Chaucer (as I've said), perhaps a relative of the late Robert. Richard, too, was a vintner who would become deputy to the king's butler in the London area; and Mary Chaucer's son by her first marriage, Thomas Heyroun, would also grow up to be a vintner— as would her son John, the poet's father.

Judging by his holdings and those of his descendants, Robert Chaucer (and others of the family) may have risen partly through shrewd acquisition of real estate. Both among the rural barons and among wealthy members of the urban middle class, buying up real estate in town—that is, getting it assigned in fief—was one of the roads to power in Robert Chaucer's day, as getting hold of land in the country would be one road to power in his grandson Geoffrey's day, after wave on wave of pestilence had decimated England's shires, making room for new landlords, and the fury of the disease in crowded quarters, not to mention the rush of hungry peasants to town, had made life in the metropolis less attractive than formerly. Court records give some clues to the value of the property the family owned.

On October 29, 1315, Robert Chaucer's widow Mary acknowledged she owed £70 (modern value, $16,800)[8] to a man named Nicholas of Halweford and promised to pay half of what she owed by the following February, that is, within about ninety days, and the other half at Easter. As security she offered her lands and chattels in the city of London and elsewhere. This has sometimes been interpreted as proof that Robert Chaucer left his widow in debt, but it is probably nothing of the kind. Considering the amount owed, the payment schedule would be stiff for any but the fairly rich; yet the securities are accepted and not seized. As J. M. Manly was, I think, the first to point out, the debt may have had to do with a loan to Mary Chaucer herself; "in any event," Manly says, "it is clear that she owned in London and elsewhere property which was regarded as good security for the amount."[9] When her son Thomas Heyroun (Geoffrey's uncle) died, in 1349, he left numerous London tenements to be sold by the executor of his will, his "brother, John Chaucer." And when John Chaucer's stepfather Richard died, also in 1349 (a plague year), he bequeathed property that would cover the cost of a perpetual daily requiem Mass for himself, his late wife Mary, and his stepson Thomas Heyroun. (How long perpetuity lasted in practice I've been unable to discover.) Earlier proofs of Richard Chaucer's wealth include the heavy sums he was several times assessed as his fair contribution to loans made by London's chief merchants to the king, and his contribution of £500 (modern value, $120,000) to the company headed by Walter Chiriton and John Wesenham, another organization which made royal loans.

But the most interesting records that come down to us are those dealing with the curious Agnes Malyn affair.

In Ipswich lived Robert Chaucer's contentious sister Agnes—she was also his sister-in-law, as widow of Walter of Westhale, Mary Chaucer's brother. Agnes of Westhale, née Malyn, is a lady remarked by history because after the death of Robert Chaucer (Geoffrey's grandfather), she made a snatch at his Ipswich property, hoping to consolidate his holdings and her own by conspiring with one Geoffrey Stace and others, and abducting the late Robert Chaucer's son John, then in his early teens, and trying to force the boy to marry her daughter (his double cousin) Joan. In righteous indignation John Chaucer's stepfather Richard and John's half brother Thomas Heyroun, probably with armed and eager servants, rode to Ipswich and captured young John Chaucer back, along with property worth, according to Agnes Malyn's suit, £40 (about $9,600). In the drawn-out counter-suit proceedings which followed, the Chaucers of London were awarded damages of £250 ($60,000) and both Agnes of Westhale and Geoffrey Stace, her collaborator, were imprisoned in Marshalsea Gaol for inability to pay. Two years later, Stace, now Agnes Malyn's husband, testified that John Chaucer had been satisfied concerning the fine, and the pair was released from prison. Geoffrey Chaucer's biographers have sometimes imagined that John Chaucer generously forgave the debt. But that seems unlikely. Just a few days before he testified that his debt was taken care of—on July 13, 1328—Stace had borrowed exactly £250.

Geoffrey Chaucer's forbears were, in short, a tough, grasping, fairly well-heeled breed, typical of the early fourteenth-century merchant family of rising fortunes, quick to draw their swords (John Chaucer was kidnapped by force of arms, "viz. swords, bows, and arrows"), quick to marry, if it seemed profitable, and quick to call in lawyers. They were not the type to throw away money with indifferent and saintly *caritas*— though neither was John Chaucer the type to nurse grudges. Not long after the debt to him was paid (if it was), he allowed his Aunt Agnes and Geoffrey Stace to buy the property they'd tried to steal from him.

But John Chaucer was perhaps at that time more mellow than usual. In the train of John Bedford, London skinner, he had followed the noble old earl of Lancaster in a rising against Roger Mortimer—adviser and consort to Queen Isabella (mother of Edward III) and chief architect of the recent ignominious peace with Scotland—and had shared in Lancaster's defeat. In January 1329 John Chaucer had been indicted for his part in the revolt, and when he failed to appear in court to defend himself, he'd been declared an outlaw (May 22, 1329), which he remained until Mortimer's overthrow and execution, engineered by the young king, Edward III, in 1330, at which time the now blind earl of Lancaster ("blind Henry") and all those charged with him received pardon. Resurfacing in public, a well-built, war-toughened man of nearly twenty, John Chaucer was in a mood to forget old annoyances, especially those far off in Ipswich. Once he had comfortably settled into life as a London businessman, petty official, and social climber, drawing on his service to the house of Lancaster, in all probability, and doubtless on friendships among the wealthy importers with whom he now moved daily and from whose ranks (lest anyone underestimate their clout) London would choose a good number of its mayors—he showed no more disposition than would his gifted heir, in later years, to let any opportunity for increased prosperity or advancement slip past, much less to leave debts uncollected.

John Chaucer was by all evidence an admirable and extraordinary man, well liked by his fellow vintners, respected by the courts and moneylenders, amiable, gracious, and properly deferential in the presence of the nobility, who frequently employed him, yet decisive, even fierce, when times required—not a man to flinch from a just war or a tavern brawl. His work was heartily approved and regularly rewarded, as his son's was to be. He was apparently elevated, by 1338, when he was twenty-five or -six (early middle age by medieval standards), to the

train of King Edward III when the king and his entourage visited
Flanders and then traveled up the Rhine to negotiate an alliance with
the Flemish king, Louis IV. (Since records are sketchy, there is a faint
possibility that we may be dealing here with some other John Chaucer
and that the mission was a military expedition, but it is very faint indeed.)[10]

What John Chaucer's function was on that occasion is uncertain; his
letter of protection says only that he went in the king's service and at
the king's command. He may have gone, as scholars have traditionally
assumed, as an authority on wine, a provider for the king's vast, sprawling household. If so, and if Edward III followed, in general, the household and wardrobe ordinances of Edward II, John Chaucer traveled
around the countryside as a member of the chief butler's staff on the look-
out for first-class wines and buying them "for the sustenance of [the
king's] household," making sure that "the purveiances & buyinges be
made to the le[a]st damage & disturbance of the merchants as the butler
can or may devise, so alwaies as our lord the kinge have his auncient
prises & al other advantages which of right he ought to have bi reson of
his seigniory."[11] If the wine so bought proved undrinkable, men with
axes would split the staves on the bottom of the tun, allowing the con-
tents to run gushing through the cellar or soak into the ground, and the
man who, in the king's name, had purchased the wine must stand the
price of it himself—emotional and financial humiliation cold-bloodedly
designed to break a man, on the presumption that he intentionally mis-
used the king's funds. (Ironically, the younger Hugh Dispenser, who
drew up these rules, was notorious for such thievery, though on a far
grander scale.) If not a searcher or buyer, John Chaucer may have served
as an experienced taster, passing judgment on the wine just before it was
served, or recommending, as a member of the butler's staff, what wine
should be served to particular guests or to the king on particular occasions; or he helped to convey, unload, and store the wine; or, finally, he
scheduled and kept records on the use of wine (also beer and ale) by
the king's household, and kept track of the king's expensive cups.

Some such job as one of these may have been John Chaucer's in 1338.
So his later employment as deputy to the king's butler for the London
area might seem to imply. No such task would be beneath the dignity
of a wealthy Londoner. This was, after all, the late Middle Ages, when
kings were very nearly gods, the foundation of the social order, and a
gentleman granted the privilege of carrying away the king's bed sheets
—that is, being close to the king at his most vulnerable—could consider
himself, and be considered by others, the holder of an awesome responsibility. Nevertheless, it seems to me unlikely that John Chaucer was

employed in any such capacity. The kinds of work I've mentioned—those traditionally mentioned in connection with the poet's father at this period—are all much too close to the king's inner circle. The butler and his staff, the providers, stewards, and tasters, were all regular members of the king's own household, constantly under his majesty's eye. If their work was menial, their attachment to the crown was close. (For comparison, think of the relationship of a New York corporation president and his personal secretary as compared with his relationship to his plant manager in Cleveland.) John Chaucer was not a household regular but an outsider, a specialist brought in for the occasion, apparently the diplomatic journey of 1338. Then what did he really do?

Let us look again at his later employment as deputy to the king's butler for Southampton. The position of deputy to the king's butler (or deputy to the king's anything else) involved doing the real work for some favored courtier, the actual king's butler, who received remuneration of one sort or another for his patronage job but was usually away in attendance on the king or lending prestige to some royal mission. John Chaucer's job as deputy—for which he was qualified partly by his import-export connections, partly by his father's having done creditable service both as deputy butler and as a customs collector—kept him in full-time attendance at an office of extreme importance to the crown: wine customs and taxes were a prime source of revenue, and the king's acquisition of the best wine available was a matter of prestige. It was tedious and exacting work, however rewarding financially and socially—work which consisted mainly of collecting the customs, keeping careful import-export accounts, and setting aside appropriate wines for shipment to the king, for good wages. It was drudgery in fact, though exalted drudgery. John Chaucer was thus neither as eminent as a role in the king's personal household would imply, nor as lowly as Chaucer's biographers have imagined.

It will be useful, in the long run, to pursue this matter a little further. We have seen already that among Victorian biographers we find a tendency to see the poet Chaucer as an early version of the Grub Street genius who by inspiration and perspiration climbed to at least brief prosperity. The inclination has been to make far too much of the darker implications of the numerous guildhall documents concerning Thames Street and, especially, the Walbrook, which bordered John Chaucer's property, a brook periodically, from 1278 to 1415, "stopped up by divers filth and dung thrown therein by persons who have houses along the said course, to the great nuisance and damage of all the city."[12] The rundown neighborhood such records suggest is an optical illusion. The nuisance—filth and dung—was a common one in fourteenth-century

London. Poor men accepted such things as inescapable facts of life. But some of the landholders on Thames Street were the politically powerful merchant vintners of Gascoyne, many of whom became mayors of the city; others were the holders of the imposing cutlers', plumbers', and glaziers' guildhalls and the town mansions of the earls of Worcester and Ormond, the great house of Henry Picard, vintner—of whom it is said that in the year 1363 he "did in one day sumptuously feast Edward III, King of England, John, King of France, David, King of Scots, the King of Cyprus (then all in England), Edward, Prince of Wales [the Black Prince], with many other noblemen, and after kept his hall for all comers that were willing to play at dice and hazard"[13]—and also the house of the Ypres family, where the greatest of the magnates, or super-barons, John of Gaunt, was dining in 1377 when a knight burst in to say that London was up in arms against him, and "unless he took great heed, that day would be his last. With which words the duke leapt so hastily from his oysters that he hurt both his legs against the form. Wine was offered, but he could not drink for haste, and so fled with his fellow Henry Percy out at the back gate, and entering the Thames, never stayed rowing until they came to a house near the manor of Kennington, where at that time the princess [of Wales] lay with [her newborn son] Richard the young prince, before whom he made his complaint."[14] Such men brooked no dung in their neighborhood brooks (according to one early Chaucerian, Stow, writing in the time of Queen Elizabeth, the Walbrook was still, in 1462, "a fair brook of sweet water," now bricked in), and they could afford to raise complaint about it.

If we dismiss the notion that John Chaucer was one of King Edward III's household familiars, since his name is missing from the household records, and if we abandon, on the other hand, all vestiges of the notion of John Chaucer as humble tavern-keeper—recalling the neighborhood he lived in, recalling that he was a follower of blind Henry of Lancaster important enough to be noticed and charged, and that (probably) his holdings in real estate were soon to include (or included already) some holdings in Kent where his wife had property and where (probably for the sake of advancing his position, considering the general practice of his age) he found a husband for his daughter, Geoffrey Chaucer's sister Kate—we may reasonably guess that, like the poet himself, later, he may have been valued not directly for his expertise in wine but for the charm and diplomacy of a talented though relatively minor civil servant, or as a skillful keeper of difficult accounts, or as a man whose business and social connections might prove useful to the crown.

The more one studies the few surviving facts, the more acceptable this theory becomes, I think. King Edward's mission in Flanders and up the Rhine, in 1338, was, as I've said, to gather allies and negotiate financial backing for his projected attack on the king of France. John Chaucer, who apparently went as far as Cologne, was a man familiar with imports and exports, a skillful accountant, one well acquainted with the intricacies of English law regarding customs; and he was a man who by his station and line of business must be well known (and evidently not repugnant) to the Flemish merchant community in London, and even better known to his neighbors and regular business associates on Thames Street, the merchants of Cologne. Not a stone's throw from his house, G. G. Coulton points out (without drawing the conclusion I myself would draw), "stood the great fortified hall and wharf of the Hanse merchants, the Easterlings who gave their name ['sterling] to our coinage, and whose London premises remained the property of Lübeck, Hamburg, and Bremen until 1853. Chief among the Easterlings at this time were the Cologne merchants, with whom John Chaucer had specially close relations."[15] Also on Thames Street stood the large house built of stone and timber, with storage vaults for wine, called the Vintry, the house where John Gisers lived—a vintner who later became mayor of London and constable of the town—and where after him lived Henry Picard, who was mayor of London in 1357 and the man supposed to have feasted four kings and the Black Prince all in one day. Picard and several other powerful and affluent vintners, besides John Chaucer—some of the wealthiest merchants in England—were along with King Edward on the journey up the Rhine in 1338.

John Chaucer probably traveled, then, as a minor assistant in a company of full-fledged merchant-diplomats (such as Geoffrey Chaucer would be later on his Genoa trip), men charged with working out trade, tax, and port agreements, a smoothing of operations and an inducement to greater cooperation between states soon to be allied in war. Such royally sponsored negotiations between merchants were the rule rather than the exception in an age when taxation beyond a certain limit could mean catastrophe (as the peasants showed the king's advisers in 1381)—an age when prudent kings depended, for war finance, on the ambitions of merchants and the booty- and ransom-lust of barons. That John Chaucer was only an assistant seems certain. He was probably not yet a licensed vintner at the time he followed Edward in 1338. He is first definitely identified as a vintner on August 1, 1342, when he was one of fifteen vintners who agreed to an ordinance made by the mayor, the aldermen, and the commonality of London prohibiting the watering down of tavern wine; and in all the later records concerning the property of his half brother Thomas Heyroun, he is explicitly "John Chaucer, vintner." Of course even if he was not yet a licensed vintner in 1338, his family connections might have earned him a position of moderate importance; but they had nothing like the power of the Picards.

One thing seems certain in the career of John Chaucer. Whether or not he traveled to Cologne as a junior diplomat, he was interested all his life in the lucrative business of politics: national politics, guild politics, and often both at once, as when, in March of 1356, at forty-four (distinguished, portly, and exceedingly well-to-do) he was appointed as one of two guild collectors in the Vintry Ward to gather money to equip two light boats for the English fleet—an expensive proposition. If he were not an affable, persuasive man, a gentleman to whom some in the Vintry Ward owed favors, one generally respected for his honesty and for the same cordial but unwavering firmness that would characterize his son, he would probably not have been given that assignment by his peers.

Among those who traveled up the Rhine with King Edward was another London vintner by the name of Henry Northwell—tall, lean, graying, dignified—who had a young wife named Agnes, his pride and joy, a pleasant, quick-witted, warmhearted woman for whom John Chaucer—watching her breathe in the nipping river breeze—probably felt an instant liking, though he had no idea, when he first passed the time of day with her, what it would lead to. At any rate, she was probably the same Agnes who had become, by 1354—and probably ten or fifteen years earlier—John Chaucer's wife and, presumably, the mother of the future poet. She was the daughter of a man named John of Copton, and niece and heiress to one of London's quiet rich, Hamo of Copton, citizen and moneyer (or mint-officer) of London, who died in 1349.[16]

Hamo Copton was survived by at least one son, Nicholas, upon whose death without issue the Copton property was apparently to devolve to Agnes. Her father had by now been dead for some time; he was apparently the same John Copton who lived outside Aldgate and was slain in 1313 or '14, when Agnes was a child. His property apparently went to his brother and, after the death of Hamo's son Nicholas, in the plague year 1349, to Agnes and John Chaucer. They did, at any event, get property in the parish of St. Botolph outside Aldgate. In October 1349 a man named Nigel of Hackney—son and heir of Richard of Hackney, an executor of Hamo Copton's will—brought a plea of intrusion against "John Chaucer, vintner, and his wife Agnes," with reference to the St. Botolph property formerly owned by Hamo Copton. If the property mentioned in these various records is all the same property, then what happened was, perhaps, that John Copton left his house to his brother Hamo; Hamo's executor tried to seize it for himself upon the death of Hamo's last surviving son; but the Chaucers rushed up from Southampton, where they'd been living—bringing along with them their nine-year-old son—and immediately moved in, enforcing their claim by occupancy. Agnes later proved her right to the house in court. It was property worth fighting for. It stood in a neighborhood where King Edward's mistress Alice Perrers would later hold tenements and where Geoffrey Chaucer would one day win a luxurious house lease-free by city grant.

As a Copton, it has been suggested, Agnes Chaucer may have been a member of the prominent land-rich Pelican family of Kent, a matter of possible importance to Geoffrey's later career. Hamo Copton is recorded in 1321 as living at St. Dunstan's parish, but he seems to have belonged to a family of Kentish origin.[17] It is clear, in any case, that Geoffrey Chaucer would later have connection with Kent. John of Philpot's *Visitation of Kent* records the marriage of a man named Simon Manning of Codham, Kent, to Catherina "soror Galfridi Chawcer militis celeberrimi Poetae Anglicani" (sister of Geoffrey Chaucer, soldier, celebrated among English poets) ; and we know that on one occasion Chaucer was given wardship over a minor in Kent. If Geoffrey Chaucer had not owned or overseen Kentish property he would probably not have been given that wardship and could not have become, as he did, justice of the peace and later representative in parliament for Kent. (As we'll see in later chapters, Chaucer almost certainly qualified for a parliamentary seat because he was resident representative or steward for one of Kent's greatest landowners, the king.)

Besides her immediate family background, Agnes Chaucer had high connections through her first husband, who was a kinsman of William of Northwell, a man in the lofty position of keeper of the king's wardrobe, an inner-circle position in the king's household, and no mere valet's assignment: the king's wardrobe meant all his household goods except those covered by the Exchequer, which governed the king's butler, the receiver of stores, the keeper of horses, and the royal messengers. He also served as the king's principal financial agent. This family connection may well have had something to do with the poet's later rise in King Edward's court and then Richard's. Agnes did, as we've seen, inherit at least some of the valuable and extensive Copton property. In addition to that already mentioned, she and her husband John Chaucer in 1354 held property which they granted by deed to Simon de Plaghe, physician, citizen of London, and Joan, his wife—a brewing tenement with houses, buildings, and garden adjacent, and two shops and solars, formerly just outside the city wall. And later, in 1363, John and Agnes Chaucer agreed to the transfer of some nearby property, ten and a half acres of land with valuable appurtenances—twenty-four shops and two gardens—in Stepney and in the parish of St. Mary Mattefalon, outside Aldgate.

The Chaucers may also have gained some wealth and courtly influence through the Heyroun line, the line of John Chaucer's beloved half brother—or simply "brother," as the two call each other in official records. Though they were not the direct source of Chaucer's appointment, the Heyrouns had connections with Petherton Forest, one of the huge royal estates originally set apart for the royal pleasure but later built up with manors and even towns. Late in life, after valuable personal service and risky loyalty to King Richard, Geoffrey Chaucer would become sub-forester, that is to say, deputized chief agent, over Petherton Forest.

John Chaucer's business career can be traced mainly through royal grants and appointments and through court appearances on his own behalf or on behalf of others. In 1343 he received a permit from the king to ship forty quarters of wheat from Ipswich to Flanders, with the proviso that he not take out of England any wool, hides, and wool-fells not customed. That grant, in effect, gave him large powers as an exporter, not only of wheat but of wool, etc., as long as the duty was paid; and there were few kinds of business in England more profitable—if one could get past the pirates—than trade with Flanders. In February 1347, when he was still in his mid-thirties—his son Geoffrey was now seven or eight—he was appointed deputy in the port of Southampton to the king's chief butler, John of Wesenham; and in April of the same year, his duties were increased by his appointment as deputy to Wesenham for customs collection on cloth and beds exported by foreign merchants from Southampton, Portsmouth, and three other shipping centers. The job was an important one, since, as I've said, customs were the king's primary source of revenue. John Chaucer gave up these offices, however, on October 28, 1349, perhaps because the Black Death had brought him new land holdings, including the Hamo Copton place, where the Chaucers moved that same month. As we've seen, John Chaucer's stepfather Richard, his half brother Thomas Heyroun, his wife's uncle Hamo Copton, and Hamo Copton's son Nicholas all died that year. Had John Chaucer's family been living in London, caring for their sick, the biography of Geoffrey Chaucer, now aged nine, might well have ended here.

As he grew older, increasingly sedate and substantial—that is, in 1355 and thereafter, or from his early forties onward—John Chaucer stood surety for loans and gave guarantee of good behavior for a number of Londoners of his acquaintance. He vouched for, among others, "two taverners, one of whom had been sued by a woman for drawing blood, two alien vintners who were later admitted to the freedom of the City of

London, and a tailor thrown into the Tun for being a nightwalker [curfew breaker] in the City. Most interesting of the cases in which he stood surety is that in which he and four others gave security, on 9 December 1364, that Richard Lyons, London vintner, would cause no harm to Alice Perrers [Edward III's mistress and friend of Geoffrey Chaucer] or prevent her from going where she pleased and doing the business of the king as well as her own."[18] This last especially teases the imagination. By 1364 Alice Perrers had a name for sharp practice—in fact for robbing people blind, even the king, whom she seems to have loved. Though parliament fretted, nothing could be done as long as Gaunt and his brother the Black Prince supported her. John Chaucer must have sympathized with his irate guild-fellow, undoubtedly one of that dazzling trickster's victims. Yet Alice was one of John Chaucer's son Geoffrey's most influential advocates in Edward's court. It was a perplexing dilemma for the loyal guildsman and father.

John Chaucer was involved in numerous other legal squabbles. In Easter term, 1353, when he was forty, a charge of assault was brought against him in the Court of Common Pleas by one Geoffrey of Darsham, who claimed that at Iseldon (Islington, at that time a village some distance from London on the northeast outskirts) John Chaucer beat and wounded him and "committed other outrages to his grave injury and against the king's peace." How John Chaucer came out in this suit no one knows. In 1357 he was sued for debt by John Long, London citizen and fishmonger. The outcome of that suit, too, is unknown, but the odds are, Chaucer paid. Medieval merchants were forever putting off their fishmongers and grocers, but no medieval debt collectors, with the possible exception of moneylenders, were more pertinacious or more efficient in pursuit. He also saw duty on various occasions between 1353 and 1364 as a juryman of the Vintry Ward in the Court of Husting and once (in 1350) as a juror in the trial of a false coiner, that is, an alchemist, one of that miserable type whose frustrations Chaucer immortalized in the *Canon's Yeoman's Tale*—

>   ful ofte it happeth so,
> The pot tobreketh, and farewel, al is go!
> Thisë metals been of so greet violencë,
> Oure wallës mowë nat make hem resistencë,   [*may*]
> But if they weren wroght of lym and stoon,
> They percen so, and thurgh the wal they goon;   [*through*]
> And somme of hem synken into the ground—
> Thus han we lost by tymës many a pound—
> And somme are scaterëd al the floor aboutë;

Sommë lepe into the roof. Withouten doutë,
Though that the feend noght in ourë sighte hym shewë,
I trowe he with us be, that ilke shrewë!   *[same]*

We find further mention of John Chaucer in court records, but these should suffice. He was a solid citizen, a man who did his duty, for the most part honorably paid his bills, drank his Bordeaux, and, if need arose, defended his opinions, like any respectable medieval gentleman, with his cane, if not his truncheon.

Geoffrey Chaucer's father was also—like all men of his day who had social ambitions (and thousands who did not)—a military man, though whether a good one or bad one, no one knows. As we've seen already, it may have been partly to his service with Henry, earl of Lancaster, great-uncle of King Edward III, that he owed both his rise in London and, vastly more important from our point of view, the lifelong friendship of his son Geoffrey with the greatest magnate in England in his time, King Edward's fourth son John of Gaunt, who would become, by marriage to the earl's granddaughter, the duke of Lancaster.

John Chaucer first bore arms alongside his older brother (that is, half brother) Thomas Heyroun in the disastrous campaign against the Scots which was initiated by Roger Mortimer and Queen Isabella, and led by boyish, overconfident King Edward III, then fifteen years old (about John Chaucer's age), handsome and well liked and eager to prove his superiority to his bungling, lately deposed father, Edward II. (This was in 1327, three years before the earl of Lancaster's attack on Mortimer, and eleven years before the journey with King Edward up the Rhine.) The London contingent of two hundred men, or rather men and boys, rode boldly north, joining with the rest of the army, followed by its train of provision wagons. In the beginning the army included tough Hainault mercenaries (the kingdom of Hainault included and extended west from what is now southern Belgium) ; but the hirelings got into fights with the citizens of York and had to be sent back south toward London, where they returned to the usual pastimes of unattached mercenary bands, drunkenness, theft, now and then lighthearted murder. The great French chronicler Froissart tells the story of the English campaign. The passages I quote are from Lord Berners's sixteenth-century translation, with minor changes to keep the meaning clear.

Froissart's figures, borrowed from England's official chronicles, are probably too high, but to fourteen- or fifteen-year-old John Chaucer and his older brother Tom, it must have seemed an immense force that set

out for England's northern moors, where the Scots, in a systematic program of terrorism aimed at preserving their national independence, were
sweeping down (wild of hair, half naked), burning villages and fields
with such fury that the English could follow their progress from miles
away by the billowing smoke. It did not seem systematic or even sane to
John Chaucer, devoted, like any young Englishman of the time, to the
ideal of chivalry, the armed horseman's code which began with fair play
on the battlefield, Christian nobility of spirit, that is, "courtesy" in imitation of the soldier, Christ, and ultimately extended—not only for horsemen but for all who respected good breeding—to politeness, gentleness
toward the weak, respect for women. It was in the broadest sense a
code that went back to the ninth-century Anglo-Saxon King Alfred,
took on refinements and ritual complexity in thirteenth-century France,
and was now, as an ideal, standard among all civilized soldiers, though
rarely exercised by practical fighting men.[19] To John Chaucer the
Scottish attacks were senseless and impudent, barbarian, even fiendish;
they would inevitably be punished by God and King Edward's men-at-
arms.

He marched on, his light armor growing heavier, and when he fell
behind a little, his older brother perhaps gently teased him. When their
contingent reached a hilltop they could see, moving out like giant,
dusty serpents, the army's three huge sections—"thre great batels,"
Froissart says—each with two wings of five hundred men of arms
(knights and squires on their horses), three hundred thousand additional armed men, half on small horses or hackneys, the other
half "men of the country" on foot—and also twenty-four thousand
archers on foot, not counting other "raskall and folowers of the [h]oste."
(Froissart's numbers, as I've said, are no doubt inflated.) The Scots
burned their way over mountains and through valleys, the English
pursuing them in formal and orderly military array, with banners
flying and strict rules that no man break ranks or, on pain of death,
pass ahead of the marshal's banners. It was the safest way to travel,
with bogs and marshes and places for ambush on every hand, and the
way that had served English chivalry well, making the whole army
like the best of its knights, controlled, imperturbable; but it meant the
English had no prayer of overtaking the Scots.

The English tried strategy, deciding to move at midnight to the
river Tyne, where Edward hoped he might cut off the enemy's return
into Scotland. For the sake of swift travel, and from conviction that
tomorrow the Scots would be forced at last to make their stand, they
abandoned their vast provisions train—the last they would see of it
for thirty-two days. John Chaucer and Tom Heyroun and the hundreds

all around them started forward in haste, starlight glinting on the metal of their chestplates and the full suits of armor of the mounted knights—moved "through montaignes, valeys, and rokkes, and through many evyll passages," some falling into marshes, losing horses and carriages; yet the army nevertheless pressed violently on, for they heard shouts ahead of them and believed that the vanguard had met with the Scots. They were wrong. The cries they heard were nothing but the shouting of men who'd raised harts and hinds. Dawn came, and the high grass was soaked with dew.

At last, that afternoon, after traveling all day, they reached and crossed the river Tyne—with much travail, since no one had told them it was full of big stones—and settled for the night without tents or utensils, no axes to make huts or even stakes for the horses, which meant those who'd been mounted must sit up till morning clinging to their horses' bridles. There was nothing to eat but bread soaked salty by the horses' sweat, and the ranks of the once-vast army were thinned; some of the footmen were far behind and had no idea which path might be the right one. John Chaucer and Tom Heyroun lay down shivering, to sleep—like most of the army, they'd made the march without bedrolls—but all night long iron men moved noisily back and forth through the trees, grumbling, sometimes shouting, and horses whinnied. When they awakened, half frozen, in the gray morning that followed that endless, miserable night, they stared up through the trees in sorrow and disbelief. It had begun to rain, interminably, drearily, from a charged August sky. The river grew swollen and no one could recross it to forage for food or discover where they were. There was nothing now, not even salty bread, to eat; even the horses had nothing but the leaves of trees. Around noon some peasants of the neighborhood were found, who told the English their location— there was no town within eleven miles. The following day the peasants came back, with others, to sell half-baked bread at profiteering prices.

It rained, with no hint of a let-up, all that week. Soldiers fought among themselves over bread, even murdered for it. By day the army slogged and slithered here and there, up hill and down in that vast, bleak landscape, over slippery-rocked creeks and through dripping woods, hunting for the Scots—who had no idea where the English were either—until at last King Edward found his enemy encamped on the far side of the river Were, high on a mountain, with warm, dry huts of hide and branches at their backs and, hanging from the beams of every tree, a huge store of butchered game.

After counsel, the English took battle positions and advanced, lances upright and flags unfurled, the whole army in chivalric array despite the leaden rain: light horse and foot soldiers like John Chaucer and Thomas Heyroun following behind the ponderous, splendidly skirted destriers—the so-called tanks of the Middle Ages, since two such war-horses, at a slow, clanking gallop, blindered and driven against a studded castle door, could sometimes smash it off its hinges. Young King Edward rode in front, shouting encouragement, until the army came close to the river, and there the army stopped.

What was happening, though no one fully understood it at the time, was what was to happen to the English repeatedly in France. The un-beatable tactics of the English army, horsemen in combination with archers using longbows, had one great drawback before King Edward's introduction of gunpowder: it only worked if the enemy would come out, like a sport, and fight. The Scots, no sportsmen when their numbers were overmatched, stood pat in their unassailable position overlooking the river Edward's army must cross, and skirled their obstreperous, ear-splitting pipes, ready to rain down arrows and boulders, and taunting the English: "Syrs, your kyng and his lordis see well how we be here in this realme, and have brent and wasted the countrey as we have passed through; and if they be displeased ther-with, lette them amend it whan they wyll, for here we wyll abyde, as long as it shall please us." So things continued for three days, Edward's army trying to apply to a mountain what sometimes worked on a walled city, the siege aimed at starving the enemy out. But it was Edward's army that was hungry and, moreover, soaking to the skin—saddles, bridles, and horses' skirts rotting and beginning to smell, foot soldiers like John Chaucer and Thomas Heyroun shivering, coughing from colds and from the pungent smoke of the wet brush they tried in vain to use for fire.

The third night the Scots vanished, later to be found on a second mountain. Again the English settled in, and again the Scots found a weakness in civilized warfare. When the English were asleep, Lord Douglas of the Scots came galloping across to them with two hundred howling, half-naked men, killed some three hundred undressed or half-dressed terrified young Englishmen, scornfully cut the ropes of the king's own tent, and plunged back, still howling, across the river. The fiasco went on—John Chaucer, patriot all his life, must have been furious—until the Scots sneaked off for good in the middle of the night, and King Edward, in tears, turned back to his base at Durham. There the lords found their provision carts hauled into barns and granges, neatly labeled with heraldic flags to show what baggage belonged to whom—the work of the thoughtful citizenry, done at the town's expense. The contrast was one John Chaucer would remember for the rest of his life, laughing when he spoke of it: the wild, noisy Scots, the vexed and demoralized

army of King Edward, and those tidy, scrupulous, dutiful householders
of Durham. Such comically humdrum yet substantial English virtue
would prove equally appealing to his poet son, who would affectionately
mock it again and again, in the too-prudent Monk of the *Shipman's Tale,*
in the unimaginative simplicity of the old widow who owns Chauntecleer,
prince among chickens, or in the genteel Prioress, starchy about her
French, which isn't even Parisian, and (despite her holy office) a
spiritual dimwit, but a lady whose manners at the table could never be
excelled:

> At metë wel ytaught was she with allë:
> She leet no morsel from hir lippës fallë,
> Ne wette hir fyngres in hir saucë depë;
> Wel koudë she carie a morsel and wel kepë,
> That no dropë ne fille upon hirë brest.
> In curteisië was set ful muchel hir lest.   [*much*]
> Hir over-lippë wyped she so clenë
> That in hir coppë ther was no ferthyng senë   [*farthing-like*
> Of grecë, whan she dronken hadde hir draughtë.   *grease droplet*]
> Ful semely after hir metë she raughtë.   [*reached*]

In the dark times that young John Chaucer saw—especially the last
days of Edward II—and in the dark times his son would see—the
days of another king fated to be murdered, King Richard II—the age-
old single-mindedness of the English middle class, "due and regular
conduct," as Defoe would say, would give comforting proof that not
all the old verities were fallen.

It was not long after his return from the north that John Chaucer
began hearing, on the streets and in his stepfather's wineshops, that
Edward's army would certainly have won had not Sir Roger Mortimer,
the power behind the throne, betrayed the king, "for he toke mede
[bribery] and money of the Scottis, to th'entent they might departe
pryvely by nyght. . . ." If Mortimer was guilty, it was the least of his
crimes. Everyone who was anyone in England knew the story, the
whole sorry chronicle of the mistakes by Edward II that brought
Mortimer to power. Since it bears indirectly on the fortunes of John
of Gaunt and directly on the behavior of Richard II toward the end
of the century—a matter of the greatest importance to Geoffrey Chaucer
—the story is worth recalling. It's a story the young John Chaucer knew
well, in one version or another. Mortimer's improbity sufficiently
offended John Chaucer's sense of what was right that he would join the

risky cause of blind Henry, earl of Lancaster, and try to strike Mortimer from power.

During the reign of Edward II (1307–1327) the king and many of his more powerful barons, including the great house of Mortimer, in the Welsh marches, were frequently at odds—as Richard II and his barons would be at the end of the century, and for some of the same reasons. But whereas Richard had a deep concern for the idea and practice of kingship (a concern Geoffrey Chaucer shared and would write about), Edward II thought the whole thing a nuisance. He was athletic and physically powerful—like Edward I, his father—and had certain more or less appealing qualities. He delighted in swimming, boating, and theatrical entertainment, loved the company of minstrels and commoners (with whom, according to hostile chroniclers, he told indecent jokes), had a gift for architecture and shipbuilding, apparently wrote poetry,[20] and, prompted perhaps by that pious streak of which Richard II would make so much, borrowed the lives of St. Anselm and St. Thomas from Christ Church, Canterbury—and failed to return them. But whatever his appeal, Edward II was a petty, ineffectual politician, a homosexual who was all his life fatally liable to fall under the influence of ingratiating young men.

May McKisack sums up Edward's failure as follows:

We may, indeed, pity the weak-willed prince, successor to a famous father, to whom fell not only the administrative problems endemic in the medieval state, but also the *damnosa hereditas* of a hostile Scotland, financial chaos, and an over-mighty cousin. We may take a less hard view than did the chroniclers of Edward's rustic tastes, his preference for the company of simple people, his delight in music and acting. Yet underlying such contemporary criticism was the sound instinct that the second Edward lacked altogether the dignity and high seriousness demanded of a king. Our sources afford us no evidence that at any time he tried to rise to his responsibilities or to learn from his misfortunes and mistakes. Alike in his relations with his friends and with his enemies, he showed himself a weakling and a fool. His mishandling of the Scottish war and his neglect of the safety of the north proved him wanting, not only in military capacity, but also in imagination, energy, and common sense. Reforms achieved in household and exchequer were the work of capable officials, not of the lazy and indifferent king. Edward lived a life devoid of noble purpose or of laudable ambition. He lowered the reputation of his country abroad and at home he was the means of bringing the monarchy into the most serious crisis that had faced it since 1066. It was his own folly which delivered him into the hands of his cruel foes; and the consequences of his disposition reached far beyond his own generation. Memories of it were to haunt the dreams of his great-grandson, Richard II; it smoothed the path of the revolutionaries in 1399 and it opened the way for dynastic conflict and the decline of medieval monarchy.[21]

Contrary to the opinion of some historians, Edward II was well liked when, at the age of twenty-four, he ascended the throne. He was strikingly handsome and muscular, and had an education that befitted his rank. He had for years been suitably betrothed to Isabella, daughter of Philip IV of France, and under his father he'd fought in Scotland four times and, as Chaucer might say, "had borne him well." While still a prince—it was the last year of his father's reign—he had once behaved foolishly; but it was a thing now forgotten. Wishing to show his special love for his fop of a friend Piers Gaveston, he had begged the old king to grant Gaveston one of the crown estates—estates old Edward had intended for no one but a prince of his house. Such a threat to the hard-won solidarity of crown holdings put the king into a passion, and he drove his son from his presence with furious reproaches and banished the favorite—but with such care for his maintenance as to show he was angrier at Edward than at Gaveston. When the old king died, Edward II's first act was to take revenge for that scolding. He recalled Gaveston, and though the man was a Gascon, scorned by the native nobility, and only the younger son of a knight, Edward put him in possession of the vastly rich earldom of Cornwall and made arrangements for his marriage to no less than the king's niece, Margaret of Clare, sister of the earl of Gloucester.

That was only the beginning. It was standard opinion in the Middle Ages that homosexuals were arrogant, vengeful creatures, mockers of decency—implacable miscreants like Chaucer's "gentil Pardoner." Homosexuality was an "outer sign of the soul's corruption," a heretic state in violation of God's first commandment: Go forth and multiply. Perhaps the universal judgment made the caricature true—so Chaucer suggests in the *Canterbury Tales*. In any event, the king all his life flaunted his scorn of the nobility and the needs of government, choosing and dismissing his officers not by policy but by favor or grudge; and Gaveston aped him, showing even greater scorn than Edward's for his former superiors. Powerful barons with private armies and gigantic estates—men like Thomas, earl of Lancaster, elder brother of Henry, who would succeed him as earl—stared dumbfounded or shook with rage at the antics and airs of this puffed-up French donzel who dared to insist that he be present whenever King Edward gave audience, even with the mightiest in the realm.

The result was inevitable. Great magnates, some of them of royal blood, who cared about the nation as the king did not, began, half un-wittingly, to move toward power almost equal to the king's, even power that "accroached," that is, usurped the king's. This was not—perhaps even in Mortimer's case—their original intention. Part of the agony in the struggle of king and parliament in this century was that nearly everyone involved held the crown in awe, willingly accepted the king's absolute power over life and death, dreaded shame, and hated the smell of treason. But once a baron's movement toward accroachment began, it often proved uncheckable.

Not the first to encroach on royal privilege, but one of the most tragic and important, was Thomas, earl of Lancaster. He was a sober, never overhasty man, graying at the temples and at the sides of his beard. After repeated attempts to humble Gaveston, whose favor with the king was making him the richest parasite in England, and whose banishment by parliament repeatedly proved unenforceable, subject utterly to the king's whim, Lancaster and others reluctantly decided on a showdown. In open defiance of the king's decree, Thomas of Lancaster and other earls ap-peared in parliament fully armed and laid a statement of grievances before Edward. In substance, their complaint was that, led by evil counsellors—by which they meant chiefly Gaveston—the king was so impoverished as to be forced to live by extortion, that the tax grants made to him had been wasted, and that by the loss of Scotland—where Edward had repeatedly refused the gauntlet (as would Richard later)— he had dismembered his crown. They forced him to agree to the appoint-ment of "ordainers" with power to reform his house and realm; and the result of the ordainers' work was the forty-one Ordinances, beginning with the removal of bad advisers, the foremost of whom was, of course, Gaveston, and covering such matters as the removal of foreigners like the king's Italian banker, Amerigo dei Frescobaldi, from the position of collector of customs.

The king was indignant. Though he could do nothing for the moment, he too had his opinions of what royalty meant, and this meddling with his personal affairs by his subjects was an outrage. He was not altogether alone in that opinion. Many of the magnates were doubtful themselves that it was right to impose ordainers on a chrisomed king; but he'd given them no alternative.

Again Gaveston was not banished for long. When word reached the ordainers that Gaveston and the king were traveling through the northern counties, mustering an army, they felt they had no choice but to meet the king's challenge. Using tournaments as a cover, and with Queen Isabella's approval, they called up their large private armies and prepared for war.

On May 4, 1312 (approximately the year John Chaucer was born),

Edward and Gaveston were at Newcastle when warning came that Thomas of Lancaster, with a large force, was descending on the town. The king and Gavetson fled by boat down-river to Tynemouth, and the next day set out for the walled town of York. The people of Newcastle were in no mood to fight; the town and castle fell without a siege. Lancaster rounded up the royal servants, weapons, treasure, and horses, and arranged his army to block Gaveston's flight if he should double back. Meanwhile other lords, the earls of Pembroke and Warenne, chased Gaveston and the king northeast toward the sea—old Robin Hood country—caught them at Scarborough, and soon forced Gaveston's surrender.

The earl of Pembroke was a mild and moderate man, sandy-haired, hesitant, devoted to old books and the golden haze of chivalry as it once was; so when Gaveston begged that they stop and rest on the way to Gaveston's own castle of Wallingford, where Pembroke meant to hold him in house arrest, Pembroke, after some thought, agreed and took the opportunity to visit his countess at the neighboring manor of Bampton, leaving Gaveston in the charge of his servants. While he was gone a less chivalrous, more modern knight, Guy Beauchamp of Warwick, came with his small army and surrounded the rectory. When Gaveston saw them, the chronicles say, he ran from window to window in fright, but there was no escape. "Get up, traitor, you're taken!" his enemy shouted, and Gaveston was forced to throw on some clothes and descend the stairs. Barefoot and bareheaded, he was forced to walk on the ground like a captured highwayman, crying and complaining, for half of the long way to Warwick Castle, then to ride for the rest of the trip like a woman, on a mare.

Pembroke was dismayed. He begged the earl of Gloucester, a member of the king's party, to help him—to save his name from dishonor and his property from forfeiture. Gloucester pursed his lips, black brows lowered, and refused. He next begged help from the clerks and burgesses of Oxford, imploring them to attack Warwick Castle and recapture his prisoner. They, too, looking soberly at the ground, refused. Meanwhile Thomas of Lancaster and his friends made their decision. They removed Gaveston to Lancaster territory, led him up onto Blacklow Hill, and there two Welshmen in Lancaster's retinue beheaded him. Lancaster kept the once beautiful head; the boyish, gray body they rolled onto a ladder, which four bent-backed shoemakers carried to the earl of Warwick, who prudently refused it.

Lancaster's success was notable—however dubiously legal—but not final. The king found new favorites, the elder and younger Hugh Dispenser. Moderate barons like Pembroke, men of the so-called middle party, thwarted Lancaster's ambition of limiting the power of the king and changing the government of the realm. At last Lancaster and those who sided with him (the barons whose lands were in the north midlands and the west,[22] among others the great western family of Mortimer, a barony that dated back to William the Conqueror) were forced to conspire with Scotland to safeguard their holdings. As Gaveston had done, the younger Hugh Dispenser made a personal fortune on the king's favor, though unlike Gaveston he did more to earn his keep than amuse the king: he reorganized the royal household and, with the help of carefully chosen servants, imposed more order on the king's complex and confused affairs than even the Ordinances could do. But his access to the king, his ruthlessness and greed, stirred jealousy and dread among the barons, exactly as Gaveston's had done, and his rapacious seizure of other men's lands, sometimes legally, sometimes by force of arms, led at last to parliamentary rebellion and the banishment of both the elder and younger Dispenser. The elder acquiesced and went to France; the younger scornfully turned to channel piracy, robbing merchant ships with the knowledge and even connivance of the king. Like Gaveston's, the banishment of the Dispensers proved unenforceable: Edward had both Hughs back within the year.

Thomas of Lancaster, seated in his great hall at Pontefract Castle, brooded. Though not yet forty-five, he was looking old. He knew well enough that he was caught up in what could be construed as a movement toward accroachment of the royal power. His brother Henry, younger by three years, was even more distressed. The future was dark; no doubt of it any more. Good and evil were less clear than in King Alfred's time, the great, by now quasi-legendary age to which all Englishmen rich or poor looked back for their principles. The house of Lancaster had never been treasonous, was even now more intensely devoted to the welfare of the kingdom than any other earldom a man could name; yet Thomas, earl of Lancaster, Steward of England, had allied himself with men like brash, unprincipled young Roger Mortimer and, however tentatively, with a long-time enemy of England, a barbaric Scot. There seemed no hope any longer for compromise with London. Henry Lancaster had urged conciliation—acceptance of the unacceptable—from the beginning. He urged it still. But it was already too late. Though he'd been known in his day as a fair jouster, a faithful soldier (his son and heir, young Henry, would prove magnificent at both), he was a patient, lenient man, a Christian fatalist who would prefer, if possible, to leave Edward's foolishness and the ills of the nation to God. But could he leave his brother Thomas to God?

At his brother Henry's prodding—and that of his conscience—Thomas

Lancaster took the most moderate course available to him. He organized, with Roger Mortimer and other great barons, what some historians have dubbed "counter parliaments," claiming a duty never claimed before in the name of his hereditary title, Steward of England. But soon, with the Dispensers back in power and seizing land that bordered on his own— their banishment outlawed by parliament's moderates—Lancaster was forced, as it seemed to him, to more desperate measures. He called up his troops for war. Edward at once marched north to arrest him. The Mortimers crumpled without offering a fight—too many magnates had chosen the other side or refused involvement, and surrender might win leniency. "Death For Principle" was not Sir Roger's motto. Other lords, seeing his surrender, followed suit, until finally, deserted by most of his allies and by much of his own army, Lancaster was taken. In what has sometimes been viewed as a parody of Gaveston's "trial" and execution by the barons, Lancaster was read the charges against him, which were presented as "manifest and notorious," thus admitting of no answer, condemned by seven of his coerced peers, and sentenced to death as a traitor. Within the next few days news reached the taverns and wine-shops of England that Sir Thomas of Lancaster, one of the greatest and most beloved of magnates, had been led out of prison in penitential dress "on a lene white Jade with owt Bridil"—his near-blind younger brother watching sorrowfully, helpless, with his son Henry the younger beside him—and executed.

Though the rabble jeered at the time of his death—the human filth that would go anywhere to see an execution for treason, a beheading, drawing, and quartering—Thomas of Lancaster became, almost instantly, a popular saint. In order to keep off the weeping crowds, Edward had to place an armed guard around Pontefract Priory, where Lancaster was entombed, and soon afterward a chapel, financed by donations from all over England, was built on the scene of his execution. For fear that blind Henry or his twenty-two-year-old son might become the center of a dangerous popular movement, blind Henry was immediately relieved of much of his suzerainty. Now the greed of the Dispensers increased by leaps and bounds, and soon opposition to Edward was greater than ever. And now—if not from the beginning—the heart of the opposition was Edward's beautiful, slightly mad French queen, Isabella.

Though she bore the king four children, it had never been a love match. Isabella had been a child of twelve when Edward had brought her to England and married her. When Thomas of Lancaster—Isabella's uncle—went north to hunt Gaveston he wrote to her in a tone which suggests that she was closer to her uncle's side than to her husband's. She had repeatedly interceded for men of Lancaster's party—for, among others, her younger uncle, Thomas of Lancaster's weak-eyed brother Henry, who'd been stripped of so much power after Thomas's death that for the honor of his house he could no longer afford to be moderate.

But it was the younger Dispenser who finally forced Isabella's hand. There were rumors, probably true, that he was trying to engineer annulment of her marriage to Edward; and in 1324, on the pretext of danger of a French invasion, he sequestered her estates. The queen was paid well for the sequestration; but the blow was a cruel one nevertheless: in the Middle Ages money was no substitute for property. When the king, on the imprudent advice of the Dispensers, sent Isabella to Paris to arrange an understanding between himself and her brother, Charles IV, king of France, she went eagerly, and stayed there, making France the base of her plot to wreck her husband. There she met dashing Sir Roger Mortimer, who had escaped from the Tower, and who now became her lover and fellow leader of the conspiracy. Soon, thanks to another error of the overconfident Dispensers, they were joined by the king's son Edward, heir to the crown. He immediately became the plot's kingpin.

With continental help—not from France but from Hainault, Holland, and Zeeland, whose ruler, William II, was willing to exchange military support for the promise of the marriage of his daughter Philippa to Edward III, who happened to be in love with her—Isabella and Mortimer invaded England. Edward II ordered a muster of his fleet, but the sailors of England, according to the chronicles, refused to fight because of their hatred of the Dispensers. Edward II's land forces were not much more helpful. He was soon captured, and after repeated attempts by his friends to rescue and reinstate him, agents of Roger Mortimer arranged his murder.

As for the Dispensers, the elder was tried and condemned in an explicit parody of the so-called trial of Thomas of Lancaster. He was brought before a group of magnates which included Henry Lancaster, and the proceedings against him read, in part: "Sir Hugh, this court denies you any right of answer, because you yourself made a law that a man could be condemned without right of answer, and this law shall now apply to you and your adherents." Like that of Thomas Lancaster, his conviction was "by notoriety." Soon after, his son, Hugh the younger, was tried and condemned in the same way.

Now Isabella and Mortimer ruled, with Edward III as their resentful puppet. And like Gaveston and the Dispensers before him, Roger Mortimer proved so greedy and unprincipled that all Englishmen soon hated him as devoutly as they'd hated the earlier royal favorites, the various so-called evil counsellors to the crown. As Gaveston had made magnates jealous and fearful through his acceptance of crown gifts—

drains on the treasury—and as the Dispensers had stirred the magnates to wrath by their legal and illegal seizures of land, so now Roger Mortimer became the universal enemy by legal and illegal confiscations and profligate waste. Lancaster quietly raised an army to oppose him— once gentle Henry, now virtually blind—and was beaten and outlawed, with all his followers, including John Chaucer. The ruinous policy of Isabella and Mortimer was at last ended by the young king himself, who in conspiracy with the Pope and certain English lords (among them his cousin, Henry Lancaster the younger) seized and killed Mortimer and placed the queen in house arrest, where she remained, now quite mad and therefore harmless, until her death.

The judgment has been universal against Mortimer as chief engineer of the deposition and murder of Edward II and later shameless thief of royal lands and prerogatives, as adulterous lover of the queen of England, and as cynical architect of the Treaty of Northampton, which ceded to the Scots—though they'd never won the field—all that they'd fought for, and freed Mortimer to selfish and acquisitive rule of England through his doting royal mistress, without fear of trouble on the border, those Scottish raids which had so stirred the people of the north against Edward II. The judgment is fair in a sense, but it requires some comment.

In the fourteenth century, neither Edward II nor his barons were in a position to understand fully what was wrong between them. The endlessly repeated complaint against Edward II—later to be raised against the far more popular King Edward III and, still later, against his unlucky grandson Richard—was that through the influence of evil counsellors he was driving the kingdom to bankruptcy. The lavish outlays of Edward II and his court favorites, the endless travel from castle to castle, grandiose and expensive tournaments and entertainments—a manner of living which drove the crown to legal and illegal seizures of land and to unprecedented taxation and demands of land grants whose rents might help support the household—gave color to the complaint. But the complaint missed the point. For all his high living, Edward II's real expenses were the inescapable expenses of a government larger and more complex than any formerly known in England. Because of the disorder of the king's affairs—a tangle the Dispensers did much to straighten out—the king himself had no clear understanding of how much it cost to be a late medieval king. The baronial Ordinances imposed on Edward II reveal that the barons, too, had no clear idea of the magnitude of the royal enterprise. The Ordinances removed evil counsellors and drove out foreign parasites (as the barons saw them); but they made no solid arrangements for bringing money into the treasury for payment of the hundreds of civil servants, armorers, shipbuilders, architects, and diplomats (with their households and assistants) required by a monarchy involved in international trade and perpetually at war or threatened by war. Collection of the king's customs by Englishmen meant only that, instead of foreigners, men like John Chaucer and later those collectors responsible to comptroller Geoffrey Chaucer could do the skimming.

The real problem, in other words, was the necessary expense of bureaucracy. Gaveston, as Professor McKisack points out, "was innocent of any notions about government: the household arrangements were much as they had been in the latter years of Edward I"[23]—when all the trouble started. It was the financial predicament of late medieval kings which drove them to dependence, not only on foreign bankers, but also on skilled administrators of the household, the only people who had even the faintest hope of keeping them solvent. The result was an impasse. Thomas of Lancaster's solution, blocked by the king's favorites and by his own peers, was to create, in effect, a puppet king who would be controlled by a baronial council under the presidency of the Steward of England—himself and those who followed in his title. Had Lancaster been successful, and had he managed to put England in the kind of order that obtained in his own household, he and his fellow barons might not have solved the problem but they would at least have learned how immense it was. As a loyal Englishman, Lancaster had no personal ambition of controlling the crown, much less of seizing it. He sought only financial order for the kingdom and, concomitantly, the safety of baronial wealth mainly threatened (he believed) by the insatiable favorites of the king. Because his program failed, the struggle had to be resolved largely by men of self-interest, royalist versus rebel.

Insatiable the favorites certainly were, but their appetite has sometimes been misunderstood. Men like the Dispensers cannot have failed to recognize that their survival depended on more than Edward's favor: they must have land, rents, armies. Snatching land from their neighbors, they roused an ire that must sooner or later swarm over them in any case, owing to their unaccountability, their access to the king. Since Edward II stubbornly refused to rule—refused as long as possible to deal with the terrorist raids of the Scots, refused to intercede in the squabbles and private wars of his magnates—those in charge of the king's business must save themselves however they might, and those not in charge of the king's business must either lose all or destroy the favorites, bring the king to terms. When the magnates were united that was easy to do (though not emotionally easy), for all of them had armies and they need not commit the treason of admitting opposition to the king himself. On the contrary, they could argue, and devoutly believe, that they attacked to rescue the king from pernicious advisers. But for the magnate whose peers refused to support him, who would allow his ancestral rights to be extingiushed rather than defend him against the power of the crown, survival became the only law. Mortimer, more unscrupulous and reckless than Thomas of Lancaster, survived, but in the process showed himself so cynical about law, even the laws of polite society—even the emotionally deep prohibition of regicide—that all who had a trace of devotion to decency were repelled. For young Edward III, whose devotion to the chivalric code was fanatical, and whose ambition was as great as his warrior grandfather's, Mortimer's very existence was an intolerable affront, and so he ended it.

If knighthood was declining, young Edward was not yet aware of the fact. His chief friends and counsellors were men like his cousin, Henry Lancaster, son of blind Henry—an athletic, keenly intelligent young knight, Edward's frequent companion, the man often cited as the probable model or partial model for Chaucer's Knight in the *Canterbury Tales*. He would become in his maturity one of the greatest fighting men in England, yet a man at the same time gentle, generous, compassionate, a man of whom, apparently, it could truly be said that

> everemoore he hadde a sovereyn prys;
> And though that he were worthy, he was wys,
> And of his port as meeke as is a maydë.   [*deportment*]
> He neverë yet no vileynye ne saydë
> In al his lyf unto no maner wight.
> He was a verray, parfit, gentil knyght.

With the backing of young Lancaster and other lords, Edward III seized his rightful powers as king, married his princess, and maneuvered his exhausted and demoralized country into war. All England rejoiced. War was the way to wealth in the late Middle Ages—or so it seemed to businessmen like John Chaucer, who helped to organize syndicates to loan money to the crown, for substantial returns,[24] and to barons who rode out in proud array to ransom or be ransomed for incredible sums.

It was of course a mistake, as Richard II would perceive. War was the way to national bankruptcy, to the death of the Christian chivalric ideal, and to further weakening of the royal prerogative. King Richard would close down England's multi-front wars and work for his own version of what was right in "the marriage of king and state"; the barons would once more fight for their ancient privileges; and Chaucer's poetry would, in various disguises, lay the comedy and tragedy of the love conflict bare. Like his father, like his close friend John of Gaunt, or like Gaunt's father-in-law, the younger Henry Lancaster, Geoffrey Chaucer would be unshakably a king's man, one who seriously believed the words Shakespeare gives to his foppish King Richard:

> Not all the water in the rough, rude sea
> Can wash the balm off from an anointed king.

Yet Chaucer would understand, too, the feelings—and the threat—of the tyrannized, whether in the marriage of the king and the state or in the ordinary household—feelings like those of the unsinkable Wife of Bath:

> Experiencë, though noon auctoritee
> Were in this world, is right ynogh for me
> To speke of wo that is in mariagë!

But in 1340, the year Edward III of England assumed, on questionable grounds, the title "King of France," neither the effects of war nor the effects of weakened monarchy were obvious. That was the year the English navy won its stunning victory over the French at Sluys. It was also the year John of Gaunt was born and, probably, Geoffrey Chaucer. It was a wonderful time to be an Englishman.

Meanwhile, in India and throughout Europe, there was famine that year. All over the world the weather was gradually, mysteriously changing—black, smoky rains, colder winters, unheard-of droughts. The next year, India would have plague, which would soon move northward.

Two: Chaucer's Youth and Early Education—Life and the Specter of Death on the Ringing Isle (c. 1340~1357)

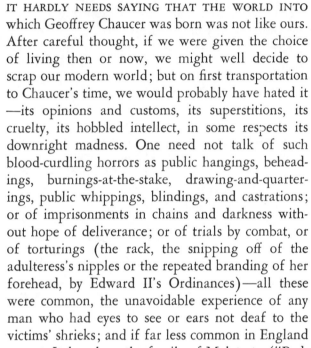

IT HARDLY NEEDS SAYING THAT THE WORLD INTO which Geoffrey Chaucer was born was not like ours. After careful thought, if we were given the choice of living then or now, we might well decide to scrap our modern world; but on first transportation to Chaucer's time, we would probably have hated it —its opinions and customs, its superstitions, its cruelty, its hobbled intellect, in some respects its downright madness. One need not talk of such blood-curdling horrors as public hangings, beheadings, burnings-at-the-stake, drawing-and-quarterings, public whippings, blindings, and castrations; or of imprisonments in chains and darkness without hope of deliverance; or of trials by combat, or of torturings (the rack, the snipping off of the adulteress's nipples or the repeated branding of her forehead, by Edward II's Ordinances)—all these were common, the unavoidable experience of any man who had eyes to see or ears not deaf to the victims' shrieks; and if far less common in England than in France or, worse yet, Italy, where the family of Malatesta ("Badhead") filled a deep well with the severed heads of victims, the difference would strike a modern visitor as trifling. England's great poet of gentleness and compassion walked every day in a city where the fly-bitten, birdscarred corpses of hanged criminals—men and women, even children—draped their shadows across the crowded public square. If the crime was political, the corpse was tarred to prevent its decaying before the achievement of the full measure of its shame. As Chaucer strolled across London Bridge, making up intricate ballades in his head, counting beats on his fingers, he could see, if he looked up, the staked heads of wrongdoers hurried away by earnest Christians to their presumed eternal torment. With our modern sensibilities we would certainly object and perhaps interfere—as Chaucer never did—and for the attempt to undermine the king's peace, not to mention God's, our severed heads would go up on the stakes beside those others.

To call it an age of—at least in some quarters—downright madness is not as extreme as it may sound: Chaucer's time was one in which official doctrine split human personality in ways we would now call schizophrenic. All violence, all aggression, all selfishness and cruelty in everyday activity were sternly condemned, though they were in fact not uncommon. For many people, the model of virtue, as all pious literature and painting shows, was the hangdog saint, hands limply extended in a gesture of helplessness and self-effacing acceptance of providential whim, or fingertips touching in timid prayer, pale eyes rolled up. (Such attitudes, admittedly, must have been more common among artists who served the Church than they were on London streets.) Yet it was an age of crusades, Jewish ghetto burning (in places like Germany, where there were still Jews*), judicial murder, legally sanctioned wife-beating (it was legal to beat a wife into unconsciousness, but not acceptable to beat her until her inert body farted, a sign that she was in shock and might possibly be dying). Outside the more sophisticated courts of the nobility and such centers of liberal thought as Oxford, it was an age of misogyny, when women were regularly and insistently viewed as the source and symbol of all human wickedness, yet at the same time it was an age of Mariolatry and courtly love—two systems (loosely speaking), one religious, one secular, which made women the pattern and vector of all human goodness. Nor is it mere hindsight that shows us these deep and, from our point of view, psychologically deadly paradoxes. They are the subject matter of the period's finest poets. Men like Dante and Chaucer, in different ways and to different degrees, analyzed these conflicts and worked, consciously or otherwise, toward a gradual softening of the official hard line. A modern humanist might have thrown up his hands in dismay.

But in small things, too, we might be bothered, at least at first, by life in the Middle Ages—for instance, by Chaucer's annoying habit (or any other well-educated man's) of always reading to himself aloud, never silently, "barking on books," as one fifteenth-century playwright puts it; or, to speak of things less petty, we might be bothered by the general manners of the better class of people in the fourteenth century. They ate with their fingers, except for the occasional employment of a knife or soup spoon, and even the fingers of courtly ladies were not impeccably clean. People washed before meals, but often in plain cold water; soap and hot water, though available if the occasion warranted, were more troublesome to come by then than now. And since meat dishes were normally sharp and spicy stews—because of men's limited knowledge, at that time, of refrigeration, and the resultant need to disguise the taste of rottenness (only after hunts or at holiday festivals were there broiled meats and roasts)—the business of taking one's supper with one's fingers, even if managed with the aplomb of Chaucer's Prioress (whom Chaucer gently mocks as a touch too fussy) made for mess. According to medieval handbooks on manners, correct form, if one had a stuffed-up nose, was

* On the outlawing of Jews in most European countries, see chapter 1, *n*. 24.

to blow it on one's clothing—the underside of a skirt or, say, a sleeve-flap. When Richard II introduced the handkerchief at court, it was considered by his enemies a further sign of his intolerable, effeminate aestheticism. Why a handkerchief is preferable to the skirt or sleeve-flap is perhaps a question for scholastic philosophy; what difference, after all, which abditorial vestimentum should collect the germs? Nevertheless, a twentieth-century visitor to the past might well be put off by a gray-eyed Queen Guinevere who happened to be down with a cold when he met her, or even by Chaucer's beautiful Blanche of Richmond, blind Henry's granddaughter, "fair Lady White." The modern man's revulsion, I hasten to add, might not last long, if we assume a man of sense. Custom is everything. "Ecch contree hath his lawës," as Chaucer writes. "For every wight which that to Romë went / Halt not o [one] path, or alway o manerë." But even so . . .

A modern visitor might be distressed, too, by the living arrangements: no glass windows except in the houses of the rich—places like John Chaucer's house on Thames Street and, better yet, John of Gaunt's palace on the Savoy, where the glass was stained. At night all light that might have labored in through the coarse glass windows, or the parchment windows or nothing-covered windows in poorer houses, was tightly sealed out by wooden shutters. (It made, of course, for a coziness we miss.) There were no chairs, only benches or cushioned trunks for a lady or a gouty old gentleman to sit on; at meal-times the servants brought out trestles and table-boards. There was no privacy, even in a vintner's big house. Whereas the poor lived in only one room, or at most two, in company with their chickens, pigs, geese, cats, and mice, a vintner's house might have numerous rooms, but none to be alone in. A house like Chaucer's father's would be a large building with a high stone wall and gardens around it, perhaps a few fruit trees, a house with a steeply pitched tile roof and leaded-glass bay windows projecting from the second and third floors. There were various outbuildings, including a pigpen (the livestock of the citizenry was a persistent problem for town magistrates, who repeatedly issued ordinances forbidding the inhabitants to let their horses, swine, and geese run loose in the streets); and inside the house lay a labyrinth of corridors and chambers, dark arches, stairs. There would be a garret, or coalhouse, set over the great gate opening onto Thames Street and extending over whatever humble tenantries were built into the wall; there would be a "pastry house" or bakehouse, connected with the kitchen, which stood next to the central hall; a vaulted cellar and a larder house, with a buttery above, and above that a chamber, all connected by stairs; beyond the hall, the great parlor, with small chambers around it, a chapel, perhaps a privy; and there would probably be, elsewhere, a cloth-house with closets, a bolting house, third-floor garrets, and various chambers for storage, laundry, and so forth. A rich splay of rooms; but the rooms—queerly small, from a modern point of view—were for working in, never for getting away by oneself. For living there was only the great parlor and the hall, which doubled as a dining room.[1] In the bedrooms the inhabitants slept several to a bed, usually naked, though sometimes in heavy, long nightgowns and night-caps. (Nightgowns and nightcaps are frequently mentioned in medieval wills.) Though today we might object to sleeping several in a bed, no objection seems to have crossed medieval minds; even the gentlemen-servants to the king slept two to a bed, as Edward's Ordinances show. It may be, however, that we pay dear for our privacy. The loneliness, ennui, and alienation now so common seem to have been rare diseases in the late Middle Ages.

There were other disadvantages in the living arrangements. The walls of a good medieval English house were cold, sometimes damp and, in general, sparsely adorned except for dish-and-mug shelves, though doors had carved figures, in the better houses, and pillows, coverlets, and draperies had pictures—sometimes bright flowers, sometimes beauti-fully fashioned crucifixions or depictions of the gruesome deaths of saints—and often in the best houses rooms boasted tapestries and hang-ings or even "halls," tapestries that covered the whole room. For the arts it was an unusually good time, of course. William Morris was not exaggerating when he wrote in *Gothic Architecture* (1893), "Every village has its painters, its carvers, its actors. . . . The few pieces of household goods left of [that time's] wreckage are marvels of beauty; its woven cloths and embroideries are worthy of its loveliest building; its pictures and ornamented books would be enough in themselves to make a great period of art." On the floor, however, beneath the feet of those long-gowned, high-hatted, white-breasted ladies, lay straw or sometimes reeds for covering, and, here and there, dogshit. Derek Brewer reminds us of Erasmus's remarks about the filth on floors, more than a century after Chaucer's time, and suggests that things were prob-ably worse rather than better in the fourteenth century. Both Brewer and Erasmus perhaps overdraw, or at any rate impose on the late Middle Ages a standard of cleanliness that would probably strike a medieval gentleman as overscrupulous if not bizarre; nevertheless Brewer's sum-mary and comment on Erasmus seems worth quoting:

> The floors . . . are usually of clay, upon which are placed rushes, which are occasionally added to but never changed. They remain for twenty years, warming beneath them spittle, vomit, urine, spilt beer, the remains of fish, and other filth not to be mentioned. This would be in the hall, where people ate, rather than in the other rooms, but still it

gives point to the foot-cloth that John Russell's valet must put down on the ground for his master to step onto when he dressed, even in his own chamber; hence the point of Chaucer mentioning that Criseyde's parlour was paved—it showed how fine it was. When a knight was being armed, of which there is a colorful description in *Sir Gawain,* it was customary to put down a rich cloth on which he stood and on which the armour was laid. When the armour had been "rocked," that is, rolled, to free the rust, and polished, and oiled, one would not want it to pick up the mess on the floor.[2]

Not that Englishmen in 1340 were savages. They'd been horrified by the behavior of the Scots in war—striking castles, villages, and thorpes without warning, often leaving behind them nothing still alive, not even dogs and cats (the religion Christianity supplanted was not dead, we've begun to see, a religion which warned of shape-shifting, so that not even an English sheepdog could safely be trusted); and they were horrified, too, by their equally Celtic allies the Welsh, who, like the Scots, went into battle half-naked, their bodies greased, and took such devilish delight in cutting heads off—as Celts had been doing since time began— that whenever some head was needed (like Gaveston's) the English nobility sent for Welshmen to deal with the unpleasantness. When law and order broke down entirely in Edward II's time, for example, and war and famine drove both Celtic (especially the Irish) and Anglo-Saxon peasants to acts of cannibalism, the whole of the British Isles was sufficiently civilized to be deeply shocked.[3]

Needless to say, in highly sophisticated cities like London, men behaved rather better than elsewhere. There, where law and order were mainly in the hands of the guilds, no cheating of the people was tolerated, once it had been noticed. A man who sold charcoal in shorted measure— or sold pies made of entrails instead of decent meat, or flogged off rotten fish and swore it was wholesome—might be clamped in the pillory, and his foul goods burned under his nose.[4] Strict laws prohibited the befouling of highways and waterways—though the laws were frequently ineffective—and saw to the fining or imprisonment, or worse, of every kind of public nuisance from the cutpurse to the gentleman-robber to the tavern-keeper whose sign was so large it interfered with passing traffic.

But for all the care of English law, and for all the high-mindedness of English guildsmen (who were, after all, protecting their own interests in their attempt to keep up quality), crookedness and violence were standard in the Christian Middle Ages. The more ferocious the punishment, the more ingenious the crooks. Chaucer, Langland, the monk John Lydgate—for that matter, most of the better English poets—tell of the

cunning and cynicism of society's parasites and of the helplessness and fury of decent men undone by them. One vivid description of crooked merchants is John Gower's in the *Mirour de l'Omme* (translated here from the original French):

> There is one merchant in these days whose name is on most men's tongues: Trick is his name, and guile is his nature: though thou seek from the East to the going out of the West, there is no city or good town where Trick doth not amass his ill-gotten wealth. Trick at Bordeaux, Trick at Seville, Trick at Paris buys and sells. . . . In the mercer's trade also doth Trick, of his cunning, practice often divers guiles. . . . Birds of that feather never want a tongue, and Trick is more clamorous than any sparrowhawk: when he seeth strange folks, then shalt thou see him pluck and draw them by the sleeve, calling and crying: "Come," quoth he, "come in without demur! Beds, kerchiefs, and ostrich feathers—sandals, satins, and stuffs from oversea—come I will show you all. What d'ye lack? Come buy, ye need go no further, for here is the best of all the street. . . ." Sometimes Trick is a draper. . . . Men tell us (and I believe it) that whatsoever is dark by nature hateth and avoideth the light: wherefore when I see the draper in his house, methinks he hath no clear conscience. Dark is the window where he bargaineth with thee, and scarce canst thou tell the green from the blue; dark too are his ways, none may trust his word for the price of his goods. Darkly will he set thee his cloth at double price, and clinch it with an oath; darkly thus will he beguile thee all the worse, for he would persuade that he hath done thee a friendship, wherein he hath the more cozened thee, saying that he hath given thee the stuff at cost price to get thy further custom; but the measure and the market price will tell thee afterwards another tale. . . .[5]

All the poets agree, and so do the surviving court records,[6] on the darkness and closeness of the con artists' shops or the underground dens of alchemists and "jugglers" (conjurers) and on the danger of alleyways and even main streets after curfew rang, where men were murdered for trifling reasons or no reason at all, stabbed by daggers, run over by horsemen, smashed to the ground by a quarter staff or door-bar in an argument over (in one recorded case) ten apples, or robbed and beaten by midnight roisterers in animal masks or the terrifying chalk-white mask of that pagan remnant Robin-o-the-Green, "the lily-white boy." Those streets were darker than even the worst in New York are now, lighted only by the occasional flimmer of a torch behind iron-barred gates; and they were darker yet, subjectively: there were ghosts in those days, as all commoners knew for a certainty, though educated people were inclined to scoff, and there were preying devils in the shape of men—"passing men," as Chaucer calls them in the *Canon's Yeoman's Tale*.

But no one went out, if he could help it, after curfew. It was against the law. Except for ghosts, criminals, and a few harmless rowdies— the notorious smithies who delighted in keeping their neighbors awake with their hellish music of hissing steam and iron striking iron (the subject of a famous Middle English poem)—men went to bed soon after sunset (candlewax was expensive) and rose with the chickens who crowed all over London and awakened the bells. And morning in London—once a man grew accustomed to the pillories, the gallows, the eyeless, putrid heads (in many districts, of course, one never saw such things)—was another matter entirely.

To foreigners England was "the Ringing Isle," thanks to all those bells. Bells had spread over England early—they're mentioned in Anglo-Saxon times—and were used to call Christians to their religious Hours, that is, the seven daily periods of prayer (matins, lauds, etc.). But measured time reached the island only in the early fourteenth century. (The first striking clock in Europe was probably built around 1290.) In the district of John Chaucer's Thames Street house, where in all probability Geoffrey Chaucer was born, there were no less than thirty-nine parish churches; and, dominating them all with its majestic wooden spire, the highest in the world, gold painted, out-thundering them all with its deep, rich boom, stood St. Paul's Cathedral. The city's bells rang as if endlessly, sometimes in the dazzling, intrinsicate rhythms that can still be heard when the bellringers ring the "changes" in York. It was impossible to sleep on, with all that noise, and dawn coming in, as it does much earlier in England than in America. So all London got up, unbarred and threw open its windows, pissed, drew water, fed the dogs, the chickens in the room off the stairs, the pigs and geese in back, and got the charcoal fires going in the grim little ovens—or in the huge stone "chimneys" (that is, fireplaces) if the house was large, like John Chaucer's. The long, laborious day began, a work day of nine or ten hours for the rich; for the poor, three or four hours longer.

Such was the world into which Chaucer was born, some summer or winter, spring or fall, around 1340—the year of the birth of the king's fourth son, John of Gaunt. Gaunt opened his eyes in a palace, attended by physicians, courtiers, and royalty—relatives of his mother, Queen Philippa. As for Chaucer—low born and obscure by comparison—no one can say where or when he first saw light. Probably London. Servants, sleepy-eyed, went out to bring in wood, or straw for the parlor, the buttery, the second-floor sitting-room bedrooms, and the first floor's low, close garret apartments—domestics on one side of the steep, narrow stairs, on the other side the chickens, in the room above the privy. The Chaucer servants met servants from next door and relayed the night's gossip: a new son born to the Chaucers.

A difficult delivery, the midwives up till dawn; it was feared they'd be forced to toss the mother in a blanket to get the labor spasms right (or else it was not a difficult delivery and took place in, say, the afternoon, and the midwives stood beaming in their nunnish attire, blowing on their fingers because the winter was cold; or they were absent, having gone to the wrong address). He was born, at any rate. His older brother John, Agnes Chaucer's son by her former husband, was perhaps thrilled and proud, perhaps secretly terrified: now no one would love him.

More gloomy nights came, and bell-filled days. Little Geoffrey began to find the world predictable, this morning the same as all other mornings ("For the whichë," his mother said, "thankëd be God!"). His ears grew attentive: the sad, ghostly cry of the conch-shell horns on the merchant ships; the lapping of the water; the clean, hard echoes from the wharves of stone. His nose grew attentive: his big stepbrother's funny smell, the fierce, slightly frightening animal smells of his father and uncle Tom, the smell of his mother, as wide and sweet and otherworldly as a meadow. He slept again. And again the chickens, the bells, the windows thrown open to let in the resurrected air. (Dawn was now one of the Church's great symbols—the resurrected Lord with his brides all around him, and behind them, sunrise, as Chaucer would impishly set Chauntecleer and his hens. It was the prominent picture in every cathedral.) The city gates opened, not far away, and into the room where the child lay asleep came the clink of horses' hooves in their heavy iron horseshoes, the clatter of wooden or iron-rimmed cartwheels, the yapping of dogs as men kicked them aside—the fourteenth century was overrich in dogs—the musical, almost operatic cries of London's innumerable hard-sell vendors ("Hot peascods!" "Ripe strawberries!" "Paris thread, sirs, finest in the land!" "Mackerel!" "Green rushes!" "Hot sheep's feet!" "Pewter pots!"), and the future poet, wrapped and tied in his cradle like a papoose on his papoose-board—as were all English infants in the days of cold houses and prowling demons, if we can judge by the paintings—opened his eyes and smiled at the motes in the sunbeams, though he couldn't move a finger to catch them, and after a while changed his mind, being wet and hungry, and bawled for help.

Childhood in some respects is always the same, in other respects different from age to age. Medieval children were apparently suckled for a long time, not weaned until five or so; and, because of the high rate of

infant mortality, they seem—judging by hints in the poetry and plays—
to have been treasured in a way that would make modern doting parents
seem cool and indifferent. In the Chaucer house, little Geoffrey went at
once into the care of a wet nurse, a virtuous girl who if all went as expected in a medieval merchant home would be, with the possible exception of his brother, the child's closest friend and companion for several years. She served his every whim—spoiled him utterly, from a
modern point of view. Chaucer's contemporary, Bartholomew the Englishman, says of the ideal wet nurse that she is

> like as the mother . . . glad if the child be glad, and heavy if the
> child be sorry, and [she] taketh the child up if it fall, and giveth it
> suck; if it weep she kisseth and lulleth it still, and gathereth the limbs,
> and bindeth them together, and doth cleanse and wash it when it is
> defiled. And for it cannot speak, the nurse lispeth and soundeth the
> same words to teach more easily the child. . . . And she cheweth meat
> in her mouth, and maketh it ready to the toothless child . . . and so
> she feedeth the child when it is hungered, and pleaseth the child with
> whispering and songs when it shall sleep, and swatheth it in sweet
> clothes, and righteth and stretcheth out its limbs, and bindeth them to-
> gether with cradlebands, to keep and save the child that it have no
> miscrooked limbs. She batheth and anointeth it with good anoint-
> ments.[7]

Medieval Englishmen were not, like stereotype modern Englishmen,
calm and sensible people: they were as passionate, as affectionate, as quick
to change moods, and as easily stirred to violence as, say, the stereotype
modern Italian. When greeting each other, they hugged and kissed like
modern Frenchmen; when insulted or injured they snatched at their daggers without thinking. The younger Henry of Lancaster once, in a fit of
pique, forgot and drew his sword on the king himself. To show just how
little such things meant in that age, nothing came of it. Without inhi-
bition they showered their affection on their children and, whenever possible, took them with them wherever they went, especially to church, to
general fairs, to holy-day outings (which averaged one a week), and to
Friday horse fairs. On those days when all England got off work, London
and the countryside surrounding became tumultuous with games—
noisy, often dangerous games, frequent cause of riots. Even those noble
games tennis and chess were illegal inside London, though often played
—the one because of the riots tennis regularly incited (this was "real"
or "royal" tennis, fast and ferocious), the other because chess, a gamb-
lers' game, had a name for provoking murders.

The games played by girls are recorded, in poetry and censurious
religious writing, merely as dancing until moonrise; but what is usually

meant is the ring-game, a kind of dancing that goes back to pagan times and has been preserved until the present in folk tradition. Older girls played ring-dance with boys, especially parish clerks (or so we're told in popular poetry), and had a way of dropping gloves or scarves which had to be returned late at night through a bedroom window, much to the increase of the population. Everyone played games with balls, from city officials to the smallest children, and older boys played, in summer-time, at archery, running and jumping contests, wrestling, putting the stone, sling-shot play, and duelling with shields and swords. In winter, an early English writer says, boys like John and Geoffrey would play on the ice:

> . . . some, striding as wide as they may, do slide swiftly; others make themselves seats of ice, as great as millstones; one sits down, many hand in hand draw him, and one slipping on a sudden, all fall together; some tie bones to their feet and under their heels, and shoving themselves by a little piked staff, do slide as swiftly as a bird flieth in the air, or an arrow out of a crossbow. Sometime two run together with poles, and hitting one the other, either one or both do fall, not without hurt; some break their arms, some their legs, but youth desirous of glory in this sort exerciseth itself against the time of war.[8]

Broken bones were no trifle in medieval England; if not fatal, they could leave a child crippled for life. Yet parents rode out to watch their children's games, shouting encouragement and frequently joining in.

Though he was coddled in infancy, a child in a house like John Chaucer's had his fair share of troubles. For all the spontaneous displays of affection from his parents, his older brother, and those servants who looked after him, the official view was that a child Geoffrey's age was a wicked creature, no better than an intelligent wild animal, who must be whipped into humanness, beaten and scolded until his bestial side —province of the Devil—was subdued and enchained, and his higher faculties aimed in the right direction, namely, toward heaven. Consider Bartholomew the Englishman's remarks on the child between seven and fourteen, from the time "when he is weaned from milk and knoweth good and evil" to what amounts to adulthood. Such children, Bartholomew says,

> are soft of flesh, lithe and pliant of body, quick and light to move, in-telligent enough to learn, and they lead their lives without thought and care, and set their hearts only on mirth and pleasure, and dread no perils more than beating with a rod, and they love an apple more than gold . . . they are quickly and soon angry, and soon pleased, and easily they forgive; and because of tenderness of body they are soon

hurt and grieved, and cannot well endure hard work. . . . Through
great and strong heat they desire much food, and so by reason of excess
of food and drink they fall often and many times into various sick-
nesses and evils. . . .

Since all children are spotted with evil manners, and think on things
that be, and regard not of things that shall be, they love playing, and
games, and vanity, and forsake learning and profit; and things most
worthy they repute least worthy, and least worthy most worthy. They
desire things that be to them contrary and grievous, and set more
store by the image of a child than the image of a man, and make
more sorrow and woe, and weep more for the loss of an apple, than
for the loss of their heritage; and the goodness that is done for them
they let it pass out of mind. They desire all things that they see, and
pray and ask with voice and with hand. They love talking and counsel
of such children as they be, and avoid company of old men. They keep
us no counsel, but they tell all they hear or see. Suddenly they laugh and
suddenly they weep. Always they cry, jangle, scorn, or disdain, that
hardly they be still while they sleep. When they are washed of filth,
straightway they defile themselves again. When the mother washeth
and combeth them, they kick and sprawl, and put with feet and with
hands, and withstandeth with all their might. For they think only on
belly joy.[9]

That this was merely the official view, not necessarily the actual opinion
of every London vintner's wife, is clear enough from the patristic ring
of so many of Batholomew's phrases—"belly joy" (from St. Paul), "regard not of things that shall be," or the juxtaposition of "apple" and
"gold" (from exegetical tradition). Indeed, we may be sure that the
frequent admonitions of public officials, priests, and irascible old
rhymers, that parents should never spare the rod, are proof that many
parents did. We have no evidence, in short, on how Chaucer was raised.
But though a sober biographer's hands may be tied, no novelist can doubt,
when he considers the impishness of the poet in maturity, or recalls the
almost certainly true story of his beating a friar during his student years,
that Chaucer, like Lydgate and Froissart, was helped by an occasional
thwack to the piety and gentleness, not to mention the learning, of his
adulthood.

There is no evidence, either, that young Chaucer's parents and their
servants told him stories, but they must have. It was a great age for stories,
as great as any the world has ever known. Priests told them, minstrels told
them, shopkeepers, workers, beggars, and wandering friars told them.
Songs, poems, and stories were a way of breaking up the endless, heavy
work and expressing the feeling of community that makes Chaucer's
time so profoundly unlike ours. He heard ballads, some of them still

heard today in later versions: "The Fox Went Out on the Town One Night," "The Clerk and the Mermaid," "The Coventry Carol" . . . He heard wonderfully obscene poems and blasphemous poems too funny to suppress. He heard, perhaps from his brother and his friends, a thousand farmer's daughter stories, except that the maiden was seldom a farmer's daughter; and stories of lecherous old men, lascivious monks, and delicious, brainless nuns; perhaps also stories of impotent old clots like January in Chaucer's *Merchant's Tale,* who labors all night to consummate his marriage to delicious young May, trying to inspire his indifferent member by madcap antics and suggestive songs—alas, all in vain!

> He was al coltissh, ful of rageryë,
> And ful of jargon as a flekked pyë.   [*magpie*]
> The slakkë skyn aboute his nekkë shaketh,
> Whil that he sang, so chaunteth he and craketh.
> But God woot what that May thoughte in hir hertë,
> Whan she hym saugh up sittynge in his shertë,   [*saw*]
> In his nyght-cappe, and with his nekkë lenë;
> She preyseth nat his pleyyng worth a benë.
> Thanne seide he thus, "My restë wol I takë;
> Now day is come, I may no lenger wakë."
> And doun he leyde his heed, and sleep til prymë.

From everyone around him, chances are—from his grandfathers, his father and his uncle Tom, his great, fat, bald uncle Nicholas Copton, and from Wat the Yorkshireman, his father's apprentice—little Geoffrey heard stories, partly true, of terrible battles with the Scots, French, and Irish, stories of whole wide kingdoms burning, and of times of starvation when even warlords of royal blood were reduced to eating horsemeat or dog. In his father's house—sitting restless on the bench, swinging his legs beside his mother and brother John—he may sometimes have heard popular romances read, also classical tales of Orpheus, Theseus, and Theodosius, tales from the (early fourteenth-century) *Gesta Romanorum* of magicians and monsters, ladies in distress, thrilling escapes from perilous situations, all with appended allegorical interpretations. And undoubtedly, late at night, with the rain drumming steadily on the baked-tile roof, he heard stories of ghosts and mysterious creatures and the Devil.

Even in the absolute darkness of his bedroom, John in bed beside him, young Geoffrey's London seemed comfortable and safe—light sounds of breathing in the chambers all around him, an occasional cough from the garret, the cluck of a chicken, the sigh of a dog, and behind the house, the startled grunt of a pig in the middle of a dream. But outside London there was another world, he knew. A world of forests and wilderness where devils prowled and only monks dared molest their ancient, solitary reign. There were many who, like the chronicler at Novalese, under Mont Cenis, had seen devils in the woods in the form of serpents and toads, or, like St. Guthlac, heard devils booming like bitterns and sometimes speaking in the Celtic tongue. "Devils rode in the storm that unroofed the monks' cloister," G. G. Coulton tells us, "or in the fire that fell from heaven upon their steeple and burned the church." Coulton tells the story of St. Edmund Rich, who when a young man "saw at sunset a flight of black crows: these he recognized at once as a swarm of devils come to fetch the soul of a local usurer at Abingdon; and sure enough, when he came to Abingdon, the man was dead."[10]

Particularly from the north—Macbeth country—came stories of witches, changelings, and other diabolic things. The regions of cold and bad weather were the Devil's special province, as Chaucer makes plain in the *Friar's Tale* and as texts such as Jeremiah 1.14 and 4.6 make clear: "Out of the north an evil shall break forth," and "I will bring evil from the north, and a great destruction." Chaucer heard, for instance, northern tales like this one:

> There befell a detestable and marvellous thing in the western parts of Scotland, in Clydesdale, some four miles from Paisley, in the house of one Sir Duncan of the Isles, which should strike terror into sinners and demonstrate the appearance of the damned on the day of the final resurrection. A man who lived wickedly under the habit of holy Religion, and who came to a most evil end under the curse of excommunication for certain sacrileges committed in his own monastery—this man's corpse, I say, long after his burial in the said monastery, haunted many men with illusions that could be seen and heard amid the shades of night. After which this son of darkness transferred himself to the aforesaid knight's dwelling, that he might try the faith of the simple and by his adverse deeds deter them [from evil] in plain daylight, or perchance that, by God's secret judgment, he might thus show who had been implicated in this crime of his. Wherefore, taking to himself a body (whether natural or aerial we know not, but in any case black, gross, and palpable), he was wont to come in noonday light under the garb of a black monk of St. Benedict, and sit upon the gable of the barn or corn-grange; and whensoever a man would shoot him with arrows or pierce him with a pitchfork, then whatsoever material substance was fixed into that damned spectre was burned forthwith, more swiftly than I can tell the tale, to ashes. Those also who would have wrestled with him he threw and shook so horribly as though he would break all their limbs. The lord's firstborn, a squire grown to man's

estate, was foremost in this attack upon the phantom. One evening, therefore, as the master of the house sat with his household round the hall fire, that sinister shape came among them and troubled them with blows and throwing of missiles; then the rest scattered in flight, and that squire alone fought single-handed with the ghost; but, sad to tell, he was found on the morrow slain by his adversary. If however it be true that the Devil receiveth power over none but such as have lived like swine, then it may easily be divined wherefore that young man met with so terrible a fate.[11]

Young Chaucer, as he grew older, would learn to laugh at such stories, and in comic poems like the *Miller's Tale* would poke fun at the ignorant and credulous. Yet it seems likely that Chaucer may have harbored—as Dr. Johnson would, four centuries later—a superstitious streak. Chaucer's was an age, we must remember, in which belief in the miraculous was sometimes the most natural available means of accounting for nature's more mysterious processes. If the ignorant of the time held curious beliefs, so did those wise men who scoffed at them—that sage thirteenth-century philosopher Thomas Aquinas, for instance, who says that "to the ignorant it seemeth miraculous that the magnet draweth iron, or that a little fish holdeth back a ship." Aquinas's fish, here, is the *remora,* an imaginary beast less than a foot in length, through whose queer activities sailors explained otherwise unaccountable hindrances or disturbances of navigation.

Even within the safe walls of London, magic and witchcraft were everywhere. Little Geoffrey's playmates could frighten him with stories of the Evil Eye—stories both they and (at least in some instances) their elders believed, not altogether without reason. Witches were not, in Chaucer's day, bent, warty strangers who lived in shanties far from town and had little intercourse with ordinary Christians. Except among the well-educated, Christianity and the old pagan religion were interlocked like two tree trunks grown together; the practice of witchcraft was not a separate way of life from the Christian but a matter of degree—not a question of whether one said magic spells or engaged in ritual acts but of how many spells one said and how benevolent one's choice of acts. Berthold or Regensburg had said in one of his sermons about a hundred years earlier, "Many of the village folk would come to heaven, were it not for their witchcrafts. . . . The woman has spells for getting a husband, spells for her marriage; spells on this side and on that; spells before the child is born, before the christening, after the christening; and all she gains with her spells is that her child fares the worse all its life long. . . ."[12]

If it wasn't from the old religion that the magic was drawn, it came from the new: the old woman who crumbled consecrated Hosts over her cabbages to kill the caterpillars, the priest who used a Host as a love philtre, the innumerable priests who used holy water to drive off grasshoppers or exorcize ghosts. Chaucer, like all medieval children, filled his head with such things and presumably, like most medieval people, had terrible nightmares. (The "night mare," technically, was a horselike thing that came to your bed and sat on you.) In his maturity, of course, Chaucer would make distinctions between things Christian and things not; but there would remain all around him—no doubt to Chaucer's delight—men like his carpenter in the *Miller's Tale* who, to save his seemingly ensorcelled guest Nicholas, cries out in a hodgepodge of old and new,

> "What! Nicholay! what, how! what, looke adoun!
> Awak, and thenk on Cristës passioun!
> I crouchë thee from elvës and fro wightës."   [*sign with a cross*]
> Therwith the nyght-spel seyde he anon-rightës
> On fourë halvës of the hous aboutë,
> And on the thresshfold of the dorë withoutë:
> "Jhesu Crist and seintë Benedight,
> Blessë this hous from every wikked wight,
> For nyghtës veryë, the whitë *pater-noster!*   [*the meaning of*
> Wherë wentestow, seintë Petres soster?"   verye *is unknown*]

When he was seven or so (in 1347), Geoffrey Chaucer moved with his parents, his older brother, and by now, probably, his younger sister Kate, to the city of Southampton, where his father had been made deputy to the king's butler. As deputy, John Chaucer was mainly responsible, as I've said, for collecting import duties on each shipment of wine that came into the Southampton area (Chichester, Seaford, Shoreham, and Portsmouth). He was made, the same year, collector of the king's customs on woolen goods made in England for export. Meanwhile, since a child's formal schooling began at about seven, Geoffrey was about now entering a new period of his life. In all probability the future poet had already learned to read a little, with the help of a clerical tutor back in London. Now he perhaps, along with his brother, began study with whatever rector served as schoolmaster in the Chaucers' district, giving lessons in the vestry of the church, in a room above it, or in his own home. The school may have been a song-school of the kind we read of in the *Prioress's Tale*, a small school attached to some church or cathedral, where children were taught manners, prayers, and hymns, and introduced to the rudiments of reading and writing Latin.

Something of what he learned in the way of manners can be gathered, perhaps, from a set of rules written for boarding-school children in the fifteenth century. The child was to get out of bed promptly, cross himself, wash his hands and face, comb his hair, "ask the grace of God to speed you in all your works, then go to mass and ask mercy for all your trespasses" and to "say 'Good morning' courteously to whomsoever you meet by the way." He was to make the sign of the cross over his mouth before eating ("Your diet will be the better for it"), then say his grace ("it occupies but little time"), and after that say a *Pater Noster* and an *Ave Maria* for the souls that lie in pain, and then—only then, apparently —begin eating. He is told to be truthful, to keep his promises, to be silent when his betters address him, "and in speaking to any man keep your hands and feet quiet, and look up into his face. . . ." The rules admonish the child:

> Point not with your finger at anything, nor be ready to tell tidings. If any man speaks well of you or of your friends, he must be thanked. Have few words and wisely placed, for so may you win a good name. . . . Get your money honestly, and keep out of debt and sin. . . . Whether you spit near or far, hold your hand before your mouth to hide it. Keep your knife clean and sharp, and cleanse it on some cut bread, not on the cloth, I bid you; a courteous man is careful of the cloth. Do not put your spoon in the dish or on the edge of it, as the untaught do, or make a noise when you sup, as do boys [i.e., ruffians]. . . . When your better hands you a cup, take it with both hands, lest it fall, and drink yourself and set it by; and if he speaks to you, doff your cap and bow your knee.
>
> Do not scratch yourself at the table so that men call you a jackdaw, or wipe your nose or nostrils, else men will say you are come of churls. Make neither the cat nor the dog your fellow at table. And do not play with the spoon, or the trencher, or your knife, but lead your life in cleanliness and honest manners.[13]

The likelihood is that a boy with Geoffrey's background had been given already a fair start on his manners. All the same, it was a painful time for children, especially the energetic child with a lively sense of humor. Medieval teachers were notoriously stern, though there were of course some teachers, then as now, who were less stern than they pretended. And so that cold eye was always on him, as he sneaked his gristly mutton to the dog or by a sudden movement upset his cup. The reproach of the teacher or usher came, and if Geoffrey was so wicked as to repeat his mistake or, what was worse, laugh, a more ferocious reproach came—perhaps that theologically stupid cliché from the time of St. John Crysostom, "Christ is crucified, and dost thou laugh?"—and the boy was snatched from the table and given his beating.

At elementary school Chaucer began his study—reading and writing Latin—with the help of a hornbook, that is, a piece of parchment protected by a transparent layer of horn on which were written the alphabet, the Lord's Prayer (in Latin), and one or two other things useful to beginners. When he'd learned the rudiments of reading and writing, he moved on to the Psalter, from which he learned more complicated Latin. The lessons were taught in French. (By 1385 all lessons would be in English, with the result, a writer of the time tells us, "that now the children of [English] grammar schools know no more French than their left heel."[14]) But French was no problem for the children of gentlemen or well-to-do merchants in Chaucer's day, though it was by no means the language of the London streets. Children of the better families, we're told, were taught French "from the time they are rocked in their cradles, and can speak and play with a child's brooch."[15] Possibly in Chaucer's time, though the invention is thought to be somewhat later, the so-called Primer was used. Chaucer's seven-year-old "clergeoun" in the *Prioress's Tale* is still at his Primer, a book mainly of psalms and ordinary church prayers but also containing the alphabet and other things suitable in a textbook for the very young. The Primer was supposed to give the child his start on both literacy and religion, and if Geoffrey used one, it was probably, in his case, successful; but quite commonly, it seems, children learned their songs and prayers, as does Chaucer's little clergeoun, without understanding a word or letter of what they said.[16]

At just about this point, Geoffrey's studies were briefly interrupted; his family moved back to London, where schools were closed.

The Chaucers had been in Southampton for two years. It was probably a peaceful time for them, though by 1347 evils were brewing in the rest of the world, evils of which John Chaucer, at the customshouse, was one of the first to hear. There was war on the continent—civil war in Rome and war on land and sea between the English and French. (The English fleet had again proved its might, defeating the French at Le Crotoy, on the Somme; and in a siege of Calais, Edward III had introduced a new weapon—cannon, strange machines used primarily for frightening horses.) War raged everywhere, in fact, the king of Hungary fighting Apulia, the king of Bohemia fighting Bavaria, the Eastern Empire fighting the Turks.

But there was also stranger, more frightening news reaching England by 1347. In Constantinople, Naples, Genoa, and south France there was pestilence. There were stories of whole cities depopulated, great castles abandoned, and drifting Genoese merchant ships—a great, dark cog riding deep in the water, loaded down with treasure, and not a live man on board and no pirate who'd touch her. In 1348—the year Edward founded the Order of the Garter—the Black Death reached England. It reached Dorset in August, crept to Bristol, then to Gloucester. It reached Oxford by September, and in October struck London.

Modern historians agree that the effect of the Black Death has been exaggerated, though no one denies that it was the greatest single disaster in European history. It is true in only the most general sense that—as F. A. Gasquet claimed in 1893, in his book *The Great Pestilence*—the plague marks the dividing point between medieval and modern history. Europe entered a period of social and economic crisis in the late thirteenth and early fourteenth centuries, and the Black Death capped it; but the Black Death was not the cause. At the beginning of the thirteenth century all Europe was greatly overpopulated—not in modern terms, of course, but in terms of what medieval farming and manufacture could support. With or without the plague, the medieval way of life was failing. By 1250 population had already begun to decline, but migration into towns made for desperate overpopulation there and resulted in increased sickness, starvation and bloodshed. By the 1340's, conditions had grown stifling. Even in an exceptionally clean town like London, there was some unavoidable piling up of garbage, poor people lived in dangerously overcrowded houses, rickety firetraps in a city where fires were not easy to put out, and rats bred everywhere along with rat-fleas, vectors of the pestilence. Feeding and clothing this population was a clumsy business, since guilds jealously guarded their privileges, including all conceivable kinds of job segmentation and featherbedding (the man who carried in kindling must have a helper to stack it), and since guilds similar enough in function to allow possibilities of job overlap (for instance, the fullers and weavers, both processing wool) frequently had street wars, in which many people died. The year 1340 had been one of famine—the worst since 1315–17. Seven years later England had still not fully recovered. The weather was changing, all Europe entering a new climatic phase involving longer, colder winters and cooler, wetter summers, so that farming was hard to plan. (A century earlier, England could still grow grapes for wine.) As Professor Nicholas has pointed out, "Europe was undernourished at the best of times. . . . [T]he diet of most was grain, chiefly wheat and rye. The carbohydrates were supplemented with some poultry and eggs, but there was little milk, since it soured so rapidly. . . ."[17] As for meat, the upper class got some from hunting, and some was available at the town markets; but the need for animals to sell, to use in war, and to pull plows ruled them out as food for the lower classes. Since animals were so valuable, providing grazing space put severe pressure on arable land used for feeding human beings. And so it was to an undernourished, grossly inefficient, sick and overcrowded London that the Black Death came.

The pestilence, we know now, was not one plague but two simultaneously: bubonic plague, which sent the victim's fever soaring and raised ugly pustules on his armpits or groin, and which in many instances did not kill him; and pneumonic plague, which attacked the victim's lungs and was therefore much more contagious and almost invariably fatal. Before the first wave of pestilence was finished (late in 1350), it had killed perhaps as many as twenty-five million people, between one-fourth and one-third of the total population of Europe. Statistical examinations show that the plagues struck mainly the weakest—the aged and the young—and those most frequently in contact with the dying, the clergy. (The Dominican order, once the intellectual élite of Christendom, suffered so severely that it was forced to accept postulants with little education or culture, and as a result, by the end of Chaucer's century, the quality of the order had so greatly declined that it could no longer compete for first-rate minds.) Partly because those who did the everyday work were least hard hit, that is, young adults and the early middle-aged, business went on almost as usual in London, strange as that now seems. Parliament's meeting was canceled in 1348 and many schools closed down, but bread was baked, church bells were rung, arrests were made, wills were probated, and the war with France ground on.

Men of vision and imagination—for instance Chaucer in the *Pardoner's Tale,* and in modern times Edgar Allan Poe and Ingmar Bergman— have left us grim images of the pestilence, stories which form their own literary genre, the so-called plague legend: maniacal revelers, drunkenness and blasphemy in a tavern or castle, some bright place buzzing and full of life, then a dark shadow, a hooded old man (sometimes woman) in black or red (Death!), then pain, anger, recriminations, hellish dancing, finally darkness and silence. Because of such images handed down by poets, we probably do not see the plague in at all the way ordinary Londoners did in 1348. Let us try to get closer to the reality of that time.

The official word was of course that the plague was a punishment for sins, a view promoted in colorful terms all over Christendom. For instance, the Leicester cloisterer Knighton writes:

> In those days [1348] there arose a huge rumour and outcry among the people, because when tournaments were held, almost in every place, a band of women would come as if to share the sport, dressed in divers and marvellous dresses of men—sometimes to the number of 40 to 50 ladies, and the fairest and comeliest (though I say not, of the best) among the whole kingdom. Thither they came in party-coloured tunics,

one colour or pattern on the right side and another on the left, with short hoods that had pendants like ropes wound round their necks, and belts thickly studded with gold or silver—nay, they even wore, in pouches slung across their bodies, those knives which are called *daggers* in the vulgar tongue; and thus they rode on choice war-horses or other splendid steeds to the place of tournament. There and thus they spent and lavished their possessions, and wearied their bodies with fooleries and wanton buffoonery, if popular report lie not. . . . But God in this matter, as in all others, brought marvellous remedy; for He harassed the places and times appointed for such vanities by opening the floodgates of heaven with rain and thunder and lurid lightning, and by unwonted blasts of tempestuous winds. . . . That same year and the next came the general mortality throughout the world.[18]

Langland and nearly all other poets say the same. "Tremble, brothers! Fear the Lord!" and a favorite theme of mid-fourteenth-century European painters is the dying rich glutton, the dying beauty, the wealth and power of Babylon overthrown.

But that official view was very strange. Most Londoners who lost children or elderly parents were not drunken revelers or people given to such buffoonery as mock transvestite dress. They were imperfect, occasionally sinful, but not so imperfect as to deserve this strange divine wrath, and they knew it. Some, in other parts of Europe, sought scapegoats. In Germany, in 1349, it was decided that the fault must lie with the Jews (who for some reason tended to be immune to the plague, as if protected by Satan), or must lie, rather, with the Christian citizenry which allowed Jews to remain in German ghettos; and so God's side launched a bloody, pious massacre. (God's mysterious purpose held firm.) There was some scapegoat hunting in Scotland, too; but this was not the usual way with Londoners, much less the way of those who lived in white, sea-breeze-filled Southampton, where, in any case, the death toll was light.

The rich of London, like Thomas Heyroun or John Chaucer's step-father Richard Chaucer, or leviathan, white-bearded Hamo Copton and his large son Nicholas, looked out from their gates, numbly sorrowing and full of bafflement, watching the cartloads of dead men pass, a bell-ringer walking by the blind lead ox as the heavy wooden wheels jerked and rumbled toward the city's two communal graves. Their servants watched beside them, keeping their distance, and as the carts came even, and they saw the blank, dehumanized stares or heard the jokes, like garbage men's jokes, of the ward collectors, both servants and masters glanced away, as if vaguely recalling something, some dream or old saying, and crossed themselves—"*I am come to set fire on the earth,*" perhaps, or "*The end is at hand,*" or "*Watch and wait!*"—some such mumble out of childhood or last Sunday's sermon, a statement no sensible man much thought about, with the sun streaming in through the stained-glass windows and the incense welming up from thick white smoke; a vision of the world not to be taken too seriously, yet secretly believed, secretly perceived on every side to be true, however incredible, gradually and terribly fulfilling itself. The poor, like the rich, came together in groups yet avoided touching—came together out of fear and to escape too much thinking—yet avoided contact because they partly understood how the disease was passed, by some demonic power that took possession of a body and grew stronger in its ruin and groped out toward others with invisible hands.

That ghost was all over London now, rising from the bodies of the dying and dead, cowering in doorways, wine cellars, bright gardens where rats lay dead along the walls. Outside London it was killing so many sheep, according to the chronicles of Henry Knighton, "that in one place more than 5000 died in a single pasture; and they rotted so much that neither bird nor beast would touch them." He adds, "Sheep and oxen strayed at large through the fields and among the crops, and there were none to drive them off or herd them, but for lack of keepers they perished in remote by-ways and hedges. . . ." The Scots were at first not infected, Knighton tells us, and "believing that a terrible vengeance of God had overtaken the English, [they] came together at Selkirk forest with the intention of invading the realm of England. . . . [There] the fierce mortality overtook them and their ranks were thinned by sudden and terrible death. About 5000 died in a short time. And as the rest, the strong and the feeble, were making ready to return to their own homes, they were pursued and intercepted by the English, who killed a very great number of them." It must have seemed that the weird, vengeful spirit had power even over wood and stone. Knighton writes: "After the pestilence many buildings both great and small in all cities, boroughs and vills fell into ruins for lack of inhabitants, and in the same way many villages and hamlets were depopulated, and there were no houses left in them, all who had lived therein being dead. . . ."[19] A thousand English villages disappeared forever during the fourteenth century's fifty years of plague.

It was an unbelievable thing that God should make use of such a creature as the pestilence. *All* medieval religious doctrine was unbelievable, in fact; and though we find no evidence that skepticism, to say nothing of atheism, was ever seriously argued in the late Middle Ages, we can be sure there were thousands who felt baffled and helpless—the cautious half-doubters we encounter in sermons and mystery plays. The probability, in fact, is that when the pestilence arrived the Age of Faith came to be made up almost wholly of people riddled by doubts, people who could deal with doubt only by the assertion, common in the religious writing of the time, that the human mind is by nature incapable of even the dimmest understanding of God—people who consciously and in a sense bravely abandoned hope of understanding and simply prayed to the unfathomable.

At least part of what made the coming of the pestilence such a jolt was that, as a judgment from God, it seemed to confute the past half century's optimistic tendency in Christian thought. Against the darker visions of some of the early Church Fathers, Aquinas had persuasively argued a theology and metaphysic which justified full confidence in man. Systematically developing ideas of Aristotle and, to a lesser extent, Plato, he'd shown that both man and the lower creatures have a natural tendency or love toward God, and that God's grace could perfect and elevate man's tendency, bringing knowledge and full love of the divine. Though sin might be tempting, it was not, for Thomas, the crushing weight on the soul it had seemed to some earlier patristic and conciliar writers. Even the secular state was good. Borrowing from Aristotle, Thomas had raised the dignity of civil authority by declaring the state one of this world's two perfect societies (the other was the Church), a positive good for the promotion of man's temporal welfare, and a necessary good inasmuch as man cannot live without civil order. Even angels, Thomas argued, must have government.

Optimism like that of Thomas would equally characterize the philosophical movement that followed and to some extent eclipsed him. Thomas had argued the existence of a "human nature" which might be united to the divine through the person of Christ. Philosophers of the "nominalist" school argued that no reality exists besides the simple entity, that is, that we can find no universal human nature but only individual human beings. Thus nature and supernature, reason and revelation, parted company; natural science was set free of the wide embrace of metaphysics and might pursue facts and concepts one by one; and civil rights and obligations need be referred no higher than the prince. Though these were still basically university ideas, they had at least some effect on every parish priest and were disseminated throughout society by the Dominicans (Thomas Aquinas's order) and Franciscans (the order of such nominalists as Bacon).

Whatever their disagreements, both Thomists and nominalists celebrated human reason and tended to check the tradition of *contemptus mundi*. "My sons have defeated me, my sons have defeated me!" the Holy One might have cried. Instead, he sent the pestilence. The nominalist idea (flatly opposed to the opinion of Aquinas) that God's nature, being unapproachable by science, is unknowable, joined unexpectedly with a less noble line of thought, the older, far gloomier view of human nature, that man is a worm, man is mere clay; and the result was a notion of man as not only base but virtually helpless.

Intelligent Englishmen like the men and women in John Chaucer's London family, not trained theologians, had no choice but to leave their feeling of helplessness in the hands of "clerks," clinging as firmly as they could to their Christian optimism, praying and obeying the commands of the Church—like John Massey's "jeweler" at the end of *Pearl,* courageously pushing away doubts, submitting. Supported by beautiful pictures, magnificent Church architecture, great music, and sermons that were themselves works of art—sometimes richly dramatic, as when the carved wooden eagle on the pulpit turned its head and seemed to argue with the priest—they struggled for Christian patience. Insofar as possible, they resisted the panic common among the less stable, who wooed God with assurances of love and loyalty—prayed long and hard, because God could be dangerous, he had loosed upon the world already the fifteen signs of the coming universal destruction—or they sought to appease him with pilgrimages, pardons, and the relics of saints. They prayed, then ran back to life like children who have at last escaped the stern paternal eye, and having escaped for the moment, they laughed and worked or fought their wars with an abandon that would fill them with alarm when they returned to the chapel. Having accepted as their standard an unattainable ideal of saintly virtue, they disbelieved, denied belief in action, and when they saw their doubt, they were alarmed and sought help in their pieces of Mary's veil or St. Guthlac's bones. Wherever we look in the Middle Ages, in the period of the plagues, we see signs of this paradoxical doubt and overheated faith. When observers speak of trials by ordeal of combat, supposedly determined by God, they include like a piece of litany some such phrase as "if God indeed be judge of these matters," a phrase undoubtedly intended ironically, as a man of faith's assertion that God is certainly judge—yet a phrase so inevitable, so impossible to leave out, that one wonders if the speaker doth protest too much. In the same way, when they speak of men harmed by ghosts or goblins, they unfailingly include some such ironic aside as, "If it be true that the Devil receiveth power over none but such as have lived like swine. . . ." Yet whatever their doubts, perhaps their admission of absolute ignorance about God's huge ways proved helpful at the last. They died clutching their rosaries, and gave large portions of what wealth they had for requiem masses in perpetuity, but they died well, by all accounts, died perhaps more nobly than we do.

It was the dark undercurrent of fear and confusion—which was sometimes transmuted to sublime faith but more commonly expressed itself as stoic calm, and evaded confrontations of doubt and doctrine by, at best, celebration of heaven's wonder, at worst, wretched cowering and the mortification of the flesh—that made Boethius' *Consolation of Philosophy* the most important single book of the age and perhaps the key element in Chaucer's education. It was a book that took medieval Christianity back to its idealist roots, the Neoplatonic doctrines on human potential and the goodness of the universe that had helped move Augustine toward his Christian conversion and had inspired and fortified King Alfred when Viking barbarism, with its belligerent espousal of murder, rape, and the destruction of all things "effete"—all beauty—made civilized and Christian virtue seem a dream of fools.

In the fourteenth century, Boethius' popularity was founded, at least in part, on his usefulness as an interpreter of the slightly schizophrenic condition of the late medieval Christian. The truth of the priest's darker warnings seemed evident: God was indeed loosing the seven angels of death—evil weathers, pestilence . . . Yet such divine severity was unthinkable for human minds, especially if God was, as Christianity asserted and one could reasonably believe, a loving father. Given this unbreakable double-bind, whose effect was imprisonment, loss of free will, man must find some way to live free though in chains, doing his work and maintaining his dignity as moral agent in a universe fundamentally foreign and tyrannical (however secretly benevolent), a "wilderness" he must survive without rationally intelligible rules. Boethius offered an account which meshed with Christian doctrine yet had the advantage of seeming clarity, a doctrine which allowed moral agency and did not too obviously violate actual human emotion and intellect, and one which, finally, was not explicitly Christian—Boethius spoke, like Aristotle, of the Prime Mover, never of God—and thus related Christian experience to non-Christian and gave sometimes baffling Christian doctrine philosophical credibility. "The world is very queer," said Boethius, in effect. "The Prime Mover understands things we don't, not that he causes them, and with his clear vision of past, present, and future, he knows that all is for the best: the plan of the universe (that is, divine providence) is beautiful and serene. Therefore do not put your money on private hopes or personal plans, but joyfully, freely accept whatever is, however terrible it may appear; work with it as a wise swimmer works with and not against the river's current; for everything in the universe is in fact linked and orderly and intended for our good, as the soul will recognize when it escapes this physical darkness to spirit's pure light." If he'd known about railroads, he might have expressed his idea of freedom with an image Bertrand Russell used (though to darker purpose): The universe is like a train. You can ride on it, freely joining your will to the will of the railroad company, and it will take you to Philadelphia. But if you stand on the track, stubbornly (and freely) seeking to impose your wish on the will of the company, things may not go well for you. Boethius went further, following Plato and (perhaps incidentally) reviving a fundamental teaching of Jesus: One single principle, according to Boethius, governs everything that exists, from winds and tides and inanimate matter to the Prime Mover's character, namely, the principle of universal attraction degree by degree— the inherent love of "natural place" and overall accord which "inclines" or encourages stones to move downward and souls to fly upward, establishing the stable and orderly ladder of existence, the "fair chain of love." (This is of course the idea behind Aquinas' "tendency" of human and lower creatures toward God.) One may, with mad obduracy, deny the principle, closing up one's heart into selfishness and envy, resisting one's natural, spiritual place, thus stepping outside the universal order and losing its benefits. (We do this, Boethius might say, when we cynically deny that love, or duty, or heroism exist, or when we impute base motives to seemingly noble acts and thus greed, cruelty, and indifference to our fellow creatures, ultimately undermining our own self-respect and even our will to live.) But however we may resist love's natural pull, the divine, all-ordering principle is still there, awaiting the will's free surrender.

The practical result of the Boethian view was that a man could watch his children die, could weep, then put his grief aside, exercising his free will by rejoining the community, the "common profit"; could "make a virtue of necessity"—as Chaucer was to write in his *Knight's Tale*—doing his small but necessary part of London's business or Southampton's. In the short view, the temporal view,

> This world nys but a thurgfarë ful of wo,   [*is not*]
> And we been pilgrymës, passyngë to and fro.
> Deeth is an ende of every worldly soorë.

But God's domain and the soul's possibilities are larger than the world we see.

The Boethian doctrine was of course not available to everyone. One of Chaucer's services to his age would be his translation of Boethius' book into English, and later his dramatization of the Boethian message in poem after poem. The Chaucers themselves, as we've seen, had need of such comfort in 1349. The future poet's life was at that time changed utterly: the emotionally close extended family he'd formerly known, the crowd of grandparents, uncles, aunts, and cousins that seems one of the most typical and attractive features of life in the Middle Ages, had been abruptly snuffed out.

Sometime after the Chaucer family had moved back to the Thames Street house in London, and after the plague had begun to burn itself out, Geoffrey began school somewhere in the Vintry Ward area, probably the Almonry Cathedral School attached to St. Paul's. It was not quite the closest to his house. St. Mary-le-Bow was slightly nearer, and a third school was situated in this part of London, St. Martin-le-Grand, somewhat farther away. St. Paul's was almost certainly the best of the three.[20] Derek Brewer writes:

> About the middle of the century this song school [attached to the grammar school] had an unusual schoolmaster, William Ravenstone, who had a large collection of books in Latin. Although he was a chaplain, he seems to have had very few theological books, but a great many other books of various interest, including some practical teaching books and a large number of Latin classics. When he died he left these books to the school, to the number of eighty-four, and with them a chest to keep them in, and provision for an annual gift of money to the boys. To feel the full significance of this one must realize the extreme booklessness of the fourteenth century. There are some 76,000 wills surviving from the fourteenth and fifteenth centuries in England. Of these [one researcher] examined 7,568, and found only 388 which bequeath books; yet this was a period when books were valuable and so likely to be mentioned. . . . So Ravenstone's eighty-four are really outstanding. Furthermore, it was extremely difficult to get the use of a library. Most of those that existed were in monasteries, and restricted to the use of monks. On the other hand, Chaucer himself from an early period shows a quite unusual knowledge of the classics. So it is possible that Chaucer got his knowledge from Ravenstone's collection, and that the learned and kindly Ravenstone may have been Chaucer's own teacher. . . .[21]

Another collection of books was also available at St. Paul's, a collection left in 1328 by William Tolleshunt, "almoner and schoolmaster of the Almonry School at St. Paul's Cathedral in London." Tolleshunt left works of grammar, logic, natural history, medicine, and law,[22] and evidently Chaucer could use these books if he wanted to, since boys were apparently permitted to take books to their rooms. But the subjects he principally dealt with, during those five remaining years of grammar school, were not history, medicine, and so forth, but early stages of the three courses of language study—grammar, logic, and eloquence (or rhetoric)—which made up the *trivium* (the word from which, I'm sorry to say, we get our word "trivial").

The order of studies in the Middle Ages was more flexible than educational programs are now, depending on the interest of teachers and students, the availability of specialists in a given field, and so on. Ideal patterns for the student's progress were set out by educational theorists, but such patterns were probably not often followed. Whereas we think, nowadays, of a child's moving from the subject matter of the first grade to that of the second, then to that of the third, and so forth, medieval teachers worked like teachers in the American country schoolhouse, mixing up the studies of fifth grade and first and emphasizing pretty much whatever they pleased—logic at the expense of grammar or even arithmetic at the expense of language. Since we have no way of knowing how Chaucer's teacher worked, we must describe not the education he got but the one the theorists of his age recommended—beginning with grammar.

Having learned the basics of reading and writing at his school in Southampton, Chaucer moved on, in his London school, to more complicated segments of "grammar," that is, the branch of the trivium which had to do with understanding letters (or *grammata*)—everything from how to make an "A" to how to interpret Christian four-level allegory. The parts of speech he learned out of Aelius Donatus's *Eight Parts of Speech,* which schoolboys called their Donat, their "given." It was a book of questions and answers on Latin grammar, a little catechism that ran to what would now be about ten printed pages. It was studied in both prose and rhymed versions and cost about threepence. He then moved on to a collection of alphabetically arranged adages and proverbs attributed to Dionysius Cato—a writer repeatedly mentioned in Chaucer's poetry. He went next, if his teachers followed the advice of the best educational theorists, to more advanced grammatical problems (shading toward logical problems) with the shorter and longer works of Priscian, where he encountered some ten thousand lines of quotation from the Roman classics—many of which Chaucer would incorporate into his own work years later. Sometime after this, Chaucer read Ovid's *Metamorphoses,* the wellspring of stories for all medieval poets.

At its most advanced, grammar dealt with the interpretation of texts, biblical, religious, or literary, and with what was known as "translation" (*translatio*), not in our sense but instead in the sense of retelling old stories in a way that reinterpreted them or heightened their original meaning. Interpretation was grounded on the standard view, which was to some extent correct, that the Bible, properly understood, is composed not entirely on a literal level but in more poetic fashion, using language "other than that of the market place" (the meaning of the two Greek words from which we get the word "allegory"). To understand this poetic speech, which might be found not only in scripture but also in certain pagan poets, notably Virgil and Ovid, one had to understand the principal ways in which "deeper meanings" are expressed in poetry. The clue came from ancient studies of Homer, and by the third century A.D. something approximately like the method of early Homeric critics was established as the method of Christian exegesis. The Bible could be read on four "levels," namely: (1) the *literal* or *grammatical,* what the words say letter by letter, in other words the level on which the Bible says exactly what it means; sometimes called the "historical" level; (2) the *allegorical* or figurative, as when the Philistines' hearts are said to be stone but no physiological miracle is implied, or, again as when man is figuratively represented by the Garden of Eden, and his rational, irascible, and concupiscent faculties are represented by (respectively) Adam, the serpent, and Eve; (3) the *anagogic* or mystical, wherein Old Testament and New Testament events are found to be harmonious, the Old Jerusalem foreshadowing the New, as when Noah's ark is recognized as an ante-type of the Body of Christ, or the Church; and wherein "last things" —death and resurrection, etc.—are subtly revealed; and (4) *tropological* or figuratively moralizing—the parables of Christ, for instance. Needless to say, this complicated way of reading scripture made for heresies and confusions, yet it is not altogether unfaithful to the way Jewish thinkers, as well as other Mediterranean writers like Homer, and much more obviously Virgil, did in fact sometimes express themselves. For authority for such a way of reading one need look no further than St. Paul.

The allegorical approach to reading had become also, early in the Middle Ages, a way of writing. The man from whom the young Chaucer got his first instruction on the parts of speech, Aelius Donatus, also wrote books (now lost) interpreting the allegory in Virgil, and, as the teacher of St. Jerome (early fifth century), helped foster among Christians a tendency to see pagan literature as poetry composed, unwittingly, under the true God's inspiration. This led immediately to imitation, chiefly of Cicero and Virgil, and to exegetical "translation," poems in which men like the *Beowulf*-poet (seventh or eighth century) and later Dante (1265–1321)—and soon after him Petrarch and Chaucer—turned old or original stories, or in Dante's case real-life experience, to new allegorical uses by introducing symbolic elements, puns, and allusions. Thus the monster in the source of *Beowulf* becomes a devil-figure, and so on.

Chaucer was to make fun of this sort of grammatical "translation" in the first major section of his rich and complex *House of Fame.* (In the second and third sections of the poem, he parodies "logic" and "eloquence.") What Chaucer's "translation" does—as we might expect, knowing his essential impishness—is confuse rather than clarify, since part of his purpose in the *House of Fame* is to dramatize, with much tomfoolery, the nominalist notion that all human knowledge is suspect, mainly (according to Roger Bacon and others) because fallen man is stupid. Chaucer caricatures himself as not just dim-witted but *magnificently* dim-witted, an unexpected proof, in fact, of God's grandeur, for, to paraphrase William Blake, "What immortal hand or eye / Dare frame such Vast Stupidity?" For a man like the "Geffrey" of Chaucer's poem, not even the "divine theologian" Virgil is above the improvement and clarification of *translatio*. With high-spirited jingling he reduces the prince of poets to—

> "I wol now singen, yif I kan,
> The armës, and also the man   *Arma . . . virum*
> That first cam, thurgh his destinee,   *primus . . .*
> Fugityf of Troy contree,
> In Italyé, with ful mochë pynë   [*much pain*]
> Unto the strondës of Lavynë."   [*shores of Lavinium*]

Though he jokes about the exegetical method of translation, Chaucer of course took it very seriously. His epic poem *Troilus and Criseyde,* drawn from a poem by Boccaccio, is an example of the method, and though the *Troilus* has wonderfully funny passages, it is finally a philosophical poem whose author history has indeed judged worthy to follow in the steps of "Virgile, Ovide, Omer, Lucan, and Stace [Statius]."

As its title suggests, the second general course of study, or second branch of the trivium, "logic," dealt with the critical analysis of true and false arguments and the valid construction of original argument. The basic matter of the course was no doubt less lively then than now— Charles Dodgson's (Lewis Carroll's) style of making logical terms of gorillas, uncles, and alligators was still centuries away—but the texts Chaucer read were anything but dreary. It was here that he met writers he'd go on reading all his life—Aristotle, Boethius, and Macrobius—and it was here that he was encouraged, almost incidentally, to reflect on how the universe is built. The question would fascinate him for the rest of his days, would lead him to the study of astrology and alchemy (the legitimate astronomy and chemistry of the day), to pursuit of arithmetic, physics, and "musical" relationships (from angels and planets to the notes on a scale; we have no related branch of study now), and would lead him, through Roger Bacon and the Oxford rationalists, to fundamental questions of epistemology—how we know what we know if, in fact, we know anything. He was on his way to becoming a "noble, philosophical poet," as his disciple Thomas Usk would call him—the first philosophical poet in English and founder of a line that would include some of England's noblest minds, among them John Milton, William Blake, and William Wordsworth.

It was no doubt also his work in "logic" that gave Chaucer his lifelong love, like Dodgson's, of loblogic. He has in the *House of Fame* a splendid piece of clown philosophy. The great, golden eagle bearing the worried, wide-eyed Geffrey higher and higher above the shrinking earth proposes to explain how the legendary House of Fame, toward which they're ascending, can really exist. His disquisition is a masterpiece of late fourteenth-century reasoning, except that it's nonsense. In his first verse paragraph the eagle appeals to "experience" (Roger Bacon's term for scientific experiment), and in the second verse paragraph he supports "experience" with "authority" (Bacon's secondary test for knowability), in this case ludicrously misapplied Boethius. The eagle says, extravagantly proud of his own brilliance, poor Geffrey unhappily wriggling in his claws:

> "Now hennësforth y wol the techë   [1]
> How every speche, or noyse, or soun,
> Thurgh hys multiplicacioun,
> Thogh hyt were pipëd of a mous,
> Mot nedë comë to Famës Hous.   [*Must needs*]
> I preve hyt thus—take hedë now—
> Be experiencë; for yf that thow   [*By*]
> Throwe on water now a stoon,
> Wel wost thou, hyt wol make anoon   [*knowest . . . soon*]
> A litel roundell as a sercle,
> Paraunter brod as a covercle;   [*pot-lid*]
> And ryght anoon thow shalt see wel,
> That whel wol cause another whel,   [*wheel*]
> And that the thridde, and so forth, brother,
> Every sercle causynge other
> Wydder than hymselvë was;
> And thus fro roundel to compas,   [*small circle*]
> Ech aboute other goyngë,   [*going*]
> Causeth of othres steryngë   [*stirring*]
> And multiplyinge ever moo,
> Til that hyt be so fer ygoo   [*gone*]
> That hyt at bothë brynkes bee.
> Although thou mowe hyt not ysee   [*may*]

Above, hyt gooth yet alway under,
Although thou thenke hyt a gret wonder.
And whoso seyth of trouthe I varyë,
Bid hym proven the contraryë.
And ryght thus every word, ywis,   [*in truth,*
That lowd or pryvee spoken ys,   *or assuredly*]
Moveth first an ayr aboutë,
And of thys movynge, out of doutë,
Another ayr anoon ys mevëd,
As I have of the watir prevëd,
That every cercle causeth other.
Ryght so of ayr, my levë brother;   [*dear*]
Everych ayr another stereth   [*stirreth*]
More and more, and speche up bereth,
Or voys, or noyse, or word, or soun,
Ay through multiplicacioun,
Til hyt be attë Hous of Famë—
Take yt in ernest or in gamë.
    "Now have I told, yf thou have myndë,
How speche or soun, of purë kyndë,   [*nature*]
Enclynëd ys upward to mevë;
This, mayst thou felë, wel I prevë.
And that samë place, ywys,
That every thyng enclynëd to ys,
Hath his kyndelychë stedë:
That sheweth hyt, withouten dredë,
That kyndely the mansioun
Of every speche, of every soun,
Be hyt eyther foul or fair,
Hath hys kyndë place in ayr. . . ."

Clearly if there is no House of Fame, there ought to be.

The third segment of the trivium was eloquence, or rhetoric. (In some medieval schools this course of study came before logic, in others, after. In the experience of the Englishman John of Salisbury, the courses came in the order I've given, and Chaucer's *House of Fame* reflects this order.) I need say nothing here of what "eloquence" covered except to mention that it dealt with making an argument in prose or verse not only convincing but attractive to the hearer, that is, more specifically, well thought out in terms of what traditional and original materials were selected (*inventio*); well and persuasively organized (*dispositio*); and stylistically appealing (*amplificatio,* etc.). It was in connection with the amplification or de-

velopment of the outline, probably, that the first principles of "music" began to be introduced. For a child like Chaucer, who had apparent talent in "poetic enditing" (that is, writing verse), a shrewd teacher might introduce parts of some such work as Boethius' *De Musica,* where the student might begin to consider the mystical relationships of stresses, rhymes, numerology, and so on. The poetry gives evidence that Chaucer did at some point come to study these matters, though it may well have been much later.

In the third section of the *House of Fame* Chaucer demonstrates with comic gusto his mastery of "eloquence," his ability to make up or steal and alter elegant figures—great catalogues like Homer's, allegorical *figurae* like Boethius' "Lady Philosophy," and grand similes. Even though he's joking, his figures are very fine. He says of a great castle that it is as "ful eke [also] of wyndowës / As flakës falle in gretë snows"; and describing the entrance of those who seek judgment by Lady Fame, he writes, boldly misappropriating an image from Homer, Virgil, and Dante—

> I herde a noyse aprochen blyvë,   [*quickly*]
> That ferde as been don in an hivë   [*fared . . . bees*]
> Ayen her tyme of out-fleyngë;
> Ryght such a maner murmuryngë,
> For al the world, hyt semed me.

And for allegorical description of the spread of undeserved bad fame, Geffrey with glorious self-confidence snatches not only from the classics but from the Bible itself (the trumpet of Doom in the *Apocalypse*):

> What didë this Eolus, but he
> Tok out hys blakë trumpe of bras   [*black trumpet*]
> That fouler than the devel was,
> And gan this trumpë for to blowë
> As al the world shulde overthrowë,
> That thurghout every regioun
> Wentë this foulë trumpës soun,
> As swifte as pelet out of gonnë,   [*gun*]
> Whan fyr is in the poudre ronnë.
> And such a smokë gan out wendë
> Out of his foulë trumpes endë,
> Blak, bloo, grenyssh, swartish red,
> As doth where that men meltë led,

Loo, al on high fro the tuel.   [*chimney*]
And therto oo thing saugh I wel,   [*one . . . saw*]
That the ferther that hit ran,
The gretter wexen hit began,
As dooth the ryver from a wellë,
And hyt stank as the pit of hellë.
Allas, thus was her shame yrongë,
And gilteles, on every tongë!

A medieval education need not end with the end of the seven-year course in elementary school. One might work on the trivium for a scholarly lifetime or one might shift in early adulthood (or at any other point) to some second educational program, either civil law, the course to which Chaucer turned next, as we'll see in the next chapter, or the *quadrivium,* the higher university course of study, where the student investigated in more detail the four classical subjects arithmetic, geometry, astronomy, and music. Few got as far as serious work at this level, and fewer still got to the three highest university programs, medicine, canon law, and theology. But introduction to these subjects, within the grammar, logic, and rhetoric segments of the trivium, gave a child a start, so that if he was curious and diligent, he could do a good deal even without formal university training. Chaucer, as I've said, probably did get at least some training at university level and became later the personal friend of several Oxford scholars. His fair knowledge of math and astronomy is shown in the book he wrote for his "little son Lewis" when the boy was at Oxford, a treatise on the astrolabe, and tradition says he wrote a later book, which may or may not be the extant treatise *The Equatorie of the Planetis.* He may have written a third book, on the planet Earth. He shows something approaching a specialist's knowledge of philosophical nominalism (on which more hereafter) and other hard matter, including even the philosophy of "music"—material not easily available outside Oxford or Cambridge. Tradition in fact makes him one of the most learned men of his century. He was reported by Holinshed to be "a man so exquisitely learned in al sciences, that hys matche was not lightly founde anye where in those dayes. . . ."[23] And he was considered, down into the seventeenth century, one of the "secret masters" of alchemy. Recent critics of the *Second Nun's Tale* and *Canon's Yeoman's Tale* have shown that he did know at least some alchemy. If he was familiar with these sciences, from his own study or from discourse with scholars like his friend the Oxford logician Ralph Strode, he got his first whiff of them in his boyhood study in the trivium.

The seven years of Chaucer's study in elementary school, despite shattering experiences—the death by pestilence of family and friends—was on the whole a period of extreme happiness. For young Geoffrey it established the habits of a lifetime: the flying, too-short hours of reading and rereading, the intense though seemingly casual questioning of anyone who might answer, whether about trades and occupations or the Spanish landscape or the darkest mysteries of philosophy. He had entered as a child who, like all his kind, loved "playing, and games, and vanity"—a defect we may be thankful he never completely lost—and left a young man filled with visions and lines of poetry, his soul brimful almost to tears with a love of books and of the bustling world they reflected and made him see with new eyes. Other poets had written of how love of a woman might make a man wonder, *Do I float or sink?* Chaucer would write— joking but in earnest—of how the anguish of the artist, art so long, life so short, and the anguish of the philosopher, the "dredful joye" of knowledge that always so swiftly slides to new questions, to ignorance, has the same effect. Love, the Boethian universal principle.

> Astonyeth with his wonderful werkynge
> So sore, iwis, that when I on hym thynke,
> Nat wot I wel wher that I flete or synke.   [*I truly know not whether*]

Such was the general character of Chaucer's early education. It was by no means as varied as modern education, nor was it as rich or even as accurate, since medieval texts were full of errors that later generations have been able to remove. But it was an education deeper, less frivolous than ours, one that encouraged seriousness and the habit of hard work toward some noble purpose. In many respects, it was as good an early education as any period could offer: in a time of unpropitious weather, famine, recurrent plague, and endless, devastating war, it encouraged a philosophical approach to life's most troublesome questions—gave noble and dignified arguments on the meaning of life and death (in Boethius and the writing of the wiser churchmen); gave a combined pagan and Christian view of Creation that, except in trivial technical respects, still holds today, a view of man as responsible moral agent in a baffling but orderly universe; gave cultural emphasis to great poetry, painting, music, and architecture—all that makes the medieval period, despite its faults, the most eloquent moment of pain and courage and high aspiration in the life of Western man.

Three: Chaucer as Young Courtier, Soldier, and, in Some Sense, Lover (1357-1360)

LIKE THE KING AND QUEEN OF ENGLAND, EDWARD III'S third son, Prince Lionel, and his wife Elizabeth, countess of Ulster, kept separate servants and separate account books —or such was the case until 1359, when the two households merged. Part of the countess's record survives, freakishly preserved as the binding paper of another book held by the British Museum; and by means of it we know that on Easter 1357, Geoffrey Chaucer was a minor member of Elizabeth's household and received as a gift from her a complete set of clothes—tight, parti-colored breeches of black and red, a short jerkin, or "paltok," which cost the countess 4s. (about $48), and a pair of shoes. Until fairly recently it was assumed that he served as a page, and a picture was composed presenting "a normal teen-age youngster . . . gratified to find that he could bend over in his new clothes only with the greatest difficulty."[1] That picture is not quite accurate. In the Middle Ages, a young man of sixteen was considered an adult (Chaucer was now at very least sixteen) and was given adult responsibilities—not those of a page, a mere boy. Chaucer is not in fact identified as a page in the countess's Household Accounts (or identified as anything else, for that matter), though other servants are repeatedly described both here and in other such records as *pagettus* (page) or as the higher-ranking *valettus* (yeoman). One servant John Hinton, who like Chaucer is listed as receiving a paltok and other gifts, is described as the countess's *valettus*. And though some of the countess's employees received gifts far more costly than Chaucer's, several also received rather less, including the servant twice identified as a page, Thomas, who received a gift worth 16d. (about $15).[2] In May, Chaucer and others in the countess's retinue again got new outfits, and the following December Chaucer was given 2s. 6d. for "necessaries at Christmas."

If he was not a page but a yeoman, or *valettus,* what was the nature of Chaucer's work for the countess's household? His status among yeomen was relatively low, since his wages were unimpressive. He was well below Edmund Rose, who'd been in the countess's service as *valettus* since at least September 1352, when the lady of Clare gave him a present, and below Reginald Pierpont, in service at least since May 1354, and below John Hinton, to whom the countess showed greater largess. And there were still others above him, as well as some below him (the countess's pages). Among the servants highest above him—such things counted a good deal in a medieval house—was the countess's personal damoiselle, Philippa Pan', of whom more soon. (The countess must have had other ladies-in-waiting at this time, perhaps including Alice Dawtrey, who received an annuity in 1359 as one of the countess's *domicelle,* but the record does not mention them.)

Given his place in the scheme of the house, Chaucer must have been essentially an assistant to superiors, in his daytime labors. In the evening, when courtiers were expected to entertain with music, poetry, or conversation on noble and interesting subjects, he was presumably much what he would prove years later, deferential, not quick to speak, though the cleverest in the room. Indeed, at least during his first few weeks or perhaps even months in the countess's retinue, he probably kept his talents to himself, for the simple reason that they were not what was required, not useful. He was not of noble blood, not one of those young gentlemen who, instead of attending a grammar school and proceeding to a university, served as pages and then squires in the halls or castles of the nobility, receiving there prolonged instruction in chivalry—training designed to fit the noble youth to become a worthy knight, a just and prudent master, and a sensible manager of an estate. The nobleman's son was assigned to one responsible position after another, as assistant to the butler, assistant to the pantryman, and so on, and he received, besides, direct instruction in reading and writing, singing, playing musical instruments, dancing, horsemanship, chess, the usages of courtesy, and the chivalric conception of duty. It was this sort of youth that was expected to entertain the company in the evening, this sort of youth—not merely an elevated vintner's son—that Chaucer describes in his portrait of the Squire in the *Canterbury Tales:*

Syngynge he was, or floytynge, al the day;
He was as fressh as is the month of May.
Short was his gownë, with slevës longe and wydë.
Wel koude he sitte on hors and fairë rydë.
He koudë songës make and wel enditë,   [*Joust and also dance, and*
Juste and eek daunce, and weel purtreye and writë.   *draw well (?), and write*]

But in the close quarters of a fourteenth-century noble household, it was difficult to keep real talent down, especially in the household of the favorite, pampered son of Queen Philippa, a truly splendid lady one of whose many admirable qualities was her lively delight in poetic ability, whatever its credentials.

Whether or not he wrote for Lionel and his wife, Chaucer did undoubtedly compose songs at this period, probably love songs and probably, some of them, salacious ones. It was the standard game in the
English minor courts (as well as in the king's). And as an admirer of
the French court poet Machault—a major influence in the surviving early
poems—he could hardly help being not simply a poet but a song writer,
since in Machault's theory music was more basic than language.

Not everything in a medieval court like Elizabeth's was elegant service
or entertainment. Chaucer was expected to continue his studies—mainly the
arts, also French and Latin literature and language, which were supposed
to help make him a refined and useful servant. There was also, probably,
for a servant like Geoffrey, the endless drudgery of record-keeping and
letter-copying. He would have finished his lower-level schooling at about
the age of sixteen (1356 or earlier) and would have acquired in the
process skills not to be dismissed lightly in the countess's household.
Since royal-house patronage seems to have helped support his later education, and since in maturity he served the English crown in three main
capacities—as a favored court poet and "reader," as foreign ambassador,
and as high-ranking accountant or financially responsible overseer (while
managing the customs, borrowing for the king, and serving as clerk of the
king's works and later as subforester)—it seems reasonable to hazard
that Chaucer served the countess primarily as a scrivener and/or keeper
of accounts. If he did in fact amuse the company with poems and songs,
no evidence survives.

How Chaucer got his position with the countess is also anybody's guess.
The countess, for what it may be worth, was a granddaughter of blind
Henry, earl of Lancaster, under whom Chaucer's father fought, along
with Thomas Heyroun, in the rising against Mortimer, and that may have
helped, since no one got a job in the great minor courts without influence.
But as we've seen, both Chaucer's father and mother had at least some
access to Edward III's court, hence indirect access to the court of Prince
Lionel and his wife.

Like other great courts, the court of Prince Lionel and the countess
of Ulster was forever on the move, and young Chaucer, as a member of
the household, moved with it. They went from castle to castle, or manor
to manor, in the usual way of medieval royalty, spreading from place to
place the otherwise intolerable burden of their numerous retinue, who
had to be fed on local produce since there were in those days no trucks,
no trains; and behind them, wherever they went, groaned their endless

string of baggage carts—furniture, tapestries, candlesticks, jewelry, hunting equipment, pots and pans. In April 1356, Countess Elizabeth was in London; later she was in Southampton, then Reading, then Stratford-le-Bow. In the spring of 1357, she was in London again, for the luxurious festival of St. George at Windsor Castle. For Pentecost she was at Woodstock, for Christmas she was at Hatfield, for Epiphany she was at Bristol.

In all these places, Chaucer participated in celebrations of a sort we moderns never see, though occasionally we may glean some hint of them in movies. On holy days, in the castles of the mighty, the long hours of work and prayer and discipline that generally characterized life in the Middle Ages gave way to resplendent show, gorgeous dress, and dazzling entertainment. We have from the period several descriptions of the holy day feasts, enough to show clearly that John Massey's description in *Sir Gawain and the Green Knight* is as close to reportage as to fiction. (Because the dialect is a difficult one, I give a modernized version.)

> All these were seated on the dais and served with distinction,
> And down below many another knight ate at the sideboards.
> And quickly the first course comes in, with a clarion of trumpets,
> Hung brightly with many a blazing banderole,
> And now the kettledrums barked, and the brilliant pipes
> Warbled wildly and richly, awakening echoes
> That lifted high every heart by their heavenly sound.
> Then in flooded wonderful cates, the finest of foods,
> Mountains of splendid meats, such a marvel of dishes
> It was hard to find places to place there, in front of the people,
> The vessels of silver that held all the various stews
> > on hand.
> > Soon each to suit his wishes
> > Turned gladly, gay of mind,
> > For every two, twelve dishes,
> > Cold beer and sparkling wine.

If we can trust the testimony of the poetry and chronicles, guests began arriving days before the holiday, with their numerous servants and lavish contributions to the castle's festivities—foods, decorations, masks, skilled performers, including dwarfs, perhaps acrobats, and magicians. The men went off on hunts, not solely for entertainment but also to provide game meats; the women, highborn ladies and their well-born servants, helped prepare for the long, spectacular party on the holiday evening, which, when it came, came like an explosion of Chinese fireworks: music and

ring-dancing, poetry, feasting, perhaps a masque or, between courses, a
series of illusions of the sort brought back to England by crusaders who'd
encountered them in the magic-loving East. In the *Franklin's Tale* Chaucer
describes such illusions, or magical "Interludes," and we know by account
books and by other evidence that such remarkable illusions were actually
attempted. The Franklin tells the Pilgrims:

> For ofte at feestës have I wel herd seyë
> That tragetours, withinne an hallë largë,   [*actors, illusionists*]
> Have maad come in a water and a bargë,
> And in the hallë rowen up and doun.
> Somtyme hath semëd come a grym leoun;
> And somtymë flourës sprynge as in a medë;   [*meadow*]
> Somtyme a vyne, and grapës white and redë;
> Somtyme a castel, al of lym and stoon;
> And whan hem lykëd, voyded it anon—
> Thus semëd it to every mannës sightë.

Chaucer writes later in the same tale of even more amazing interludes, the
feats performed by a great magician for his supper guest:

> He shewëd hym, er he wentë to sopeer,
> Forestës, parkës ful of wildë deer;
> Ther saugh he hertës with hir hornës hyë,
> The grettestë that evere werë seyn with yë.
> He saugh of hem an hondred slayn with houndës,
> And somme with arwës blede of bittre woundës.
> He saugh, whan voyded werë thisë wildë deer,
> Thise fauconers upon a fair ryver,
> That with hir haukës han the heron slayn.
> Tho saugh he knyghtës justyng in a playn;
> And after this he didë hym swich pleasauncë,
> That he hym shewëd his lady on a dauncë,
> On which hymself he dauncëd, as hym thoughtë.
> And whan this maister that this magyk wroughtë,
> Saugh it was tyme, he clapte his handës two,
> And farewel! al oure revel was ago.

Interludes like these, or like the seeming interlude when the stranger
visits in *Sir Gawain and the Green Knight,* magnify actual interludes
to pure fiction; but they undoubtedly communicate the tone of those
occasions Chaucer took part in as a member of the countess's household

staff, and convey the ideal of breathtaking spectacle for which the illusionists labored.

In all probability Chaucer also took part in the countess's preparations for the betrothal of her infant daughter Philippa to Edmund Mortimer, son of the infamous Sir Roger, lover of Edward II's queen, Isabella. (King Edward III with typical "gentilessë" had refused to punish the son for the father's crimes.) Chaucer may have been present, too, at the funeral of Queen Isabella, in London on November 27, 1358, a rather eerie affair in that no one had heard of the queen in years, not since her confinement to her castle when she'd gone mad, yet now here she lay, surrounded by gloomy ceremony, as if summoned back out of the past to be given due burial. He may have been present at the Smithfield tournaments where King Edward and his cousin Henry Lancaster displayed their amazing skill—a tournament for which Countess Elizabeth had tapestried cushions prepared; and he may have been with the countess when she visited the Tower of London for a look at the lions. But most important, in the long run, was his trip to Hatfield for the Christmas holidays, in 1357, where he met the young man who would be his lifelong friend and advocate, Prince Lionel's younger brother, John of Gaunt. (Gaunt, then earl of Richmond, was apparently at Hatfield for at least part of the celebration. The countess gave two of his attendants Christmas gifts of money.)

The seventeen-year-old Gaunt was no doubt already an impressive figure and had almost certainly developed already his aloof, distant manner. His servants had the look of men proud of their good fortune in being servants to such a prince; had the look, like the servants of the king himself, of men who would die for their master without an instant's hesitation. Though Gaunt was a man of medium stature, he had, by all reports, an air of great confidence—what his enemies would call arrogance. He was the family intellectual, though what he thought of Geoffrey Chaucer, when the two first met, is impossible to say. Gaunt had of course grown up with poets, including the great French poet Jean Froissart, ever-faithful attendant to Gaunt's mother, Queen Philippa; but unlike his older brother Prince Lionel, Gaunt for the most part inclined to friendship with philosophers, theologians, and political theorists rather than with men who thought up rhymes or painted pictures. Nevertheless, whatever they may have thought of one another when they first met, Gaunt and Chaucer were in time to become fast friends.

Chaucer probably served the court of Lionel and Elizabeth for about three years (some Chaucerians think longer). He must have met at this time all the royal family and many of the great men who served them, poets and painters, statesmen, businessmen. To a vintner's son they must have seemed awesome creatures. Their manors, with their gardens, lakes, and parks, gave a man an idea of what Paradise must look like (Chaucer's poetry repeatedly makes use of such settings in this way). Their feasts and tournaments, above all their entertainments, were more spectacular than almost anything modern man has seen. It was a great age for spectacular display. Even the mystery pageants, which scholars until recently have tended to imagine as small-time and shoddy, were by the fifteenth century, and probably as early as Chaucer's time, more grand than nearly anything available to us today. These were biblical plays put on by local guilds every Corpus Christi Day in every important town in England, beginning early in the morning and lasting until after dark (in some towns they may have run two full days). They were usually presented, in Chaucer's time, from large, two- or three-storey pageant wagons, but occasionally done in fields or from enormous, complicated stages which were equipped, at least in places like fifteenth-century Wakefield, with wind machines, secret passages, devices for raising small groups of actors to heaven on invisible wires, and props for creating, among other things, a gruesomely realistic Crucifixion, in which real blood (goat's blood) came gushing from Christ's wounds.[3] It was all wonderful theater, now deeply affecting, now sweetly touching, now bawdily comic—as when some pretty fellow like squeamish Absalon, in the *Miller's Tale,* put on the ridiculous, overreaching ways of a pretender to the throne of Christ himself and "pleyeth Herodës on a scaffold hyë." Prince Lionel and the countess watched the pageant wagons come clumsily rolling into position for performance—and then afterward roll on, lurching and swaying, toward their further stations—from a costly, elevated box with a blinding-bright awning which bore their coats of arms, a box nestled among many such boxes, brightly painted, aflutter with streamers, constructed wherever there was a park or widening of the street that might serve as a playing station. Chaucer, as one of his employers' lesser yeomen, must have watched from the street or from low bleachers, craning to see, since he was not very tall, or perhaps jumping for a look, like the people in the back of the crowd in his *House of Fame:*

> And whan they were alle on an hepë,
> Tho behyndë begunne up lepë,
> And clamben up on other fastë,
> And up the nose and yën kastë,   [eyes]
> And troden fast on others helës,   [heels]
> And stampen as men doon aftir eles.   [eels]

But the courtly masques—stately dumb shows, long playlets, or sequential tableaus honoring courtly ideals or saints for whom aristocrats had a special regard (St. George, patron saint and spectral model of chivalry, St. Lucy, patroness of light, St. Cecilia, patroness of music)—made even the mystery pageants seem country trifles. There were astonishing mechanical horses (perhaps real horses inside, though only in the dreams of kings were there flying horses, like the one in Chaucer's *Squire's Tale*);[4] there were seeming forests filled with birds, descents of the angelic Host, frightening dances of witches and wild animals, and much more. Just the masks for the guests who took part in the dancing which concluded one popular form of the masque could cost a small fortune, we know from Edward's account books—masks of, for instance, lions, elephants, bat-eared men, and satyrs. The feasts on these occasions, too, were spectacular, not only for the wealth and variety of food and drink provided but also for the art that went into their presentation. The table was made a great landscape of food, with forests of parsley and watercress, lakes and rivers with bridges and tiny horsemen, and castles made out of "clean white paper," sometimes set afire in the darkened room before the feasting began. In a country where starvation was never far off for the lower classes, no wonder if preachers and popular poets occasionally howled "Wickedness!", wringing their fingers.

But the people whom Chaucer met in these courts outshone everything around them, as all the poets of the age agree. Imagine kettledrums and long, straight trumpets, servants in livery—the flashy uniforms of their various employers—ladies in high hats with trailing veils, stately gentlemen attired like peacocks (no straw on the floor here—we've entered the world of flagstone and beautifully made tiles like those in *Troilus and Criseyde*), and booming from the tapestried stone walls, echoing down from the six by six rafters made of oak-tree hearts, an oceanic roar of music and laughter.

As a servant of Elizabeth, countess of Ulster, Chaucer must have met, on numerous occasions such as the festival of St. George, King Edward himself, Prince Lionel's father. He was a handsome, fair man with a curly brown beard, gentle eyes and mouth, the eyes just perceptibly slanted like the eyes of all his sons. He was no ordinary mortal, one could see at a glance, and he liked to support that impression with a story.

Some four hundred years ago, Edward III told his friends, the founder of his line, Count Fulke the Black, ruler of Anjou, traveled to a distant land and returned with a bride whose beauty was unsurpassed in all the world. The four children she bore him were brilliant and handsome, like all Plantagenet sons and daughters after them, but they

carried also a darker heritage. She kept it secret for many years, living
a life more secluded than a nun's. Then one day the count demanded that
his wife accompany him to Mass, a thing she'd repeatedly refused to do.
She did so this time, pale and trembling. When the priest raised the
Host, the countess let out an unearthly shriek, rose into the air, flew out
the chapel window, and was never seen again. The truth was out. She
was Melusine, daughter of the Devil!

By the time Chaucer knew him, Edward III at least half believed the
story. Again and again he'd led armies into battle against Scots and
Frenchmen, and it had come to appear to him that he really did have a
charmed life. (The *Morte Arthure*-poet makes a point of this queer
belief of Edward's.) He knew by experience that the description "Scion
of Satan" struck terror into the hearts of his enemies. He half believed,
too, that he was the reincarnated Arthur—not metaphorically but literally—and established a Round Table to prove it. (Mortimer, his mother's
lover, had earlier maintained that *he* was Arthur.) At the same time,
Edward's religious devotion was by all accounts as simple and unques-
tioning as a peasant's. He regularly prayed for wealth and victory before
the tomb of Edward the Confessor in Westminster, and when visiting
Kent he never failed to kneel in obeisance to the saint, Thomas à Becket,
whom his forbears had murdered.

He could show the same noble Christianity on the battlefield, as in
one famous story of the siege of Calais. According to Froissart, when
the governor of Calais realized the force of the English king's siege, he
called together all the poorer inhabitants, those who'd been unable to
lay in food, and one Wednesday morning sent seventeen hundred men,
women, and children out of town. As they were passing through the
English army, the English asked them why they'd left, and when the
people replied that they had no food, the king allowed them to pass
through in safety, ordered them a hearty meal, and gave to each two
sterlings, as charity and alms, "for which many of them prayed earnestly
for the king."

Edward's mercy, however, was not unfailing. When Calais surrendered,
the king threatened to put the city to the sword, then offered the people
this bargain: he would spare the city if six of the chief burghers would
give themselves up unconditionally. With some courageous gallantry,
and some expectation that their lives would be saved by the wealth their
ransoms might bring to King Edward, six of the chief burghers gave
themselves up and begged the king for mercy. All the knights and barons
around Edward wept for pity, but Edward was out for vengeance, since
the people of Calais had caused him losses at sea; and despite the pleas
of his own knights, including saintly Henry of Lancaster, his cousin, he

ordered the hostages executed. Queen Philippa, who was with him, and great with child, fell on her knees to plead for them, "for the sake of the Son of the Blessed Mary, and for your love to me." Reluctantly, angrily, the king relented. Then, stubbornly cruel, as vain and overweening as the Arthur of the alliterative *Morte Arthure,* he evacuated the French inhabitants and repeopled the city with Englishmen. Ironically, it was partly in celebration of the fall of Calais that Edward instituted the chivalric and idealistic Order of the Garter, his latter-day Round Table.

But Edward's whimsy, or at least changeability, did nothing to diminish his stature with the commons, or with those at court who, like young Geoffrey Chaucer, had the pleasure of knowing this "new King Arthur" in person. His charm could be devastating, as many women found, including his good, plump wife Queen Philippa, who loved him despite his affairs, just as he loved her, as was sensible and right. He had the boyish good looks, the brash yet gentle and idealistic love of life and of his native England—also the ferocity, deviousness, and cunning—that it took to make his weak, demoralized realm a European power again, mainly perhaps because, as an athlete, an orator, and a benevolent lawmaker, he encouraged men to feel once more respect and affection for the crown and, beyond that, such love for and pride in the island of their birth as John of Gaunt's son expresses when banished from his homeland in Shakespeare's *Richard II*:

> Then, England's ground, farewell; sweet soil, adieu;
> My mother, and my nurse, that bears me yet!
> Where'er I wander, boast of this I can,
> Though bannish'd, yet a trueborn Englishman.

From boyhood, Edward III was an athlete, a lover of jousting and a dangerous opponent in that frequently deadly imitation of war. With his mother and Roger Mortimer, and with his relatives from Hainault, he'd attended a great number of magnificent tournaments, and after he'd achieved his crown and independence, he and his friends had become still more fanatical spectators and participants in military sports.

There was, to take one typical instance, the great tournament given by William Montagu in Cheapside when Chaucer was still a boy. The king and his knights paraded through London in Tartar dress, to a skirling of pipes and a brattle of drums, then entered the lists and—in armor calculated to be at once spectacular and terrifying (not for mere convenience was the helmet shaped like a hangman's hood, the eyes grimly slanted, and the codpiece of steel made enormous, as if for a bull or a stallion)—declared they would take on all comers. Such tournaments, widely publicized, were attended by thousands; and given man's age-old illicit affair with pain and death—the same dark entanglement of fear and desire that brings fame, if not fortune, to bullfighters and motorcycle stuntmen today—the heavy attendance is understandable. Though a contender could survive them, and most contenders did, jousts could make the fiercest modern football game seem a pastime for ailing young ladies. How much Chaucer knew of the deadly sport, and something of what he felt about it, is apparent in the *Knight's Tale:*

Tho werë the gates shet, and cried was loudë:	[*Then*]
"Do now yourë devoir, yongë knyghtës proudë!"	[*duty*]
The heraudës lefte hir prikyng up and doun;	[*heralds . . .*
Now ryngen trompës loude and clarioun.	*galloping*]
Ther is namoorë to seyn, but west and est	
In goon the sperës ful sadly in arrest;	[*solemnly*]
In gooth the sharpë spore into the sydë.	[*spur*]
Ther seen men who kan juste and who kan rydë;	
Ther shyveren shaftës upon sheeldës thikkë;	
He feeleth thurgh the herte-spoon the prikkë.	[*the spoon-shaped*
Up spryngen sperës twenty foot on hightë;	*depression at the end*
Out goon swerdës as the silver brightë;	*of the breastbone*]
The helmës they tohewen and toshredë;	[*hew and shred*]
Out brest the blood with stiernë stremes redë;	
With myghty maces the bonës they tobrestë.	[*burst*]
He thurgh the thikkeste of the throng gan threstë;	[*thrust*]
Ther stomblen steedës stronge, and doun gooth al;	
He rolleth under foot as dooth a bal;	
He foyneth on his feet with his tronchoun,	[*thrusts (or parries)*]
And he hym hurtleth with his hors adoun;	
He thurgh the body is hurt and sithen takë,	[*afterwards taken*]
Maugree his heed, and broght unto the stakë;	[*to the safety zone*]
As forward was, right there he moste abydë.	[*prearrangement,*
	former agreement]

For all the "stern (or violent) red streams," broken bones, and hurts through the body, Chaucer is describing here not battle-to-the-death but mere sport, a joust with nubbed lances.

The games proper opened with a parade around the tourney grounds, model of the parade of artists and animals in our modern circus. As in Chaucer's *Knight's Tale,* every champion of importance had his host of followers, all splendidly armed and mounted, and had his array of bright banners, also, in some cases trumpeters, clowns, fine hunting dogs, exotic animals. Then the jousting began—heralds riding back and forth announcing contenders, marshals establishing the positions of the players and the particular rules to be followed in this joust, whether the combat was to be between two men or twenty or, indeed, two hundred. Setting up each joust was a slow business, so between collisions of iron and iron there were various forms of interlude: displays by acrobats, animal trainers, jugglers, clowns, magicians, dancers—all the various forms of "buffoonery" that men like the Leicester cloisterer Knighton believed to be responsible for the plagues. When the jousters were ready, the bannered wooden horns rang out (horns modern man has been unable to reproduce, as he's unable to reproduce tempered brass or fused brick), and the tourney grounds fell silent. Whatever act was in progress broke off —perhaps a spatter of applause—and the contenders, alone or with their followers, rode in at the opposite ends of the field, helmets off or visors lifted, lances raised. Interluders fled out of the field, back to the stands, or if they were too late retreated to the safety of the "stake." With a sound like thunder the great gates fell shut, sealing off the field from the spectators, and the horns rang out again.

In upright position—"in arrest," as Chaucer says—its butt end supported by a cup hanging close to the rider's steel shoe, the lance could be nearly the height of a modern telephone pole ("twenty foot on highte," Chaucer says) and for much of its length very nearly as wide, though hollowed out. (Such lances have been preserved all over Europe and can be seen in, for instance, the Tower of London.) When he was ready to attack, or when the fourteenth-century equivalent to our referee gave the signal, the jouster snapped his visor shut, took in a huge gulp of air like a weight-lifter's, and heaved upward on the lance, throwing the wide steel flange onto his shoulder and clamping the butt inside his arm while in the same motion tilting the tip slightly forward, into "proffering" position—sign to his opponent that he was charging now (hence Chaucer's obscene pun in the *Miller's Tale,* when sex-hungry Nicholas, urging his attentions on the miller's wife, "spak so faire, and profrëd him so fastë")—and spurred his horse in the direction of his challenger. As the horses moved toward each other (lumbering but swift medieval destriers exactly like the Busch Beer Clydesdales), increasing their speed, the two knights gradually let their lances drop, pivoting the weight on the flange of the lance, which would in strike position rest on the right steel breastplate. If the timing was wrong, the lance might drop too far, harmless, shattering or stabbing the tourney turf, or might fail to descend to the target area, the opponent's head or chest. If the timing was right, and if the opponent was unable to deflect the blow with his enormous shield, or "targe," down he went—down quite frequently both knights went, noisily rolling underfoot. Even if the point of the lance was capped with a great, blunt ball—as it is in the *Knight's Tale* and as it often though by no means always was in the English tournaments where Chaucer sat bent forward, holding his breath, watching the combatants with partisan alarm—the damage to man and horse could be consider-able. It was not, in short, a sport for weaklings, or for men with the faintest touch of clumsiness or bad judgment, or for men perturbed by bruises. Needless to say, when the battle was in earnest, it was con-siderably more violent. The chronicles are filled with such accounts as the following:

> Then stepped forth an English squire . . . and came before the earl and kneeled down and desired that he might perform the battle; and the earl agreed thereto. Then this [squire] came forth and armed him-self completely and took his spear, and Clarence his, and so they came against each and foined and thrust so sorely at each other that the spears flew all to pieces over their heads. And at the second encounter they did likewise, and at the third also, so that their spears were broken; and all the lords on both sides thought this deed a goodly feat of arms. Then they took their swords, which were very big, and in six strokes they broke four swords. And then they would have fought with axes, but the earl would not let them and said he would not see them fight to the finish, saying they had done enough.[5]

Even more common in the chronicles are the catalogues of knights who did fight to the finish, slaughtering or dying.

King Edward, though a small man, was one of the world's great jousters. That alone might have made him into a hero to his people, with their love of pageantry and roughneck games. But he was also—after his bad start in Scotland, at fifteen—a master strategist, one devil of a man to encounter in actual war by sea or land. Around the time of Geoffrey Chaucer's birth, the enormous French fleet was a constant threat to the shores of England. It raided Portsmouth and Southampton in 1338, brazenly sailed near the mouth of the Thames, and, just off Middelburg, seized the great cog *Christopher* and four other vessels; in 1339 the French attacked Dover and Folkestone. They got their comeuppance the following year. As he was approaching the Flemish coast with a small English fleet, King Edward, aboard his cog the *Thomas,* unexpectedly came upon "so great a nombre of [French] shippes that their mastes semed to be lyke a great wood," Froissart reports. The king of England rearranged his ships, "the greatest befor, well furnysshed with archers, and ever bytwene two shyppes of archers he had one shypp with men-at-arms." He set aside three hundred men-at-arms and five hundred archers for the protection of the numerous highborn ladies who were traveling to Flanders to join the queen, then waited for favorable wind and tide, and, when the sun was in the faces of the enemy, steered full sail into the harbor mouth of Sluys and crashed into the French at their moorings. Even against overwhelming odds, Edward's combination of archers and men-at-arms—a trick he'd learned in Scotland—was devastating. Though the French fought hard, by dawn both French admirals were dead, and the fleet was in ruins.

In 1346, when Chaucer was a small child, King Edward had still more spectacular success. In what may or may not have been a brilliant last-minute change of plan, he landed not at the Bay of Biscay—where he had intended to join forces with Henry, earl of Lancaster, eldest son of blind Henry—but in Normandy, where, in the words of an adviser (according to Froissart), "ther is none that shall resyst you: the people of Normandy have not been used to the warr, and all the knyghtes and squyers of the contrey ar nowe at the siege before Aguyllon with the duke: and sir, ther ye shall fynde great townes that be nat walled, wherby your men shall have such wynning [booty], that they shall be the better therby twenty yer after." Edward's plan was a typically bold one. He risked meeting the much larger army of King Philip of France, and since, once the troops were landed, the English shipmasters were always eager to sail back home, he risked, first, loss of his line of retreat, then encirclement and annihilation. But Edward was lucky, or protected by the Devil, as usual—or perhaps had information historians lack. Even after his invasion force had been spotted, he managed by feints to evade an encounter until he'd reached Crécy and an ideal position for defense, the wood of Crécy-en-Ponthieu behind him, in front of him the broad Valley of the Clerks. Against the advice of some of Philip's generals, and despite thunder and rain that made a great flock of crows wheel crazily for fear, the daredevil French knights attacked, facing into the setting sun, with Genoese crossbowmen in the vanguard. Overmatched by English longbows, with their greater range, the Genoese spent their arrows on mere angels and empty air, then retreated in confusion. The French king was outraged, according to Froissart, and yelled, "Slay me these rascals, for they shall hinder and trouble us without reason!" The French cavalry rode down their own allies, striking them as if they were the enemy, while Edward's cool, well-ordered archers picked off both Genoese and Frenchmen, and Edward's foot soldiers hamstrung French horses with their knives and killed fallen French knights—much to Edward's displeasure, since he'd have lief had their ransom.

It was a great triumph for Edward's ideas on how battles should be conducted. The French nobility and the aristocrats among Philip's allies fought by the old, wasteful code of individual chivalry. Froissart tells how the king of Bohemia, nearly blind, asked his companions to lead him into battle that he might strike one stroke with his sword. His gentlemen linked their horses' reins, with the king at the head. When morning came, they were all found dead, their horses still tied together. The English, on the other hand, fought as a unit, efficiently controlled under Edward's direction, calm, fanatically loyal to their king. When dawn came and the countryside was blanketed in fog, any other medieval army would have scattered in pursuit of the enemy and might well have been lost. Under Edward's command, the English counted casualties, tended to the wounded, and prepared for their march on Calais.

To his contemporaries, to men like young Chaucer—whatever modern historians may say—Edward seemed an ideal king. He was widely praised for his fair-mindedness. Despite the treason of Sir Roger Mortimer, Sir Roger's son Edmund (husband to the countess of Ulster's baby daughter) was allowed to retain land in Wales; and when Edmund Mortimer died, his son, another Roger, was granted holdings, later knighthood (for bravery at the Battle of Crécy), and eventual memberhip in the Order of the Garter, restitution of all titles and family lands, and, in the end, parliamentary reversal of the judgment on his grandfather. Those close to court affairs thought Edward III politically astute, which indeed he was, though the fact is obscured by calamities no one at the time could have foreseen: the early death of his eldest son, the Black Prince, and the general bad luck of Edward's grandson, son of the Black Prince, Richard. Edward dealt justly and wisely with his magnates, keeping the loyalty of his people not just by charm or by such shrewd innovations as paying wages to his armies—a practice which freed him from that bane of the medieval general's existence, an army of feudal vassals which by law had the right to disband after forty days to go home and do its farmwork—but also by concern for the general welfare of all Englishmen. He chose advisers, generals, and civil servants wisely, and he was willing to delegate authority. He avoided clashes with parliament and the Church, still maintaining his royal rights to the best of his ability. If he was wrong in thinking war the great hope of his kingdom, his people, for the most part, wholeheartedly believed him right.

Men were blissfully proud to be Englishmen in Edward's day. When he began his reign, English military power was negligible. By the time the yeoman Geoffrey Chaucer came to know King Edward, English fighting men, both knights and infantry, were the joy of the Ringing Isle. English knights, guided by Edward, had learned respect for lowborn archers and dagger fighters—not that any English knight thought an archer his social equal. Serfs who fought bravely were regularly promoted or "released" into freemen, a practice virtually unknown before.

On the home front, common men gained power in parliament, and courts of law became considerably more liberal, since mustering troops and raising money for war were both heavily dependent on the commoners' good will. The result, despite plagues, bad harvests, and failing trade, was a general, often near-hysterical excitement, a great surge of English self-confidence.

Young Geoffrey Chaucer, whatever his sophistication and innate good sense, must have felt the same thrill every other Englishman felt in King Edward's presence. If he ever believed King Edward wrong—he leaves no sign, but other poets were occasionally critical—he doubted as one of the fiercely loyal opposition. He never for a moment shared the modern historian's distaste for Edward's love of ostentation—an objectionable trait in lowborn guildsmen, Chaucer would have said (as in the *General Prologue to the Canterbury Tales*), but a noble virtue in a man like Duke Theseus (in Chaucer's *Knight's Tale* and *Anelida and Arcite*), a godlike man such as Edward III. At sixteen or so he must have believed, as Englishmen twice his age believed, that Edward was a virtually faultless king, a shining gift to England straight from heaven. If the future poet were not already a staunch royalist, through his father's influence and later Prince Lionel's, he would have become one the day he met his king.

At some point during his attendance on the countess, Chaucer met Edward's pride and joy and the darling of all England, young Edward, Prince of Wales, more often in his own day "le Prince d'Angleterre"— later called by Tudor historians (because of his black armor, designed for the joust) "the Black Prince." He was by all accounts even more handsome than his father, as fanatically chivalric, as fond of jousting and the excitement of war—also beautiful women—and as capable as his father of stirring his followers to heroic loyalty and superhuman courage. He was a hero at Crécy and was made governor of Gascony in 1355, where he went in September with a small, top-notch army (bulky medieval equivalent of the modern commando or terrorist outfit) to make trouble for the French. He spent the autumn pillaging and burning the suburbs of the ancient cities of Narbonne and Carcassonne, then ravaging the Mediterranean provinces. He could lure no French army out to meet him, but he succeeded well in that he humiliated the enemy, kept France disorganized, depleted her resources, temporarily cemented the loyalty of the Gascons to Edward III, and, of course, enriched his raiders. The following year—he was now just twenty-six—he moved further afield, perhaps to meet Henry of Lancaster, blind Henry's son, and, with Lancaster's help, strike at central and northwest France. On September 17, 1356—at about the time Chaucer was applying for service with the countess of Ulster—the Black Prince, marching cross-country to Poitiers under a low, brooding sky, his army's horses loaded down, and every wagon he'd been able to steal piled high with booty, collided with a French reconnaissance party. Despite his overladen outfit's clumsiness, the Black Prince took prisoners—two French counts—and continued the march. The following day he met, much to his displeasure, the main French army, in the personal command of King John the Good. The French, looking up at the invaders, laughed. Young Edward treated for time. It was a Sunday, and the cardinal nuncios were able to secure a brief truce.

On Monday, as most French historians reconstruct it, and they are probably correct, the Black Prince attempted to break away, but John outflanked him. The English were almost certainly outnumbered by as much as five to one (the point has been disputed), and they were, in any case, battle-weary and laden down with the spoils of their raiding. But the countryside's numerous old, dark woods and its natural baffle of vineyards still in leaf, with swampy ground stretching between the prince and his enemy, were favorable to defense; and the prince remembered his father's tactics at Crécy: keep to high ground, with the sun behind your back.

The ensuing battle has been described as the longest and one of the most vicious in all the Middle Ages. Again and again the English broke and fled; again and again the man in black armor, visor lifted, cajoled, inspired, or cursed them back to order. By the force of his will, his own daredevil courage, his near-maniacal faith in the divine right and might of Englishmen, he inspired his troops as no English leader had done since the days of King Alfred. When the archers were out of arrows, they tore arrows from the bodies of fallen men and horses, and fired again; when their lances were broken, the English cavalry fought with splintered stubs, later with looted household knives, hammers and axes, and, in the end, with stones. Such fantastic great-heartedness—if not lunacy—was irresistible: the columns of King John's huge, seasoned army broke up in disorder and fled. The slaughter was unspeakable, the glory of the victory incomparable. Among the 1,975 prisoners rich enough to be worth taking alive were the king of France, his youngest son, an archbishop, eighteen counts and viscounts, and twenty-one barons.

Le Prince d'Angleterre wintered in Bordeaux, accepted a French truce, and waited on his captive, King John, like a servant. In May he transported his prisoners into Plymouth and made a three-week triumphal progress toward London, hailed along the way by a weeping, hysterically joyful populace. His train of wooden-wheeled, booty-laden carts stretched miles behind him like the glittering tail of a dragon.

There was probably no sign in that glorious prince, when Chaucer first knew him, of what would come later. He was still all chivalry, all beauty, in 1357. But there was tragedy ahead: sickness, mental breakdown, despair. In 1362, when he became sovereign of Gascony, his favoritism—bestowing all important posts not on Gascons but on his own followers—would lead to serious trouble and the eventual loss of Gascony; but that was mere error, not a serious deficiency of character. He was still a man of principle when, in 1367, he fought (victoriously, as always) to restore Pedro the Cruel to the throne of Navarre and refused to surrender those opponents of Pedro whom he'd taken as prisoner, knowing how Pedro would deal with them. (They later managed to assassinate King Pedro.) While in Spain the prince contracted the disease—perhaps tuberculosis—which would eventually kill him; and by 1370, he was grotesquely changed, not just in body but in mind. King Edward's European vassals and allies were by this time deserting him on every side. Since the prince was ill, apparently close to death, the king had shifted his faith to Prince Edward's younger brother, conservative John of Gaunt, now duke of Lancaster—his wife having inherited the duchy of Lancaster from her father, Earl Henry. Desperate, perhaps feeling he was running out of time, the Black Prince set his heart on teaching all potential defectors to France one final lesson.

His chance came with the defection of Limoges—a beautiful and prosperous city on the Vienne. Against the urgent pleading of John of Gaunt, his closest friend as well as his brother, the Black Prince organized an expediton and set out at its head, riding on a litter, every jolt sending agony through his body. He found the great gates of the city closed, the walls manned by citizens with makeshift weapons. For a week the prince lay, sleepless and feverish, haggard, perspiring, in his splendid battle tent, cursing his men on as they worked at a tunnel below the walls. At last they set the wooden supports afire, and about dawn, a section of the wall collapsed. The prince's servants carried the litter across the rubble as the English troops flooded in, wiping out the ineffectual civilian defenders, and, at the prince's command, began murdering every man, woman, and child in the city. To all pleas for mercy the Black Prince dramatically turned away his face. Only a small number of the leading citizens had inspired the revolt, as the prince knew full well; the common people could do nothing but obey. Yet he ordered the litter dragged through the town, from street to street and lane to lane, watching the bloody execution of his own wailing subjects.

King Edward's second son, William, died in infancy. His third son, Prince Lionel, Chaucer, as an attendant to Prince Lionel's wife, must have known intimately. The man is perhaps the hardest of all Edward's sons to understand or assess. Historians have almost universally berated him. We read, for instance: "He was lazy, cruel and vain. His good looks had ensured from childhood that there was always a woman to spoil him—first his mother and later his wife and various mistresses."[6] Except for the charge of laziness, the same could of course be said of virtually all of Edward's sons (and of Edward himself), handsome men, adored by women and extravagantly admired by men, capable of cruelty but also of fits of generosity. He was born in Antwerp in 1338 and given the romantic name "Lionel" perhaps in honor of the Lion of Brabant. Since he could expect little from the paternal estates, he must be advanced by marriage or not at all. He had the terrible luck we know now, by hindsight, to be married off to Elizabeth of Burgh, granddaughter of the Lady Elizabeth of Clare and only child of William of Burgh, earl of Ulster. This gave him, among other things, nominal control of the earldom of Ulster, an area perhaps even less comfortable then than now. King Edward sent him there as lord lieutenant, shortly after Chaucer left the service of Lionel's wife, and the prince failed miserably.

His rule in Ireland was undoubtedly tyrannical. No native Irishman was permitted to come near him, either in the castle of Dublin or when he moved through the town. He overtaxed his subjects and never appeared without numerous bodyguards, whom he is said to have permitted to rape and pillage as they liked. He manipulated passage of the Statute of Kilkenny, which prohibited all connection, through marriage or otherwise, between the English and the Irish. But bad as all this sounds, it probably reflects fairly standard feeling among the English of the day concerning Irishmen. If Lionel had been a more intelligent, less selfish man, he might have seen that in acting on his whims and prejudices he was sowing dragon's teeth for future generations; but here Lionel was like his father Edward, of whom it has been said, not unjustly, that along with more endearing boyish qualities "he retained too a certain youthful petulance and shortsightedness, a readiness to sacrifice the future for the present, to give almost any price for what at the moment he passionately desired."[7] If the Black Prince was more noble in his rule of Gascony—more understanding and generous—part of the reason is that he did not fundamentally despise all Gascons as Lionel did the Irish. Lionel, like many medieval Englishmen, judging by the chronicles, hated the Irish—disliked their outlandish dress of furs, the wild-man manners of their warrior chieftains, their reputation (largely unjustified) for treachery. When the enlightened Richard II, toward the end of the century, attempted with some success to understand and conciliate the Irish, his own people reacted with contempt.

For Lionel, things went from bad to worse. Upon the death of Countess Elizabeth, he was married off to the beautiful heiress of the Visconti family—potential heiress, too, of a good part of the fortune of her uncle, the lord of Milan. The dowry offered was two million gold florins, part in advance, along with vast estates in northern Italy. Prince Lionel was married in Milan Cathedral on June 5, 1368. Four months later he was dead, by some reports having "addicted himself overmuch to untimely banquetings," by others, having been murdered by poison.

When Chaucer first knew him, Prince Lionel had not yet left for Ireland. He was a mother's boy, certainly, though not necessarily in an ugly sense. He had no overwhelming love of athletics, but he was proud of his older brother, the Black Prince (King Edward's family, even in times of disagreement, was close), and in many respects Prince Lionel aped his elder brother: the extravagant dress, the arrogance, the flirtations. Lionel was shy, more comfortable with his mother and her intellectual friends than with his heroic father—more sure of his ground when talking about poetry or painting than when talking about war. He was a depressive, an evader. He ate too much, drank too much, avoided responsibility by humor or deep glooms. What Chaucer thought of him is impossible to say, except for this: he was loyal to King Edward's family all his life, as they were, for the most part, to each other (as all the chronicles remark). Whether or not Chaucer liked Prince Lionel, the probability is that like Queen Philippa, he could easily excuse him.

As we've seen already, King Edward's fourth son, John of Gaunt, was roughly—perhaps almost exactly—Chaucer's age. It seems highly unlikely that the two did not meet between 1357 and 1359. What they thought of each other no one really knows, but later, in his poetry, Chaucer would treat John of Gaunt as a paragon of virtue. The poet's first great poem, the *Book of the Duchess,* is an elegy to Gaunt's first wife, Blanche of Lancaster, daughter of Earl Henry, and a tribute to Gaunt. There is fair evidence that Gaunt and Chaucer became very close friends—not just brothers-in-law, though they became that too, but friends who were like brothers.

Traditionally historians have not liked Gaunt, more swayed by the hostility of the duke's contemporaries than by Shakespeare's admiration; but recent historians incline to the view that, with the exception of his father-in-law Henry of Lancaster, Gaunt was perhaps the best man in all the group. He had the usual family faults. He fell in love too easily, though he later became a model of faithfulness to Katherine Swynford, first as lover, later as husband. He was not, as some historians have imagined, a complete military incompetent. His "great march through France," which some modern historians consider a disaster, was regarded in his own time as a superb feat. His numerous retreats and doubtful compromises show sometimes a tendency toward self-interest (understandable, given his situation), but mainly show a military leader more concerned about his men than about victory at any cost. It is worth remembering that the Black Prince's glorious victory at Poitiers, when his army of berserkers took the day with stones, came in a battle only joined because retreat was cut off. Gaunt's battles in Spain, where in the 1380's he struggled to seize the Castilian crown, were not at all mere "romantic ventures," much less simply grabs at a foreign throne, as his detractors have suggested (Gaunt had at this time, through marriage to Princess Constance of Castile, a reasonable claim, as such things were then determined); they were, first and foremost, attempts, like those of his brother the Black Prince, to control the Spanish navy and establish against France a second front. Professor Williams says, rightly,

> There is no record of [Gaunt's] ever having betrayed a friend, or swerved in loyalty to a supporter. His continued protection of Wyclif, even after he broke with the Reformer on theological issues, and even after supporting him became unpopular and dangerous, is well-known. His biographer Armitage-Smith speaks of him as one who held the laws of chivalry sacred; who had a fine "knightly modesty"; who was notably courageous; who valued learning; who left behind him a record, in a century that could be savage, "extraordinarily free from acts of violence and oppression"; who sympathized with the poor and the humble; who did many an act of kindness and of charity; and who had a reputation for sincere and profound piety.

Williams adds, again rightly, "We should not feel either surprised or outraged if we find that Chaucer regarded this man as both great and good, and felt honored by his friendship. Rather (if we try to view matters with fourteenth-century eyes), it would have been surprising and even disgraceful of Chaucer not to have esteemed such a man."[8] While England's beloved King Edward was alive and England felt self-confident (or overconfident), Gaunt was a stabilizing influence, a spokesman against war's waste of money and human life. When Richard II became king and began to show his colors as an unfashionable pacifist, a stubborn advocate of royal prerogative, and an arrogant intellectual who seems to have detested from the bottom of his heart the rising power of his magnates (though he tried to be just and, by his own by-no-means-dim lights, kingly), Gaunt was a powerful spokesman for compromise and patience.

Gaunt was a lover of ideas and books, and would grow increasingly to be a supporter of inquiry and, as in his concern for Geoffrey Chaucer, a patron of the arts. He believed profoundly—like others in his family—in intellectual exploration; so much so that, years afterward, when Oxford's leading theological investigator was to be tried for his possibly heretic opinions—opinions with which Gaunt personally disagreed—Gaunt would appear with his army to defend by force, if necessary, what we now call academic freedom. Gaunt was equally dependable in the joust, though he was never as dazzling as his brother the Black Prince or his father. Like all his family, he believed on principle in ritual, pageantry, and ostentatious display; thought it shameful to explain his decisions to inferiors; and could be fierce, though never unjust (by medieval standards) in meting out punishment for wrongdoing. Unlike his relatives—his father, for instance, whose frequently ingenious moneymaking schemes were repeatedly vitiated by graft and inefficiency—Gaunt was murderously efficient, at least in his own personal affairs, in collecting what was due him. Partly for this reason, partly because of his notorious haughtiness—his bold interference in London's business when John Wyclif was being tried there for heresy—and partly for other, more complicated reasons, Gaunt's palace on the Savoy would be the number one target of rebellious peasants in 1381. But Gaunt's haughtiness was for strangers, not friends. Chaucer says of him in the *Book of the Duchess:*

> Loo! how goodly spak thys knyght,
> As hit had be another wyght;   [*wight, commoner*]
> He made hyt nouther towgh ne queyntë.
> And I say that, and gan me aqueyntë   [*saw*]
> With hym, and fond hym so tretable,
> Ryght wonder skylful and resonable,
> As me thoghtë, for al hys balë.   [*sorrow*]

In the years of Chaucer's service with the countess, Gaunt's mind can have been on only one thing: war. Or rather, two: war and women. If the two young men talked—the talented young prince and the sly young wit who was a vintner's son—war and women were, at least some of the time, the subject. Gaunt's eldest brother had just lately won his incredible war prize, King John of France, and was home again, basking in female adoration, giving away favors, moving from flower to flower like a magnificent black bee. In fourteenth-century courtly circles, war and women were pleasures inextricably linked. What Chaucer says of his Knight's son, the Squire, in the *General Prologue to the Canterbury Tales,* was true of all young soldiers of that age—if not of every age:

> And he haddë been somtyme in chyvachië . . .   [*the cavalry*]
> And born hym weel, as of so litel spacë,
> In hopë to stonden in his lady gracë.

It was partly, of course, the universal experience: men who constantly
play games with death have a sharpened appetite for the pleasures of
living, and no one has invented a pleasure more profound or intense
than the love of man and woman. But in the late Middle Ages the usual
experience may perhaps have had extra bite.

By official—by this time rather old-fashioned—Church doctrine, love
was a bad business (just as violence was). It was as likely as not to hurl
one straight to damnation, that specially grisly damnation universally
advertised by fourteenth-century painters, minor English poets, and hell-
fire churchmen: hissing serpents, monstrous fire, ingeniously sadistic
imps equipped with the latest Italian implements of torture. On the
other hand, as the example of the Virgin Mary showed, a truly good
woman could be an inspiration toward nobility and virtue. As the writers
of the *Romance of the Rose* explained in a passage much copied and
quoted throughout medieval Europe, a lover attracted to a lady of great
purity, gentleness, and goodness might rise through the influence or
"grace" of that lady to similar virtue, and thence still higher, in Platonic
fashion, lower goods awakening the soul to higher and higher goods in
the way Plato described in his *Symposium* and the way Dante treated as
the central dramatic principle in his *Divine Comedy*. Like a just and noble
war, the love of a good woman could be a knight's salvation. Like an unjust and ignoble war—a war pursued in a bad cause or by bestial, unchivalric means—the "carnality" in love, the tendency of love to collapse
into sex and selfish greed, could spell ruin. Thus the two emotions, love
of battle and love of love, became, at least for some, intrinsicate. Not only
in the joust but in battle as well, the knight wore his lady's talisman:
her virtue, her influence, would prevent any damning lapse from chivalry
on his part. And his success in the battle, which he joined in her name and
for her increased glory, would earn him his lady's "grace" or favor—and
also persuade her to his bed. For those who earnestly believed official doctrine, the love affair of the soldier and his lady was a dizzying game, a
tightrope walk over the chasm of eternal torment, as exciting as a joust.
Managing it properly became a matter of ritual, a religion (at least in
poetry, and probably to some extent in real life)—the so-called love
religion or courtly love in all its innumerable varieties and forms.

The Plantagenets were experts, though they were sufficiently sophisticated and freethinking to take official doctrine with a grain of salt. As
children of Satan—a role they played with gusto—they took the idea of

hell rather lightly, as they took the idea of death. But they enjoyed the game enormously nevertheless. Even a man thoroughly convinced that the religious reformer John Wyclif was right, or close to right, in his main points (that a man should examine the scriptures for himself and trust in the mercy of Christ, not the Pope), even a man certain of God's essentially loving and patient nature—and all of Edward's family felt certain of this—could be troubled by misgivings, the midnight uneasiness that gave zest to the game. The Plantagenets (with some exceptions) flaunted their superiority to the stern, little-minded old religion. But they were careful to be thoroughly honorable. The Black Prince had several illegitimate children and cared for them well; neither he nor anyone else in court saw much harm in it. Before his marriage to Blanche of Lancaster, John of Gaunt had a daughter by one Marie of St. Hilaire, and took care of both mother and daughter ever afterward. When the Plantagenets changed mistresses, as they frequently did (except for Gaunt's deeply, perhaps narrowly religious younger brother Thomas of Woodstock, later earl of Gloucester), they no more abandoned them than they abandoned their wives. Gaunt especially would all his life give his former mistresses and his illegitimate children tokens of affection and generous support. At least twice he would fall deeply—and faithfully—in love, once to Blanche, whom Chaucer mourns in the *Book of the Duchess,* once to Katherine Swynford, Gaunt's mistress for twenty-five years before he at last became free to marry her.

In the courts Gaunt frequented, where Chaucer was sometimes in attendance on the countess, there was a plentiful supply of worthy and noble-hearted ladies, thanks, largely, to that great and generous mother hen, Queen Philippa. She had married Edward III not merely for convenience (though the marriage was convenient), but because she loved him, and would love him, with remarkable selflessness, all her life. It has been suggested that one of her last acts was to set Edward up with a mistress who would love and care for him, Philippa's ward Alice Perrers.

Philippa and Edward had first met in the last days of Edward II when Edward and his mother, Queen Isabella, made a week-long stay with the king of Hainault, his wife, and numerous daughters in his palace at Valenciennes. That week, Edward and Philippa were inseparable. Philippa's parents and Isabella were delighted. It meant, to Isabella, a chance to get military and financial aid for her projected invasion of England with Roger Mortimer, and she at once promised that, on becoming king, Edward would marry Philippa in return for the alliance. According to Philippa, who told the story to her old friend Froissart, on the day when

Edward and his mother had to leave, Edward gave Philippa a formal kiss, and she burst into tears. Asked why she was crying, she said, "Because my fair cousin of England is about to leave me, and I have grown so used to him." Edward, too, remembered that moment. When he was told by peers and bishops, immediately after his coronation, of the tentative agreement with the family of Hainault, the boy king laughed and said, "I am better pleased to marry there than elsewhere, and rather to Philippa, for she and I accorded excellently well together, and she wept, I know well, when I took leave of her." They were married in York, snow swirling down into the unfinished cathedral. In an age when marriage was not expected to go well, Edward and his queen lived in nearly perfect matrimonial happiness until Philippa's death.

She bore Edward seven sons and, in all, twelve children. Two died in infancy, and beautiful young Joan, the favorite daughter, died of the plague in a remote French village while traveling to Castile to be married. She was fifteen. Much later, in 1361—when Geoffrey Chaucer was in his early twenties—Margaret, said to be the cleverest of the royal children, died suddenly of plague, and a few days afterwards, plague took Mary, seventeen-year-old bride of the duke of Brittany. Another daughter, Isabella—with whom Chaucer must have spoken on many occasions —was apparently a great tribulation to Queen Philippa. She was stubborn, hot-tempered, extravagant, and unpredictable, and Philippa loved her to distraction. Isabella refused many marriage contracts arranged for her. She was jilted once, and then at the age of thirty-two fell in love with a French lord who'd arrived in England in the retinue of King John. In 1365 she married him.

By this time, it might be mentioned, old Queen Philippa had other troubles. The Black Prince, her eldest son—England's brilliant and handsome prize in the marriage-of-convenience game—had married himself off, not for convenience but for love, to Joan, "the Fair Maid of Kent"—Philippa's ward ever since Roger Mortimer, ruling from behind the scenes during Edward III's first years, had executed her father. Joan was in her prime regarded as the most beautiful woman in England, and, though the chronicle reference is somewhat mysterious, she was probably that "Countess of Salisbury" whom King Edward loved and with whose garter he started his famous Order. She'd been betrothed in childhood to the earl of Salisbury, though she'd never in fact become his wife. When Salisbury, after resistance on Joan's part, sought to enforce the betrothal compact by abducting her, she revealed that she'd been secretly married for three years to Thomas Holland, Salisbury's steward. (She was already, by this time, in love with the Black Prince.) When Thomas Holland later died in Normandy, Joan rushed to the prince at his home at Berkhamsted. She was now forty, and her legendary beauty had softened toward fat, but the prince was as much in love with her as ever (as was chivalrous and right) and swept away physical and spiritual objections—her age, her probable former relationship with his father, and the fact that he himself was her son's godfather. He sent away post haste for a Papal dispensation and, before it arrived, married her.

Queen Philippa was worried. She distrusted Joan, though she loved her. Joan was too fond of the spectacular, too much the unscrupulous social climber, though famous for sweetness and generosity. And Philippa worried that the child of a woman of forty might not be healthy. She was apparently right. News came from Bordeaux that a child had been born to the heir of England's throne. "Slow," it was whispered. . . . "Straunge of eyë"—so Philippa learned, some historians believe. (The records speak only by significant omissions.) It seems at least possible that the child was mongoloid. Stowe says, when he mentions the child's death, "The death was not too soon, it was said." The Black Prince, nonetheless, was heartbroken. But in her second pregnancy Joan of Kent was luckier, or so it seemed at the time. She produced the brilliant, healthy baby with golden hair who would be Richard II—the man who, by uncommon bad luck and miscalculation, would bring on revolution.

Young Chaucer would come to know Joan of Kent well, and beyond a shadow of a doubt he would be shocked by modern historians' occasionally adverse judgment of her. However Queen Philippa may have disapproved of the marriage, if she had really disliked Joan, her devoted and sequacious old friend Froissart could never have brought himself to say that in all England Joan was "the most loving [of women], famous for her beauty and the extravagance of her dress." The loving nature of that pretty, fat, bejeweled lady shines through page after page of the story of her life. In 1381 (when Chaucer was approximately forty-one and just beginning his *Canterbury Tales,* from which he sometimes gave readings for Princess Joan and her friends), Joan was a peacemaker between Gaunt and the angry Londoners, with whom Gaunt was too busy and too self-righteous to deal. Several of her knights were important as a stabilizing influence in Richard's court, and others were among the famous "Lollard knights," pious adherents to reformer John Wyclif. When trouble broke out between Richard II and his violent half brother Sir John Holland, and Richard threatened to have him executed, their mother Joan of Kent made frequent, painful trips to reconcile them. Her apparent failure to do so may have brought on her death.

Besides Joan of Kent and Alice Perrers, the girl who would become Edward's mistress, Queen Philippa had various other wards and attendant ladies, many of whom, by the late 1350's, had courts of their own. One was Chaucer's employer, Elizabeth, countess of Ulster. Another was Blanche of Lancaster, who would become first wife to John of Gaunt.

Her father was, as I've said, the son of blind Henry and cousin of Edward III, and had become, after Henry's death, the earl of Lancaster, a distinguished general in the Scottish and French wars, a superb negotiator, a beneficent influence on the king, whom he frequently dissuaded from acts of cruelty, and one of the best jousters in all Europe. He was the richest man in England—his daily expenditure was £100 ($24,000) —and one of the most deeply devoted Christians of his day. When the king of France, John the Good, entertained Henry on the occasion of a great French tournament and wished to give him rich gifts, Henry would accept nothing but a thorn out of the Saviour's crown, which he then gave to the collegiate Church of Our Lady in Leicester. Toward the end of his life—he died of the pestilence in 1361—he wrote an honest and moving meditation called *The Book of Holy Medicines* (*Le Livre de Seyntz Medicines*).

Blanche, his second daughter, was apparently a young woman much like her father. It is true, of course, that one does not always get an accurate portrait from a funeral elegy, so that Chaucer's portrait of "Lady White" in the *Book of the Duchess* may be very much an idealization. But it is also true that good writers do not tell lies in elegies, but idealize qualities that were really there. She was, by Chaucer's elegiac account, supremely modest yet easily approachable, refined, temperate, lighthearted, and pious without sternness or coldness. Whatever Chaucer wrote for other ladies, for Blanche (when he came to know her, perhaps not until 1361), he wrote devotional pieces, notably—if tradition can be trusted—his religious poem, the *ABC,* a free translation of a religious poem in French, done at Blanche's request. It has always been taken as a straight devotional piece, which indeed it is; but its appeal in its day was its obvious relationship to the poetry of courtly love at its most spiritual. Chaucer's *ABC* is in effect a courtly-love poem to the Virgin, if not simultaneously (and only indirectly) to Lady Blanche herself. The poem strongly emphasizes the spiritually uplifting effect of the lady, as courtly-love poems, like poems to the Virgin, always do. The poet asks only that her perfection help him toward God; but his stance as worshipper is not purely conventional. He says, for instance:

> Evere hath myn hope of refut been in thee,   [*refuge*]
> For heer-beforn ful ofte, in many a wysë,
> Hast thou to misericordë receyved me.   [*mercy*]
> But merci, ladi, at the grete assysë,   [*great judgment*]
> When we shulë come bifore the hye justysë!
> So litel fruit shal thanne in me be foundë

That, but thou er that day me wel chastysë,
Of verrery right my werk wol me confoundë.

It is of course more courtly-love convention than Church tradition that
accounts for the poet's asking the Virgin to scold and correct him and
thus help him resist sin and error. Though nothing whatever need be
made of the not too serious reference in the *Book of the Duchess* to
"eight years" of fruitless devotion to some lady, the very act of Chaucer's
translating the delicate *ABC* for Blanche shows that she was his friend
long before the time of her death and his writing of the elegy.

If his feelings toward Blanche were friendship and admiration, we
have strong evidence that toward other young ladies Geoffrey Chaucer
could be something of a threat. In his old age he would speak of himself
as having written "many a song and many a lecherous lay." We have no
reason to doubt the older Chaucer's word. The venerable poet, notable
for his dignified, unfanatical piety, had no reason to claim sins never
committed, and no need to distort harmless ditties into lecherous lays.
Moreover, Chaucer's friend and fellow poet John Gower tells us, in a
poem originally written for an audience that knew Chaucer intimately,
that in "the flourës of his youthë" Chaucer was a disciple and poet of
Venus and filled the countryside with "songës gladë." Even if he were
by nature disinclined to be a ladies' man, his culture gave him hardly
any choice. G. G. Coulton points out that conditions in the courts where
Chaucer served made love affairs, Platonic friendships, requited or unrequited sexual passions "not so much natural as positively inevitable."
Coulton continues, "Within the narrow compass of a medieval castle,
daily intercourse was proportionately closer, as differences of rank were
more indelible than they are nowadays; and in a society where neither
could seriously dream of marriage, Kate the Queen might listen all the
more complacently to the page's love-carol as he crumbled the hounds
their messes."[9]

Two highborn ladies who were to be of importance in the life of
Geoffrey Chaucer were the daughters of Sir Paon of Roet, a chevalier
of Hainault. Roet was attached to the service of Queen Philippa when
she came to England, and later attended her at the siege of Calais, when
he was one of the two knights appointed to lead away the citizens she'd
saved from Edward's wrath. He also served as an official of the household of Marguerite, empress of Germany and countess of Hainault,
sister of Queen Philippa. Sir Paon's daughter Katherine, who married
a man named Thomas Swynford, was to become John of Gaunt's mistress,
later his wife. Her sister Philippa was to become—sometime shortly before 1366—the wife of Geoffrey Chaucer.

It has sometimes been suggested, and perhaps rightly, that the romance

between Chaucer and Philippa began as early as 1357 or so. The basis of
the theory is a group of references, in the countess of Ulster's Household
Accounts, to gifts and expenditures on behalf of a lady called Philippa
Pan'. The word "Pan'," by this theory as originally brought forward,
is short for *panetaria*, and means "mistress of the pantry." In that form,
at least, the theory won't work. A careful search of records shows that
Pan' was never an abbreviation of *panetaria*;[10] English pantries were run,
in all cases we know of, by men, not women; the countess's gifts to
Philippa Pan' include some which would be too fancy for a pantry mistress, for instance some furs for the St. George's Day feast of 1358; and
the abbreviation "Pan' " is more naturally explained as part of a family
name, "Pantolf, Panetrie, Panter," Manly says. But as a later scholar
pointed out, "Pan' " may also abbreviate "Panetto," a form of Sir Paon
Roet's name. It has more recently been identified as a possible abbreviation of Paon, Paonnet, and Payne, other known forms of Roet's name.[11]
Thus, though the theory is commonly described as "discredited," it is
probably quite right. Chaucer and Philippa probably knew each other as
teen-agers, and it may well have been to highborn, theoretically unreach-
able Philippa that Chaucer wrote some of his love songs.

It may be useful to pause here to answer some commonly advanced
objections to the idea of Chaucer's having served, like every adventure-
some young man around him, as a poet and disciple of Venus. It is true
that Chaucer speaks repeatedly in his poetry of knowing nothing about
love. In *Troilus and Criseyde,* for instance, he calls himself the servant of
Love's servants, because he himself is, in Cupid's court, a hopeless case.
From his earliest great poem, the *Book of the Duchess,* to some of his last,
he presents himself as a ludicrously unsuccessful lover, a man pious by
default—that is, a man devoted to God because the ladies won't have him.
That consistent stance, repeatedly adopted, must mean one of two—no,
three—things. Either Chaucer is telling the truth, jokingly apologizing
for the ineptitude or perhaps piety which keeps him aloof from the
court's normal love play; or he's telling the truth but throwing a polite
tease to the ladies in his audience (several of his patrons were noble-
women—Elizabeth of Ulster, Blanche of Lancaster, Queen Philippa,
Queen Anne) ; or he's working for a laugh because everyone in his original audience knew that his claim of innocence was the opposite of the
truth. There can be very little doubt, I think, that the last of these explanations is the right one. His early love complaints are less conventional
than most and have the unmistakable ring, or so it seems to me, of serious attempts at persuasion. They do not merely praise and flatter, like
French and Italian persuasions to love from this period. They also tease,
amuse, and hint, in the age-old fashion of successful seducers. Moreover,

no poet in the whole literary tradition of England can write more titil-
lating poetry than Chaucer's—unabashed celebrations of the joys of
swyving, as in the *Miller's Tale,* the *Reeve's Tale,* and so on. One thinks,
for instance, of that glorious moment in the *Reeve's Tale* when the clerk
plays his trick on the miller's wife. The first clerk, Allan, has crept into
bed with the miller's daughter, so the second clerk, John, considers it his
duty to mount the miller's wife. Since the room where they're all sleeping
is very dark, John moves the baby's cradle from the foot of the bed where
the miller and his wife sleep and places it at the foot of his own bed.
Result:

Soone after this the wyf hir rowtyng leet,   *[snoring stopped]*
And gan awake, and wente hire out to pissë,
And cam agayn, and gan hir cradel myssë,
And gropëd heer and ther, but she foond noon.
"Allas!" quod she, "I hade almoost mysgoon;
I hadde almoost goon to the clerkës bed.
Ey, benedicite! thanne hadde I foule ysped."
And forth she gooth til she the cradel fond.
She gropeth alwey forther with hir hond,
And foond the bed, and thoghtë noght but good,
By causë that the cradel by it stood,
And nystë wher she was, for it was derk;
But faire and wel she creep in to the clerk,
And lith ful stille, and wolde han caught a sleep.
Withinne a while this John the clerk up leep,
And on this goodë wyf he leith on soorë.
So myrie a fit ne haddë she nat ful yoorë;
He priketh harde and depe as he were mad.
This joly lyf han thisë two clerkës lad
Til that the thriddë cok bigan to syngë.

The pun in the last line, by the way, is pretty typical Chaucer. He writes
not labored puns of the sort Dr. Johnson found (rightly) so offensive
in Shakespeare—for instance, those spoken by the dying John of Gaunt
in *Richard II:*

Old Gaunt indeed, and gaunt in being old:
Within me Grief hath kept a tedious fast;
And who abstains from meat that is not gaunt?
For sleeping England long time have I watch'd;
Watching breeds leanness, leanness is all gaunt. . . .

Chaucer's puns are throwaways, easily missed until the fifteenth reading, such jokes as that ghastly *double entendre* in the portrait of the Wife of Bath, where after speaking of the Wife's many husbands and lovers and then of her three pilgrimages to Jerusalem (notorious at the time as occasions for promiscuity), Chaucer says innocently (head tipped, eyes heavenward, hands behind his back), "She haddë passëd many a straungë strem [stream]"!

But we were speaking of the knowledge of love revealed in Chaucer's poems. He knows more than just the sexual side of love. Part of what makes *Troilus and Criseyde* one of the two or three finest narrative poems in English is its detailed and wise analysis of what love feels like and does in men and women. The effect is cumulative, so that quotation cannot do the analysis justice, but one may mention as an example of Chaucer's way of working in this poem the long soliloquy by Criseyde in which she debates with herself whether or not she should allow herself to fall in love with the young prince. She reasons at length and with great subtlety but in the end still cannot make up her mind. At last she goes to bed, still torturing herself with questions. And what happens is this:

> A nyghtyngale, upon a cedir grenë,
> Under the chambre wal ther as she ley,
> Ful loudë song ayein the moonë shenë,
> Peraunter, in his briddës wise, a lay   [*Peradventure*]
> Of lovë, that made hire hertë fressh and gay.
> That herkned she no longe in good ententë,
> Til at the lastë the dedë slep hire hentë.   [*took away*]
>
> And as she slep, anonright tho hirë mettë   [*then she dreamed*]
> How that an egle, fetherëd whit as bon,
> Under hirë brest his longë clawes settë,
> And out hire herte he rentë, and that anon,
> And dide his herte into hirë brest to gon,
> Of which she nought agroos, ne nothyng smertë;   [*felt dread*]
> And forth he fleigh, with hertë left for hertë.

After passages like this one—and we find many such passages—it is hard to take very seriously Chaucer's claim that he knows nothing about love from personal experience.

Granted, writing about love was standard in the fourteenth century (though often, as we've seen, love is not the poet's real subject). But the central and most admired figure in every court young Chaucer knew was a lady-killer—Edward, the Black Prince, Lionel, John of Gaunt. How could a young man of seventeen or eighteen resist such influence, especially when the love affairs he witnessed were chivalrous and, in their own way, marked by fidelity? How could a man not conspicuously ugly (as we know from portraits), a man with extraordinary understanding of women (as we know from his poems), a man often praised by those who knew him for his remarkable charm and gentleness, and in later years a man who, as poetry reader in England's greatest courts, stood out as a sort of star performer—how could such a man be anything but attractive to women? But above all, where did he learn so much about the behavior of women and men in bed? And, finally, whether we take the "Retraction" at the end of the *Canterbury Tales* as a deathbed lament for sins committed (the sin of writing poems that pull lovers toward the woods) or as something else (a carefully planned aesthetic close after the *Parson's Tale* or a sly way of listing his most important works), the Retraction says plainly that Chaucer was aware of sex as a major theme in much of his life's work, both early and late. Sex was in fact for Geoffrey Chaucer the heart of the matter—sex and the sharpening of awareness, the heightened nobility that go with it, as they do for young Troilus:

> In allë nedës, for the townës werrë,   [*war*]
> He was, and ay, the first in armës dyght,   [*arrayed*]
> And certeynly, but if that bokës errë,
> Save Ector most ydred of any wight;
> And this encrees of hardynesse and myght
> Come hym of love, his ladiës thank to wynnë,
> That alterëd his spirit so withinnë.

> In tyme of trewe, on haukyng wolde he ridë,   [*truce*]
> Or ellës hontë boor, beer, or lyoun;
> The smalë bestës leet he gon bisidë.
> And whan that he com ridyng into town,
> Ful ofte his lady from hirë wyndow down,
> As fressh as faukoun comen out of muwë,   [*falcon*]
> Ful redy was hym goodly to saluwë.

> And moost of love and vertu was his spechë,
> And in despit hadde allë wrecchednessë;
> And douteles, no nedë was hym bisechë
> To honouren hem that haddë worthynessë,
> And esen hem that weren in destressë.   [*ease*]
> And glad was he if any wyght wel ferdë,
> That loverë was, whan he it wiste or herdë.   [*knew*]

In 1359, by his own account in the Scrope-Grosvenor trial of 1386 (where he testified on a question of heraldic precedence), Chaucer went to war. He was at least technically a soldier from that time to the time of the trial, when he testified that he had "borne arms for twenty-seven years," but it may have been only in a few campaigns, including the winter campaign of 1359–60, that he served as an actual fighting man, since he seems to have served later primarily as diplomat.

King John of France had been in England since his capture at Poitiers by the Black Prince. He'd been living in high style, mostly in Lincolnshire, with forty-some attendants: two chaplains, a secretary, a clerk of the chapel, a doctor, a *maître d'hôtel,* three pages, four valets, three wardrobe men, three furriers, six grooms, two cooks, a fruiterer, a spiceman, a barber, a washer, a chief minstrel (who also made musical instruments and clocks), a fool or jester, and so forth. He had with him his son Philip, captured in the same battle, and numerous furnishings and conveniences—hangings, curtains, cushions, ornamented chests, etc., wines, spices, sugar (he dearly loved sweets), innumerable expensive robes, one trimmed with fur made of 2,550 skins, and much, much more. He whiled away his time playing music, chess, and backgammon; his son filled his days working hunting dogs, falcons, and gamecocks. John gave parties and attended all the great English parties, but his welcome presence did nothing to settle the debate between England and France, where the young dauphin Charles now ruled in John's stead. Edward III, still claiming the crown of France through the line of his mother Queen Isabella, decided it was time to set things straight.

He made his preparations slowly and carefully, and at last, in the autumn of 1359, his knights all over England began mustering their troops. Much of the year's harvest had been transported, by the king's command, to the ports of Kent. There would be nothing much to be found in France—raiding outfits like that which had accidentally captured King John had left her rich fields in ruins. Children gathered wood for bows and arrows, lance shafts, spear handles; men who spoke strange languages arrived from Wales and the Forest of Dean to fell timber in the woods of eastern England for carts, wagons, and ships. According to Froissart, eight thousand carts were knocked together, each to be pulled by four horses commandeered from English villages, and blacksmiths were impressed into service to make portable grain mills, ovens, horseshoes, and weaponry. Butchers were issued quotas of skins to give to tanners who must cure them for footwear and the coracles needed for fishing to provide for fast days. Shipping firms gave up their most valuable cogs, twenty-ton coalboats from the Tyne, fifty-ton trading ships from East Anglican ports. And new ships were built, like the flagship *New St. Mary,* with a capacity of three hundred tons and a crew of a hundred.

On October 28, 1359, "between daybreak and sunrise," the cream of England's manhood, including the Black Prince, Lionel, and Gaunt, and including Geoffrey Chaucer—nearly a hundred thousand in all, if one can believe contemporary reckonings, though only some five thousand were actual combatants—set sail across the Channel. It was the largest invasion force Edward had ever mustered, and its size was to be its undoing.

Henry of Lancaster, Gaunt's father-in-law, had set off with his army some months ahead of the rest and had encountered at Calais a distressing situation. Various lords and knights of the empire, old allies of King Edward, had gathered up horses, harness, and attendants and had ridden to Calais to await the king's coming, which was scheduled for August. Edward failed to arrive on schedule; but more and more adventurers arrived, "so that they wyst nat wher to lodge, nor to have stablyng for their horses; also bredde, wyne, hay and otes, and other provisyons were very dere and scant, so that ther was none to gette for golde nor sylver; and ever it was said the kyng commeth the next weke." To survive in Calais, where prices had gone sky-high, the adventurers were forced to sell all they had, horses, saddles, implements and weapons. When Lancaster arrived, with "four hundred speares and two thousand archers," by Froissart's exaggerated count, they had no place to stay, nothing to eat except the rations they'd brought with them, and no way of replenishing the supplies of their volunteer allies, who were by now turning hostile. Lancaster stalled.

"Fayre lordes," he said, "the taryeng here is no profyte. I woll go ryde forthe into Fraunce, and to see what I can fynde ther: wherefore sirs, I requyre you to ryde forthe with me, and I shall delyver you a certayne somme of money, to pay withall your costes in your lodgynges, that ye have spent here in this towne of Calays, and ye shall have provision of vitayle to carry on your somers." The allies accepted, Lancaster provided down payment on his promise, and the whole mixed horde moved through France to live by ravaging. There was not much to ravage. They took the town of Bray-sur-Somme by assault and found nothing there to steal, then moved on to Cerisy, where their luck was slightly better. There they spent Halloween and the next day learned of the king's arrival at Calais. They turned back and met, four leagues from Calais, "so gret multytude of people that all the countrey was covered therwith, so rychely armed and besene, that it was great joye to beholde the fresshe shinyng armours, baners wavynge in the wynde, their companyes in good order ridyng a soft pase." One of that "gret multytude of people," wearing a vest and light helmet of iron and showing at his collar and sleeves the livery of Prince Lionel, was the twenty-year-old poet Geoffrey Chaucer.

Edward could offer no better to the adventurers than Henry of Lan-

caster had offered, but he persuaded them to follow him and take whatever Fortune might send. The unwieldy provision carts, draught horses,
and heavily armed knights kept the advance down to nine miles a day,
the huge horde moving in three parallel columns, cutting broad highways
of litter and devastation through an already abandoned countryside, many
of the adventurers now traveling on foot, having sold their horses for
bread or having slaughtered them for meat. Chaucer and his company, advancing with Lionel in the battle wing commanded by the Black Prince,
rode for days on end without encountering a soul—no French army, not
the shadow of a peasant. Wherever Chaucer looked, gazing past the blur
of his helmet's noseguard (the sounds around him muted, closed off
where the helmet pressed snugly against his ears), the landscape was
barren and black, lifeless—or lifeless except for an occasional gray specter
of smoke. Wheatfields, cottages, whole towns had been burned, some by
raiding bands of Englishmen earlier, some by the French so they could
offer no comfort to the invaders. When Chaucer rode out with small
foraging expeditions, he was forced to travel farther and farther to find
food, and as the desolation became an increasing burden, emptying the
wagons of the long provision trains, the army's three great columns were
forced to travel farther apart. The Black Prince and his army, we know
from the *Scalacronica* of Sir Thomas Gray of Heton,

> took the way of Montreuil and Hesdin, through Ponthieu and Picardy,
> crossing the Somme and passing by Neuilly and Ham into Verman-
> dois, near which place Sir Baudouin Daukin, knight, Master of the
> Crossbowmen of France, with other French knights, was taken in fight
> by the men of the Prince's train, as he would have overrun by night the
> quarters of the earl of Stafford, who defended himself well. . . . So
> the Prince held his way aforesaid by St Quentin and Retieris, where the
> enemy themselves burned their town to hinder the passage; but the
> Prince's men passed [the river] by main force at Château-Porcein. . . .[12]

We know it was with this wing of the army—the only wing that was
to pass this way—that Chaucer served, and it was sometime after the
battle near "Retieris" that he was almost certainly ambushed while on a
foraging mission, captured by the French, and held for ransom. He
would testify in the Scrope trial, years later, that before his capture, he
saw Sir Thomas Scrope bearing certain arms "before the town of Retters."
Scholars have debated whether Chaucer's "Retters" should be identified
with Retiers in Brittany or Rethel in the Ardennes,[13] but Sir Thomas
Gray's remarks in the *Scalacronica* would appear to settle the matter.
None of Edward's army went near Retiers in Brittany. The "Retieris"
mentioned by Gray no longer exists, but apparently it once did: Château-
Porcein is near Rethel.

Chaucer was captured after the army arrived at Rheims for the siege, since at the Scrope trial he speaks of "the whole expedition," implying that he made it clear to Rheims. He must have been captured between December 4, 1359, and January 11, 1360.[14] On March 1, 1360, while the siege was still in progress—Rheims was to capitulate on the 8th of May —Chaucer was ransomed, the king himself contributing £16 ($3,840). This was probably only a part of the total ransom. T. R. Lounsbury remarked some eighty years ago:

> The language of the document leaves uncertain whether this was only a part or the whole of the amount paid. The former is rather the more natural interpretation. . . . There has, however, been some comment, not altogether good-natured, on the sum paid by the king for the poet. It has been contrasted with other entries in the same roll, not very favorably to his majesty's appreciation of literature. These show that at about the same time he gave Robert de Clinton between sixteen and seventeen pounds for a horse, and John de Beverley twenty pounds for a war-horse. But . . . [Chaucer] was ransomed, so far as the king had anything to do with it, not for his literary qualifications, but for his business usefulness; as a soldier, not as a poet. The censure, moreover, is based upon a mistaken conception of the comparative value of human beings and horses. There has never been a period in the history of the race when that somewhat indefinite individual, the average man, if burdened with the encumbrance of freedom, could bring the price of a good horse.[15]

Evidence that Chaucer, serving under Lionel, was with the Black Prince, not in Edward's main army, and that after his capture and ransom he returned to the service of Prince Lionel, for whom he carried letters back to England from Calais (for which he was paid £24 10s. 8d.), supports Lounsbury's impression that the king's contribution may not have made up the whole ransom, and that Prince Lionel must also have contributed. Be that as it may, Chaucer was ransomed swiftly, as these things went. He probably rejoined the army at Guillon in Burgundy, carried Lionel's letters, then returned with answers, and after the treaty of Brétigny, on May 18, sailed home with the king's sons to England.[16]

King Edward's victory was illusory, like so many victories throughout Edward's reign—won on the battlefield, where the English were supreme, but allowed to slip away at the conference table, where no one, not even Earl Henry, could match the subtle French. Treaty negotiations dragged on for some time. (It was probably letters involving Lionel's private affairs, not, as some have thought, letters concerning the treaty, that Chaucer took to England.)[17] The ransom now finally set for King John was £30 million ($7,200 million), but England was never to get more than a trickle of it; and when spring came in earnest, and Edward was about to resume his attack on Paris and close the war, his army was struck by a freak April storm. According to Holinshed, by the end of that "Black Monday," huge hailstones and interminable ground-lightning flashes had killed or injured a thousand knights and six thousand horses. Shaken to the boots by religious fear, Edward vowed to make peace then and there and renounced before God all claim to the crown of France. He later changed his mind.

As for Chaucer, numerous scholars have suggested that having seen what he had seen of war, he may have had second thoughts about glory, at least where *he* was concerned. All things considered, that's unlikely. Chaucer was a gentle human being, that's true. But nowhere in his poetry does he draw back from violence, either the formal violence of war or jousting or the violence of an old drunken miller and a pair of Cambridge clerks. He was an Englishman. He wore his sword proudly, we may be sure—he would never have been embraced in courtly circles, otherwise—and when he swung it, after training as a courtier, he swung it with a measure of style and murderous intent. But now the time for swinging swords was temporarily over. Whether at the promptings of some royal patron or by his own inclination—probably both—he apparently settled down (more or less) and became a student. Prince Lionel stormed off to Ireland to make trouble for the natives. Chaucer bowed his humble good-byes, kissed the countess on both cheeks, and went hunting for books.

Four: Chaucer's Further Education, a Summary of Some Fourteenth-Century Ideas of Great Importance to Chaucer, and the Poet's Marriage to Philippa Roet—Speculations and Scurrilous Gossip (1360–1367)

IT WAS ONCE COMMON FOR BIOGRAPHERS TO SUPPOSE that Chaucer was with Lionel in Ireland until the end of 1367, when Lionel returned to England. That idea has been abandoned by most Chaucerians for three reasons: the absence of all mention of Ireland in his poetry, except one use of a generally Irish motif in the *Wife of Bath's Tale*; the strong circumstantial evidence that he was studying in London some of this time, or perhaps London and then Oxford; and the recent discovery that he was granted safe-conduct as king's "esquire" (a rank higher than *vallettus* if the word is used technically, as in this case it probably was not) for travel to Navarre, in northern Spain, from February 22 to May 24, 1366. (The record of this grant of safe-conduct was published in 1890 but recognized as referring to Chaucer only in 1955.) Lacking other information, early biographers kept Chaucer busy composing his English translation of the French *Roman de la Rose* and assigned him a tragic unrequited love anguish of eight years' duration, perhaps directed toward Gaunt's wife Blanche. Chaucer probably did do his translation of the *Roman* at about this time, though it hardly took seven years; and as I've said already, he probably did in some sense love Blanche, though it's highly improbable that for eight long years he adored her or anyone else from afar without revealing his love (as he claims in the *Book of the Duchess*) —improbable, in fact, that he loved Blanche of Lancaster in that way. Chaucer's self-portrait in the *Book of the Duchess* is a comic caricature designed to contrast with his portrait of the true and successful lover, John of Gaunt, and we may feel sure that whatever love he may have felt for Blanche he felt equally—judging by the poem—for her husband.

If Chaucer was at all like a modern man, the missing six years, from the time he was twenty-one to the time he was twenty-seven, were among the most interesting and rewarding of his life. They gave him his higher education; they left him in a position to be called, in a record dated June 20, 1367, *"dilectus valettus noster"*—our beloved yeoman—by King

Edward; they led him, probably by devious paths, to marriage with a lady of noble birth; and they won him, as patron and personal friend, the magnificent John of Gaunt. Perhaps more important than all the rest, they were the years of Chaucer's poetic apprenticeship.

Chaucer must have been, repeatedly, a member of the audience where poetry was read—at royal courts, in obscure country manors from just outside London clear to Lancashire, or in the wide, well-lit chambers of Gaunt's Savoy Palace—intently studying not only the poems but their presentation as well, the subtle alterations of voice and gesture that made this so basically an oral poetry. He may perhaps have lingered with other young "enditers" afterward, not intending to speak or ask questions himself, but eager to hear what silver-haired, black-robed Froissart might have to say, or the latest celebrated visitor from the continent, perhaps the young lyricist and shaper of dream poems, Eustace Deschamps, with whom, years later, Chaucer would exchange works. Young Chaucer could be found, from time to time, in one of the dining halls that served the inns of court, at one of which inns he was studying law—could be found, perhaps, absent-mindedly reaching for his pewter mug, head craned toward a parchment extended in his direction by a short, dour man we recognize at last as his fellow law student and future fellow poet in the court of King Richard, "moral" John Gower. (The poem runs on and on.)

The early poems of Chaucer—poems like his loose translation from French, the *ABC* (and by his own account he did other translations)—show talent, wit, linguistic felicity, and show too, of course, his willingness to learn his craft in the expected manner: in the Middle Ages as in the eighteenth century, translation and imitation of great older poems were the normal first steps toward a career as an original poet. His most important translation, the *Romance of the Rose,* taught him many of the techniques he would use all his life: how to create vivid allegorical figures and conventional landscapes with such original touches as would make them an extension of tradition, a lively combination of the old and the new; how to organize a long, complex poem; and above all, perhaps, how to achieve the essential of great poetry, a unique poetic voice. Partly driven by necessity, translating from a melic tongue abounding in rhymes to a less fluid language where rhymes were scant, Chaucer learned an easy, colloquial style that would serve him faithfully from that moment on, becoming, as the years passed, richer, more subtle, more capable of both comic irony and pathos, even of epic high seriousness. Notice the effortless colloquialism here, in a passage of Chaucer's *Romance of the Rose* that he would borrow later for the *Book of the Duchess.*

These trees werë set, that I devysë,
Oon from another, in assysë,   [*in measure*]
Fyvë fadome or sixe, I trowë so;
But they were hye and great also,
And for to kepe out wel the sonnë,
The croppës were so thicke yronnë,   [*crops (twigs)*]
And every braunche in other knet,   [*knitted*]
And ful of grenë levës set,
That sonnë myght there non discendë,
Lest [it] the tender grassës shende.   [*hurt*]

Or here:

About the brinkes of these wellës,
And by the stremës overal ellës,
Sprang up the grass, as thicke yset
And softe as any veluët,   [*velvet*]
On which men myght his lemman leyë,   [*sweetheart*]
As on a fetherbed to pleyë. . . .

Here we have already the authoritative voice of the mature poet. With his first reading of his delightful English version of the *Roman de la Rose,* Chaucer's reputation was established. Even so, probably no one was prepared for his first great full-length original poem. The *Book of the Duchess* is a masterpiece, and Chaucer must have known it. When it first appeared, it was a work as original, as deeply felt, and as "difficult," as T. S. Eliot's *The Love Song of J. Alfred Prufrock.* Aesthetically at least, one can speak no longer, after this splendid poem, of "the young Chaucer." From this point on, he would write as a master with only one important technical problem left to solve—the problem all first-rate poets must solve: how to simplify. Blanche of Lancaster died in 1369, and Chaucer probably wrote his elegy soon after. It was largely during the "lost years" that he learned how to do it. Whatever his love of war, diplomacy, flirtation, and the rest, nothing in his life can have surpassed the excitement of beginning to penetrate "the craft so long to lernë."

Upon returning, ransomed, from the war in France, Chaucer went to what we may loosely call law school. Some scholars still think this a matter of uncertainty, but there are numerous reasons for believing it. For one thing, we have records from 1395 and 1396 in which he signs as "attorney"; for another, in his prose and poetry Chaucer makes easy use of terms that, in the fourteenth century, no one but a man with some training in law would be likely to know—terms like those found in the *Reeve's Tale* and the *Tale of Melibee,* which is riddled with such language. Whereas a modern writer can easily bone up on philosophy, biochemistry, psychology, or whatever he may please, having available large libraries of books, a medieval poet had to learn arcane matter by rote under a teacher or from manuscripts linguistically and otherwise obscure, as well as virtually unobtainable except by professionals, since knowledge at the time tended to be prized as occult, the property of jealous guarddian "masters."

Moreover, all of Chaucer's jobs in later life were jobs which, normally, only people with legal training held. J. M. Manly describes a study made by two of his students:

> The personnel of nearly four hundred [diplomatic missions like Chaucer's to Genoa] was investigated. About eighty of them contain members concerning whose social status and business training no information has been discovered, but in all cases in which it is possible to ascertain facts, that is, about three hundred and twenty, it appears that the last-named member of the commission is always a person who has some legal training. It seems, therefore, not an unfair assumption that the frequency with which Chaucer was chosen for such negotiations was due . . . to his possession of special [legal] qualifications for the work.[1]

Manly's most telling argument has to do with an ancient tradition that Chaucer once beat up a friar. In his 1598 edition of Chaucer's works, Thomas Speght said, "Yt semethe that these lerned menne [Chaucer and John Gower] were of the Inner Temple [for the training of lawyers], for that, manye yeres since, master Buckley did see a recorde in the same howse, where Geffrye Chaucer was fined two shillinges for beatinge a Franciscane Fryer in fletestreate [Fleet Street]." The record Master Buckley saw was later destroyed, perhaps by angry peasants in 1381, but Buckley's account was accepted as true, or at least as probable, by Sir William Dugdale and later writers on the inns of court. It was rejected by an early Chaucerian Francis Thynne, in his *Animadversions* on Speght's edition, but his information was faulty. He believed Chaucer was born in 1328 and thus too "grave" a man to go beating up friars, and he believed that the teaching of law in the Temple began after 1370, whereas in fact law was taught there as early as 1347.

For these reasons and others, Buckley's account may be accepted as true. Buckley was the one man in England, Manly shows, whose particular business it was to have seen such a record if it existed. He was not only a member of the Society of the Temple but the official charged with preservation and care of the Temple records. Moreover, the fine Chaucer paid for his assault on the friar was appropriate for the time and place. No Temple records survive, but study of the records of Lincoln's Inn, a similar institution, has shown that "fighting and other disorderly conduct were among the offenses most frequently subject to fines, and that the fines imposed ranged commonly from 1s. 3d. to 3s. 8d."[2]

So the strong likelihood is that while Chaucer was studying at the Inner Temple, which at that time lay just outside the city, bounded by Fleet Street on the north, he encountered some friar, perhaps from the convent just inside the city gate, and had words with him, and eventually gave him a knock. Various scholars have pointed out that as a student seriously concerned with knowledge, Chaucer could find plenty to dislike in your average fourteenth-century friar. Though sworn to poverty, friars were often the favorites of princes—the Black Prince, among others, gave them extravagant gifts—and managed to amass such wealth as to make their wills run for pages and pages. Though notorious paraders of knowledge—some with good reason—many of the later fourteenth-century friars whose histories and opinions come down to us were humbly born, ill-educated men whose claim to scholarship cannot have been very impressive to the truly learned.

Whatever Chaucer thought of friars in general, the one friar he has immortalized in the *Canterbury Tales* is a dreadful man indeed, a fornicator, as Chaucer slyly hints through such puns as "a noble post," and perhaps a homosexual as well as a heterosexual, if "famulier" is a *double entendre;* he is a false confessor who cares more for payment than repentance, a man who actively eschews his main responsibility, ministry to the poor and ill, and who finds abhorrent his order's vow of poverty; a man, finally (as the Summoner of the *Tales* makes the pilgrims believe), who is one of the stupidest clerics in all merry England. Attacking friars was something of a literary convention in Chaucer's day and might also appeal to Chaucer because he sympathized with John Wyclif, who at almost exactly the time Chaucer was writing his *General Prologue* was in angry disputation with several Franciscans and was attacking the order's very existence as unwarranted by scripture. But however natural or conventional the lampoon against friars, no other literary attack can hold a candle to Chaucer's.

> A Frerë ther was, a wantowne and a meryë,   *[sportive (wanton)]*
> A lymytour, a ful solempne man.   *[one who begged within*
> In allë the ordres foure is noon that kan   *a designated area (?)]*
> So muchel of daliaunce and fair langagë.
> He haddë maad ful many a mariagë
> Of yongë wommen at his owenë cost.
> Unto his ordre he was a noblë post!

Ful wel biloved and famulier was he
With frankeleyns over al in his contree,   [*the climbing class just below*
And eek with worthy wommen of the toun;   *knights, often accused*
For he haddë power of confessioun,   *of prissiness if not*
As seyde hymself, moorë than a curat,   *homosexuality*]
For of his ordre he was licenciat.   [*licensed (licentious)*]
Ful swetely herde he confessioun,
And pleasaunt was his absolucioun:
He was an esy man to yevë penauncë,
Ther as he wistë to have a good pitauncë. . . .
He knew the tavernes wel in every toun
And everich hostiler and tappesterë   [*innkeeper and barmaid*]
Bet than a lazar or a beggesterë;   [*leper or begger*]
For unto swich a worthy man as he
Accorded nat, as by his facultee,
To havë with sikë lazars aqueyntauncë.   [*sick*]
It is nat honest, it may nat avauncë
For to deelen with no swich poraillë   [*poor people*]
But al with riche and sellerës of vitaillë. . . .   [*victuals*]
There nas no man nowher so vertuous:
He was the bestë beggere in his housë. . . .
For thogh a wydwe haddë noght a sho,   [*shoe*]
So plesaunt was his "*In principio,*"
Yet wolde he have a ferthyng, er he wentë.   [*farthing (fair thing?)*]
His purchas was wel bettre than his rentë. . . . [*income . . . expenses*]
His eyen twynkled in his heed aryght,   [*eyes*]
As doon the sterrës in the frosty nyght.
This worthy lymytour was clepëd Huberd.   [*named*]

To some Chaucerians, Chaucer's usually gentle nature makes the story of his beating a friar seem unbelievable. It helps to remember that the poet's father John Chaucer, though a stable citizen respected by the courts, was apparently involved in a tavern fight even at the mature age of forty, and that Geoffrey, like his father, was a wine drinker. He was of course no alcoholic—he left too much poetry and held too many positions of responsibility—but students did in the fourteenth century occasionally get drunk, as did kings. And so it may be that on his way down Fleet Street (toward nightfall, let us say, the nightingales in the vines and the thrushes in the oak trees just beginning their evening calls, and from half a mile away, where there were hedged country fields, a lowing of cattle waiting by barn doors for milkmen), young Chaucer and several somewhat flushed Temple friends fell in with a friar whose opinions struck young Geoffrey, the more he thought them over, as dangerous, immoral, and unreasonable. Then again, of course, Chaucer may have been perfectly sober. Part of his greatness as a poet resides in his sure sense of right and wrong, his nose for the excessive; and we know that in political life he was a man of great loyalty to principles and people he believed in. The Temple authorities were sufficiently in agreement with Chaucer's point of view on the friar that they let him off with a nominal fine, a mere two shillings and, probably, a warning that he be, in the future, more discreet.

The Temple Chaucer attended was one of the inns of court, institutions where young men studied common law. According to John Fortescue, who wrote an account of his legal studies with the Society of Lincoln's Inn some fourteen years after Chaucer's death, law students first entered one of the inns of chancery, "where they studied the nature of original and judicial writs, which are the very first principles of the law."[3] They then advanced into the inns of court. Fortescue writes:

> There is both in the inns of court, and the inns of chancery, a sort of academy, or gymnasium, fit for persons of their station; where they learn singing, and all kinds of music, dancing and such other accomplishments and diversions (which are called revels) as are suitable to their quality, and such as are usually practiced at Court. At other times . . . the greater part apply themselves to the study of the law. Upon festival days, and after the offices of the church are over, they employ themselves in the study of sacred and prophane history: here every thing which is good and virtuous is to be learned: all vice is discouraged and banished. So that knights, barons, and the greatest nobility of the kingdom often place their children in those inns of court; not so much to make the laws their study, much less to live by the profession (having large patrimonies of their own), but to form their manners and to preserve them from the contagion of vice.

Fortescue speaks of the inns of court as universities and claims that as preparation for practical life, the education to be had from them was preferable to the more specialized, more theoretical education to be had from Cambridge and Oxford. Chaucer's own description of the Manciple, in his *General Prologue,* shows that many leading members of the Society of the Temple taught business administration, though they perhaps did not practice business themselves. There were among the lawyers, Chaucer says,

> . . . a duszeyne in that hous
> Worthy to been stywardës of rente and lond
> Of any lord that is in Engelond,

> To make hym lyvë by his propre good
> In honour dettelees (but if he werë wood),
> Or lyve as scarsly as hym list desirë;
> And able for to helpen al a shirë
> In any caas that myghte falle or happë;
> And yet this Manciple sette hir aller cappë!

Fortescue mentions two further features of inns of court education which throw light on Chaucer's life at this time: the expense involved in achieving it, and the classes of society drawn to such education.

> In these greater inns a student can not well be maintained under eight and twenty pounds a year [$6,720]; and, if he have a servant to wait on him (as for the most part they have), the expense is proportionably more: for this reason: the students are sons to persons of quality; those of an inferior rank not being able to bear the expense of maintaining and educating their children in this way. As to the merchants, they seldom care to lessen their stock in trade by being at such large yearly expenses. So that there is scarce to be found, throughout the kingdom, an eminent lawyer, who is not a gentleman by birth and fortune; consequently they have a greater regard for their character and honour than those who are bred in another way.

As we've seen, Chaucer's father may have been sufficiently well off, though not a born aristocrat, to pay for Chaucer's education at the Temple; but he may not have found it necessary to foot the bill alone. For a century or so, by Chaucer's time, there had been conflict in England between canon law and civil law (that is, the tradition of law developed by the Church as opposed to that established by secular authority), most earlier decisions going to canon lawyers. By the time of Edward I, kings and noblemen had grown weary of seeing cases decided in favor of the Church and had developed a practice of sponsoring the education of secular "clerks" who would support their patrons in matters of legal interpretation, historical precedent, and so on. Surviving records of Lincoln's Inn show, among members of the Inn, numerous squires of the royal household and list in detail the regulations provided for special concessions to such people. (Though technically a yeoman, if Chaucer attended law school under royal protection, he was no doubt treated as a squire.) It should be added, by the way, that if the household regulations of Edward III were similar to those of Edward IV, only half the king's squires were required to be in attendance at court at a given time; hence for half his time, if a young courtier had ability and royal favor, he could pursue his education.

If anyone did sponsor Chaucer's education—at least between 1361 and

1366—it was probably not the king but John of Gaunt. The evidence, complicated and wholly circumstantial, is as follows: (1) Chaucer biographers used to hold that the language of his grant from the king in 1367 implies that Chaucer had already been in the king's personal service for some time; but it has recently been shown that the language is similar to that used when Philippa Chaucer was appointed *domicella* to Gaunt's second wife, Constance of Castile, who had only recently come to England. Hence it is possible that Chaucer was in the service of someone other than the king in the early sixties. (2) On September 12, 1366, "Philippa Chaucy," that is, Philippa Chaucer, was granted a lifetime annuity, from the royal treasury, of 10 marks (c. $1500) in addition to her regular wages as lady-in-waiting. Chaucer himself is not mentioned in this record, which probably means that, though he was already married to Philippa, he was not yet a member of the royal household. He did become one sometime before June 1367, when he is mentioned as a yeoman, but he was apparently not yet in the king's service during the summer of 1366, for which we have a very full list of household members who were at that time granted robes. (3) If he was with Prince Lionel in Ireland (highly unlikely), he reached England and married Philippa well before Lionel himself got back, in November 1366. (4) If Chaucer's reference to an "eight-year love sickness" in his elegy to Blanche of Richmond (Gaunt's wife) has anything to do with Blanche, who died in 1369, it must have been in 1361 that he came to know her well, that is, perhaps, became one of her attendants. (5) John of Gaunt, who had not been out of England since 1360, except for a brief diplomatic mission to Flanders in 1364, was preparing, in September 1366, to leave England on a military mission, which might account for Chaucer's showing up as one of the royal household at about this time. In other words, not wishing to go to the wilds of Ireland with Prince Lionel, Chaucer persuaded Countess Elizabeth to transfer him to the household of her young cousin and only sister-in-law, Blanche. (Such transfers were common.) When Blanche's husband, John of Gaunt, was preparing for war—Blanche was to cross the Channel with him—Chaucer secured a second transfer, this time to the court of Gaunt's father, Edward III.[4]

Though the evidence is circumstantial, it grows stronger when we consider the apparently close relationship, later, between Gaunt and the poet. A reasonable guess, then, is that Chaucer was assisted in his studies by Gaunt, not the king.

There is a long tradition that he also studied at Oxford University, though again the evidence is indirect and, one may as well add, extremely weak. It was first suggested, so far as we know, by the antiquary Leland, who died insane in 1552. Leland says Chaucer was a studious Oxfordian who ended up a master logician and profound student of philosophy, and that in later years, or perhaps earlier, he studied at the Inner Temple. Much that Leland says we know by other evidence to be true, for instance that Chaucer was admired by the best French poets of the day; but also much that Leland says is mere legend or demonstrably false; hence Leland and those antiquaries who copied his account, Bishop Bale and John Pits, dean of Liverdun, have not been taken very seriously. (Bale begins his history of English poetry with the Flood.) Yet for all that, Leland's account may be more or less right; at any rate, only the foolhardy can claim, as some have done, that the tradition has been "long since exploded."

One of Chaucer's friends, Ralph Strode, to whom (along with the poet John Gower) Chaucer dedicated *Troilus and Criseyde,* was a tutor at Oxford in the 1360's, and in Chaucer's *Treatise on the Astrolabe* (written when his son Lewis was at Oxford), Chaucer mentions two men contemporary with himself who were Oxford professors. His religious views seem largely in accord with those popular at Oxford—views which interested John of Gaunt, who once visited the religious reformer John Wyclif there (Gaunt visited Oxford on several occasions). We have no good records for the 1360's, but in later years Gaunt maintained several students at Oxford, establishing them afterward in the king's court, and he may well have begun this politically useful practice early.* It may be added that one of Chaucer's most flattering portraits in the *Canterbury Tales* is that of his Oxford Clerk, and one of his funniest is the Oxford student "hendë Nicholas," in the *Miller's Tale* (perhaps the Miller's wicked version of that same Oxford Clerk in his youth). As various Chaucerians have pointed out, the poet knew Oxford life in detail; for instance, he mentions the town of Oseney and causes his Oxford carpenter to swear by the locally popular S. Frideswide. Moreover, the books we know to have been available at Merton College, Oxford, before 1385, would go a long way toward accounting for Chaucer's scientific and philosophical sources. Many of the manuscripts recall specific citations by Chaucer, ranging from religious works to, for instance, all twelve medical writers mentioned by Chaucer's Doctor in the *General Prologue,* ll. 431-4. In later life, Chaucer was undoubtedly familiar with affairs at Oxford. Most of his significant astrological allusions appear in poems which can be dated after 1385, when Merton acquired the Rede Library, from which Chaucer could easily have drawn them.[5]

The theory that Chaucer started at Oxford sometime between 1360

---

* He also sent to Oxford both his son Henry Beaufort (his son by Katherine Swynford) and his grandson Henry (King Henry V, son of Gaunt's son by Blanche of Lancaster, Henry Hereford, later King Henry IV).

and 1367, and revisited his old school later, off and on, accounts for what is otherwise hard to explain in his poetry and prose: his sure grasp of all the standard material of the arts course, the trivium, and much of the quadrivium. Except for some knowledge of medicine, Chaucer was probably not familiar with the highest university programs, medicine, canon law, and theology. He may have studied at Oxford first (if he went there at all) and only later at the Temple, as Professor Williams thinks (medieval course levels were not graduated, as we've noticed, in the modern way), may have studied at both places more or less concurrently, or may have moved from the Temple to Oxford.

He never became a full-fledged sergeant of the law, which took at least sixteen years, Fortescue tells us. Chaucer's work in later life required no such expertise. As a justice of the peace for Kent he served, in all important cases, with another man who would not have been needed if Chaucer himself had reached that rank. But it has been shown that a smattering of legal knowledge would be necessary for him as clerk of the king's works at Westminster Palace, the Tower of London, and elsewhere; and it has been shown that as subforester for the royal park of North Petherton in Somerset, he would again need some legal ability, since the forest was ruled by a curious special body of laws, different from both common and civil law and enforced in special courts. On the other hand, without university training it seems unlikely, though not impossible, that he could ever have become the "noble philosophical poet" he was, a thinker admired far and wide as one of the most original and learned of his age.

What he chiefly learned, wherever he may have studied, was the enormously complex art of poetry. Just what this entailed can only be suggested here. For one thing, it meant mastering rhetoric, or eloquence, a rich, confused, and lively field of study in Chaucer's time.

Motivated by his discovery that many important ideas brought down from ancient times had been misunderstood because of inaccurate translation, Robert Grosseteste—at Oxford a century before Chaucer's time and one of the truly outstanding scholars of the period—had developed elaborate and rigorous theories concerning translation from the classics, had promoted the revival of Greek studies in England, had brought Greek scholars from abroad (a minor innovation but one that incalculably broadened and enriched the university program), and had arranged that Greek manuscripts might be brought from Athens and Constantinople. He himself made what were for the time superbly accurate translations from Greek into Latin and organized the work of collaborators in translation, insisting on correct interpretation of the originals and establishing new standards of accuracy.

To appreciate Grosseteste's achievement in this regard, we need to recall that before his time "translation" often meant, in effect, rewriting, and though various schools followed various persuasions, the "rules" of translation normally did not deal with exactly recapturing the original text in a more accessible language but, on the contrary, involved altering the original by compression or expansion, by inserting moralizing asides, enlivening figures, and so forth. It is worth noting that those prose treasures we find most appealing in King Alfred's translation of Boethius' *Consolation of Philosophy,* such as his beautifully poetic axletree simile on limited free will, are none of them present in the original.

After Grosseteste's time, the Franciscan Roger Bacon, in his work at the universities of Oxford and Paris, had carried Grosseteste's ideas further, working on and supporting word for word translations from Hebrew, Greek, and Arabic, and developing principles for grammatical studies in languages other than Latin. Though he was not himself much interested in the study of vernacular languages, his emphasis on the commercial and political advantages to be won from a wide extension of language study did result in a general reassessment, especially in France and England, of the language men really spoke. (By 1362, the lord chancellor of England would be opening parliament in English, making it the nation's official tongue.) Another great contributor to the Oxford revival of letters—in this case not so much an innovator as an apologist for the exciting new techniques worked out by Grosseteste, Bacon, and their students—was Richard of Bury, bishop of Durham (d. 1345), a famous collector and book-lover and author of the *Philobiblion (On the Love of Books).*

By Chaucer's time, three generations of Oxford professors had been picking their cautious way through the classics, encouraging translation in prose and verse, and in bold new ways—without exegetical predispositions—examining the style and structure of ancient literatures. Factions arose, and heated debates, some men judging all writing by Aristotle's rule, "To speak as the common people do, but to think as the wise," some stumping for Seneca, "Nothing is pleasing unless refreshed by variety of effect." On the authority of Augustine and Paul, men like John Wyclif spoke sternly of the dire need for plain, direct speech and scoffed at the rich efflorations of, say, Geoffrey of Vinsauf, the rhetorician who had taught at Oxford his doctrine of decorum, the adaptation of style to hearer and occasion, allowing to the "high style" all manner of verbal flash and structural intricacy. The debate was not, as it may seem, merely academic. It had to do quite fundamentally with the question of how the human mind works, what relationship obtains between language and thought; in short, with the whole fiery question of "nominalism"—to which we'll turn in a moment. To work out his answers, the Oxford student read all the available masters, old and new, translated what they wrote—concentrating not only on the meaning of words but on the intellectual and emotional effects of subtle repetitions, juxtapositions, and so forth—and then composed, by old and new principles, works of his own. If he believed that thought is essentially rational, he followed Wyclif. If he believed that meters and poetic phrasing can touch the inexpressible, he inclined toward Vinsauf. An early mark of Chaucer's genius was his recognition, in the *Book of the Duchess,* that both points of view are valid. Let me try to explain.

The "Black Knight" of the poem, grieving over the death of his lady, evades direct confrontation of his grief by poetic artifice and figurative, poetically conventional language. He speaks, for instance, of losing a game of chess with Fortune:

> The falsë thef! what hath she doo,
> Trowest thou? By ourë Lord I wol the seyë.
> At the ches with me she gan to pleyë;
> With her falsë draughtës dyvers
> She staal on me, and tok my fers.   [*stole; fers, an Arabic piece,*
> And whan I sawgh my fers awayë,   *the Queen or Counsellor*]
> Allas! I kouthë no lenger playë,   [*could*]
> But seydë, "Farëwel, swete, ywys,
> And farëwel al that ever ther ys!"
> Therwith Fortunë seydë "Chek her!"   [*here*]
> And "Mat!" in myd poynt of the chekker . . .

The narrator of the poem, to cure the knight of his crippling melancholy, must bring him to the plain English—the direct admission, "She is dead." But if plain speech has value, so does artful, suggestive speech: only poetic circumlocution can carry the subtlest emotions, surprise the mind by subliminal innuendo, give expression to that side of reality we feel but cannot see. In the poem's surprising closing lines, a hart-hunt, a heart-hunt, and a darkened, grief-sick soul's search for God are simultaneously, mysteriously resolved and the poem's central characters are suddenly, through puns, identified: John (St. Johan!) and Blanche of Richmond ("ryche hil"—Gaunt's title before he became duke of Lancaster) and Lancaster ("long castel"). The narrator's love, forcing the Black Knight to the painful admission "She ys ded!", brings to an end the heart-hunt—what we would call psychoanalysis—putting him once more in touch with his feelings, forcing him to look for help to the

huntsman-lover Christ on his rich hill (Paradise), as reported in the
*Apocalyps*e of "St. Johan." The mysterious dream ends:

> "She ys ded!" "Nay!" "Yis, be my trouthë!"
> "Is that yourë los? Be God, hyt ys routhë!" . . .   [*loss . . . sorrowful*]
> With that me thoghtë that this kyng
> Gan homwardës for to rydë
> Unto a placë, was there besydë,
> Which was from us but a lytë.
> A long castel with wallës whitë,
> Be seynt Johan! on a ryche hil
> As me mettë; but thus hyt fil.   [*dreamed*]
> Ryght thus me mette, as I yow tellë,
> That in the castell ther was a bellë,
> As hyt haddë smyten hourës twelvë.—   [*struck*]
> Therwyth I awook myselvë
> And fond me lyinge in my bed,
> And the book that I haddë red . . .

By the time he began on the *Book of the Duchess,* Chaucer had a master's
command of the "colors of rhetoric"—those figures such as hyperbole,
metaphor, verbal repetition, and so on, that make poetic suggestion
possible. He had translated at least one, and probably several, stylistically
and philosophically difficult poems and had steeped himself in Latin and
French poetry, so that he could twist allusions with effortless cunning,
much as T. S. Eliot twists allusions, and could elaborate a poetic structure
more intricate and rich in symbolic implication than anything written in
English since *Beowulf.*

Just how much Chaucer really knew about matters other than *ars
poetica* has been endlessly debated by modern scholars, though none of
his contemporaries seem to have had doubts. For all the debate, the question can be answered simply: he knew enough to be a serious medieval
"philosophical" poet; in other words, he knew a great deal. Unfortunately, this simple answer requires some explaining, and though the
explanation may take us far afield, it is one over which we must pause
at least briefly. It will provide a clearer sense of Chaucer's intellectual
habits and interests, and it will provide the only kind of argument available in support of the tradition that Chaucer shows in his work effects
of an Oxford education.

In the Middle Ages people took it for granted that the very best poetry
is metaphysical; that is, the poet sought to understand and express man's

nature, his place in the universe, his meaning. As in medieval philosophy and political theory—as in metaphysical speculation in any age, and as in all great poetry—this meant what is now sometimes casually dismissed as "argument by analogy." If we understand the exact relationship between gold and lead, between Christ and the Virgin, so this argument runs, we can determine the proper relationship between, say, a king and his subjects. (The medieval English political theorist Henry Bracton argues his "king's pleasure" principle from the status of the Virgin.)

Though not much favored by modern logicians—rightly enough, from a certain point of view—argument by analogy is as much the method of our most serious modern novelists and some of our most penetrating recent philosophers (for instance, Alfred North Whitehead) as it was of Geoffrey Chaucer or the ancient Chinese. It begins—to take a simple but not facetious example—in the intuition that if a drop of water, a planet, and the universe all tend to circularity, then they are in some respect inherently the same, and that ultimately all that exists may be the same. Compare Boethius' notion of "love" as the world's unique principle, a natural law in the same class as the Newtonian laws of thermodynamics but broader in its sphere of operation, drawing sparks toward the sky, odd numbers toward even, waves toward shore, or the spirit of man toward its maker; or compare the Oriental "unique principle" of *yin* and *yang*. Medieval thinkers assumed that the way to truth was through metaphor, that is, through a search for the essence of the world's relationships. To a serious medieval poet, it was not enough simply to state what one believes about a given situation, as Robert Frost might do; one must discover an essentially analogous situation and expose the identical process of decline or growth (or whatever) in operation there, as T. S. Eliot liked to do. Thus Chaucer, in the Prologue to the *Second Nun's Tale,* uses language drawn from alchemy to speak to the purifying powers of sainthood. Though not obvious at a glance to the modern reader, the following lines imply a comparison between heaven, the Philosopher's Stone, and the saintly life:

> And right so as thisë philosophrës writë
> That hevene is swift and round and eek brennyngë,   [*also*]
> Right so was fairë Cecilië the whitë   [*St. Cecilia*]
> Ful swift and bisy evere in good werkyngë,
> And round and hool in good perseveryngë,
> And brennynge evere in charité ful brightë.

When Chaucer tells, later in the poem, of the martyrdom of St. Cecile, he compares her to the Philosopher's Stone burning in its alembic or, as some English alchemistical treatises say, "house":

And he weex wrooth, and bad men sholde hir ledë   [grew angry . . .
Hom til hir hous, and "In hirë hous," quod he,   bade]
"Brenne hire right in a bath of flambës redë."
And as he bad, right so was doon the dedë. . . .   [deed]

No one need know all medieval arts and sciences to understand and enjoy Chaucer's poetry, since there as in the Bible (at least as the wiser Church Fathers read it) nothing is revealed obscurely in one place that is not revealed plainly in another; but it is important—aesthetically as well as philosophically—to know that, for Chaucer, all the universe is connected, blood-related.

Whatever objections we may have to argument by analogy, we still use it, as Ludwig Wittgenstein pointed out, whenever we speak of "mental circuits" as if the mind were a switchboard or "channels of thought" or "rivers of feeling" as if wisdom were a sea we might arrive at like stout Cortez. But we use the method ineptly, from a medieval point of view. We have nonce metaphors, but no totally organizing system. We focus on individuals, ignoring universals. Medieval and ancient philosophy, on the other hand, untouched by the thought of Descartes and Leibnitz, was holistic. Take an example: whereas modern Western medicine examines the patient's area of pain and ignores the rest of the universe, medieval and (in some cases) ancient medicine considered the position of the stars and planets, the patient's life-long diet, his physiognomy, his family relationships, sometimes the entrails of a freshly killed goat. Whereas the Western doctor cuts out as much as practicable of the patient's diseased liver, the medieval doctor, convinced that the microcosm (man) and the macrocosm (the universe) are intimately related, would as part of his cure cast an "image," a small model of the zodiac in which each stone or metal is designed to attract the healing power or inhibit the destructiveness of a particular planet, and (in addition to prescribing drugs) would determine which of the four humors—blood, phlegm, choler (yellow bile), and melancholy (black bile)—was the source of the problem and how the patient's diet should be altered.* Though Chaucer scoffs at the Physician in the *Canterbury Tales* for such faults as greed and self-righteousness, he is perfectly serious in his praise of the Physician's techniques of cure—

For he was grounded in astronomyë.
He kepte his pacient a ful greet deel

---

* Oriental medicine, more inscrutably, invented yoga, *do-in,* dietary balance of sodium and potassium—basis of the electrical charge in cells—acupuncture, moxaburning, and so on, which are essentially systems for altering the body's electromagnetic fields in accordance with a theory of the balance of *yin* and *yang* forces in the universe.[6]

In hourës by his magyk natureel.
Wel koude he fortunen the ascendent
Of his ymages for his pacient.
He knew the cause of everich maladyë,
Were it of hoot, or coold, or moyste, or dryë,
And wherë they engendred, and of what humour.
He was a verray, parfit praktisour:
The cause yknowe, and of his harm the rootë,
Anon he yaf the sikë man his bootë.   [*cure*]

   Given the holistic premise of his age, Chaucer felt he had no choice, if he wished to be a first-rate poet, but to pursue by whatever means available what we might call, loosely, metaphysics, the interrelationship of form and matter, higher and lower living orders (from worms to angels or Platonic spirits), geometry, numerology, astrology, alchemy, the philosophy of music, and so on—in other words, the university matter of the so-called quadrivium. His writing shows that he did just this and did it well, for his own purpose, not as a specialist in each discipline, but as a poet seeking grist for his mill. Chaucer was no professor of mathematics (if the last page of the *Equatory of the Planets* is Chaucer's work, as it may well be, he was capable of amazing blunders), but he was usually an excellent amateur mathematician, no mere reckoner of sums but a man who understood the mystical properties of numbers and geometrical forms as they were brought down from Pythagoras, Plato, and Aristotle by Macrobius, Boethius, and others, and applied to physics, optics, and so forth (in ways we need not pause here to detail) by men like Robert Grosseteste and Roger Bacon—understood them well enough that he could without heavyhandedness manipulate numerology in his prose and verse, reinforcing ideas, deepening symbolic structures, instructing and delighting by his dazzling plays of wit.
   He eventually came to know enough alchemy that he could load his *Canon's Yeoman's Tale* not only with the language of alchemists but also with the emotions such men went through—fiery curiosity, ambition, rage and frustration, despair—and beyond all that, knew enough alchemy that he could rightly interpret the difficult alchemistical text which closes the poem. These were, as we've said, not pseudo-sciences in Chaucer's day, though they involved what we now would call magic; nor were all their practitioners such bunkum artists as we encounter in the *Canon's Yeoman's Tale*. At best, mathematicians and alchemists—"philosophers"—were diligent theoretical and practical scientists struggling to unlock nature's secrets. In their own view and Chaucer's, a bad man might seek knowledge for personal gain, but good men sought it for its usefulness and interest. The good deserved respect, especially at Oxford, where

occult studies had a noble tradition going back at least to Roger Bacon, whose later name as a great magician derived mainly from his original, from our point of view far-fetched, speculations in astrology and alchemy.

Chaucer must have only begun on these disciplines in the 1360's. His philosophical stance in his 1369 or 1370 elegy for Blanche is generally Boethian: a major theme is free will as a quality of mind in a world wherein Fortune seems omnipotent; he uses, in a general way, the Boethian contrast of darkness and light (related to matter and form, or spirit) and the Boethian idea that we must work with, not against, the drive of nature; and he uses also several images drawn directly from Boethius' *Consolation of Philosophy*. But only in poems later than the *Book of the Duchess* does Chaucer depend heavily on Boethian quotation and allusion, for instance, his use in the *House of Fame* of the Boethian idea that all existents have their natural place on a ladder running from the lowest sort of matter to the purest sort of spirit:

> . . . every kyndëly thyng that is   [*natural*]
> Hath a kyndely stedë there he   [*natural place*]
> May best in hyt conservëd be;
> Unto which place every thyng,
> Thorgh his kyndëly enclynyng,
> Moveth for to comë to
> Whan that hyt is awey therfro. . . .

Astronomical and musical allusions in the *Book of the Duchess* are conventional, and if the poem contains alchemistical elements, scholars have found no trace of them. What the poem does contain in abundance is proof that Chaucer had been through the standard matter of the trivium and knew—like the back of his hand—the *Canticle of Canticles,* the *Apocalypse,* French poetry, and Ovid. He also knew contemporary psychology, not only dream theory but also theoretical approaches to madness and its cure ("heart-hunting" as Oxford medical men called it). In all likelihood he had only just begun his work in the mathematical and scientific fields that would be important to him later, and had not yet proceeded far into speculative philosophy. He may possibly have touched on optics as developed in the somewhat queer tradition established at Oxford a century before Chaucer by Robert Grosseteste, who studied light in simultaneously Neoplatonic and scientific ways, as "light metaphysic," having to do with divine illumination (hence with the relation of God's nature and man's, with epistemology, and psychology), and as natural or secondary light (having to do with physics). In Chaucer's thoroughly Neoplatonic elegy—Neoplatonic in that matter is informed by spirit and freedom accompanies an escape from devotion to the material—light is a central motif, and Grosseteste's ideas could easily account for the double use of the image throughout, even, perhaps in the opening lines: "I have gret wonder, by this lyght, / How that I lyve . . ." But of course no medieval Christian poet needed Oxford scholarship to tell him that light could be symbolic.

Oxford was a liberal and exceedingly vital university in the fourteenth century. Partly this was an effect of its power and security, its right and its sometimes ferociously demonstrated will to rule itself; and partly it was an effect of the climate created by the bold ideas of the line of thinkers which began, in a sense, with Robert Grosseteste. Thirteenth-century Franciscans took the lead in the development of medieval thought when the Dominicans hobbled themselves, in 1286, with an obligation to defend the doctrine of St. Thomas Aquinas. Grosseteste, the Franciscans' teacher, founded a school at Oxford which Roger Bacon and others would make the most important of its day. It stood for independent judgment and firsthand knowledge, the study of languages (as we've seen) and physics, not merely "old authorities."

In the Franciscan dismantling of the Thomist system, the great Duns Scotus pressed further than Grosseteste had gone. Duns Scotus was a brilliant critic of systems and was able to show that Aquinas' harmony of revelation and philosophy was illusory. But Duns Scotus drew back from the final step, reluctant to admit a fundamental divorce between reason and faith, philosophy and religion. Then into mid-fourteenth-century Oxford came William of Ockham and the revival, or rather revision and flowering, of the old twelfth-century philosophical position known as nominalism.

Ockham is now remembered chiefly for the dictum known as Ockham's razor, *"Pluralites non est ponenda sine necessitate"*—Multiplicity ought not be posited without necessity—a principle not in fact original with Ockham but important to the history of philosophy and the sciences, not only because it is of logical convenience (asserting that a simple explanation is logically preferable to one more complicated) but also because it turns out to be true to nature's way of working: when a modification is needed in the process of animal evolution (for example), nature does not create from scratch but elongates, flattens, or otherwise alters cells already at work, patching and toggling, following the line of least resistance. But Ockham's importance in his own day lay in his original speculations in political theory, where he powerfully defended civil authority against claims of temporal authority by the Pope, and in philosophy, especially psychology, metaphysics, and logic. He was the first to formulate the persuasive nominalist attack on universals, arguing that only singulars exist—particular cows or trees or men—and that the universal (e.g., the nature of man) has objective value or actual existence only as it is *thought up*. He argued, foreshadowing Schopenhauer, that will, not intellect, is the primary faculty of the soul, since ideas, that is, abstractions, follow naturally from perception and intuition, the fundamental forms of human knowledge; and he taught that since universals are mere concepts, there can be, between "essence" (the *idea* of the thing) and "existence" (the thing itself as grasped by our senses) no real distinction.

Medieval philosophy, before and after Ockham, had two main tendencies, known to the history of philosophy as "realism" and "nominalism." The controversy arose from a passage in Boethius' translation of Porphyry's *Introduction to the Categories of Aristotle,* which treated the problem of genera and species (for example, "animals" and "horses"). The question was: (1) Do genera subsist in themselves or only in the mind? (2) If they're subsistent, are they corporeal or incorporeal? and (3) Are they separated from sensible things or placed in them? To put this very simply, (1) Can one think of an "animal" without thinking of a horse, cat, dog, or cow? (2) If there is such an "animal," does it have a body? and (3) If "animals" exist, do they exist by themselves or do you have to, so to speak, cut open a rhinoceros to get one out?

The realists, whose position went back to Plato, were inclined to the persuasion that behind and before my dog Fred, my horse Alexander, and my ape named Jim stands God's idea, "animalness," and that only God's idea is ultimately *real*. The rest is, as Chaucer says, borrowing from Plato, mere "shadows passing on a wall." According to the nominalist, on the other hand, words like "animal" (i.e., universals) are mere names we invent to express, or abstract, the qualities we have observed in particulars. Such a view leads to an interesting problem in which Chaucer would take great delight. If ideas are abstractions from the concrete, I can neither know that my idea is "right" nor—since you too abstract from concrete particulars—can I meaningfully communicate my idea to you. (Though answered many times, this error is still around, for instance in the positivists' claim that one man "cannot have another's toothache.") If all ideas are necessarily private, then all debate, all judgment must collapse to passion and opinion, so that Chaucer in the Invocation to his mock-nominalist *House of Fame* is quite right to bawl out, anticipating critics who dislike his poem:

> And whoso thorgh presumpcion,
> Or hate, or skorn, or thorgh envyë,
> Despit, or jape, or vilanyë,   [*jape—humor*]

Mysdeme hyt [i.e., my dream], pray I Jesus God
That (dreme he barefot, dreme he shod),
That every harm that any man
Hath had, syth the world began,
Befalle hym therof, or he stervë,   [e'er he die]
And graunte he mote hit ful deservë,
Lo, with such a conclusion
As had of his avision   [dream, vision]
Cresus, that was kyng of Lydë,   [Lydia]
That high upon a gebet dydë!
This prayer shal he have of me;
I am no bet in charyté!

Though the whole "realist"-"nominalist" dispute may at first appear vain scholastic subtlety, it involves issues of the greatest speculative and practical importance. Especially in its early eleventh- and twelfth-century form, nominalism implied an anti-spiritual view of the world, whereas "realism" implies a spiritual view. More important, since Church doctrine—established over centuries by careful students of the meaning of scripture—purports to describe what is ultimately real (such actual but invisible existents as, say, the Trinity), a strictly pursued nominalism would imply that the writings of the Fathers might as well be discarded.

In rethinking nominalism, Ockham, as a devout churchman, of course disavowed such heretic implications; he simply (in accord with the intuitive St. Francis, founder of his order) abandoned all attempts at the reconciliation of human understanding and God's mysteries. Removed to the realm of the incomprehensible, God became a baffling Absolute Will bound by no human concepts of justice or reason, a Being about whom it was futile to ruminate. The idea was not in itself new. Augustine had long before proclaimed that he believed because he could not understand. But Ockham's purpose was new, the freeing of philosophy. He never presumed to question the truth of Christian revelation, but he turned it, in effect, into a subject no longer open for discussion. He opened the door to the layman and the scientist, free to ask questions untrammeled by theological presuppositions. His followers would study human history, politics, and the world of sense without undue concern for the authority of the past; and the independence his ideas inspired would lead to Wyclif, and through Wyclif, to the Bohemian religious reformer and martyr Jan Hus, and to Calvin and Luther.

John of Gaunt's friend and apologist, John Wyclif, ten years older than Geoffrey Chaucer, wrote largely in reaction to nominalist ideas, though he sometimes reached similar conclusions. He was a moderate realist, a partial follower of Aquinas who admitted that universal ideas are only substances "in an equivocal sense": their existence is only separable, on the one hand, from the particulars in which they are made palpable or, on the other, from the mind of God, where they have their ghostly eternal existence. Given his Platonic idea of God—his idea that God's will and nature are unalterable, like a Platonic "form" (e.g., Plato's perfect, insubstantial chair, of which all actual chairs are mere approximations)—Wyclif necessarily rejected the idea of arbitrary divine decree, rejected the notion that the Pope and his delegates could receive or confer upon others arbitrary privileges, for instance, pardons and dispensations—rejected Papal authority in temporal matters (as Ockham had done), rejected the doctrine of transubstantiation as historically newfangled and philosophically absurd, and, more and more as he grew older, inclined to accept theological determinism and a notion of election (grace in a special sense) much like Calvin's. For all his dislike of nominalism, he shared the nominalists' concern about translation, and, arguing the literal inspiration of the Bible, he accepted the scriptures as the sole basis of the law of God and urged that they be placed in the hands of the laity. The clergy, he thought, should be stripped of worldly offices and surplus wealth, and though he did not in fact argue against wealth in general, he was interpreted as doing so, and thus gave solace to the peasants who rioted in 1381, burning rich men's houses, including Gaunt's. Actually, of course, Wyclif was a Gaunt apologist, "running about from church to church" in London, attacking Gaunt's clerical enemies, especially William of Wykeham, bishop of Winchester, who in 1376 had briefly overturned Gaunt's control of parliament. It was in support of Wykeham that young William Courtenay, bishop of London, cited Wyclif to appear before Archbishop Simon Sudbury—the trial which Gaunt helped break up, to all London's indignation.

The main popularizers of Wyclif's ideas were the Oxford-based "Lollards" or "mutterers." Among other points, they argued in their *Twelve Conclusions,* drawn up for presentation to parliament in 1395, that the Church in England had become unduly subservient to her "stepmother" in Rome; the present priesthood was not the one ordained by Christ, and the ritual or ordination had no warrant in scripture; clerical celibacy caused unnatural lust; transubstantiation was a "feigned miracle" which led toward idolatry; the hallowing of bread, wine, vestments, and the like was necromancy; prelates should not be temporal judges and rulers; prayers for the dead, pilgrimages, and offerings to images were heathen; confession to a priest was unnecessary for salvation; and warfare was "express contrarious to the New Testament." Though some famous Lollards were wealthy knights, particularly certain followers of the Black Prince, Lollardy came to be associated in the popular mind with lower-class puritanical self-righteousness and with a sort of ignorant biblical fundamentalism, especially a cranky, eccentric glossing of texts. It's in this sense that Harry Bailey and the Shipman think of the Lollards when they speak of them in the *Canterbury Tales:*

> "Sir Parisshë Prest," quod he [the Host], "for Goddës bonës,
>   Telle us a tale, as was thi forward yorë. . . ."   *[bargain]*
>   The Parson hem answeredë, *"Benedicite!*
> What eyleth the man, so synfully to swerë?"
> Oure Host answerde, "O Jankin, be ye therë?
> I smelle a Lollere in the wynd," quod he.
> "Now! goodë men," quod oure Hoste, "herkeneth me;
>   Abydeth, for Goddës dignë passioun,   *[noble]*
>   For we schal han a predicacioun;
> This Lollere heer wil prechen us somwhat."
>   "Nay, by my fader soulë, that schal he nat!"
> Seydë the Shipman; "heer schal he nat prechë;
> He schal no gospel glosen herë ne techë.   *[gloss, explain]*
> We leven alle in the gretë God," quod he;   *[believe]*
> "He woldë sowen som difficulte,
> Or springen cokkel in our clenë corn. . . ."

But despite the commonplace association of Lollardy with the ignorant and unsophisticated—despite Lollardy's natural appeal to the barely literate, who by Lollard theory might read the Bible in their own tongue, not Latin, and understand it without background or training—the movement remained a part of the intellectual climate of fourteenth-century Oxford. In his association with the university, whether as student or only as an occasional reader of poems, visiting parent, or guest in the rooms of his tutor friends, Chaucer cannot help having picked up and sympathized with some Lollard ideas. Like Gaunt, Chaucer had no wish to follow Wyclif into heresies—such as his dismissal of transubstantiation—but many Wyclif notions, especially Wyclif's hatred of the rich, corrupt clergyman, are featured in Chaucer's poetry.

For much of the fourteenth century Oxford was the best university in all Europe. Yet for all its prestige, it was a violent place. The university chancellor, elected by the highest branches of the senior faculty (theology and canon law), was the principal executive officer of the university and had wide jurisdiction in both criminal and civil actions where members of the university were implicated. His duties virtually assured the university of self-regulation—not only the right of self-government, making, itself, all decisions on moral and academic standards, but also the right to protect its members from civil law and even to try townsmen whenever one party to the dispute was a member of the university. These jealously guarded rights were continually threatened from without and within, but they held firm down to the time of the temporary closing of the university for Lollardy in 1382. Battles flared up from time to time with the town of Oxford, which not unreasonably objected to the sometimes inexcusable liberties taken by students on Oxford's streets (for instance, murder) and objected still more to the university's claim to jurisdiction in such cases. There were also times of internal conflict, sometimes between the various faculties, more often among Oxford's students of different nationalities—the English, Scottish, and Welsh. The disputes were so violent that, according to one writer, more than one famous battlefield might perhaps be found upon which less blood had been shed per square yard than upon the Oxford High Street.[7]

The most famous of Oxford's riots, still vividly remembered when Chaucer knew Oxford, was the "Great Slaughter" of St. Scholastica's Day, February 10, 1355. (Chaucer was then fifteen.) It began when some students went to a tavern, disliked the wine, and commented on it. When the taverner answered them incautiously, the students threw the wine pot at his head. Before long the bell of St. Martin's Church was calling the citizens to arms, and the bell of the university church was tolling, by order of the chancellor, to call out the university. When it was over, townsmen and men of the surrounding countryside had on two successive days broken into the halls and killed sixty-five students. Most of the scholars left alive fled the town, but the town's victory was Pyrrhic. The university exacted heavy damages, imposed a stiff fine on the burgesses, and received extension of the chancellor's jurisdiction, giving him sole custody of the assizes of bread and ale and of weights and measures, along with other privileges which in effect placed the town under university rule. Right up into the nineteenth century, the mayor of Oxford was still doing annual penance for town sins in a formal procession to the university church.

Though the Great Slaughter claimed more lives than any other Oxford riot, murderous battles between Town and Gown or between students of different nationalities were common throughout Chaucer's time, and he may well have taken part himself in such battles, tiptoeing down alleyways, pressed close against the walls, making use, perhaps, of old war skills. G. G. Coulton quotes a Coroner's Roll of 1314 as a typical specimen of the kind of thing found throughout the period— a jury report of how Scottish students and southern and western students met at Grope Lane "with swords, bucklers, bows, arrows and other arms, and there fought together." Robert of Bridlington and some of his fellows, the report tells us, stood in an upper chamber window,

> and there the said Robert de Bridlington with a small arrow, smote
> . . . Henry of Holy Isle and wounded him hard by the throat, on the
> left side in front; and the wound was of the breadth of one inch, and in
> depth even to the heart; and thus he slew him. . . . And in the same
> conflict John de Benton came with a falchion into Grope Lane and
> gave David de Kirkby a blow on the back of the head, six inches in
> length, and in depth even unto the brain. At which same time came
> William de la Hyde and smote the aforesaid David with a sword
> across the right knee and leg: and at the same time came William de
> Astley and smote the said David under the left arm with a misericorde,
> and thus slew him. . . .[8]

The same kind of thing was still going on in 1389–99, when Adam of Usk, a solemn old lecturer in canon law, led his Welsh and southern students in their battle against Northerners, with numerous deaths on either side.[9]

Some of Oxford's troubles came from intellectual earnestness. Derek Brewer writes:

> In the Lollard controversies, one of the disputants on the orthodox
> [anti-Lollard] side (which was not popular in the university) lost his
> nerve when he saw, or thought he saw, that twelve of his listeners held
> weapons concealed under their robes. He believed that death was
> threatening him unless he got down from the chair in which, ac-
> cording to custom, he was maintaining in public his argument.[10]

Brewer comments that "against such rowdiness we should balance the intense zeal for intellectual matters which in a rather odd way it bears witness to." Possibly. But whatever the cause of the rowdiness in a given case, the numerous records of beatings and street wars give a slightly chilling dimension to Chaucer's merry fabliaux of rough-and-ready Oxford and Cambridge students, the *Miller's Tale* and the *Reeve's Tale*. In the latter, when the miller is beating up the young clerk Allan, punching him in the nose so that the blood gushes down, Allan's companion John—and also the miller's wife—leap up to help as best they can in the dark:

> And by the wal a staf she [the wife] foond anon,
> And saugh a litel shymeryng of a light,
> For at an hole in shoon the moonë bright;

And by that light she saugh hem bothë two,
But sikerly she nystë who was who,   [*truly, she knew not*]
But as she saugh a whit thyng in hir yë.   [*eye*]
And whan she gan this whitë thyng espyë,
She wendë the clerk hadde werëd a volupeer,   [*weened, or believed . . .*
And with the staf she drow ay neer and neer,   *nightcap*]
And wende han hit this Aleyn at the fullë,
And smoot the millere on the pylëd skullë,   [*bald*]
That doun he gooth, and cride, "Harrow! I dyë!"
Thise clerkës beete hym weel and lete hym lyë;
And greythen hem, and tooke hir hors anon,   [*dressed*]
And eek hirë mele, and on hir wey they gon. . . .   [*meal*]

Both the rowdiness and the zeal were conspicuous elements of Oxford student life in Chaucer's time, and both come through powerfully in Chaucer's verse, the rowdiness in characters like John and Allan and "noble Nicholas" in the *Miller's Tale,* the zeal in Chaucer's own explorations of experience and authority, or in his Lollard-like attacks on the corrupt religious.

From February to May 1366, Chaucer was away from England's snow, traveling the glorious mountain roads of Spain. In England's war against France, the king's two sons, Gaunt and the Black Prince, were now seeking to establish a second front by allying themselves with France's Spanish enemies, and one theory has it that in 1366 Chaucer was traveling in connection with the preparations of Charles the Bad, king of Navarre, for war against France. The Black Prince is known to have been in Navarre at this time, as was the then well-known English military leader Dauberchicourt (or Daubrichecourt), perhaps for negotiations with Charles the Bad. Another theory (untenable) is that Chaucer was in Spain to help Henry of Trastamara—pretender to the throne of another Spanish kingdom, Castile—in his attempt to unseat the legitimate ruler, Pedro, called by later historians Pedro the Cruel. The truth is probably that Chaucer's job was to fight or (more likely) negotiate on Pedro's side against Trastamara. To John of Gaunt and the Black Prince, it was imperative that the powerful Castilian navy not fall into the hands of England's enemy, France (to whom Trastamara looked for help), and since the French army's escape route lay through Navarre, it was important that King Charles be kept friendly. Thus Chaucer may have seen both Spanish courts at this time. He gained from the trip, if nothing else, one striking image for his poetry. In the

House of Fame he finds a mountain of ice with a building on top, and recalling his Spanish trip—recalling the amazing peaks, the frightening sudden drops to valley floors, perhaps the occasional monastery high on a crag above one's head as one moves along what was then the only pass through the Pyrenees—he says of Fame's false Paradise, tawdry imitation of the medieval white castle of heaven, "Hier stant ther non in Spaynë." He may have brought back much more besides—ideas from the highly sophisticated Spanish Moors he would have met in the various Spanish courts, and perhaps the idea for his later *Parliament of Birds,* since a poem somewhat similar in general conception and identical in title had been composed in Spanish before 1366.

In 1366 or 1367, John Chaucer, the poet's father, died, and in May 1367, his widow married a vintner named Bartholomew Attechapel (or atte Chapel, or, simply, Chapel). Also by 1366, and perhaps earlier, Geoffrey Chaucer had married Philippa Roet, damoiselle of the queen. As a daughter of Sir Paon Roet, Philippa was considerably above her husband in social station, and in recent years, if not at the time, the marriage has given rise to gossip. For one thing, the marriage is said to have proved an unhappy one; for another, it is said to have been arranged by John of Gaunt as a means of disposing of his pregnant, highborn mistress. To this thoroughly mysterious business let us turn at once.

Geoffrey's father, as I've said, had died the previous year—he was alive in January 1366 but dead by May 6, 1367, when his widow remarried. However rich he may have been by vintner's standards, John Chaucer cannot have left his son sufficiently well off that he would seem an attractive catch to the Roets, prominent in Hainault, for many years intimately associated with the queen, and rich in land (if we may judge from the fact that Philippa's sister Katherine had married into the ancient family of Swynford, English landed aristocrats). Neither rich nor highborn, not yet established as a poet of high, international stature—in fact nothing but a squire—Chaucer captured one of Queen Philippa's own wards. How can it have happened? He may have loved her, of course, and because he was likable and clever at "dalliaunce," she may have loved him in return; but love was rarely a major consideration in the marriage of fourteenth-century heiresses.

Certain evidence suggests (though by no means proves) that John of Gaunt, who had a reputation in his day for amorous adventures, seduced Philippa, got her with child, and persuaded his attendant Geoffrey Chaucer to marry her. In that very September of 1366 when Philippa is recorded as married to Chaucer,[11] Gaunt was preparing to leave England to join his brother the Black Prince in war against the French and Henry Trastamara, a war from which, given the way medieval wars were fought, especially in Spain, he might never return. As a man devoted, like his father, to chivalry—as a man who all his life would prove unswervingly loyal to friends and dependents, a paragon of faithfulness in that ofttimes faithless, licentious age—Gaunt would have found it unthinkable to abandon a girl who was, after all, no strumpet but the daughter of one of the queen's old friends, indeed, the queen's own damoiselle and ward. Perhaps, then, the lifetime annuity he granted to Philippa that September was a consolation and marriage gift. Nine months later, apparently at about the time Elizabeth Chaucer, daughter of Philippa (probably), was born,[12] Geoffrey (now a member of the royal court) was granted a lifetime annuity of 20 marks (c. $3,000). Obviously the grant might be simply a recognition of the poet's new parental responsibilities, or a favor granted for some other reason; but just as obviously, if Elizabeth Chaucer was the illegitimate daughter of John of Gaunt, it would be natural that the duke, through his father (who made the grant; but Gaunt was in full control of the government), should take care of his own. Professor Williams, whose conjectural account I'm summarizing, notes a curious parallel:

> Whether such procedures [as the marriage "at his owene cost" outlined above] were common in this corrupt court, I do not know; but there is a teasing little record of one of Chaucer's fellow employees in the court, Edmund Rose, being granted a royal annuity "because he has taken to wife Agnes Archer, Damoiselle of the Queen's chamber." The wording is suggestive—and Agnes retained her maiden name.[13]

Gaunt continued to be kind to Elizabeth Chaucer and to another of Chaucer's children as long as he lived. When Elizabeth entered the convent of Barking to become a nun, Gaunt presented the convent with £51 8s. 2d. (c. $12,235), partly as a gift, partly for "various expenses" incurred. Since Elizabeth was the niece of John of Gaunt's beloved mistress (later wife) Katherine Swynford, since Gaunt and Geoffrey Chaucer were evidently friends for many years, and since Gaunt, as duke of Lancaster, was by now the richest man in England, no dark explanation of the gift need be sought. All the same, the gift is large enough to suggest that Gaunt may have had special reasons for concern about Elizabeth.

Professor Williams finds numerous hints that Gaunt felt a concern about Philippa not related to his interest in and friendship for Chaucer. He granted Philippa, in August 1372, an annuity of £10 ($2,400) "by our special favor, and for the good and agreeable service" she had done for "our very dear and much loved companion the queen." Later he granted Chaucer an annuity of £10 not only for the services of "our well-loved Geffray Chaucer" but also "for the good service that our well-loved Philippa, his wife, has done to our most honoured lady and mother the queen. . . ." Queen Philippa had at this time been dead for five years. Just before his departure for the Great March through France, in 1373, Gaunt gave presents to his second wife (after the death of Blanche of Lancaster) Queen Constance of Castile, to his father, his sister, his daughters, Alice Perrers (King Edward's mistress), and, among others, Philippa Chaucer. To his wife he gave four gold buttons, and to Philippa he gave a buttoner with six silver buttons worked with gold. On New Year's Day, 1380, he gave Philippa a silver cup worth 31s. 5d. ($377); in 1381 he gave her another silver cup, worked with gold, which was one of a pair worth £10 4s. 2d. ($2,570), and the next year he gave her another silver cup. Gaunt was of course generous to everyone around him; nevertheless, the steady recurrence of Philippa Chaucer's name in his household accounts, even granting the fact that she was the sister of Gaunt's beloved Katherine, is interesting.

The evidence, or possible evidence, can be spun out indefinitely. In May 1379, when Gaunt was in complete control of public affairs in Lincoln, the sheriff of Lincoln for some reason sent Philippa and a Mary St. Clair (another of Gaunt's pensioners) £26 13s. 4d. From 1381 to 1386 certain receipts from the customs were not paid entirely to Geoffrey, the controller, but were divided between him and Philippa, which perhaps suggests (or so Williams speculates) that Geoffrey and Philippa were not at this time living together, and that someone was taking care of Philippa's interests. At any rate it is certain that Philippa Chaucer had a life independent of the poet's and was esteemed in her own right in the Gaunt circle. On February 19, 1386, she was admitted to the fellowship of Lincoln Cathedral, along with Gaunt's sons Henry Bolingbroke (his son by Blanche), and John Beaufort (by Katherine), Katherine's son Thomas Swynford (Gaunt's stepson), Robert Ferrers (who would soon be Gaunt's son-in-law, husband to Gaunt's daughter by Katherine, Joan), and other of Gaunt's retainers. Chaucer himself was not admitted. Neither was Katherine Swynford, but she may well have been a member already (and, indeed, she may have been the arranger of the whole initiation).

To all this it can of course be answered that Gaunt showed his fondness for Chaucer in other ways. He seems to have placed Chaucer in the king's service in the beginning, in 1366 or 1367, and, contrary to the rather queer opinion of J. R. Hulbert,[14] seems often (though not always) to have had a hand in Chaucer's political and financial advancement. In 1369, when Chaucer was paid £10 ($2,400) on account of wages and expenses to be incurred in the war with France, Gaunt was the leader of the troops to be sent to France. In 1370, when Chaucer received letters of protection for a journey across the sea, Gaunt was in England taking a leading part in public affairs. In 1372, when Chaucer was commissioned to go to Italy, Gaunt was in London, had for some months been the lover of Katherine Swynford, Chaucer's sister-in-law, and was by far the most powerful figure in the government. In April 1374, when Chaucer was granted his pitcher of wine daily for life, Gaunt had probably just returned from his Great March through France, which had ended that month. He was certainly back in England on May 10, two and a half weeks later, when Chaucer was granted a free lifetime lease on the house above Aldgate, probably in order that he might (as Margaret Galway suggests) be close to his new work as customs controller—a job already awarded though not yet granted officially. Four weeks after that, he was appointed controller of customs and subsidy of wools, hides, and woolfells for the port of London; four days after that he was made controller of petty customs of wines for the port of London; and the following day he was granted a lifetime annuity of £10 by Gaunt himself. And so it goes to the end of Gaunt's days.

Williams' analysis, I think, greatly underestimates the influence of King Richard II on Chaucer's later fortunes; but it is true, certainly, that whatever he could do for Chaucer, Gaunt did. Beside such favors —it can easily be claimed, in opposition to Williams' position—Gaunt's gifts to Philippa were mere tokens of friendship to the family of a man Gaunt esteemed. It might be claimed that Gaunt was telling the truth: he gave gifts to Philippa because she'd been extraordinarily kind to his mother Queen Philippa in her last years (except that we know Gaunt used the same formula on one woman who really was his mistress) ; and it might be claimed that later he was kind to her because she was Katherine's sister and had perhaps helped them in their love affair. We'll never know the truth, but however we may wish to deny the rumor, the whole business looks exceedingly suspect. Why did John of Gaunt give such a very large gift to Elizabeth Chaucer—and not to Katherine Swynford's son Thomas, by her earlier marriage, a boy Gaunt loved?

Part of what makes the whole puzzle so dark is that Gaunt and Chaucer do indeed seem to have been friends, as Gaunt's account books insist: other recipients of Gaunt's largesse are often simply named; Chaucer is always "our beloved." Though all the evidence is indirect, Chaucerians have generally formed the impression that the two were quite close friends, not because of what Chaucer owed Gaunt or Gaunt owed Chaucer, not because Philippa and Geoffrey helped the duke in his affair with Katherine (though they may have), and not because Chaucer's marriage to Philippa and, after Philippa's death, Gaunt's marriage to Katherine made the two men relatives, but because they were brilliant, in many ways like-minded men, intellectually daring, scrupulously honorable, at least by their own medieval code, and emotionally useful to each other. Gaunt could give Chaucer the station and self-respect that Englishmen of the middle class hungered for (as no one knew better than Chaucer himself, who dramatized that hunger in the *Canterbury Tales*),[15] and Chaucer could give Gaunt a sense of participation in the contemplative, artistic life he was fitted for by nature but largely denied, except as patron and collector, by his responsibilities and station. He was—as we've said—a prince who'd grown up in a household where ideas were celebrated, where sage and polished old Froissart and his friends were never beyond Queen Philippa's call; a prince who in later life would haunt the halls of Oxford and pay visits to scholars among his enemies the French, and who would defend with armed soldiers the right of theologians to free inquiry—not that we need deny the element of self-interest in Gaunt's stand, since Wyclif's inquiry favored civil power. Yet all we know of Gaunt suggests that his action was not pure self-interest.

Nothing would be more natural, though of course the suggestion is pure speculation, than that Gaunt and Katherine Swynford, with a few attendants, should from time to time spend an evening with the Chaucers, the sisters talking of whatever it is medieval sisters talked about—a certain cool distance between them, it may be, young Katherine sometimes made suddenly timid by some hint of irritation in her older sister's voice, forced to be cautious about showing too openly her affection for the duke, never reaching for his hand when Philippa was in the room (even a smile shared between them could make Philippa's eyes go quiet) yet at other times standing firmly, younger sister or no, unwilling to take any more blame than she deserved, even defiant, however guardedly, taking with Philippa the attitude Criseyde had taken in the temple where Troilus first saw her,

> . . . somedel deignous . . . for she let fallë
> Hirë look a lite aside in swich manerë,   [*little*]
> Ascaunces, "What! may I nat stonden herë!"   [*askance*]

—and while the sisters worked out their difficult truce, the two men, great in their extremely different ways, discussed, for Gaunt's benefit, the difficult question of animals versus cows, and, for Chaucer's benefit, the fascinating intricacies of a double-front French war.

Though described as "mediocre" by most modern historians since the nineteenth-century Bishop Stub, that was by no means what Gaunt seemed to Chaucer. That very moderation, that very reasonableness which makes Gaunt seem pale in comparison to his dramatic father and older brother—pale even in comparison to his stern and monklike younger brother, Thomas of Woodstock, later earl of Gloucester, doomed to die for treason against King Richard II, or to his still younger brother, Edmund Langley, later bishop of York, who cared more for the pursuit of fox and deer than for pursuit of empire or justice or salvation—Gaunt's balance, his good sense, was for Chaucer a high and noble virtue, indeed the apex of virtue, the chief point of praise he'd offered in his elegy for Blanche:

> Therwith hir lystë so wel to lyvë,
> That dulnesse was of hir adrad.
> She nas to sobre ne to glad;
> In allë thynges morë mesurë
> Had never, I trowë, creaturë.

According to Professor Williams, the likelihood, or anyway suspicion, is that not only Chaucer's daughter Elizabeth but also his son Thomas was biologically a child of Gaunt. The idea is an old one, but it became a matter for serious consideration in 1932, when Russell Krauss wrote his elaborate study, "The Paternity of Thomas Chaucer." Like many Chaucerians who have followed him, Krauss began his study, he tells us, in hopes of disproving the old contention that Gaunt could have been Thomas Chaucer's father, but ended up convinced that there was no other way of accounting for the facts.

The tradition begins with Speght, who reluctantly reports, damaging his own case, "Yet some hold opinion (but I know not upon what grounds) that Thomas Chaucer was not the sonne of Geffrey Chaucer, but rather some kinsman of his whome hee brought up."[16] Krauss comments: "Speght was undoubtedly reporting a genuine opinion—an opinion of a sort that can hardly arise without some basis in fact. Unless we are to assume that some one sat down and made it up, which seems gratuitous, how are we to account for it?"[17] Various kinds of evidence can be adduced. The weakest piece of evidence (though one repeatedly brought forward) is the fact that John Lydgate, who revered Geoffrey Chaucer and knew Thomas sufficiently well to address a complimentary poem to him, says nothing in that poem about Thomas's paternity. If the argument is worth answering at all, the answer is that even if Geoffrey was Thomas's father and Lydgate knew it, Lydgate would not necessarily have thought that relationship an appropriate detail for inclusion in his verses. It is true of course, though it carries no weight, that if Lydgate knew Thomas Chaucer to be Gaunt's son, he'd have been a fool to have mentioned it.

Two slightly stronger bits of evidence are, first, Thomas Chaucer's various coats of arms, one of which is preserved on his tomb, and second, his apparent failure to claim his Roet property in Hainault. The heraldic evidence is complicated, but in brief it comes to this: On his tomb Thomas Chaucer takes his mother's Roet arms, not Geoffrey Chaucer's, and elsewhere, when he displayed the arms of Geoffrey Chaucer as his own, he seems not to have adopted them outright but to have used them in an altered form. It was not uncommon in the fourteenth and fifteenth centuries for a man to choose his mother's coat of arms when her station was higher than her husband's; but given Geoffrey Chaucer's fame and favor—*pace* the usual opinion of Chaucerians, the poet was chiefly admired not for his diplomacy but for his brilliance as a poet, the greatest since Dante in all Europe—the omission is curious. Thomas's apparent alteration of his father's arms is even stranger. The seal used by Thomas Chaucer at Ewelme in 1409 is marked "s [G]HOFRAI CHAUCIER"—it is, in other words, not Thomas's seal at all but Geoffrey's—and on this seal we find a bend *entire*. All other surviving coats of Thomas Chaucer exhibit a bend *countercolored*. Though this might be explained as a personal whim, the explanation is a little unconvincing, since the alteration could be construed as a sign of bastardy. The suggestion that the Ewelme seal may be an engraver's mistake is also unconvincing. Ordinarily one does not pay for work that might be construed as critical of one's mother.

Since Philippa Chaucer was a Roet heiress, Thomas Chaucer ought to have been in line for property in Hainault; but there is no evidence that he ever held land there. There are several plausible explanations. One is suggested by the difficulty encountered by Thomas Swynford, Katherine's son. In 1411 Thomas Swynford was unable to claim his share of the Hainault property, his inheritance through Katherine, because those who held it maintained that he was illegitimate. Henry IV rescued him by issuing a writ proclaiming his legitimacy. Perhaps for Thomas Chaucer, no such writ could honestly be issued.

None of this evidence is conclusive, but, for what it's worth, we have more. Generous as he was to Geoffrey Chaucer, Gaunt was far more generous to Thomas Chaucer. Among other grants, he apparently arranged for Thomas a reward, additional to Thomas's pension, of 20 marks ($3,000) in 1394–95 and in the same year doubled Thomas's pension, as we learn from King Richard's confirmation of Thomas's £20 annuity after Gaunt's death. Though the later records of Gaunt are scant, we know from Richard II's Patent Rolls that when, in the last year of his reign, King Richard took over the late duke of Lancaster's holdings, he infringed on provisions Gaunt had made for Thomas Chaucer and felt obliged to make amends, granting Thomas, for life, 20 marks a year as

compensation for offices (unfortunately not described) which Richard
had now given to the earl of Wiltshire. As Krauss remarks,

> If we compare this treatment of Thomas with that accorded Geoffrey,
> we cannot but be struck by the disparity. If we were to say that Geoffrey
> was a protege of Gaunt's, how would we describe Thomas's con-
> nection with him? John of Gaunt extended his bounty to Geoffrey in
> the year 1374 very possibly in recompense for an injury done him [the
> affair with Philippa]; he continued in warm and generous intimacy
> with Philippa throughout her life; but Thomas he received into his own
> retinue and provided for from the year 1389 [probably just after the
> death of Philippa] until he died, when the task passed to his sons.[18]

Gaunt's son Henry Bolingbroke, when he became King Henry IV, was
extraordinarily generous to Thomas Chaucer; but, Krauss writes,

> Gaunt and [Henry IV] were not the only Lancastrians to heap good
> fortune upon him. Henry Beaufort [Gaunt's son by Katherine] . . .
> made him constable of Taunton Castle in 1406, calling him in the writ
> "nostro Consanguineo." This was a munificent reward. Chaucer was to
> have £40 yearly with "supervision of his manors, lands, and possessions
> in Somerset with all due fees, profits, emoluments and commodities."
> When it is brought to our attention that no duties were attached to the
> appointment and that the office might be exercised by deputy, we must
> recognize that the salary amounted to an out-and-out gift. Writing of
> Thomas to his nephew Henry V in 1420, the cardinal called him "my
> Cousin." Such a term would have been eminently fitting and generous
> for a great prelate to use in reference to his illegitimate half-brother.[19]

Krauss's final point here, I must admit, eludes me. The two men *were*
cousins. But the rest is sound and it does seem curious that Gaunt and
his sons and heirs gave no such lavish treatment to Katherine Swynford's son, Thomas, Gaunt's stepson.

The early Chaucerian Thynne reported in his *Animadversions* (no one
knows on what grounds) that Gaunt "had mayne paramours in his youthe
and was not verye contynente in his age," and Chaucer with careful
politeness implies the same in his *Book of the Duchess*. Who these paramours were, besides Katherine Swynford and Marie St. Hilary (mentioned by Froissart), no one has discovered. Marie, like Philippa Chaucer, was a damoiselle of the queen and received gifts from Gaunt, as
did Philippa, "for the good and agreeable service she has rendered for
a long time to our Lady and Mother Philippa, late Queen of England,"
almost the same formula Gaunt used in giving gifts to Katherine Swynford. He used the same formula on other women, not all of whom,
surely, can have been his mistresses; but the size of his gifts to Marie
(later married to one of his retainers), to Katherine, and to Philippa is
suggestive.

Several objections are commonly raised to the theory that Philippa Chaucer was Gaunt's mistress and that Thomas Chaucer was Gaunt's son. One is the testimony of Thomas Gascoigne, of Oxford, who undoubtedly knew Thomas Chaucer, and who states plainly that Thomas was Geoffrey's son. But Gascoigne may not have known Thomas Chaucer well—though they were Oxfordshire neighbors, their worlds were far apart—and Thomas, brought up by Chaucer, may not have advertised his illegitimacy. (Thomas once signed himself in court "son of Geoffrey Chaucer," which may mean simply that he grew up in Chaucer's house, though it may also mean, of course, that he was really Chaucer's son.) No one else from the Chaucers' time says a word about any relationship between Geoffrey and Thomas Chaucer, a fact which has made such eminent Chaucerians as Furnivall, Tyrwhitt, Kirk, and Lounsbury feel, at best, uncertain that Geoffrey and Thomas were father and son. A stronger, though strictly emotional objection is that, while one can understand Geoffrey's marrying his friend's cast-off mistress to help the cast-off mistress and the friend out of their trouble, it seems incredible that three to six years later (the probable time of Thomas's conception), he should still be putting up with their love affair. This has been answered in several ways. Krauss's view is that the love affair took place while Philippa was serving in Gaunt's household, Geoffrey being away in Italy (December 1, 1372 until May 23, 1373), and that when the poet got home he was wild with indignation, which Gaunt assuaged by his largesse of 1374 (the pitcher of wine, the house over Aldgate, and so on). Professor Williams, bearing in mind Chaucer's evident close friendship with Gaunt, takes a different tack. It should be remembered, he says,

> (1) that Chaucer never expressed contentment with his married life or his love life—quite the contrary; (2) that if he really married Philippa at Gaunt's behest in 1366, he went into the arrangement with his eyes open, and had no cause to feel deceived; (3) that he was well remunerated; and (4) that he may actually have regarded it as a high honor to be so closely connected with the royal house of England, and the kingdom's greatest nobleman. Alice Perrers' husband accepted with excellent grace his wife's role as mistress to the king, along with the incidental perquisites to himself; and many a subsequent husband of the royal mistress in France and England has managed to view a similar situation with philosophic aplomb.[20]

Another mainly emotional objection is that it seems to us offensive that Gaunt, even in that age, should be making love to two of Sir Paon Roet's daughters simultaneously. Professor Williams' answer is that Gaunt wasn't. By a careful examination of the dates involved, he gets Thomas conceived and Philippa paid off (the annuity grant of August 1372) before Gaunt's affair with Katherine began, so that the pension to Philippa "may have been granted at the behest of Katherine, and to please her; or it may have been granted as a kind of peace offering from Gaunt because he had deserted Philippa for her sister."[21] The argument, though tenable, may seem a trifle weak, resting as it does on our desire to believe that Gaunt failed to notice for several years the beautiful woman in his household whom he would later keep as mistress for decades and ultimately marry. Katherine had been in the Gaunt household at least since 1369,[22] and had probably served for some while by then, whereas it was only after Queen Philippa's death that Philippa Chaucer was officially transferred to the Gaunt retinue—though Gaunt and Philippa had known each other, and had perhaps been lovers (as we've seen) earlier. Although it's conceivable that Gaunt made no move toward Katherine in all that time, despite her proximity and golden-haired beauty, or that Katherine, from regard for her sister, rebuffed him, it is not much more than conceivable. Gaunt was in England from November 1369, shortly after Blanche's death, to June 1370, when he left for France and Spain; and he returned to England in November 1371. If he really did love first Philippa and only later Katherine, as we hope, he was—and they were—lucky. From the medieval point of view, it was incest either way.

J. M. Manly raised one important objection to Krauss's argument, that Gaunt's marrying Katherine after he had had carnal relations with her sister would have violated canon law; hence Philippa can never have been Gaunt's mistress. Williams has tried to prove that Manly was mistaken about canon law.[23] Perhaps a safer argument—supported by what we know of Gaunt's agreement with Wyclif, especially with regard to civil and canon law—would be an assertion that Gaunt didn't give a damn about canon law.

But let us return to the troublesome fact that, if it is true that Thomas Chaucer was really Gaunt's son, and true that Chaucer and Gaunt were good friends, then Chaucer's marriage was, at least from a modern point of view, strange. He was married to Philippa by 1366; sometime between 1369 and the spring of 1372, Gaunt begot Thomas on Chaucer's wife. We can blink Chaucer's marrying his friend's cast-off mistress, but why did he let the affair drag on? One natural reaction is to scoff at the whole idea, as B. J. Whiting does, alluding ironically to Chaucer's "pretty role as a contented cuckold." Another equally natural reaction is Williams' assertion that Chaucer felt no pain in the matter, since he didn't really like his wife.

That notion, far from original with Williams, has taken a strange hold on Chaucer biography. The only evidence comes, naturally, from Chaucer's verse, especially the *House of Fame,* wherein Chaucer speaks of worshipping at the shrine of St. Leonard (patron saint of prisoners and henpecked husbands, among other things), and later tells how, fallen into a state of suspended animation in the claws of a soaring eagle, he is awakened, or indeed brought back to life, by an eagle's imperious cry of "Awak[e]!" which is spoken

> Ryght in the samë vois and stevenë   [*sound or pitch*]
> That useth oon I koudë nevenë;   [*name*]
> And with that vois, soth for to seyn,
> My myndë cam to me ageyn,
> For hyt was goodly seyd to me,
> So nas hyt never wont to be.

Pointing out that the eagle wakes Chaucer in the voice of Philippa, but more kindly than Philippa, critics have repeatedly drawn the conclusion that Philippa really was, in Chaucer's view, a shrew. They add Chaucer's assertions in the *Book of the Duchess, House of Fame, Parliament of Birds, Troilus and Criseyde,* and so on, that he knows nothing of love, and conclude that his marriage was a disaster. For instance, J. W. Hales, after reviewing the literary evidence, says, "It seems impossible to put a pleasant construction on these pages. It is incredible that they have no personal significance. The conclusion clearly is that Chaucer was not happy in his matrimonial relations."

One dissenter from this view is T. R. Lounsbury, who writes, on the passage just quoted:

The lines are unmistakably pure banter—banter doubtless understood at the time. . . . To attach a serious meaning to [them] would render it necessary for us to revise our whole conception of the poet's charac- ter. From the little we know of his life and from the great deal we find in his writings, we recognize him plainly as a man of the world in the best sense of that much-abused phrase. He had all that tendency to self-revelation in unimportant matters and to reticence in important ones which distinguish men of his kind. We can be certain that he was not one to wear his heart upon his sleeve, not one to take the world into his confidence in things wherein it had no concern, or to parade before it his domestic grievances, if any he had.[24]

Two further points might be made. First, if the lines do refer to Philippa (and that seems the easiest reading) they say, for all their teasing, that her voice has roused Chaucer from a deathlike state. Since the whole poem parodies Dante's *Comedy,* wherein Dante is elevated by the love of Beatrice, Chaucer's lines suggest, delightfully and it may be truly, that the everyday love of a wife can also save the soul. The idea that in a woman's love, as in Christ's, a man can be resurrected is a commonplace of love-religion poetry, including that of Chaucer. For instance, he has the Black Knight say in the *Book of the Duchess*, "As helpe me God I was as blyve / Reysed, as fro deth to lyve . . ." This idea that married love is as beneficial as courtly love turns out to be one of the consistent idiosyncrasies in Chaucer's verse. Chaucer repeatedly celebrated the love of man and wife and suggested the analogy between love of this kind and that between God and man, that is, Christ the Bridegroom and his Church, and he frequently compared wedded happiness with happiness in heaven. In the *Man of Law's Tale,* for instance, we find:

> And swich a blisse is ther bitwix hem two
> That, savë the joye that lasteth everemo,
> Ther is noon lyk that any creaturë
> Hath seyn or shal, whil that the world may durë.   [*endure*]

The most fortunate kind of married love and the love of God are com-pared, too, in the *Franklin's Tale.* In this marriage, where each party has renounced tyranny over the other, love is "patient," like that of the mightiest of all lovers, God:

> Love is a thing as any spirit free.
> Wommen, of kyndë, desiren libertee,   [*nature*]
> And nat to been constreynëd as a thral;
> And so doon men, if I sooth seyen shal.
> Looke who that is moost pacient in lovë,
> He is at his advantage al abovë.

Though comic and ironic, Chaucer's jibe at Philippa in the *House of Fame* carries the usual love-religion comparison of woman's elevating love and God's love.

The second point which I think should be made is that neither Chaucer's repeated claims that he knows nothing about love nor his "obsessive" concern with faithless wives can fairly be read as evidence that he was unhappy with his wife. The claim that he knows nothing about love, as I've suggested already, has the ring of an in-joke. As for Chaucer's fas-cination with unfaithful wives, it was stock material for the poets of his day, including sober Gower. What sets Chaucer apart is his insistent *de-fense* of unfaithful women. Surely the following is not mocking or ironic:

> But trewëly, the storië telleth us,
> Ther madë nevere woman moorë wo
> Than she, whan that she falsëd Troilus.

> She seyde, "Allas! for now is clene ago
> My name of trouthe in love, for everemo!
> For I have falsëd oon the gentilestë
> That evere was, and oon the worthiestë!"

When Chaucer speaks of men who try to "cage" their wives or daughters (in the *Miller's Tale*, the *Reeve's Tale*, the *Wife of Bath's Prologue*, the *Merchant's Tale*, and the *Manciple's Tale*), he always comes down on the side of the wife and against the jealous male. If the gossip is right and Chaucer's wife was for a time Gaunt's mistress, Chaucer was equally sympathetic in real life. He and Philippa were frequently apart, usually when Chaucer was away on business, perhaps sometimes for other reasons we do not know; but apparently they also spent a good deal of time together, right to the end of Philippa's life, as they need not have done judging by other marriages we know to have been contracted for the sake of appearances in that century.

So the marriage was perhaps odd, but nothing urgently suggests that it was loveless. A thoroughgoing Freudian slightly in his cups might argue that Chaucer's consistent defense of faithless women, his idealization of married life, and his insistence that a wife should be allowed to roam freely, are all indications of repression and desperate neurotic facade. But Chaucer's poetry has the unmistakable ring of good health. Perhaps one of the best things that happened to him in the 1360's was that by a wild stroke of luck—which secured him the lifelong gratitude, friendship, and patronage of the most powerful baron in England—he fell into marriage with a rich and beautiful heiress whom he had known and liked for years and whom he liked well enough now, or generously enough, that he would not cage her like a bird, though he felt the need, from time to time, to defend his point of view, slyly glancing around the audience, because they knew his situation but were hardly in much of a position to judge him since they too, most of them, had their vulnerable points, as Chaucer knew:

> For O thyng, sirës, saufly dar I seyë,
> That freendës everych oother moot obeyë,
> If they wol longe holden compaignyë.
> Love wol nat been constreynëd by maistryë.
> Whan maistrië comth, the God of Love anon
> Beteth his wyngës, and farëwel, he is gon!

This is not to say, necessarily, that the marriage of Geoffrey and Philippa was absolute bliss, like the pure-fiction marriages he'd created for the Black Knight and Lady White, or Alla and Custance. He may per-

haps sometimes have been uncomfortably aware of his lower station, for
instance when they visited the great Swynford estate. Chaucer knew
Philippa's relatives were in no rational sense his betters. By Christian doctrine, all people had pretty much an equal claim to true "gentilessë." So
Chaucer's character the old hag would argue with comic long-windedness,
in the tale of the Wife of Bath, telling her young knight that it's better to
be married to a woman old and foul but virtuous than to a beautiful, faithless woman:

> "But, for ye speken of swich gentillessë
> As is descended out of old richessë,   [wealth]
> That therforë sholden ye be gentil men,
> Swich arrogance is nat worth an hen. . . .
> Crist wolë we clayme of hym oure gentillessë,
> Nat of oure eldres for hire old richessë.
> For thogh they yeve us al hir heritagë,
> For which we claymë to been of heigh paragë,   [lineage]
> Yet may they nat biquethë, for no thyng,   [bequeath]
> To noon of us hir vertuous lyvyng,
> That made hem gentil men ycalled be,
> And bad us folwen hem in swich degree."

But all that was mere talk, as the canny hag knew. Philippa's kinsmen
might perhaps speak no Latin (such knowledge was relatively uncommon among rural aristocrats), but their power and wealth, their ancient
pedigree made a difference only a fool could pretend not to notice. There
was a line, a barrier that closed him out, and though jealousy and envy
were laughable to Chaucer—he'd mocked them many times—his poetry
shows that he understood such emotions well. He would set down
jealousy with deadly accuracy in *Troilus and Criseyde,* and because of
his knowledge of how jealousy felt he would be able to inject authentic
pain and anger into one beautiful conventional lyric on the subject of
unfaithfulness:

> Madamë, for your newefangelnessë,
> Many a servaunt have ye put out of gracë.
> I takë my leve of your unstedfastnessë,
> For wel I wot, whyl ye have lyvës spacë,
> Ye can not lovë ful half yeer in a placë,
> To newë thing your lust is ay so kenë;
> In stede of blew, thus may ye were al grenë.

Right as a mirour nothing may enpressë,
But, lightly as it cometh, so mot it pacë,
So fareth your love, your werkës bereth witnessë.
Ther is no feith that may your herte enbracë;
But, as a wedercok, that turneth his facë
With every wind, ye fare, and that is senë;
In stede of blew, thus may ye were al grenë.

Ye might be shryned, for your brotelnessë,
Bet than Dalyda, Creseyde or Candacë;
For ever in chaunging stant your sikernessë;
That tachë may no wight fro your herte aracë.
If ye lese oon, ye can wel tweyn purchacë;
Al light for somer, ye woot wel what I menë:
In stede of blew, thus may ye were al grenë.

[*fickleness, or breakableness*]
[*surety*]
[*blemish . . . erase*]

We cannot know what lady he wrote this lyric for. There is even some doubt, certain scholars think, whether the poem is by Chaucer; but it would not, perhaps, be unduly surprising to learn that he wrote it, in an angry moment, to Philippa herself.

Yet whatever its oddities, the Chaucers' marriage was probably not an especially bad one. They stayed together, with only occasional interruptions which may have had nothing to do with how they felt; they seem to have been comfortable with the same friends; they raised children. Indeed, there is so much good said of marriage in Chaucer's poetry, and there are so many signs of his subtle understanding of how married men and women feel and behave toward each other, that one is inclined to believe theirs must have been an excellent marriage, that sometimes Chaucer lay at night with Philippa's head against his shoulder, listening to her breathing and the breathing of the children—Elizabeth and little Thomas, later little Lewis—and thought, half-smiling in the room's complete darkness, how strange and unpredictable are the ways of this world, and felt the emotion he'd give later to Troilus, a wish that all lovers might fare as well as he, a prayer, almost, that would surface out of memory and slip into the *Knight's Tale:*

. . . God, that al this wydë world hath wroght,
Sende hym his love that hath it deere aboght!

Five: Significant Moments and Influences: Pedro the Cruel, Two Deaths, that Shameless Woman and Wanton Harlot Alice Perrers, and Italian Artistic Humanism (1367-1373)

WHEN GEOFFREY AND PHILIPPA CHAUCER were just beginning their married life together, in 1367, the Black Prince was at war in Spain, enforcing the foreign policy Chaucer had had a hand in working out the year before. The immediate significance of the war was the English government's wish to keep the French from control of the Castilian navy, tipping the balance against England in Edward III's war with France; but in the long view, the Spanish troubles with which England involved herself in the late 1360's are perhaps chiefly interesting as an instance of that conflict which was beginning to crop up here and there over the length and breadth of western Christendom, the conflict that would bring out the best and worst in Chaucer's later friend and patron King Richard II, ultimately leading to Richard's deposition and murder—the conflict, that is, of limited versus absolute monarchy, magnates versus king.

The Spanish troubles came about, briefly, as follows. When the plague of 1350 killed Alfonso XI, king of Castile—the rich Spanish peninsula kingdom of mountains and wheatfields and the innumerable castles that gave the place its name—Alfonso left behind him five bastard children by his favorite mistress, Doña Leonor de Guzmán, and one legitimate son, the man whom Chaucer would address as "O noble, O worthy Petro, glorie of Spayne," remembered by history as Pedro the Cruel. Alfonso had been strong. Though his forbears had left him a weak throne and a strife-torn kingdom, he'd been able to impose some order on the anarchic nobility, had brought his towns back to prosperity, and by long, fierce struggle had beaten back the Moors, recapturing the provinces of Granada and Morocco. But his death reawakened the old factionalism, the old lawlessness and oppression by noblemen and prelates, and his illegitimate line, guided and encouraged by Doña Leonor, stood as a powerful threat to the legitimate, so that Pedro had his hands full maintaining his authority against treason and revolt. Like many absolute monarchs of the period, Pedro looked for inspiration, on the one hand, to renascent Roman political theory, which was now being much discussed throughout Europe, offering, as it did, a creditable alternative to the theory that

168

temporal power derived from spiritual authority, that is, from the Pope; and he looked, on the other hand, to the living model of successful medieval absolutism as practiced by Moorish princes. Neither Roman theory nor Moorish practice, as Pedro understood them, made high moral demands on the monarch. Power and authority were his by right, and were the sole basis of happiness in the state. And so, to end her dissentious influence on her children and his magnates, Pedro murdered—or perhaps his mother and favorite counsellor murdered—his father's mistress, Doña Leonor, and the result was the beginning of as ugly a blood feud as history records.

His quasi-mystical notion of what kings might do with impunity led Pedro, in 1353, to a more dangerous error. For centuries France had been exerting influence on the affairs of kingdoms in the Spanish peninsula. The rulers of Navarre, Castile's neighboring kingdom to the northeast, controlling the upper Pyrenees, were of French lineage, and the powerful French navy rivaled the Castilian for control of the European Atlantic. To seal a peace with France, Pedro married a French princess, Blanche of Bourbon, and then, indifferent to the concern expressed by his barons and even his close friends, immediately locked his French queen in a dungeon for the sake of his mistress, Doña Maria de Padilla. It was an act of madness. Rich and splendid as his court might be, graced by Moorish philosophers and musicians and supported by the marvelous powers of sorcerers, it was still a foolish business to stir up that hornet's nest, France. His favorite counsellor, the bastard brothers, and the queen mother united in a rebellion, which Pedro crushed.

But since the injury to France invited invasion and thus involved not Castile alone but also her neighbors, and since a strong Castile, united under an absolute monarchy, could be a threat to smaller, less wealthy kingdoms nearby, Pedro's success was temporary. Neighboring kings joined in, notably Peter IV of Aragon (also in the mountainous northeast, next door to Navarre), supporting the eldest bastard, Don Henry of Trastamara. Pedro won for a time and shocked Christian, chivalric Europe by executing his captives, both women and men, including two of his half brothers, and killing with his own hand the suppliant king of Granada. France was persuaded to enter the conflict, not only to punish the offense to Blanche of Bourbon and Pedro's scorn of the chivalric code, but also to prevent, if possible, an alliance of Castile with England, and, incidentally, to give employment to the "free companies," the roving bands of mercenaries who were then ravaging southern France. The king of France and the Pope at Avignon sent one of the finest French generals of the day, Bertrand du Guesclin, with a large army of mercenaries, into Spain. They won the throne of Castile for Trastamara in 1366, and Pedro, exiled, turned to the Black Prince for help. With some reluctance but very little choice from the point of view of international politics, since the Castilian navy under Trastamara would certainly side with France, the Black Prince came, leading his crack army and a bevy of diplomats (probably including, as we've seen, Chaucer), and in a typically brilliant victory at Nájera, in 1367, placed Pedro once more on his throne. Pedro slaughtered his captives as usual, and the Black Prince, indignant—and also suffering from the disease that would finally kill him—angrily returned to England, where he and his staff would advise abandonment of Pedro's cause, support for a government of Castilian magnates, and the partitioning of Castile.

So began the English involvement in Spain. Meanwhile, left to face his enemies alone, and believing implicitly in the strategy that had worked so well for the Moors, Pedro stepped up the atrocities. Then, near Montiel, in 1369, his castle under siege, he was tempted out by du Guesclin for truce talks and murdered by his bastard brother in the Frenchman's tent. Pedro's daughters by Maria, whom the Cortes (heraldic judges) acknowledged legitimate heirs to the throne, made war against Trastamara, whose weakened Spanish neighbors now deserted him. In 1372—three years after the death of John of Gaunt's beloved Blanche— the daughters of King Pedro secured England's continued alliance by marriage of Pedro's daughter and heiress, Constance, to John of Gaunt, duke of Lancaster, making Gaunt, according to Spanish law, the legitimate king of Castile, if he could snatch his legitimate throne from the usurper Trastamara.

One may wonder what "glory" a man like Chaucer could see in King Pedro. Yet Chaucer's attitude need not surprise us. For one thing, whatever he may have thought of Pedro as a man, the poet naturally favored Pedro's side on the issue involved. Like Gaunt and the Black Prince (until revulsion caused the latter to abandon his stand), Pedro stood for strong central government as opposed to government by a puppet king supported by rival, frequently warring magnates, government that historically, in Britain, had seldom proved efficient either in organizing for war or in maintaining peace and prosperity. (Turning against Pedro, Prince Edward had not changed his mind about how government ought to be run; he had merely given up on Spain and Pedro.) Praising Pedro after his death, when his friend John of Gaunt was married to Pedro's daughter and stood as rightful claimant to Pedro's legitimate power, Chaucer was perhaps more honoring the Castilian throne than the man who had held it.

It seems probable, moreover, that the stories Chaucer heard, not from the Black Prince but from men who served under him, made Pedro appear at least nobler than his opponents. Chaucer may have received his information from old Sir Guichard d'Angle, a man of some importance in Chaucer's life, though we know less of their relationship than we might wish. Guichard was a man with whom Chaucer would serve on various important diplomatic missions including royal marriage negotiations in 1376, and a man whose word would count with Chaucer or, indeed, with any Englishman.

He was a Frenchman by birth and training, known in Chaucer's circle as a man of exceptional chivalry and valor. He'd fought courageously on the side of the French in the Battle of Poitiers in 1356 and had been left for dead on the battlefield. Soon after, from admiration of the Black Prince and in faithful service to the code of chivalry, which obliged a knight always to fight on the side he believed to be just, he'd switched his allegiance from France to England, abandoning everything he had, though a wealthy man. He'd been appointed marshal of Aquitaine by the Black Prince and later Lord Playnmartyn and captain of Aquitaine; and because he was a cultured and noble-spirited knight, he was repeatedly sent on errands for King Edward—to Rome in 1369, for example, to confer with Pope Urban V. (There he met his fellow ex-Frenchman, Froissart, who shared his great passions, including poetry, and his company on the journey home.) Guichard distinguished himself, as did his two sons, fighting with the Black Prince in support of King Pedro at the Battle of Nájera, and was present at the ceremonious meeting of the Black Prince and King Pedro. He escorted Pedro to Burgos when the Spaniard, surrounded by jubilant, cheering friends, resumed his title to the throne. In 1372 Guichard was captured by Trastamara and spent two years in a Spanish dungeon, a grim place even by medieval standards, where, according to the report of Owen de Galles one month after Guichard's capture, Guichard and his companions lay in darkness, chained two by two. They were fortunate at that, since many of Trastamara's captives, whatever their rank and nobility of lineage, were summarily executed, blinded, had their ears cut off, or were castrated. And while Guichard was suffering the misery of his dungeon—this too Chaucer knew in all its grisly detail—his wife was persecuted and humiliated by the French generals allied with Trastamara and was forced to surrender and flee her castle of Achart. She escaped to the protection of the duke of Berry, who eventually—in 1374–75—won by bribery and a prisoner exchange the release of Guichard and his fellow knights.

Back in England, that long nightmare finally behind him but so deeply cut into his memory that he must have spoken of it frequently, Guichard met Geoffrey Chaucer often, since they both were favored diplomats and both in the inner circle of Gaunt's friends. As Guichard grew older, his interests, not least of them his love of poetry, drew him closer still to Chaucer. Guichard remained in the retinue of the Black Prince, whom Gaunt and his mistress—and probably the Chaucers—frequently visited until the prince's death, and when the prince saw death approaching in 1376 he made Guichard guardian of his young son Richard, the future king. It was Guichard d'Angle who first suggested to John of Gaunt a marriage alliance with Constance of Castile, an alliance that, with luck, might permanently remove Castile from French influence; and it was Guichard who negotiated and finally achieved the marriage. When Guichard died, in 1380—beloved old hero and a faithful friend of King Edward's sons and grandson, now king—John of Gaunt, as a sign of the depth of his mourning for that emblem of steadfast faith and true chivalric valor, ordered payment "for 1000 masses sung for the soul of Guychard Dangle."

Listening to the stories Sir Guichard had to tell of dungeon murders, torture, cruel disfigurings, starvation, chains, and filth—mistreatment bad enough if dealt out to peasants but outrageous when bestowed on a man like Guichard—Chaucer must have felt that Pedro was at least a lesser evil compared with his enemies. In any event, when cool, black-eyed Constance, Pedro's daughter, arrived in England a few years later to take her place as Gaunt's wife, whatever doubts Chaucer may have harbored about Pedro were forgotten.

Meanwhile Edward's war with France dragged on. While the Black Prince had been fighting in Spain there had been between France and England a cessation of hostilities; but in January 1369, a rebellion had flared up against Edward in Gascony, with the tacit approval of the French king, Charles V. On May 21, Charles officially declared war on England, and on June 3, soon after he received the news, Edward reassumed the title "King of France." In September, Gaunt attacked, raiding France from Calais to Harfleur. Geoffrey Chaucer was with him.

It was a grim time to be trying to fight a war. England had been sunk in deep spiritual and economic depression since the autumn of 1368, when abnormally heavy rains had flooded the lowlands and made higher land so sodden it was difficult or impossible to plow. The acreage of sown wheat and other grains was low; and spring planting failed to make up for it, because that spring the pestilence struck again and by June was soughing through London. The court sealed itself off in Windsor, on the theory that the vast belt of park and forest made it relatively safe. Plague was kept at bay, but Death, as the *Pardoner's Tale* reveals, has schemes upon schemes. By July Queen Philippa was desperately ill and bedridden, though not with the plague. Her attendant ladies, including her beloved young Alice Perrers, who would later become King Edward's mistress—and including also Philippa Chaucer—sat beside her bed to read to her, kept hot cloths on her forehead, trying to break the fever, and watched in sorrow, probably, as her physicians bled her, unwittingly helping death along. The queen had none of her family around her but the king and their fourteen-year-old son, Thomas of Woodstock—the devoted, model child who would later become the earl of Gloucester and would be executed by King Richard for treason—and she had few of her beloved old friends near either, not Joan of Kent, not even Froissart, who was away accompanying Prince Lionel to the wedding that was soon to prove the death of him. On August 15 the queen received last rites. Froissart got there barely in time to see her die. He wrote later:

> And the good lady, whanne she knewe and parceyved that there was with her no remedy but dethe, she desyred to speke with the kynge her husbande, and whan he was before her, she put out of her bedde her right hande, and toke the kynge by his right hande, who was right sorowfull at his hert; then she said, Sir, we have in peace, joye, and great prosperyte, used all oure tyme toguyder: Sir, nowe I pray you at our departyng, that ye wyll graunt me thre desyres. The kynge, ryght sorowfully wepyng, sayd, Madame, desyre what ye wyll, I graunt it.
>
> Sir, sayde she, I requyre you firste of all, that all maner of people, suche as I have dault with all in their marchaundyse, on this syde the see or beyond, that it may please you to pay every thynge that I owe to theym, or to any other. And secondly, sir, all suche ordynaunce and promyses as I have made to the churches, as well of this countrey as beyonde the see, where as I have hadde my devocyon, that it maye please you to accomplysshe and to fullfyll the same. Thirdely, sir, I requyre you that it may please you to take none other sepulture, whan soever it shall please God to call you out of this transytorie lyfe, but besyde me in Westmynster. The kynge all wepynge, sayde, Madame, I graunt all your desyre. Than the good lady and quene made on her the signe of the crosse, and commaunded the kyng her husbande to God, and her youngest sone Thomas, who was there besyde her; and anone after she yelded up the spiryte, the whiche I beleve surely the holy angels receyved with great joy up to heven, for in all her lyfe she dyd neyther in thought nor dede thyng, wherby to lese her soule, as ferr as any creature coulde knowe. Thus the good quene of Englande dyed. . . . Of whose dethe tidynges came to Tornehen, into the Englysshe hoost, whereof every creature was sore displeased, and ryght soroufull, and specially her son the duke of Lancastre [John of Gaunt].

For all he had seen of plague and war, Gaunt was not a man who took the death of friends easily. For every loved one he lost, including his retainers and some of the retainers of his brothers, he established costly requiem masses and memorials, and he regularly did everything possible for the survivors of the deceased. Froissart's remarks suggest that Gaunt's grief, when he heard the news of his mother's death, was terrible indeed. Yet there was further sorrow to come to him in that plague year 1369, sorrow that would be shared to the fullest by his attendant Geoffrey Chaucer.

With a vast army and an unusually large and unwieldy store of provisions—it was a time of famine—John of Gaunt, probably with Chaucer in personal attendance, crossed the Channel on a military expedition into France. (Chaucer received £10—$2,400—"for reward or wages of war.") Gaunt's duchess, Blanche, with numerous retainers, accompanied her husband part way to the front, as was customary in knightly wars, and a part of Chaucer's business—he was now almost thirty—may well have been the care and entertainment of the duchess. No record spells out Chaucer's office, but years later he would receive the exact same amount for a job which included attendance on Queen Anne when Richard II was at war in Scotland, and we know that for much of his life, from the days with King Edward to the death of Queen Anne, Chaucer was valued partly for his ability to entertain ladies of the nobility with poetry and conversation, much as Jean Froissart used to entertain and provide company in the household of Philippa.

Perhaps Sir Richard Stury, one of the Black Prince's most trusted retainers, was also in France, probably with Gaunt. (No evidence survives, but it's certain that the Black Prince had one or two of his best men there to give advice as seasoned veterans of the prince's great battles.) The prospects for the campaign were bad, in fact dismal. Chaucer, Stury, the whole company knew it. They'd landed in a city that shrank back in alarm from strangers, shrank even from friends, for no one could say who might be bringing "the death." If there was merriment anywhere, it was the poisoned merriment Chaucer would write of in the *Pardoner's Tale,* the riotous debauchery of seedy taverns, churches of the Devil, where prostitutes frolic with drunken dancers and shooters of craps:

> tavernës,
> Where as with harpës, lutës, and gyternës   [*guitars*]
> They daunce and pleyen at dees bothë day and nyght,   [*dice*]
> And eten also and drynken over hir myght,
> Thurgh which they doon the devel sacrifisë
> Withinnë that develës temple, in cursed wisë . . .

Such pleasures were not for Chaucer and his friends. They settled the ladies into a castle in the country, a place they could hope might be safe from the plague, and while the lesser attendants brought in equipment from the wagons, opened wine, served food, and covered the cold bed-boards with mattresses and featherbeds, blankets and bolsters, Gaunt and his friends sat talking, since tomorrow they must ride out to the sprawling encampment and begin the slow trek into France.

Gaunt, that night, at the table beside his beautiful, pale wife, perhaps seemed for the moment to have put away his grief to speak easily, almost cheerfully, of how changed things were since their earlier visits, though autumn in France was always beautiful, of course. In the past the English had struck France from Flanders, sent on their way by eager allies. Not now. Back in 1363, when a wool staple had been established at Calais—a boon to the Flemish, who were thus made firm allies of England—King Edward had begun negotiations for marriage between his sixth son, Edmund Langley, earl of Cambridge, and Margaret, heiress not only to Flanders but also to the counties of Burgundy and Artois. Charles V of France, determined to block that dangerous alliance, had persuaded Pope Urban V to refuse the necessary dispensation, then himself had entered into the bargaining and, in this dark year 1369, had won Margaret as bride for his brother, Philip the Bold. English domination in Flanders was at an end.

That was no doubt at the back of Gaunt's mind too, as he talked on, speaking lightly of the world's great changes as if they had to do only with the weather, old friends moved away.

But beauty passes "like a shadow on a wall." Perhaps it was a servant, an old woman, who came hurrying from the pantry. Conversation broke off. Timidly, she asked permission to speak with the duke. Stury signalled to her; she spoke to him instead. He paled, then rose quickly, a little stiffly, and went to whisper with the duke. Gaunt said nothing for a moment, then at last announced that the company must move on to another place. A rat had been found dead. No one knew at the time exactly how it worked—how with the death of the rat, the rat fleas shifted not to cats or dogs but to the rat's age-old companion and ancient kinsman, man—but they knew what the death of the rat meant, and the whisper went round: "Pestilence!"

The damage was done. Four days later Blanche of Lancaster's skin had gone dark in patches like ink stains: Black Death. On parts of her body there were lumps the size of eggs; if they broke, there was a chance —but the pustules would not break. Her fever soared, she could not hear or see them. When Gaunt bent down to kiss her, a servant drew him back. And so Gaunt's beautiful young wife died. His grief was frightening, and though he turned his mind at once to war, his spirit was in ruins; he rode at the head of his army like a ghost.

There are politicians capable of taking deep grief in stride, ambitious men—which is not to deny that they may also be good men—for whom even the most terrible personal tragedies do not rob life of meaning, because power, for them—often the power to do good—is itself life's meaning. But John of Gaunt was no such man. Though it was rumored otherwise by those of his contemporaries who envied or feared him, he never sought power for himself or his sons, but supported the throne, as Steward of England, because he believed it was his duty. And though duty can be a strong motivating force, it gives cold comfort to a man whose beloved mother and wife have just died and whose dearest friend in the world, Gaunt's elder brother the Black Prince, is hurrying toward the grave. Chaucer watched Gaunt's sorrow, no doubt grieving himself for Blanche, and did for Gaunt the only thing he could do, began a poem. To be true to his feelings, true to the dignity of Gaunt and Blanche, it must be the finest elegy ever written in English; and in fact it would be, when Chaucer finished—long after he began, because a poem in memory of Blanche must be as large and airy and full of subtleties, teasing in-nuendoes, oddly lighted beauties, as a Gothic cathedral. Though a diffi-cult poem for modern readers, it stands today as one of the four or five great elegies in our language, a poem full of mystery and the queer shape-shifting common in our dreams. In her husband's memory, Lady White—Blanche—sums up all the beauty of the universe:

> For I dar swerë, withoutë doutë,
> That as the somerës sonnë bryght
> Ys fairer, clerer, and hath morë lyght
> Than any other planete in heven,
> The moone, or the sterrës seven,   [*the seven fixed stars*]
> For al the world so haddë she
> Surmounted hem alle of beauté . . .

And her death becomes one with the mutability of the universe, a source of absolute despair. Yet finally her love, like that of Dante's Beatrice, is the key to the knight's return to health, since her nature is not merely physical but spiritual as well: human love and divine love work by one same principle:

> My lady yaf me al hooly   [*gave me wholly*]
> The noble yifte of hir mercy . . .
> As helpë me God, I was as blyvë   [*swiftly*]
> Reysëd, as fro deth to lyvë . . .   [*raised*]

Lady White, in other words, sums up not only all that gives us delight in nature but also the benevolence of the unseen power nature veils. The

Book of the Duchess does, of course, far more—a lyrical and philosophical masterpiece—but the heart of its greatness is its convincing expression of Gaunt's love and grief, and Chaucer's anguish and concern.

Not too surprisingly, Gaunt's campaign in France went badly. Even if he'd been at his best, there was little he could do. Under the brilliant du Guesclin the French fought methodically, with infuriating patience—keeping out of sight, refusing battle except when they knew they had the clear advantage—as the Scots had done forty years ago, during Edward III's first campaign. Gaunt's army had no choice but vain ravaging marches, hunger and pestilence moving along with them, snatching at the stragglers. The duke was back in England from November 1369 to June 1370, consulting with his father and the Black Prince.

It must have been a painful meeting. It was the first the two brothers had seen of each other since the death of Blanche, and the Black Prince was much worse now, his once powerful body wasted to a skeleton. Yet they were king's sons; they got down to business quickly. What was wrong was clear enough. Whatever a man's courage and will to fight, he can't kill shadows and empty air, an invisible enemy like du Guesclin. But not even the Black Prince was sure, at first, what to do against the Frenchman's strategy. In September, sick of body and mind, furious at the war's dragging on and on, more allies abandoning the English every month, the Black Prince—over Gaunt's strong protest—turned on Limoges the tactics he'd despised when he'd seen King Pedro of Spain use them, and for him as for Pedro, they backfired. Former neutrals and indifferent peasants became fanatical Anglophobes. The Black Prince, feverish and raging, sailed home.

England's depression, and no doubt Chaucer's, deepened. In plague-gutted France and England, it was beginning to be remarked, chivalry was dead. Gunpowder was standard, and no longer used merely to frighten the horses. As defense against the longbow, breastplates and leg armor of leather were being added to chain mail, with the result that a knight was virtually helpless when down off his horse, hence easy to capture or—by the increasingly popular strategy of King Pedro—kill. Though there were still noble gentlemen of the kind that had rushed to their death at Crécy—still men like Richard Stury and Guichard d'Angle—they were becoming increasingly inferior, in general, to the seasoned and able, thoroughly unchivalric mercenary companies who would fight on any side, in any cause, whatever its morality, for cash. The "new English gentlery" was on its way, men whose code was that of the crusaders who would shame Christendom in the European campaign of the bishop of Norwich, slaughtering and seizing booty not from the infidel

but from Christian European burghers, or that of the knights who would
swear by the solemnest of all Christian oaths to give Richard II safe-
conduct, then treacherously seize and kill him. Not that French or English
gentlemen necessarily understood the extent to which ideals had declined
by the 1370's. Some remembered the code men once had served and believed that chivalry might even now be revived. But Geoffrey Chaucer,
for one, was not fooled. Late in the noble old poet's life, when chivalry
was in ruins—the genteel Christian code set forth in the thirteenth-century French poem *L'Ordene de Chevalerie* and dramatized in Wolfram
von Eschenbach's *Parzival,* and even practiced, to the letter, by Christian
knights like St. Louis and Henry of Lancaster—Geoffrey Chaucer would
create, with gentle irony, his "verray, parfit gentil knyght" and give him
a story, the magnificent *Knight's Tale,* which at once celebrates the ideals
of chivalry and reveals the old Knight's awareness of the code's decay.
In the tale the Knight tells, blood-sworn oaths mean nothing to his
knightly characters: in blatant violation of the knightly code they serve
a tyrant, Creon, and they lightly abandon their oaths to one another for
love of a woman they cannot even get to from their prison. Yet Chaucer's
storytelling Knight takes it casually enough, even shows affection for his
ignoble young heroes; and in the end that was no doubt Chaucer's stance.
For most men, especially the younger generation of poets and painters
from Italy to Scotland, the world had grown harsher, more desperate;
it was becoming the dark, endless forest of Sir Thomas Malory, a grim
cosmic joke redeemed only—if at all—by "courteous love." But Chaucer
was a wise and compassionate man, a man secure in his faith that God
had things in hand.

Devoted, like Gaunt, to the English royal court, he nevertheless knew
well enough that since the death of Queen Philippa it had decayed. Increasingly, it was ruled not by Edward himself but by his mistress Alice
Perrers, "the Lady of the Sun," a woman Chaucer undoubtedly admired,
though she had faults enough, and though history has taken a dim view
of her. Since her story is interesting, since she was a friend and in some
sense patron of Chaucer's, and since her rise to power provides insights
into the general moral decline at this period, it seems worth telling.

Chaucer may have known her, or known about her, from childhood,
since she came from his own class, his father's merchant circle. Like all
royal favorites, she came to be hated, at the peak of her power, and
contemporary stories of her background tell us only the extent to which
she was hated by those who made up the stories. Recently champions
have arisen to defend her, foremost among them F. George Kay, who has
written the first sympathetic biography.[1] Even Professor Kay has perhaps
been too cautious in giving Alice Perrers her due. At any rate, she was

Chaucer's good friend and saw to his welfare for as long as it lay in her power to do so, and she was equally a friend of John of Gaunt and others of Chaucer's circle. She was a woman of conviction; she was ferociously loyal; and if she fought tooth and nail for her own selfish good, she also fought for the rights and privileges of the crown, more on principle than for selfish gain, when King Edward, grieving, disillusioned, sick at heart, and tired half into his grave, no longer cared.

She was probably born in the plague year of 1348 or 1349, of middle-class parents, and no doubt she received some education or she would not have become lady-in-waiting to Queen Philippa. Her background may have been much like Chaucer's, since in court records she and Chaucer are frequently associated—they repeatedly received gifts on the same occasions, and Alice was serving at Gaunt's Savoy Palace at the same time as Philippa Chaucer, when both, on May 1, 1373, were given presents by the duke. It may be that one of Alice's early relatives had dealings with Chaucer's grandfather Robert, for Haldeen Braddy points out that

> . . . it was no other than Elias Pier (Peres, Piores, Pieres, etc.) who on September 14, 1309, succeeded Robert Chaucer (appointed November 15, 1308) as Deputy to the King's Butler in the City and Port of London. Moreover, on August 2, 1310, Robert le Chaucer and this same Elias Perr' (Perrers) were appointed, jointly or severally, to collect at the port of the City of London the custom on wines brought by merchant vintners from the Duchy of Aquitaine.[2]

When Alice was about eighteen, Queen Philippa was living in her favorite rural retreat at Havering, the unostentatious house in the woods that Edward the Confessor had praised as the most peaceful of residences —the house that by this time had become, traditionally, the personal property of a reigning monarch's consort or the permanent home of a widow queen. It was from this house, surrounded by huge, dark trees, old bridges, and flatlands reminiscent of the landscape of Philippa's birth, that tidings came of the queen's wish to hire a new maiden for her personal retinue.

The queen was fifty-four when she engaged Alice. She was no longer the vigorous woman she'd once been; she'd been thrown from a horse when she was forty-six and had suffered a dislocated shoulder, perhaps other injuries as well, and she was plagued now by abdominal pains and, within the year, would for a time take to her bed with dropsy. She was of course no complainer. She was the most beloved woman in all England, with a gift for arousing the immediate affection of everyone who met her. What she needed at the moment was a pleasant young lady to "do" for her, keep her company and take care of the tiresome, troublesome things that the queen was too weary and stiff to attend to. Alice's role with the queen's personal staff, in other words, was like that of lady of the bedchamber when that office was not a mere sinecure.

They obviously got on well. All her life Queen Philippa had surrounded herself with attractive, clever women and noble-hearted, cultured men. Such matters as birth and rank did not impress her. When young Jean Froissart had come to England to study the manners of the country traditionally hostile to his own, he was the son of an artisan, but Philippa in an instant saw through to the young man's true "gentillessë," as Chaucer would say, and invited him to be her guest in the royal household, where he remained for the rest of her life as her loyal servant, clerk, and diarist. She showed the same insight in choosing Alice Perrers, whose meteoric rise would have been impossible without Philippa's help. For example, within months of her arrival, Alice received a grant from the king of two tuns of Gascony wine to be delivered to her annually. This was no small gift—four hundred gallons of wine a year, worth as much as £10 ($2,400)—and since the king had had virtually no opportunity to know Alice at this time, Philippa must have suggested the gift herself, as an assurance of the new damoiselle's permanent security in the household.

When Alice was nineteen or so she met, through her attendance on Queen Philippa, Sir William Windsor. He had served with Prince Lionel in Ireland and, before that, with the Black Prince at the Battle of Poitiers. Despite the fact that his beginnings were relatively humble, though aristocratic, he did well for himself, eventually becoming "an active and valorous knight rich with great wealth which he had acquired by his martial prowess."

He'd returned with Lionel to England for discussions with the king of the thorny Irish question. He must have acquitted himself well, at least in Edward's opinion, since he was ordered back to Ireland as an assistant to the new governor, and later was made himself king's lieutenant for Ireland. He was in his thirties when Alice met him—nearly twice her age—but he must have had the usual chivalric accoutrements. When he and young Prince Lionel came to visit with Queen Philippa, Alice sat quietly listening, waiting for her mistress's commands. If her eyes shone, watching the old warrior, Queen Philippa surely knew. When Windsor returned to Ireland he left behind him a girl who would gladly keep him informed on court opinion and policy with regard to Ireland. She would later become his fiancée and, eventually, his wife, and when, long afterward, parliament condemned him, she would throw all caution to the winds to set Windsor free.[3]

When Philippa died, King Edward conscientiously carried out her

last requests and rewarded her faithful servants. His order to the Exchequer for such payments began with the sum of "ten marks yearly, at
Easter and Michaelmas, to our beloved damsel Alicia de Preston [a
scribal error for Perrers], late damsel to Philippa, late Queen of England." He gave similar gifts to eight other ladies who had served the
queen, but he described only Alice as "our beloved damsel." The phrase
carried no sexual or romantic significance; it marked only a subject whose
loyalty and position are especially deserving of mention. But those in the
know in King Edward's household understood his mentioning, with
special favor, and first on the list, a maiden of junior status on the late
queen's staff. And they probably approved. Weighed down by grief,
taxed by problems of war, desertion by his allies, and grim financial
troubles, and sorrowing over the continuing decline of his beloved Prince
Edward, the king could easily be forgiven his attachment to the not-
especially-beautiful but yielding and devoted—and intellectually remarkable—young Alice. In time she would become his sole reason for living,
and his subjects' approval would, little by little, be withdrawn. But for
a time at least she seemed a gift from heaven, a lady capable of keeping
the court a bustling, happy place where the king, for all his sorrow and
weariness, felt amused, felt even that he was still a great king, surrounded by bejeweled and interesting ladies, entertaining knights, rich
merchants of London (over whom Alice had particular influence), musicians, painters, the poet Geoffrey Chaucer, who was so regularly in attendance and so often seen with Alice that to strangers it seemed he was
her special protégé. F. George Kay writes of her,

> . . . this woman was no brainless doll with a pretty face and a be-
> witching sexuality. No one who rose from utter obscurity and for eight
> memorable years reigned as uncrowned Queen of an England where
> monarchy was almost absolute could be without feminine qualities near
> to genius. That she was not beautiful but had a beguiling tongue was
> intended by her contemporary critic as a damning criticism. It is, of
> course, a testimonial. Women with the personality and brains of the
> quality enjoyed by Alice Perrers are rare phenomena. Still fewer man-
> age to exploit them in a man's world.[4]

Whatever her ambition—and no one denies that Alice Perrers was ambitious, as Chaucer was (though Chaucer was more discreet)—all signs
agree that she loved King Edward and that Edward would scarcely have
survived without her calming devotion. Kay writes:

> The times of greatest infatuation on the part of the King . . .
> occurred when Alice was about twenty-eight. This was a mature age for
> a woman who proved to have the attraction of beauty and vigour as

never before. The average woman was regarded as entering middle age in her early thirties. She was more often than not dead before she reached thirty-five. But Alice Perrers was no average woman, and lived no ordinary life. Her adult days had been spent in the comfort and good living of the court, even if her childhood had been hard. . . . She had not been worn out by recurrent childbirth. The few descriptions of her, for the most part compiled in the crisis period of her life in the late 1370's, give grudging concession to her healthy physical appearance.

Perhaps more important is the fact that Edward III, through the experiences of his childhood, was the type of man who needed maternal love rather than a pretty toy. He got it from his Queen for more than forty years. And he enjoyed the same mixture of maternal and sexual love for the remaining eight years that were left to him as a widower.[5]

It must certainly have been her devotion to the king, rather than her notorious cunning, that won Alice the friendship of both the Black Prince and John of Gaunt. These things are of course impossible to decide, since some people see plots everywhere, while others see nothing but the best of intentions even in the most deadly vipers. (Chaucer, if asked, would surely have insisted that snakes have, like people, good intentions.) Certainly it must be admitted that Alice's admiration of the two great princes did not greatly interfere with her ambition. On the other hand, the princes were not slow to make use of Alice Perrers's easy access to the king, whether of necessity or because they admired her, agreed with her, and felt gratitude for the health she gave their father, whom they both loved.

As for Chaucer, who during this period had to deal with that group in government with whom Alice was most influential and to whom she was most beholden, corrupt political London merchants—customs collectors skimming the king's profits, and moneylenders lending to the king at inflated interest rates—there can be no doubt that her cunning and self-advancing machinations were the qualities he liked least in her; yet he could blink such faults, since for all her ambition, Alice Perrers could be selfless too. And in any case, her freedom was limited: she loved her husband, as royal mistresses seem frequently to have done; yet, as any devoted medieval subject would have done, she returned the king's love and did everything in her power to make him happy. To Chaucer, in short, she was a study for art—a brilliantly entertaining wit, a good, gentle woman, a thief, a harlot; she was, as a child of the poet's own merchant class, an astonishing success, and at the same time a woman dissatisfied, as firmly locked out of the aristocracy as Chaucer was himself—a kind of pet, a failure. Chaucer watched, forgiving and fascinated, hands behind his back, prepared to trade lightning fast puns with Dame Alice, discuss biblical exegesis or astronomy or, if she liked, perform some recent poem for the dazzling company she'd assembled for King Edward's amusement.

Her star was rising fast in the early 1370's, a woman in her early twenties, ten years younger than Chaucer. She persuaded the king—or the king decided without Alice's persuasion—to grant her Wendover, which had been, ever since Edward the Confessor had held it, one of the most desirable manors in the possession of the crown. It was a beautiful little township in the shire of Buckingham, with fertile land and access to valuable timber and swine food in the wooded hills. It was thirty miles from London but easy to reach, since it straddled Icknield Way, one of the busiest trading routes across the windmill-strewn flats from the ports of East Anglia to the green and rolling wool, leather, and grain-producing areas of the English southwest; and it was also approached by another major road, the ancient, chestnut-lined *Via Londoniensis*. Wendover was in the district where both John of Gaunt and the Black Prince had country estates. The Black Prince was living in the great castle of Berkhamsted, an excellent place for displaying his booty and receiving official guests, but draughty and uncomfortable and not good for his health, more a fortress than a home. He had also a smaller place in the same general area, a fortified castle at the foot of a steep escarpment, an ideal part-time home and stud farm for breeding warhorses. John of Gaunt was lord of the manor of Chalfont St. Peter, which he used only as a source of food and revenue for his vast household at the Savoy Palace in London; and he was also lord of the manor of Weston Turville, which almost adjoined the Wendover lands and was one of his favorite country residences.

The three near neighbors may not have seen each other often, since the king did not like Alice Perrers to leave his side, and since the princes were constantly involved in the crown's troubled business; but they got along amicably, despite the fact that Joan of Kent, wife of the Black Prince, did not care for Alice. (Though known once herself for extravagant dress, Joan found Alice vulgar and thoroughly distrusted her.) The peace between Gaunt, the Black Prince, and Dame Alice, their apparent agreement on all important issues, was a remarkable thing in fourteenth-century England and attests to the basic nobility of all three, whatever the general moral flaccidity of the Edwardian court or the flaws of character in Edward's mistress. If the Black Prince should die, leaving his young son Richard heir to England's throne, it was possible, especially if the child too should die, as medieval children all too commonly did, that John of Gaunt might succeed to the throne; and it was almost equally possible, as shown by England's position on the succession in Castile, that if Alice should bear an illegitimate child to King Edward, that child might also have a claim. Equally striking, Alice's ties were, as we've said, with the mercantile class of London, chief source of royal revenue (through customs) and with the mayors and moneylenders whom England's barons distrusted, even hated. Gaunt and Prince Edward were not only landed aristocrats but were, indeed, the two most powerful magnates in England. All this might have made for friction; yet in all important business, the three were in agreement, impartially and staunchly defending the rights of the crown, whoever might wear it. When outsiders needed help from England, now that Edward was growing more and more uninterested—he was in fact incapable of remembering even the names of his chief enemies—it was to the two princes and Alice that they appealed. For instance, when the new Pope, Gregory XI, crowned at Avignon on January 5, 1371, needed help in persuading the constable of Aquitaine to ransom the Pope's captured brother, he sent his appeal to the prince of England, John of Gaunt, and Alice Perrers.

King Edward was sliding into senility. He could no longer dream up, as once he'd done, brilliant or crackpot schemes for saving England from her financial woes; and this, along with the tendency of all favorites to snatch at whatever wealth they could, led Alice into evil ways. Even Queen Philippa, who lived very simply for a royal consort of her time and place, had grappled continually with domestic crises, loaded down with bills, frantically struggling to cope with the problems of keeping a half dozen houses ready for his majesty's use: Westminster, the Tower, Eltham, Sheen, Woodstock, Havering, and Wallingford, not to mention the houses farther from London where the king might need to go if there were trouble with Scotland or he felt inclined to do some hunting. To pay such bills—and to add to her own power—Alice turned to connivance with her old friends and cohorts, the less honest London merchants, many of them Chaucer's intimate associates, and also, by subtle and somewhat shocking means, to dipping into the royal till. One method she used— one of the least offensive—was to borrow money from the king personally, taking care that the amount was meticulously entered by the clerk of the wardrobe, and then to persuade the king to excuse the debt. Another trick, a good deal meaner, was to show Edward jewels he himself had given her, explaining that a merchant had let her borrow them to show him. The vague old king, for love of Alice, would desire the jewels now as much as he'd desired them the first time he'd seen them and would happily give her the money for them. On one occasion, or so it was later alleged by parliament at the time of her downfall, she obtained £397 ($95,280) in this way. Eventually she got, by the king's grant, all the jewels of Queen Philippa.

Despite such faults, which old King Edward clearly failed to remark and his sons, apparently, were willing to overlook, King Edward's love for Alice grew to manic proportions. The extreme was the great celebration of the Lady of the Sun. At a time when England was financially desperate and Londoners were furious at the crown's unending and merciless taxation, King Edward decided (or someone decided) to give Londoners a spectacle they would never forget. He, or someone, arranged a great procession and a seven-day tournament in honor of Alice Perrers—ostensibly a celebration of the end of Lent. Princes from all over Europe came, as well as street vendors, fortune-hunting mercenaries, pardoners, whores, friars, and cutpurses. The procession formed on the hill behind the Tower, Geoffrey Chaucer taking his place with the rest of the royal courtiers, arrayed in his finest, looking dignified and exceedingly pleased with the celebration, whatever he may privately have thought of it. The noisy, colorful procession moved along Tower Street into Chepe and on through Aldersgate to the area of the joust, and all the way, in the center of the glorious cavalcade—everyone else walking—rode the Lady of the Sun in her golden chariot. It may have been about this time that Chaucer began composing his *Anelida and Arcite,* which contains a striking image Chaucer might well have drawn from this very spectacle. Theseus returns from war with the Amazons leading his queen and a great procession:

[His lady] Faire in a char of gold he with him laddë,
              That al the ground about her char she spraddë
              With brightnesse and the beauté in her facë,
              Fulfillëd of largesse and of allë gracë.

The broad hint of paganism in the title given to Alice Perrers, "Lady of the Sun," was no accident. She was meant to be viewed as the courtly lover's mistress *par excellence.* As we see throughout the poetry of Chaucer, including his majestic *Book of the Duchess,* the poetic scheme of courtly love made Neoplatonic Christianity and a fanciful version of pagan religion or nature worship (with the lady as emblem of idealized nature) into analogues: as the Christian loves God, or Christ, or the Virgin, and is purified and improved by that love, his soul rising higher and higher toward the perfection of heaven, so the pagan worshipper of Pan, Cupid, or Venus—the god or goddess embodied in his lady—is purified and improved, provided, of course, that the lady and the love are "worthy." Just as pagan and Christian religion interpenetrate and at best present man with the same ideals, as even St. Augustine had grudgingly admitted and as classicists like Boccaccio now boldly asserted

—that is, just as pagan religion, especially in the writings of inspired men like Virgil, "touched and almost grasped the truth"—so this neo-pagan love religion, or this curious acting out of the *Canticle of Canticles,* might elevate the spirit by the metaphor of desirable flesh.

To Edward it must have seemed literally true that his lady had raised him "fro deth to lyve." His sons—and all London—apparently agreed that Alice had done a splendid thing in giving King Edward the will to live. If the whole festival seems to modern historians a trifle outrageous, it did not seem so then. The king's rejuvenation, the end of Lent, nature's springtime "resurrection," all called for observance, as spring always does in Chaucer. Even the sober Knight of the *Canterbury Tales* wholeheartedly approves, telling of the May worship of beautiful Emelye,

> that fairer was to senë
> Than is the lylie upon his stalkë grenë,
> And fressher than the May with floures newë—
> For with the rosë colour stroof hire hewë,   [*strove*]
> I noot which was the fyner of hem two—   [*know not*]
> Er it were day, as was hir wonë to do,   [*habit*]
> She was arisen and al redy dight;
> For May wole have no slogardie a-nyght.
> The sesoun priketh every gentil hertë,
> And maketh hym out of his slep to stertë,
> And seith, "Arys, and do thyn observauncë . . ."

It was only later, when her ambition and greed became boundless, that Englishmen began to say of her, as the allegorist William Langland did in his portrait of Alice as Lady Meed, or Reward/Bribery:

> I looked on my left hand, as the Lady [the Church] told me,
> And was aware of a woman [Lady Meed] wonderfully clad,
> Her robe fur-edged, the finest on earth,
> Crowned with a crown, the King hath no better;
> Fairly her fingers were fretted with rings,
> And in the rings red rubies, as red as a furnace,
> And diamonds of dearest price, and double sapphires—
> Sapphires and beryls, poison to destroy.
> Her rich robe of scarlet dye,
> Her ribbons set with gold, red gold, rare stones;
> Her array ravished me; such riches saw I never;
> I wondered who she was, and whose wife she were.
> "What is this woman," said I, "so wonderfully clad?"

> Quoth she, "That is Meed the maid; she oft hath harmed me;
> She hath slandered my love that is named Loyalty,
> And belied her to lords that have laws to keep.
> In the Pope's palace, she is private as I,
> But Truth would not have it so, for Meed is a bastard . . ."

The so-called Good Parliament of 1376—which Chaucer and John of Gaunt despised—would demand that Alice be stripped of all honors and removed from Edward's court. Chaucer could well understand, of course, the Commons' annoyance at the strain crafty Alice could put on the treasury; nevertheless, from Chaucer's point of view (as, of course, from Gaunt's), the Good Parliament was not only grossly unfeeling but it also, and more important, meddled with the crown's personal business and thus dangerously eroded the king's "ancient right." Nevertheless, Alice was forced out, and though she would return briefly from time to time, her power would from this point go down and down, one great drop after Edward died, in 1377, and another on the death of her husband, Sir William Windsor. One hopes she was not the lady mentioned in the Monmouth court record of 1397: *Item quod Jankyn ap Gwillum fornicatur cum Alicia Parrer*—a woman caught in fornication with a Welshman. (Alice would have been about fifty at the time.) However she may have ended up, it is certain that Alice Perrers became, as the years passed, increasingly cynical, increasingly litigious, increasingly corrupt. Declines of that sort were not uncommon in the late fourteenth century.

The eminent French historian Simeon Luce speaks of Chaucer as "le protégé de la favorite Alice Perrers."[6] Whether or not he has direct authority for the statement, it is undoubtedly true, at least in a broad sense. At very least they were a part of the same world, and if Chaucer had met with Alice's displeasure he would never have thrived there. Connections between Chaucer and Alice show up everywhere. Sir Philip la Vache, the friend to whom Chaucer addressed his short poem *Truth*, was associated in 1375 with Sir Philip of Courtenay, "admiral of the fleet towards the west," in the "gift and sale" of the marriage of a ward to "Dame Alice Perrers."[7] Chaucer's friend Sir Lewis Clifford, and Sir Guichard d'Angle, Prince Edward's beloved old retainer and the poet's fellow ambassador to France in 1377, were two of the seven mainpernors or guarantors of good conduct who, on August 20, 1376, won the release of Alice's husband William Windsor from the Tower. Sir Richard Stury, who was with Chaucer on numerous missions in England and abroad, was one of Alice's most fervent supporters. One anonymous contemporary chronicler asserts, no doubt correctly, that (along with Gaunt and Prince Edward) Stury, Lord Latimer (whom Chaucer knew well), and that "shameless woman & wanton harlott, called Ales Peres" were all close friends of Edward III, "That att there beck the Kynge permitted all matters of the realms to be disposed, & commyted also the government of hym selfe."

On some occasions, Dame Alice seems to have been either Chaucer's direct patron or the means by which John of Gaunt was able to get advantages for the poet. In 1374, Chaucer received free lease for life to the mansion over Aldgate. Most Chaucerians agree that Gaunt must have been influential in getting this prize for his friend. But Haldeen Braddy points out, rightly, that Gaunt had never owned property in the Aldgate area, whereas Alice had there valuable holdings, and that the rent-free grant (from London merchant-politicians) was one of Alice Perrers' specialties. She repeatedly won from the king rent-free holdings for herself and others, usually—as probably in this case—by finagling favors from London moneylenders, especially mayors (who controlled the property), when short finances were cramping the king. (Braddy goes on to say, "It is interesting that Chaucer's loss of the deed to Aldgate in 1386 should coincide so strikingly with Alice's own waning prosperity."[8] We now know that, almost certainly, Chaucer did not "lose" Aldgate but instead took a royal promotion and a much better house as a faithful friend of Richard II in his time of troubles.)

No one has suggested that Alice Perrers shows up in Chaucer's poetry. But given the way writers alter and redesign experience, we may well suspect that this brilliant and attractively vulgar woman did indeed leave her traces. Chaucer's court audience, who knew Alice well, may have thought of her briefly when they heard of that wonderful sex-kitten by the same name and the same affectionate diminutive, "Alisoun," who purrs and romps through the *Miller's Tale*. There is, heaven knows, nothing courtly about the Miller's Alisoun; nothing directly connects her with Alice Perrers but her name and the fact that, as Alice Perrers must sometimes have done, despite hostile chroniclers, she oozes sexuality:

> She was ful moorë blisful on to see
> Than is the newë pere-jonettë tree,   [*a kind of*
> And softer than the wolle is of a wether.   *pear tree*]
> And by hir girdel heeng a purs of lether,
> Tasselëd with silk, and perlëd with latoun.   [*a cheap metal*]
> In al this world, to seken up and doun,   [*seek*]
> There nys no man so wys that koude thenchë   [*think up*]

> So gay a popelote or swich a wenchë.   [*doll*]
> Ful brighter was the shynyng of hir hewë
> Than in the Tour the noble yforged newë.
> But of hir song, it was as loude and yernë
> As any swalwe sittynge on a bernë. . . .

Without rashly insisting that the portrait is anything like a lampoon aimed at Alice, we may note that here and throughout the tale the country wench and the king's mistress have certain trifles in common. The *pere-jonette*, or early pear, is associated in popular lyrics of the fourteenth century (for reasons no longer entirely clear) with illegitimacy; Alice was regularly accused by her enemies of bastardy. The cheap purse of latten, or imitation gold, might seem to the audience appropriate, since gold in the Middle Ages often symbolized (as for Plato) the aristocracy, and Alice was not quite the real thing. The image of the bright "shynyng of hir hewë" might easily suggest her character as Lady of the Sun; and she was indeed, to Edward, more precious than the "noble," a coin he invented and one which earned him both profit and prestige, as much profit and prestige as, loosely speaking, he lost on Alice Perrers. To elaborate the parallels would be to distort the poem, since the Alisoun of the *Miller's Tale* is much more and much less than Alice Perrers. The point is merely this: Chaucer's audience could hardly help but think of Alice Perrers from time to time as they listened to the poem.

Similarly, Alice Perrers, famous for her wit and intelligence, sexuality and ambition, may have provided part of the inspiration for Chaucer's single most magnificent character, middle-aged Dame Alice, the inexhaustible Wife of Bath. As J. M. Manly proved years ago, Chaucer and his audience delighted in in-jokes, personal satire or praise. It's true that, because of his association with Petherton Forest, Chaucer may have known various weavers, even some named Alice, from Walcot, the tiny village "besyde Bathe," and his courtly audience may just possibly have known this. Nevertheless, they might not unnaturally have remembered Alice Perrers when they considered the intelligence, humor, shameless sexuality, greed, ambition, sensitivity to slight, and, above all, the opinions of the Wife of Bath—her comically over-protested conviction that birth is irrelevant to true "gentillessë," her sympathetic view (which she shared with John of Gaunt and the Black Prince) of certain Lollard tenets, and her ability, given the right lover, to love truly and well. They might think of Alice, too, when it occurred to them that the Wife's tale is Irish in part of its origin, that is, that it came from the country where Alice Perrers' husband was lord lieutenant. The magical hag in the *Wife of Bath's Tale* is the traditional ghostly figure of Erin; and the implied political philosophy of the Wife's tale is the Irish persuasion that the subject should have a say in things. As the Wife claims that women, subject to men, should have a voice in family government, Irishmen claimed that the Irish, subject to England, should have a voice in the governing of Ireland. Needless to say, Chaucer's Wife of Bath, as a character in a fiction, is drawn from any number of real-life and literary models, but it may well have seemed to his original audience that Alice Perrers was one of them. If so, his at once comic and sympathetic portrait can have done her no harm with those in a position to support her.

In the heyday of the Lady of the Sun, Geoffrey Chaucer thrived. It was probably during this period that he began his significant travels for the crown. He'd traveled briefly to Spain in 1366, but he was apparently at that time a minor attendant. It seems barely possible that in 1368 he may have traveled to Italy to visit Prince Lionel. Speght, writing in 1598, quotes an old report that Chaucer was in attendance on his former master when Lionel went to marry Violante Visconti. That, we know, is not exactly right, since the wedding party left in May, and Chaucer not only received his annuity on May 25 (though not "into his own hands") but was still in England two months later (July 17, 1368), when he received a license to sail from Dover with £10 in exchange. If Chaucer was not back in England before October 31, 1368, when a half-yearly payment on his annuity was made, he may have been gone for 106 days. The £10 Chaucer was allowed to take with him was easily enough to carry him to Milan; but it's unlikely that he could make the long round trip, which in those days was usually taken overland, in 106 days. It therefore seems more likely that he traveled to Flanders in connection with the marriage negotiations involving Margaret of Flanders and Edward's son Edmund Langley (Chaucer would travel often as a marriage negotiator); or he may have gone as a diplomat to France or, possibly, Spain.

In 1369, as we've seen, he was with Gaunt in France, and he was again "abroad in the king's service" during the summer of 1370. Since his absence was brief, he may have gone to the Netherlands, or possibly to northern France, where Sir Robert Knoll's small army was raiding. The likelihood is that his business, once again, was diplomacy. A new treaty with Flanders was just at this moment about to be completed, and when Chaucer sailed home, negotiations with an envoy from Genoa were about to begin.

What may have been Chaucer's first major diplomatic assignment came in November 1372, when he was appointed to serve in a commission with two men of Genoa, Sir James of Provan and John of Mari (apparently head of the commission), to negotiate with the duke, citizens, and merchants of Genoa over the choice of some English port where the Genoese might form a commercial establishment. For his journey Chaucer received 100 marks ($16,000) in advance of the day he left London, December 1. He was away for about a year and eventually received for his expenses 138 marks ($21,480), calculated at the rate of 13s. 4d. ($160) a day. As his expense account suggests, his business was important. Foreign commercial establishments in English ports meant revenue for the English crown, and England was now—as usual—in desperate straits. But the trip was perhaps even more important for Chaucer the poet. The roll which records the payments made to him mentions that Chaucer's business had taken him to Florence as well as to Genoa, probably to negotiate a loan to King Edward, who depended heavily on the Bardi and Florentine financial houses; and there is reason to believe that he also saw Padua and there met the great Italian scholar-poet Petrarch. The trip is usually called Chaucer's first Italian journey, and though doubts have been expressed, the description is probably accurate. He was probably chosen for this present mission because he spoke some Italian. He had known Italians since his youth in London, where his father and mother had been associated with pepperers—guildsmen who dealt mainly with that exotic Italian fruit—and when he returned from Italy he would again be associated with Italians as controller of customs for the port of London, where he would deal with both royal creditors and Italian merchants.[9] Whether or not he knew Italian when he left for Italy, Italian poetry would be the chief influence on his own poetry when he returned.

The trip down to Italy was laborious and dangerous. Channel crossings —the first small step—could in themselves be murderous. Froissart tells us that Harve of Leon once set sail from Southampton with "the intent to arrive at Harfleur; but a storm took him on the sea which endured fyftene dayes, and lost his horses, which were cast into the sea, and Sir Harve of Leon was so sore troubled that he had never health after." King John of France, a few years later, took eleven days to cross the Channel, and King Edward once had a passage so grim he was convinced he was the victim of necromancers and wizards. Since Chaucer's main ambassadorial missions came after the English naval defeat of 1372, he had reason to fear not only rough weather but also French privateers.

Though winter had set in when Chaucer began his long journey, the trip down through France was serene enough. The weather was cold and the party had to press through heavy snow and wind, but it would warm as he moved southward; and as for the troubles between France and England, his papers from the king protected him. His party would encounter, in that bitter season, no battles in progress. But crossing the Alps in the dead of winter was an enterprise now almost unimaginable —"travel" in the original sense of "travail." The mountain trails were narrow, crooked, and badly kept up, roads the width of modern broad sidewalks that wound up mountainsides heavy with snow when Chaucer passed. (He would look down tentatively past his furs and the flanks of his wary horse and make out, far below him, dazzling icy rocks and that gray rushing water one sees only in Switzerland and the Himalayan mountains, and he would close his eyes for a moment and whisper, "A Goddes half!"—to which his fur-draped horse with a shudder expressed agreement.) The inhabitants of the mountains were queer, dour people, herdsmen and bandits who could appear from nowhere and vanish, it seemed, into the ice of the cliffs—though they would hardly dare trouble a large, well-armed party like Chaucer's. Then, when the Alps were towering behind his back, came what Dante called, in his *Purgatorio,* that "most desolate, most solitary way between Lerici and Turbia." For us, heirs of the Romantic poets, the dangers and privations of the long, hard trek would be redeemed by the breathtaking beauty of it all, but that sentiment would seem to Chaucer outlandish. There were, of course, some men of his time who liked such things—Yorkshiremen, for instance, like the *Gawain*-poet, who could say in *Sir Gawain and the Green Knight,* after scrutiny of the scene,

> They rode by hills where every bough lay bare
> And climbed in the bloom of cliffs where coldspots hung—
> The dark sky overcast, the low clouds ugly;
> Mists moved, wet, on the moor, and the mountain walls
> Were damp, every mountain a huge man hatted and mantled;
> Brooks boiled up muttering, bursting from banks all about them,
> And shattered, shining, on the stones as they showered down.
> The way through the wood wound, baffling, out and in,
> Till the hour of sunrise came and the sun rose cold
>   and bright.
>   They rode on a high hill's crown,
>   The snow all around them white . . .

But the beauty of the landscape, to Chaucer's way of thinking, would be curious stuff for a man to be squandering his wits on. Genoa, on the other hand, where the weather was as warm and fresh as an English summer, where highly civilized, artistic eyes had transmuted nature to a celebration of man's will—Genoa was something else again.

Italy was far ahead of England in many respects, though hindsight may tell us she was behind in others. England had what we now call Oxford rationalism, sire of modern science and industry; and England had the old Anglo-Saxon respect for human life, a sentiment Chaucer would find less primary, despite the influence of great men like Dante, in the land of ingenious torturers and poisoners. But Italy was, for Chaucer, as it would be for Henry James long afterward, impressively old and, however perilous, at least in an aesthetic sense, highly civilized. In England the Renaissance would be a startling discovery. In Italy it was already in full bloom.

Chaucer left a London of quaint stone, plaster, and wooden houses, winding streets like alleyways, lumbering cogs that could be broken to splinters by a good Channel storm, and arrived in a Genoa of Roman and mock-Roman (or Romanesque) columns—the Genoa Ruskin recorded in its decline—wide, smooth old streets, great domes and portals, a harbor where the fleet was, from an English point of view, futuristic. What Chaucer had grown up with, the wonderful rough-and-ready character of Englishmen, the blunt honesty and childish impulsiveness that could lead a devoted retainer to forget and draw his sword on the king himself, was a matter for aloof amusement to the Genoese. At least in the eyes of an Englishman like Chaucer, they were cool, darkly impressive, these Genoese. They had the aplomb we associate with English bank clerks, and they had, besides, a reputation as sharp traders. That Chaucer should be sent to deal with them is an indication of the respect his employers had for his facile tongue and canny eye. He was beginning to be known as an unusually good poet, and in fourteenth-century diplomacy, tone was important.

Not the least of Italy's charms was its music—a charm not lost on Geoffrey Chaucer, whose poetry makes repeated reference to music of every kind, from the singing of the old carpenter's young wife, "like a swallow on a barn," to the devilish thrum of tavern guitars in the *Pardoner's Tale* or the raucous brattle of bagpipes that brings the Canterbury pilgrims out of Southwerk. Leaning from his carriage, bending toward the window of his urban palace, or walking somewhat cautiously through the crowded, noisily polyglot markets, Chaucer heard music brimming, as it seemed, from all directions. Italy, then as now, was a country of song. Ancient Rome's musical leavings had become common street songs, as Puccini's arias are in our time the property of Naples' garbage men. In France, Chaucer knew, music was more experimental, more advanced—Machault was at about this time composing the first musical Mass by a single composer—but in Italy serious music, both religious and secular, was popular with all classes, as popular as were, back in England, barbaric lays like "Little Musgrave." In Italy as in England and throughout much of Europe, court composers wrote motets in the style of Machault, but in Italy, where so many kinds of music thrived, the delightful and intricate motet went more or less unnoticed.

Even more important, for Chaucer's future career at least, was Italian architecture. He would become, late in life, clerk of the king's works, that is, the public official responsible for most of the crown's great building projects; and it seems likely that Chaucer was involved, in one way or another, with repair or building projects throughout much of his career. He would be appointed controller of customs just when repair and rebuilding of the custom office and wharf were in progress, and he would move from that job to another involving building and maintenance, clerk of the king's works at Eltham, Sheen, and Greenwich. None of these jobs involved Chaucer directly as architect, but the hiring of architects was partly or wholly his responsibility—along with the buying and transporting of materials, payment of workers, and inspection of the work done—so his first-hand knowledge of Italian architecture was an important qualification. Since he began as controller immediately after his return from Italy, and since years later he would be sued for debt by (apparently) the carpenter in charge of the custom-office work (one never sued the crown, only the officer in charge of crown work; hence this suit against Chaucer may indicate that he was the supervisor of custom-office renovations), it seems possible that in choosing Chaucer for the mission to Italy, his employers instructed him to take a more than casual look at Tuscany's famous program of construction.

Especially in Florence, Italian architecture was a thing to widen a sophisticated Englishman's eyes. Chaucer saw, for instance, the extraordinarily beautiful double belt of stone walls that encircled the city, and the even more impressive ancient baptistry of St. John—to this day one of the most distinguished Christian monuments in Europe. Modern experts have been unable to determine whether it was built in the period of declining Rome, that is, sometime in the seventh century, or later;[10] but to the courtly nobleman who showed the baptistry to Chaucer, it was definitely known to be the oldest building in the world, going back to pagan times, when it was a temple of Mars (a legend believed until the end of the nineteenth century, when excavations proved the building was, *ab origine,* Christian). Actually, of course, Chaucer and his Italian guide were right, standing in that great, dim, mysterious building, imagining it filled with pagan specters performing the solemn and terrible rites of Mars; for whatever the persuasion of the unknown architect, those

majestic columns, capitals, and architraves he'd assembled from abandoned pagan temples had kept, as they keep even now, their ancient mood.
Other northern poets might take a small-minded view of the old religion,
imagining its rites to have taken place in huts, old mounds, dripping
caves; but Chaucer, having seen the baptistry, knew better and could
give ancient worshippers dignity and space:

> This Troilus, as he was wont to gidë   [*guide*]
> His youngë knyghtës, lad hem up and down   [*led*]
> In thilkë large temple on every sidë,   [*this same*]
> Byholding ay the ladiës of the town . . .

And he knew by those massive columns and stern, spare capitals the
solemnity and threat in the old religion, so he could write with grim
humor of Troilus' comeuppance when he mocks the God of Love, and
then

>   caste up the browë,   [*raised his eyebrow*]
> Ascauncës, "Loo! is this naught wisëly spoken?"   [*askance, as if to say*]
> At which the God of Lovë gan loken rowë   [*began to gaze down ruefully*]
> Right for despit, and shop for to ben wroken.   [*planned to be avenged*]
> He [Troilus] kidde anon his [Cupid's] bowë   [*found out pretty soon*]
>   nas naught broken;
> For sodeynly he hitte hym attë fullë . . .

When Chaucer saw it, the incrustation of white and green marble, inside
and outside the baptistry, had been in place for many years, as had the
glowing mosaics of the interior (far brighter then than now), the mosaic
envelope of the apse with its triumphal arch, and the mosaics of the
cupola, source of some of Dante's most striking images.

A few hundred steps eastward of the baptistry rose the palace of the
podesta (now known as the Bargello), one of the most impressive piles
reared anywhere in Italy in the age of the emerging third estate. Though
it was built by burghers—strong competitors, in Italy, of the old feudal
class—it outwardly followed the model of the square, stiff feudal castles
that dotted the hills of Tuscany, equipped with gates, moats, draw-
bridges, and battlements. But if, from outside, its imposing walls of
rough-hewn stone and its vigorous battlemented tower made it seem
the soul of Italian feudalism, it was something else altogether within: a
people's palace with a large and handsome inner court, columns supporting a spacious vaulted portico, and a great ceremonial stairway
leading to an impressive loggia at the level of the first storey.

Chaucer saw other great buildings throughout Florence, many of which survive today. The Dominicans had constructed, over the past century, their splendid monastic group of structures—churches, including Santa Maria Novella, cloisters, a refectory, a library, a chapter house, and a great bell tower. The Franciscans had constructed Santa Croce, a striking departure from stern, squared-off Florentine tradition, not quite northern Gothic but capturing some of that style's best features—well proportioned, rising on slender piers, the spacious interior flooded with light from choir and clerestory. There was the palace of priors—the present Palazzo Vecchio—and the bright, warm piazza created by the clearing away of the wrecked Uberti houses—the present Piazza Signoria.

There was the graceful hexagonal campanile still admired today, at that time part of the church of the Badia (the church itself was vulgarly rebuilt in the seventeenth century); the newly dedicated Or San Michele with its great covered loggia; and the rose-colored, marble-encrusted campanile of Santa Maria del Fiore, generally regarded as the loveliest architectural work in Florence. Much of this was new when Chaucer saw it: the thirteenth and fourteenth centuries made up a great period in Florentine building, though also there were structures as old as the Tuscan hills.

The crowning architectural pleasure of Chaucer's tour, a work that cannot help having influenced his artistic vision, subtly moving him toward his late, so-called realistic style (whether or not it left its mark on some English building long since fallen), was Giotto's campanile, just nearing completion when Chaucer first looked at it. (Giotto had died in 1337, at the age of seventy; the tower was not completed for another half century.) Though its effect was achieved not by buttresses and windows but by the ingenious patterning of light stone and dark, it made most other towers seem old-fashioned and sunk in gloom. Giotto had lived to carry his project only to just above the first row of sculptures, but that was enough to give his stamp to the entire work, and it was finished with only minor deviations from his plan. Probably the first seven panels on the west face of the campanile are Giotto's own. In any event, it is in their subject matter and style that these were chiefly important, we may imagine, for Chaucer. The series begins with the creation of Adam, continues with the creation of Eve, then depicts the Fall. On this third panel, Adam is delving and Eve spinning, in accord with the curse they've drawn down on themselves. From this orthodox beginning Giotto and his disciple, Andrea Pisano, move, in a continuous band enclosing the four sides of the tower, to a record of the inventions and occupations which measure the rise of civilized man. (The tower's fourth side was blank when Chaucer saw it, to be filled in long afterward.) It was this startling development from the populist premise of Florentine architecture—this "humanism" in Giotto's work, not only in the sculptures but in his paintings and richly colored frescoes as well—that made his art so new and exciting and for a time informed the vision of every artist around him.

No doubt Chaucer saw, too, the greatest surviving example of this new humanistic movement in art, Pisano's chief work, carried out between 1330 and 1336, the magnificent bronze doors for the baptistry. Andrea Pisano's relief figures—the eight single figures representing the theological and moral virtues, and the numerous figures making up the twenty scenes from the life of St. John—have not only the simplicity and directness of Giotto's imagery but also a new delight in the free movement of the human body that Giotto, in pursuit of his ideal of static dignity, had avoided. Such "realism"—whatever that elastic term may mean—became the mark of Florentine art in the latter half of the fourteenth century, appearing on carved altars, doors, and windows, in piazza sculptures, and the ornamentation of books. It marked a vision of man that went back to classical times, recalled by Virgil's parting speech to Dante in the *Purgatorio*, "Henceforth take your own will as your guide . . . I make you king and high priest over yourself." It was the vision being expressed, in the north, in scholastic and post-scholastic pursuits—in the emphasis on "experience" as opposed to "authority," in the concern of Oxford scientists with the discrete scientific question without relation to metaphysics, and in the independent thought of religious reformers that would ultimately, through Hus, Calvin, and Luther, take Dante's words "high priest" in earnest, launching the Protestant Reformation. But in Italy, especially in Tuscany, the new focus on human experience was not abstract and intellectual, but palpable art, the kind of humanistic argument one actually might, in the words of the eagle in Chaucer's *House of Fame*, "shake by the bills," because it was concrete and physical, not crepuscular logic; it was such argument as Chaucer would himself advance in his greatest Italian-influenced works, *Troilus and Criseyde* and the *Canterbury Tales*. Wherever he went in Florence, Chaucer saw frescoes, paintings, and sculptures that celebrated humanness: man's warts, the roughness of his elbows, the distortion of his shoulders when he walked with a Bible clamped under one arm, and also man's inclination toward nobility and goodness.

"*Chè bello,*" said Chaucer, no doubt, like all tourists to Italy then and now, and (if he knew no Italian) closed his phrasebook.

Phrasebooks for medieval travelers, I might mention, could be had in all the major languages. They were approximately as ridiculous as the ones we use today, as an example will show—I quote only the English:

"God commend you and guard you from evil, my friend."

"Sir, you be welcome."

"What hour of the day is it, prime or tierce, noon or nones? . . ."

"Between six and seven."

"How far is it from here to Paris?"

"Twelve leagues and far enough."

"Is the road good?"

"Yes, so God help me."

"Of these two, is this the right road?"

"God help me, sweet sir, no."[11]

Scholars have debated whether or not Chaucer ever met Italy's two greatest literary humanists, Francesco Petrarch and Giovanni Boccaccio, and have tended to conclude that he probably did not. But at least in the case of Petrarch, we have more to go on than our romantic wish that great poets should know each other. In the Prologue to the *Clerk's Tale,* Chaucer's Oxford Clerk tells the Canterbury pilgrims that he learned his story of patient Griselda from the Italian scholar Petrarch "at Padua." As it happens, during the very year of Chaucer's visit, Petrarch had just translated the tale into Latin from the *Decameron,* and during that same year, a time of war, Petrarch was forced to flee his home in Arquà for refuge inside Padua's fortifications. Such accurate information about the Italian poet's whereabouts and poetic occupation strongly argues that Chaucer met him.[12] If they did meet and talk, it seems incredible that the name of Petrarch's brilliant young disciple Boccaccio should not come up, especially since the old man had recently deemed one of his disciple's works worthy of elevation into Latin.

Nevertheless most scholars believe Chaucer did not meet or, perhaps, even know the name of Boccaccio, even though Chaucer left Florence only a short time before Boccaccio's first lecture there on Dante. Chaucer borrows from the writings of Boccaccio even more frequently than he borrows from Petrarch, but he never names Boccaccio as his source, and often when he quotes from Boccaccio or acknowledges indebtedness, he gives some name other than Boccaccio's. Such evidence, of course, hardly closes the case. As a medieval poet, Chaucer is not always careful to give credit. He names his sources only for artistic reasons—to achieve a certain tone, to deny personal responsibility, and so on—never from the modern sense that a literary source is some other writer's property. For all we know, Chaucer and Boccaccio may have been well acquainted, may have laughed endlessly at each other's bawdy stories, and may simply not have had occasion to mention their acquaintance in any of their writings. But it seems more likely that the two did not meet and that in

borrowing from Boccaccio Chaucer worked from anonymous or pseu-
donymous manuscripts of the sort more common than not in the late
Middle Ages.

Boccaccio's influence on Chaucer's poetry is in any case second only
to that of Dante. One sees the Boccaccio influence everywhere, not only
in the plot and general approach of major poems like *Troilus and
Criseyde* but also in the easygoing irreverence, the unabashed delight in
obscenity that makes the erotic in Chaucer so much more vivid, in fact
so much more healthy, than the erotica of our own day. Think, for instance, of his wickedly, deliciously voyeuristic passage, developed from
an image by Boccaccio, on Venus reclining on her couch in the temple
of Love:

And in a privë corner in disport	[*secret; in pleasant activity*]
Fond I Venus and hirë porter Richessë,	[*Found; Wealth*]
That was ful noble and hautayn of hyrë port.	[*haughty*]
Derk was that placë, but afterward lightnessë	
I saw a lyte, unnethe it myghtë be lessë,	[*not easily*]
And on a bed of gold she lay to restë,	
Til that the hotë sonne gan to westë.	
Hyre gilte herës with a golden thred	
Ibounden were, untressëd as she lay,	
And naked from the brest unto the hed	
Men myghte hire sen; and, sothly for to say,	
The remenaunt was wel keverëd to my pay,	[*delight*]
Ryght with a subtyl coverchef of Valencë—	
Ther nas no thikkerë cloth of no defensë.	

As everywhere in Chaucer, and as in Boccaccio's best-known tales, the
naughtiness is blatant, the narrator creeping up in what at first seems
perfect darkness to spy on the lovemaking of Venus and her porter, then
his undisguisedly wicked description leading to the transparent cloth
which provides "no defense." We see the same openness in all of Chaucer's
bawdy scenes—when Pandarus throws poor young Troilus, who has
just fainted from embarrassment, into bed with Criseyde and hurriedly
tears from him everything but his shirt, or when young May, in the
Merchant's Tale, climbs up her blind husband's back to be swyved by
her lover in the pear tree. Such stories were of course not unknown in
England. We find bawdy enough in the thirteenth-century debate, *The
Owl and the Nightingale.* But it was in the work of Boccaccio that sex
came to be humanized, so that its pleasures might be mentioned in con-

nection not only with fools and country wenches but even with noble
and sympathetic characters like Prince Troilus.

It was also during his first diplomatic visit to Italy that Chaucer encountered the poetry of Dante Alighieri. We have no reason to believe
that Chaucer was at this moment "going through an intense religious
crisis," or that "Dante's mysticism may well have carried Chaucer off
his feet for a time."[13] But it is certainly true that the influence of Dante
on Chaucer's later style and way of thinking is incalculable. Though
Dante was typically medieval in his Thomistic Christianity, one special
quality impelled him forward toward the Renaissance: his all-consuming,
unsubmergeable personality—what he might himself have called his
pride. In a city of factions, where his role was laid down by heredity, he
was, as he says, his own party in politics. His minutely accurate observation of individual human characters and events, his eye for the fine details of nature, from rocks to warring lizards—above all his ability to
suffuse the allegory of his *Commedia* with personal emotion, made him
the unrivaled master poet of his age and the founder of all modern literature, with its characteristic emphasis on personal vision, that is, art
as "a portrait of the artist." Dante's genius would cast strange reflections
in Chaucer's poetry—the sublime landscape of the *Commedia* becoming
the burlesque-sublime scenery of the *House of Fame,* the precise, often
tragic characterization in, especially, the *Inferno* and *Purgatorio* becoming
the comic and satiric portraiture of the *Canterbury Tales*—but however
transformed by Chaucer's art, Dante's powerful influence would from
now on always be visible.

That influence is clear as early as Chaucer's *Parliament of Birds,*
probably written around 1377. Dante's third canto of the *Inferno* opens:
"Per me si va," "Through me the way," or "Through me one goes . . ."
repeated three times, like strokes of doom—the message on hell's
gate warning of the terrible significance of sin, man's refusal of God
and all God is: power, wisdom, love. Dante is "arrested" by the gate's
"dreadful sense" and can for a moment move no further. Chaucer can
hardly have missed the power of Dante's image: the towering portal of
hell with its message of "Abandon hope all ye who enter here"; but in
his own dream in the *Parliament,* it is not the gate of hell he stands before but the gate opening into the garden of Love, which can either
uplift or destroy, and so Chaucer is arrested not by awe and fear but by
confusion, since the gate's two signs (one on each gatepost) contradict
each other:

> "Thorgh me men gon into that blysful placë
> Of hertës hele and dedly woundës curë;

Thorgh me men gon unto the welle of gracë,
Therë grene and lusty May shal evere endurë.
This is the wey to al good aventurë.
Be glad, thow redere, and thy sorwe of-castë;
Al open am I—passe in, and sped thee fastë!"

"Thorgh me men gon," than spak that other sidë,
"Unto the mortal strokës of the sperë
Of which Disdayn and Daunger is the gydë,
Ther neverë tre shal fruyt ne levës berë.
This strem yow ledeth to the sorweful werë   [weir]
There as the fish in prysoun is al dryë;
Th'eschewing is only the remedyë!"

Dante is guided out of his dread by Virgil's sound reasoning; Chaucer is comically dragged into the garden by force. As Dante well understood, Love can lead either to hell, as it led Paolo and Francesca, or to heaven, as Dante's beloved Beatrice hopes to lead Dante. Dante is therefore a willing and virtuous lover. Chaucer, poor comic clod, has "lost his taste for love," as his guide tells him. In short, though Chaucer's poem is comic, not a noble vision but the vision of a clown, it plays with and develops ideas out of Dante. The same might be said of innumerable short passages or whole poems by Chaucer. But Dante's influence is also visible in ways more fundamental. It is largely Dante's compassionate view of the sinful that makes possible Chaucer's similar compassion toward people undone by love, like Troilus. After Dante has seen Paolo and Francesca buffeted through hell to the end of time on the wind of their passion, he falls silent, grieving, thinking how many sweet thoughts brought them to this pass. However one may judge them from a Christian point of view, one cannot help but pity them and partly admire them. In the same way, Chaucer pays beautiful tribute to Troilus' perhaps excessive but nevertheless sincere and devoted love. In Book V he has, for instance, a magnificent scene in which Troilus finds Criseyde's house closed and shuttered, and knows she has left Troy. He weeps at sight of the barred doors and cries out to the house as to a body from which the spirit is gone, or a "lanterne of which queynt [quenched] is the light," and soon after, Chaucer writes,

Fro thennësforth he rideth up and down,
And every thyng com hym to remembraunce
As he rood forby placës of the town   [past]
In which he whilom hadde al his plesaunce.

"Lo, yonder saugh ich last my lady dauncë;   [*saw*]
   And in that temple, with hire eyen cleerë,
   Me kaughtë first my rightë lady derë. . . .

"And at that corner, in the yonder hous,
   Herde I myn alderlevest lady deerë   [*most beloved*]
   So wommanly, with vois melodious,
   Syngen so wel, so goodly, and so clerë,
   That in my soulë yet me thynketh ich herë
   The blisful sown; and in that yonder placë
   My lady first me took unto hirë gracë."

Many a medieval poet before Dante had experienced love, but Dante's poetry, more than that of any other poet of his time, made the subject legitimate and noble.

Dante's disciples Petrarch and Boccaccio were of course more openly "modern." Though it has been argued, in recent times, that Petrarch's *Canzoniere* are allegorical as well as literal, it is nevertheless true that the poems are—whatever else—the introspective record of a poet's moods. It was the same self-conscious individualism, the same self-regarding restlessness, that sent Petrarch wandering over Italy and France and even to Bohemia, like some enthusiastic nineteenth-century impression seeker; and it was the same restlessness, or anxious modern search, that impelled him to study ancient Latin literature and comb the south of Europe for manuscripts of new works and forgotten authors, picking through old libraries, laboriously copying or buying dim, cracked parchments. It was much the same with his Florentine disciple Boccaccio. He too has been accused (not convincingly) of allegorical intentions, even in the *Decameron*,[14] but the *Decameron* is, whatever else, a collection of tales instinct with humanness precisely and sensually observed, exactly the kind of work Chaucer would repeatedly produce after his first trip to Italy. Like Petrarch, Boccaccio devoted himself to ancient Latin writers, wrote scholarly Latin on eminent lives and ancient mythology, and hunted for old manuscripts. He even housed an apparently repulsive Calabrian, who for Boccaccio's benefit miserably translated Homer into Latin. Chaucer would follow much the same pattern, collecting books, studying ancient writers, and writing about life for its own sake.

Chaucer's first ambassadorial mission to Italy, in short, was a turning point in his poetic career. He would immediately begin writing short lives (preserved as the *Monk's Tale*) of the sort Petrarch and Boccaccio were writing, and he would turn more and more from now on to themes and techniques out of Dante.

The trip to Italy also seems to have boosted his career as servant to the king. Within three months of his return from Italy he was sent on a related journey, escorting an arrested ship from the port of Dartmouth to her master, a merchant of Genoa. (It was while he was at Dartmouth, presumably, that he found suggestions for his portrait of the Dartmouth Shipman in the *Canterbury Tales.*) Life was soon to improve still further for Chaucer: in recompense for arduous but important journeys, and other business for the crown, he would be rewarded with a fine house, lucrative opportunities, and, above all, time to write.

Six: Chaucer's Adventures as Celebrated Poet, Civil Servant, and Diplomat in the Declining Years of King Edward III (1374-1377), with Some Remarks on Chaucer's Honesty and Comments on his Art

IN 1374, IMMEDIATELY AFTER JOHN OF Gaunt's return to England from abroad, honors began falling to the poet thick and fast. On St. George's Day, the great time of religious and chivalric celebration for the Order of the Garter, the king granted him a pitcher of wine for life, a gift commuted in 1378 to cash. On May 10, Chaucer was given a lifetime rent-free lease on a fine house built over Aldgate on the London city wall, probably in connection with a government post he'd already been granted informally and was officially awarded on June 8, the office of controller of customs and subsidies, with the obligation of regular attendance at his office in the port of London, and of writing the rolls with his own hand. On the 13th of June, five days after his appointment to the controllership, Chaucer received yet another prize, an annual pension of £10 ($2,400) from John of Gaunt.

From these records and others we can deduce a good deal about how Chaucer occupied himself in the last years of the reign of King Edward III. The pitcher of wine for life, granted on the day of the Festival of St. George, patron saint of Edward's Order of the Garter, was probably —as were similar prizes to later poets—an award to Chaucer for his reading of some poem at court. Judging from other medieval English poems probably associated with St. George's Day—the alliterative *Winner and Waster,* which makes explicit reference to the Order of the Garter, and *Sir Gawain and the Green Knight,* which has the motto of the Order tacked on at the end (though not by the same scribal hand that had copied out the poem)—we may assume that Chaucer's poem for the court was a long one, an assumption we would make in any case, recalling how luxurious and lengthy these Garter festivities were in the fourteenth century. Garter knights were wealthy men and came, as did their ladies and servants, dressed in their finest, all the nobility adazzle in jewels, wrapped in splendid cloaks and capes trimmed with silver and gold or with costly furs.

As star poet of the occasion, Chaucer too came dressed to the nines. He was not, after all, some poor traveling minstrel who would be ushered into the dining hall for one quick performance, paid a few pennies, and whisked away by the royal marshal. (It was because of the marshal's absolute sway over visiting poets, some critics think, that Sir Kay, the marshal in King Arthur's court, is regularly presented in the Arthurian legends as a philistine, dimwit, and scoundrel.) Like Froissart, or like Deschamps and Machault in France, Chaucer was an intellectual ornament of the court, one of those government treasures, so to speak, that proved the court's worth and class. We have a record from much later of his receiving from the king a fine scarlet robe. He no doubt received similar, though perhaps less spectacular, gifts earlier, though no records survive. At any rate, we may be sure Chaucer's performance that day was a central event, second only, perhaps, to the closing masque—the play and magic show that led to general dancing of the guests and closed the festivities. His performance of his poem probably took place not inside the castle but outdoors, perhaps at the entrance of a gorgeous pavilion as large as a small circus tent but infinitely more costly, decorated all around with flowers, huge battle shields, and heraldic flags and banners. As he read he may have been flanked, like the speakers in *Winner and Waster,* by knights in odd costumes, some wearing the heads of symbolic beasts. It was now early spring in Chaucer's England, and the mysterious connections between the physical and the spiritual were always a central element in celebrations of the festival of St. George.

It's natural to wonder what poem it was that Chaucer read on St. George's Day, 1374—if the wine-gift was really for his reading of a poem. Most Chaucerians agree that it cannot be among the surviving works and that it can therefore never be identified; yet it's interesting to notice that on the basis of Chaucer's lists of his poems (in the *Legend of Good Women,* the Prologue to the *Man of Law's Tale,* and the "Retraction") no major work seems to be missing except for the mysterious "Book of the Lion," which was probably a translation from a famous French poem of the same title. A first-rate translation of a courtly French poem might well qualify for Order of the Garter festivities, especially when we remember that "translation" in the Middle Ages often meant imaginative reworking. We know that, not too much earlier than 1374, Chaucer had borrowed heavily from French poetry for his *Book of the Duchess,* and despite his borrowing had made that work a poem of extraordinary originality. We know too that soon after his first Italian trip, Chaucer began to draw more and more from Italian sources—

Petrarch, Boccaccio, and Dante. It is thus quite possible that the lost "Book of the Lion," still largely French in influence, if the title gives us any clue, was the poem with which Chaucer won his pitcher of wine.

When he was made controller of customs and subsidies for the port of London, Chaucer was required, as we've said, to attend to the work in person and write the rolls with his own hand. These obligations were not, as some writers have thought, mere technicalities. They involved Chaucer in personal hard work of great importance to the crown finances. It is true that, by means of an official or unofficial deputy, the obligation to do the work in person could sometimes be sidestepped or temporarily dropped, if the king had need of his controller's talents elsewhere. We know that Chaucer went abroad more than once during his years as controller. But the *House of Fame* tells us that Chaucer did fulfill his obligations in person much of the time, or at least wanted his courtly audience to think he did, and that like most of Chaucer's work for the crown it was laborious. In that poem, in a passage I've quoted earlier in this book, the eagle says of him:

> Thou herist neyther that ne this;
> For when thy labour doon al ys,
> And hast mad allë thy rekenyngës,
> In stede of reste and newë thyngës,
> Thou goost hom to thy hous anoon,
> And, also domb as any stoon,
> Thou sittest at another book
> Tyl fully daswed ys thy look. . . .   [*dazed*]

There was good reason for the requirement that Chaucer do the customhouse reckonings himself. Aside from borrowing from London merchants or foreign bankers, customs collection was the crown's chief source of revenue, and in Chaucer's time, as throughout the fourteenth century, customs collectors—the men whose figures Chaucer must audit and check against his own—were notoriously crooked. They were also, as it happens, men of great power, often London mayors with a penchant for hanging their enemies without trial. Needless to say, this put Chaucer in an awkward position. Most Chaucerian scholarship assumes that Chaucer deplored the goings on of the crooks all around him. But one may wonder if that is so.

As controller Chaucer dealt with a number of important and influential London merchants, all friends of Alice Perrers, all of doubtful character. The city's economic life was for the most part dominated by the powerful victuallers' guild, which was dominated in turn by a few wealthy merchants who, according to complaints in the House of Commons, conspired to keep up food prices, lent money to the king at inflated interest, and through their personal and financial influence persuaded the king to issue edicts profitable to themselves. Among these wealthy merchants, the ringleaders were William Walworth (the man we will encounter later as the murderer of Wat Tyler), John Philipot, and Nicholas Brembre. Their main competition, which had the support of John of Gaunt, came from the mercers' guild (traditional enemies of the victuallers), led by two merchants, Richard Lyons and John Northampton, men of perhaps equally doubtful character. The extent of these merchants' dishonesty is a little uncertain—the "trial" which sentenced Brembre to hang was hardly a fair one even by medieval standards—but Professor George Williams' assessment is probably not far wrong.

> Brembre, the victualler, turned out to be a political gangster and murderer, as well as a large-scale grafter, who was later hanged for his crimes; Lyons was an utter scoundrel who was beheaded by the peasants in the rising of 1381; Northampton was imprisoned for his lawless and dictatorial deeds as Lord Mayor (and £22, or $4,400 [now as much as $5,280] was paid to his enemy Brembre for conducting him to Corfe Castle!). Walworth and Philipot were far less crude operators than these three. Indeed, there is nothing especially heinous in the records of either. Yet Walworth kept a string of bawdy houses, was one of those who lent money to the government and, by devious means, secured an exorbitant rate of return, was the leader of a monopolistic group of food profiteers, influenced the government that was in debt to him to issue trading regulations that profited him and his clique enormously, was closely associated for years with Brembre, and (despite his extensive interests otherwise) found time to be a customs collector in a port whose mere wool trade alone grossed, in customs fees of various sorts, sums mounting up to $4 million [now $4,800,000] annually. Philipot is also pictured in conventional history as an honorable man devoted to his country, and hostile to the evil machinations of John of Gaunt. But he too was a food monopolist, a lender to the king, a collector of the customs, and an associate of the unspeakable Brembre.[1]

During all but two of the twelve years Geoffrey Chaucer was controller, one of the trio of Brembre, Walworth, and Philipot was a collector of customs, paying Chaucer's salary of £10 ($2,400) out of their immense takings in fees, and dividing fines and bonuses with him. How did Chaucer feel about these shady associations? He himself, after all, was in a position for considerable crookedness, if he felt the inclination.

In Professor Williams' view—the standard view in Chaucer studies—

the poet invariably sided with John of Gaunt and Gaunt's friends or political supporters the mercers against victuallers Brembre, Walworth, and Philipot. But issues in the court of senile King Edward, those last three years, and in the court of his grandson and successor Richard II, afterward, were not so clear-cut. Young Richard's advisers, as we'll see, urged a theory of monarchial absolutism, and the victuallers, who opposed moderates like Gaunt, were among King Richard II's most loyal supporters.[2] The "unspeakable Brembre" died, in fact, because instead of fleeing with his friends he stayed in London trying to raise an army for the king. Chaucer's later career—his promotions and favors while Gaunt was away from England in the late 1380's, his diplomatic associations with Ricardian absolutists like Simon Burley, his known friendship with men like Richard Stury, who were at various times jailed for profiteering and the like, and his choice, almost certainly manipulated by Richard, as representative from Kent in the opposition parliament of 1386, a parliament Richard knew would be devoted to clipping the wings of his favorites—suggests that Chaucer was in his earlier days not merely tolerant of Richard's supporters but was himself one of the principles. This is not to deny that he was John of Gaunt's friend; but he was also (as was Gaunt, despite disagreements) a friend of the king. Compared to men like Brembre, Chaucer was a relatively powerless royalist, of course, but royalist and absolutist he surely was; in other words, he was one of those troublesome "court favorites." The view that Chaucer was infallibly high-minded and incorruptible requires us to believe that Chaucer was the exception to the rule among Richard's courtiers and friends. Possibly that view is right, but in general, at least, corruption corrupts, and in a whole barrel of rotten apples it is extraordinary to find one absolutely sound one. The truth is perhaps that we're applying here modern standards of morality (standards seldom realized even in modern politics) to a world that would blink at such standards in amazement.

At very least we must say that if Chaucer was a devotedly honest man, he was certainly fortunate in always happening to be looking the wrong way. A few of his friends and fellow poets spoke out or took action against government corruption, and some of them—for instance, young Thomas Usk—were hanged for it. Geoffrey Chaucer was a survivor and, incidentally, a man who repeatedly fell into appointments normally sought after by people notoriously unscrupulous. (His later office as justice of the peace was outrageous in this regard.) And surely we may add that if Chaucer was not himself a rascal, he certainly is, in the poetry he wrote, one of the world's great celebrators of rascals.

But whatever Chaucer thought, there was nothing he could do about his friends' or, at the least, associates' activities in those last years of King Edward's reign or later when he served Edward's grandson. Brembre and company could be dangerous enemies to anyone who opposed them. Though he may have disliked Nick Brembre personally and may perhaps have preferred John of Gaunt's friend, the rival crook Northampton (who achieved the execution of the poet Thomas Usk), Chaucer stirred up no trouble, merely waited for things to mend.

Meanwhile, the office he received under Edward III in 1374 had its good points, among them the mansion over Aldgate. It was a grand house, a veritable town castle which had sometimes been used as a prison. The grant from the mayor and aldermen gave Chaucer "the whole dwelling house above Aldgate Gate, with the chambers thereon built and a certain cellar beneath the said gate, on the eastern side thereof, together with all its appurtenances, for the lifetime of the said Geoffrey." The mayor and aldermen promise in this grant to lodge no prisoners in the place during Chaucer's tenancy, but stipulate that the city may take the gate back if that should prove necessary for London's defense. It was, for the time, a "good address"—an earlier occupant had paid 13s. 4d. ($160) a year besides upkeep and repairs, high rent for the time. In fact it was the kind of house not beneath the notice of the Black Prince, who for one of his followers, Thomas of Kent, personally asked the mayor for a similar mansion, Cripplegate. Aldgate was splendidly furnished, if we may judge by the expensive cups the duke of Lancaster was to give Philippa Chaucer on New Year's Day, 1380, 1381, and 1382; and not the least of its appointments was Chaucer's for-the-time enormous library of sixty books. Chaucer would keep the house until 1385, when he would move to Kent.

As we've said, five days after his appointment to the controllership, Chaucer received an annual pension of £10 ($2,400) from Gaunt. He was now firmly established in government—as he would remain all his life—a valuable servant of unquestionable loyalty, capable and politic, not tiresomely fussy (from the king's point of view) about ideals irreducible to practice. One sign of the esteem John of Gaunt and the crown had for Chaucer is the fact that he was frequently abroad on the king's business in the next few years. According to one record, dated April 11, 1377, the year of Edward's death, Chaucer had already at that time made "divers voyages" to France; and in a record dated May 10, 1377, he is mentioned as having been "often" abroad in the king's service.

Most if not all of Chaucer's diplomatic missions at this time, the late seventies, seem to have involved, at least in part, proposed peace treaties and marriage alliances. On December 23, 1376, he set out through snow and ice for a journey abroad on some secret mission with Sir John Burley, captain of Calais. A month and a half later, on February 13, 1377, he received a letter of protection for another trip in the king's service, and from February 17 to March 25 he was in France. His friend Richard Stury was in France at exactly the same time, also on some secret mission, and from Froissart we learn what the mission was. Stury and Chaucer—along with his old friend Sir Guichard d'Angle—were in France to negotiate a marriage agreement between young Richard and King Charles V's daughter Marie.

Since Chaucer's mission with John Burley and his later mission with Stury and Guichard came so close together, and since Chaucer would later work with Burley toward marriage treaties, we may assume that both Chaucer's December '76 and February '77 missions dealt with the same matter. The proposed marriage was of course of the greatest possible importance to England: King Edward's health was rapidly slipping, and the war he had begun with such gusto had long since lost its appeal. Repeated truces had broken down, driving both England and France back to costly and, especially on the English side, futile war. Plagues, crop failures, and social changes of a kind still obscure in most men's minds but decidedly ominous—a rumbling among the peasants of both England and France that had already led, in France, and would soon lead, in England, to rioting and widespread destruction and to still more serious social change—had made the danger and waste of war all too obvious. The exorbitant cost of war had given new power to the English Commons, on whom Edward largely depended for funds and to whom he had granted, through the years, such concessions that the ancient prerogatives of the throne were now threatened or even, in some respects, irretrievably lost. Not only was parliament seeking to oversee the king's expenses; outrageously, as it seemed to John of Gaunt and Geoffrey Chaucer, who would put some of his annoyance into a poem, the Commons made a serious try in 1376, at driving some of the king's most loyal servants out of government, among them John of Gaunt and Chaucer's fellow diplomat in 1377, Richard Stury. And England had other, even more serious troubles.

Edward's practice of paying wages to his army to avoid its dissolution every forty-five days (the maximum legal stint of the unpaid army of feudal vassals) and the general practice in both England and France of hiring foreign mercenaries had filled all Europe with a battle-trained peasantry—a dangerous element in times of peace, capable of stealing, kidnapping, or murdering with terrorist efficiency—and had created roving "free companies" often indifferent to the laws and customs of the lands through which they roved. Also, as often happened when the throne was weak, England was now troubled by quarrels and bloody private wars between rival barons ("birds of rapine," Chaucer would call them). Achieving peace with France had become a necessity, and the old sovereignty dispute which kept the war alive could only be resolved, it seemed, by marriage between the two royal houses.

By all rights, the commission on which Chaucer served ought to have been successful. It was as prestigious and elegant a diplomatic team as Gaunt, who was running the government, could put together—three men picked for their devastating charm more than anything else, but men of proven ability as negotiators. Chaucer himself was a poet much admired in France, where his poetry was considered an artistic advance on French poetic tradition. Like the greatest of the young French lyric poets, he was a master at working out intricate schemes and discovering new uses for old conventions, yet he was equally at ease with the longer, more substantial form, the allegorical dream vision. Guichard d'Angle, of course, was honored everywhere, even in France, for the chivalric integrity which had made him a follower of the Black Prince, for his heroism in every battle he joined, for his sufferings in Spain, for his rare knowledge of visual art, music, and poetry, and above all for his basic gentleness and wisdom. The third member of the commission, Sir Richard Stury, was a man loved and respected in aristocratic circles, however he might fare with the Commons in the English parliament.

Throughout Stury's career, he and Chaucer would be closely associated.[3] Stury had been with Chaucer in the campaign of 1359–60 and, like Chaucer, had been taken prisoner. For Stury, who was apparently in the king's direct employ, Edward had paid a ransom of £50 ($12,000). (Toward Chaucer's ransom, as we've seen, the king contributed £16.) The 1368 royal Household Accounts show payments for Christmas robes to Geoffrey and Philippa Chaucer, Richard Stury, and others, and Chaucer's name appears again with Stury's in a record dated July 26, 1377—Chaucer as *"scutifer regis,"* Stury as *"miles."* Some years later, in March 1390, Chaucer and Stury would again be appointed together, partly because both had middle-class experience, as members of a commission to repair the dikes and drains of the Thames from Greenwich to Woolwich. Stury was a knight of the privy chamber, a recipient of numerous royal grants, and, like others of Chaucer's circle, a man who loved poetry. His will includes an expensive manuscript of the *Roman de la Rose*—what we would call an art treasure—and he had various other literary interests and connections. He was a staunch loyalist all his life; an intellectual, a Lollard, a gentle and chivalrous knight, also a brave one.

The marriage commission failed, tragically enough, not because its members were unpersuasive but because, as they neared conclusion of their work, Marie of France quite suddenly died. Chaucer and his fellow diplomats shifted their attention to King Charles's second daughter; but now, for reasons not entirely clear, the French apparently drew back. King Edward was dead and England weakened by the struggle of Commons against barons, barons against barons, and upper classes against peasants. French raiders were hitting England's coasts with impunity, and French pirates controlled the Channel. For all these reasons and, perhaps, others, those in the French government who opposed the alliance won the day; at any rate, the commission turned homeward. Almost at once, Chaucer was chosen, again in company with Sir John Burley, former retainer to the Black Prince, to set off on a new diplomatic mission, this time to Lombardy to negotiate, among other things, a proposed marriage alliance of young Richard and Caterina, daughter of the duke of Milan. The idea of course was to secure the Italian state as an ally against France, threatening King Charles V with war from the south. At least with respect to the marriage alliance, the mission failed. Chaucer once again made the tedious, seemingly endless trek back to England and was no doubt glad enough to see the house over Aldgate, the scales and piled-up goods of the customhouse. He went back to his reckonings, perhaps also to examining plans for the building projects that were beginning now, the expansion and renovation of the government's dock facilities. And nights, when his work at the customhouse was finished, he went back to his endless reading, poring over volumes of Boethius and Macrobius and now, increasingly, Dante.

Busy as he was in public affairs between the early 1370's and the death of King Edward, Chaucer wrote a fair amount of poetry, although just which poetry and just when he wrote it is to some extent uncertain. In the beginning, as we've seen—before his first trip to Italy—he favored French masters, poetic techniques, and forms. Aside from his innumerable allusions to the *Canticles,* he had depended almost entirely, in the *Book of the Duchess* (probably written in the very early seventies) on French poets like Machault as his base of imitation and allusion. His technique in all these early poems is approximately that generally practiced in France, a complex interweaving of allusions and original material, all in the "high style," with intense concern about musical effects (echoes, repetitions, various kinds of word play); and his favorite forms are the typically French "dream vision" and "complaint." Both are restrained, highly intellectual forms which take strong emotion as their subject matter (a death, the anguish of a lover, etc.) and deal with that emotion by freezing it to elegant crystals. It will be useful to pause here for a word about these forms, Chaucer's point of departure as a literary artist.

In the complaint, the poem's speaker is some fictional persona or caricature of the actual poet, commonly some variation of the stock suffering lover more familiar to us, since the Renaissance, as the mournful but ever-optimistic complainer in sonnet sequences. As in the sonnet, what makes a first-class complaint is not necessarily its power but, normally, its cleverness and elegance, its ingenious rhyming (much freer than sonnet form), its effortless intellectual juggling. Chaucer's early *Complaint to His Lady, Complaint Unto Pity, Complaint of Mars,* and the complaint which makes up part of his unfinished *Anelida and Arcite,* to say nothing of the complaints incorporated into the *Book of the Duchess,* are all models of the form. Biographically, as we've said, they tell us nothing, since the form is stock, much like such forms as the "Prelude" or "Suite of Country Dances" to a composer. They do tell us that he had, from very early in his career, an independent, somewhat impish eye (although he could also write serious lyrics), and that he loved invention and poetic complexity. Sometimes the complexity exists at least partly for its decorative value, as in the *Complaint of Mars,* where a neatly worked out astronomical pattern embellishes the old Mars-Venus-Vulcan story and perhaps also, for the original audience, some courtly liaison—some say an affair between John Holland, the Black Prince's stepson, and Isabel, duchess of York (as the early Chaucerian Shirley believed), others say an affair between John Holland and Gaunt's daughter Elizabeth, and one critic imagines the poem has to do with Geoffrey Chaucer, Katherine Swynford, and John of Gaunt.[4] But as a rule (and finally this is true even in the relatively slight *Complaint of Mars*), Chaucer's ingenious tricks contribute to meaning.

The dream vision is a longer, more complicated form, symbolically intricate, built in sections or "panels" which may or may not have obvious superficial relationship, but which are enclosed, normally, by a frame story of the kind found in the *Book of the Duchess,* where Chaucer begins and ends with scenes involving the narrator's insomnia. The individual sections of the narrator's dream are linked symbolically, often by subtle forms of verbal repetition and by the kind of thematic punning we do in fact experience in dreams—for instance, the juxtaposition in the *Book of the Duchess* of a deer hunt (a quest for the hart) and a love quest of sorts (a pursuit of a heart). But since the dream's connections are obscure (far less obscure for the original audience than for modern readers), individual panels may be filled out in any of a variety of ways, each fairly conventional—a hunt, a courtly lover's complaint, description of a strange landscape, formal debate between people or animals, and so forth. In this kind of art, needless to say, the reader's pleasure comes not from original plot, characterization, and so on (though these may occasionally contribute), but from the subtlety and authority of the poet's manipulation of stock devices, moving them around, presenting them in startling new ways, or juxtaposing them in such a way as to achieve new effects.

At least in England it seemed that there really were only two kinds of poetry one could write: short poems and long poems made of short poems strung together (panel-structure poetry). Think of the work of John of Massey, that is, the *Gawain*-poet, in his four-part linked work *Pearl, Purity, Patience,* and *Sir Gawain and the Green Knight,* or of the Wakefield *Second Shepherd's Play,* a three-act pageant in which the three sections have only the feeblest sort of plot connection—certainly nothing of the inevitability Aristotle recommended.[5] Or think of such collections, framed and linked, as the *Canterbury Tales.* In Italy, with huge dramatic poems like his *Africa,* Petrarch was struggling to overcome this limitation by returning to classical forms; and Boccaccio, working to solve the same problem, provided Chaucer with his source for the *Troilus.*

All his life Chaucer would be experimenting with ways of solving the problem of the long, "important" poem, and some of the poems he abandoned unfinished in this early period—possibly the *Squire's Tale* is an instance—he may have quit on because he saw that the experiment was failing. With the exception of the *Troilus,* no experiments he was ever to make would prove more important for his later poetry than those in the *Book of the Duchess* and the *Parliament of Birds.*

For the elegy and the *Parliament,* some critics have suggested, Chaucer brought together fragments or whole poems already written, added new material, then shuffled and patched, working toward a total, panoramic canvas, a unity. The theory must be rejected in the end, I think, but the unity problem which gives rise to the theory is an interesting one. In both these poems, the unity Chaucer finally achieved was typically medieval, more intellectual than "dramatic." By playing idea against idea, image against image, genre against genre (this last was common practice in the fourteenth century—think of, for instance, *Sir Gawain and the Green Knight,* where elegant romance and earthy fabliau interpenetrate), Chaucer had learned to make poetry philosophical. It would be a while yet before he would achieve anything approaching full emotional coherence, and in my view—though most Chaucerians think otherwise—that coherence would remain to the end of Chaucer's career not a product of his whole soul's conviction (like the coherence in the poetry of Dante or Goethe) but dramatization with the poet's judgment mostly suspended. Chaucer takes, that is, exactly the nominalist stance of philosophers like Roger Bacon, for whom truth is, outside doctrine, finally unknowable. When the Italian influence had deepened in him, strengthening his confidence in realism, Chaucer would create characters like the Wife of Bath, the Nun's Priest, and the Canon's Yeoman, who could so infuse their own personalities into the stories they told us as to create what Poe would call unity of impression. But for all the brilliance of his characterizations—his mimickry, if you like—Chaucer was never a man like Shakespeare, or like his own less philosophical contemporary, the *Gawain*-poet, who "saw life whole." Anything and anyone he saw, Geoffrey Chaucer could mock or defend at will; he could tell you the opinions of dogs, cats, carpenters, or the Man in the Moon, and he could set against that the orthodox Real Truth—the great universe "set all on sevens" which he reflects numerologically in the *Parliament*. But never, even in his old age, could Chaucer firmly make up his mind, at least in his poetry. If that was a fault, a problem in his character (surely it was not!), no one was more concerned about it than he was. Every major poem he wrote is a philosophical search, a careful, intelligent balancing of alternatives, an attempt to see clearly, state plainly, and above all feel emotionally what he believes; an attempt, to put it another way, to harmonize the two "Chaucers" of his standard technique—Christian master poet, and comic, myopic narrator caught up in sympathy with the things (and people) of this world. As in the work of all great modern writers, for whom Melville may stand as representative, every attempt fails, or rather, struggles to a draw. Thus for example in *Troilus and Criseyde,* Chaucer-the-narrator shows by every conceivable sign that he understands and sympathizes with his characters and that he believes that their problems—universal problems—are desperately important, yet at odd moments throughout, and more forcefully at the end, he remembers, as if suddenly—or Chaucer-the-controlling-artist reminds him—that *on the other hand* . . . One can of course "explain" the ending of *Troilus and Criseyde,* where Chaucer turns more or less unexpectedly to Christian moralizing, condemning human love, at least in comparison with the love of God. One can *justify* the abrupt shift both aesthetically and philosophically, and numerous critics have done so, very well; but philosophical justification does not change the fact of the sudden shift of tone: what Chaucer believed about adultery was flatly unorthodox. He saw it all around him in the court of King Edward and later Richard; he admired John of Gaunt, for whom adultery was a way of life; yet Christian doctrine on the matter was firm. With daring like that of the bold religious reformer Wyclif, Chaucer faced the problem and tried to resolve it. Philosophically, he succeeded, but on the emotional level he failed—as perhaps we all do. It would be the same still later in the

Canterbury Tales, where the Knight's secular, philosophical vision stands balanced with the Parson's sermon on withdrawal from this life: and it was no doubt the same in Chaucer's real-life experience. It was in his first two dream visions, the *Book of the Duchess* and the *Parliament of Birds,* where opposite positions struggle to a draw, that Chaucer worked out his method.

How these two poems work, philosophically and aesthetically, need not detain us here; but two lighter matters do need mention, the dating of the poems and what they tell us, in the most general terms, about Chaucer's personality and opinions.

Though critics have often done so, no one can say with any confidence when either poem was written. Since the *Book of the Duchess* is an elegy for Blanche of Lancaster, who died in 1369, and since it seemed to early critics a fairly simple, even mindless poem, it was once common to date it 1369. More recent critics, recognizing the poem's complexity—and remembering that Gaunt held a solemn and costly annual memorial ceremony for Blanche every year until his death, a ceremony Chaucer's poem might well have graced—have favored a later date. We know now that the poem contains both French and Italian influence (though mainly French) and draws heavily from Boethius, so it may have been composed as late as Chaucer's first diplomatic trip to Italy, 1373.

The date of the *Parliament* is equally uncertain. Some critics have insisted that like the elegy for Blanche, it is built of sections not originally intended as part of one large work. There are various indications of this, they say, mostly too complicated to mention here. One part of the vision takes place in "grene and lusty May" (l. 130), while another part of the same vision takes place in February, on "seynt Valentynes day" (l. 309). (But it is clear that time slides in the poem, and that the idea of Time's swift passage is a major motif.) Again, in some sections of the poem Chaucer uses Boccaccio and Dante as his sources, as he did in poems written after his Italian journey; other sections look like work of the so-called French period; and much of the poem's third section has the "realistic" quality of his later work. (It is of course not truly realistic, having more to do with the richly colored cartoon-like miniatures being done in Italian books at this time: people with comically big hats, warts on their noses, bedpans in the corners of their rooms. If Chaucer's first period is one of "French influence"—this may be an optical illusion—and his second, one of Italian influence, in that he quotes or imitates specific Italian poets, his final period is not one of native realism but of Italian influence fully assimilated and usually exerted on native English subject matter.) But the whole argument that the poem was made of old material reshuffled comes crashing down when we notice that the plan of the poem is numerologically tight, a tour-de-force application to poetry of musical principles drawn from Boethius' *De musica* and going back to Pythagoras and Plato; that is to say, briefly, that for symbolic reasons the poem is written in seven-line stanzas to the number of 699 lines— intentionally one line short of 700—divided into sections numerologically significant, and thematically controlled by seven kinds of music.[6]

Another approach to the dating of the poem has been the assumption of some scholars that it must have been written to some specific occasion. That was standard opinion for many years, such early Chaucerians as Tyrwhitt and Godwin arguing that the courtship of the female eagle to be married off in the poem refers to the marriage of Richard II and Anne of Bohemia[7] or the proposed marriage of Richard and Marie of France (or some other French princess).[8] Lately the search for an occasion for the poem has been abandoned, mainly for unsound reasons.

It is true that no occasion has been found that neatly explains everything in the poem. For instance, the twentieth-century theory[9] that the poem deals with Anne of Bohemia fails to account for the lady eagle's reluctance to get married and her wish to think it over for a year before deciding, whereas Anne of Bohemia herself instigated negotiations with Richard. Again, the theory that the poem concerns Marie of France claims that, since three eagles sue for the lady eagle's hand, three separate suitors, not just Richard, must have competed for Marie—which is doubtful. And the older Tyrwhitt-Godwin theory, recently revived— a theory that would date the poem as early as 1358 and claims that the poem's three eagles represent three of King Edward's sons, the Black Prince, Gaunt, and Edmund Langley, all still marriageable in 1358— fails in that it makes the poem unflattering (if we read the suitor-eagles' lines at all carefully) to Edward's two younger sons. A second reason the search for an occasion for the poem has been abandoned is that the poem makes good sense as, simply, an entertainment.

All these objections are easily answered. The year's wait before giving consent to a suitor is standard in courtly-love procedure (we see the same thing in the *Book of the Duchess*) and even if applied to Anne of Bohemia would give no one in the audience pause. Besides, of course, a poem which alludes to real people and events need not be exact in every detail. Except in the work of Alexander Pope, point-for-point topicality makes for dreary art. As for the argument that the poem deals with Marie, the disparity in the number of suitors is of no importance. The three suant eagles present the three traditional positions on love: (1) That the lady should consent out of mercy, (2) that she should consent because she owes it to her lover, and (3) that she should consent out of self-interest—in other words, the arguments descend from selfless to selfish. This debate is so stock in the poetry of courtly love (it goes back to the idea of the tripartite soul, on which we will have more to say in due time) that Chaucer had hardly any choice but to present it, whatever the situation in France. On the other hand, since in this commonplace of love debate it seems highly improbable that Chaucer would associate his friend Gaunt with one of the baser love positions, we may safely rule out identification of the three male eagles as the Black Prince, Gaunt, and Langley. (The date 1358 is of course much too early for any section of the poem, especially the comic final section. In 1358, Chaucer was eighteen.) As for the notion that the poem works aesthetically as a conventional love debate, a philosophical statement, or whatever, and therefore cannot be a topical poem as well, we need only observe that the *Book of the Duchess* is obviously both at once, that topical allusion is common in the poetry of Chaucer's age, and that as we have known since Manly's *Some New Light on Chaucer,* even the *Canterbury Tales* is sometimes topical.

Though most scholars have inclined to the persuasion that the *Parliament* refers to the marriage of Richard and Anne of Bohemia, the stronger likelihood is that the poem was composed in the year 1377, when Chaucer and his fellow negotiators were convinced that they'd finally achieved a marriage treaty between young Prince Richard and Marie. By all the theories thus far advanced, the correspondence between suitors and sued in the poems and suitors and sued in actual history is slight if not invisible; all the theories are equally well supported by the poem's one supposed astronomical reference, wherein Venus is seen in the north-northwest (but this may be, as some have argued, a joke, since the north-northwest is often associated, as is love, with insanity or confusion); but only the theory that the lady is Marie can account for the poem's chief feature, the parliament of *foules* (fowls or, by a foul pun, fools) itself. For Dame Nature, in Chaucer's poem, it is imperative that the beautiful formal eagle be married; but the debate on that great question by the assembled parliament of birds leads to comic madness and inefficiency, each of the lower species of birds slightly crazier than the last. It seems to me impossible to read the poem without at least suspecting that the crazy bird-parliament has something to do with the obstreperous Commons of England.

The so-called Good Parliament of 1376, the year in which Chaucer began negotiating for Marie of France, was the first in history to give representation to all of England's social classes. Though Sir John Knyvet, the chancellor, did not say so, the purpose of the parliament was to do something about the strained relationship between members of the House of Commons and King Edward's executives. At a time when those executives were embarking on a new program for England—peace and eventual prosperity through marriage alliance—nothing could be less welcome than parliament's attack on the chief architects of that program. The Commons took the offensive, leveling charge after charge against the favorites of the king. Conspicuous targets for attack were Chaucer's main patron John of Gaunt (who led the royalist defense), Chaucer's old friends Alice Perrers and William Lord Latimer, and Chaucer's friend and fellow diplomat in France, Sir Richard Stury. Though history has called this parliament "the Good," we may be sure that is not what Gaunt and Chaucer called it. To them it was a truculent, disorderly, almost treasonously aggressive body. The Commons insisted on informing the king against Alice Perrers and told him she was the wife of William of Windsor (which the now senile king solemnly swore he'd never heard), and despite the king's plea that Alice be dealt with gently, the Commons insisted on her banishment and the forfeiture of her property. John of Gaunt's faithful friend and Chaucer's, William Lord Latimer, was accused of unlawfully levying higher duties on merchandise than was authorized by parliament, he and his accomplices setting prices so high, his accusers said, that they "made such a great scarcity in this land of things saleable, that the common sort of people could scantily live." (He was the first minister of the crown ever impeached by Commons.) The Commons laid charges not only against John of Gaunt and his circle but also against the king himself, though they prudently kept those charges moderate. By the time it was over, numerous associates of Chaucer's—Stury, Lord Latimer, Richard Lyons, and Sir John Neville, among others, all members of Gaunt's circle—had been thrown into prison, to fret there until the "Bad Parliament" of 1377 could set them free.

All this might account for Chaucer's tone in treating the common birds' parliament. These lines, for instance:

> The noyse of foulës for to ben delyverëd   *[freed from the session]*
> So loudë rong, "Have don, and lat us wendë!"   *[leave]*
> That wel wende I the wode hadde al toshyverëd. *[I really thought the wood might shatter]*
>
> "Com of!" they criede, "allas, ye wol us shendë!   *[kill]*
> Whan shal youre cursedë pleytynge have an endë?   *[suit]*
> How sholde a juge eyther parti levë
> For ye or nay, withouten any prevë?"
>
>
> The goos, the cokkow, and the doke also
> So cryedë, "Kek kek! kokkow! quek quek!" hyë,
> That thourgh myne erës the noysë wente tho.   *[then]*

Chaucer does not, of course, condemn all birds equally, and if he devotes
many lines to the selfishness and stupidity of the lower orders, he also
gives a comic view of the tedious and intricate negotiations of the suitor
eagles—perhaps a comic reflection of the marriage negotiations in which
Guichard d'Angle, Stury, and Chaucer himself were involved. The suitor
eagles, at any rate, spend the whole long day from dawn to dusk making
"gentil ple [plea] in love and other thyng."

Professor Edith Rickert worked out the main lines of the political
allegory long ago. The "fouls of ravyne," she points out, represent the
nobility in the House of Commons,[10] the "water-fouls" the merchants,
the "seed-fouls" the country gentry, and the "worm-fouls" the citizenry.

The birds use parliamentary procedure, each group speaking through
its representative. The goose, representative of the water-fouls, says
boldly:

> "Al this nys not worth a flyë!
> But I can shape hereof a remedië,
> And I wol seyë my verdit fayre and swythë   [swift]
> For water-foul, whoso be wroth or blythë!"

The officious "foul cukoo," representative of the worm-fouls, says,

> ". . . I wol of myn owene autorité,
> For comunë spedë, take on the chargë now . . ."

And so it goes with the rest of the lower orders. Toward all the lower
orders Chaucer displays genial contempt, and in every case they are
put down at last by birds of "ravyne," that is, the noblemen, especially
by the "tercelet of the faucon," chosen by "pleyn elleccioun" by the
birds of rapine. Only the tercelet of the faucon addresses himself directly
to the three suitors for the lady eagle, saying, as if with full authority,

> "Oure is the voys that han the charge in hondë,
> And to the jugës dom ye moten stondë."

He is also the only spokesman who actually reviews the case of the rival
suitors and implies that he knows the lady eagle's inevitable decision:

> "And of thesë thre she wot hirëself, I trowë,
> Which that he be, for it is light to know."

The tercel is treated with special respect by Dame Nature, who quotes
him twice with approval:

"For sith it may not here discussëd be
Who loveth hire best, *as saydë the tercelet* . . ."

And:

"[I] Conseylë yow the royal tercel takë,
As seydë the tercelet ful skylfully . . ."

Professor Braddy remarks,

> We shall probably not be mistaken . . . in supposing that Chaucer
> in the "tercelet of the faucon" was describing a real person; and, of
> course, one to whom the royalist faction would naturally have turned
> as their leader. And if this supposition is correct, the only person who
> would have fitted such a role was manifestly John of Gaunt, Duke of
> Lancaster, who being the son of the aged King might appropriately
> have been described as "the tercelet of the faucon." Moreover, at the
> Parliament of 1376 John of Gaunt actually presided as the deputy of
> the King.[11]

All this of course strongly suggests that the *Parliament* was written
around 1377; but ultimately we can be sure of only this: when Chaucer
wrote the *Parliament* he felt at least a touch of scorn for the growing
role of the House of Commons, as he would all his life. What seems
liberal to us seemed to Chaucer cumbersome and absurd. He learned the
idea of humanism in Italy, chiefly from Petrarch and Boccaccio; but
when the idea expressed itself politically, Chaucer responded—exactly
as Boccaccio and Petrarch did—with disapproval in the form of satire.
Then King Edward died, and the son of the late Black Prince became
king. He was handsome and brilliant, like all Plantagenets; a faithful
husband and a political moderate. He would resist with all his might the
new spirit that was abroad in England, the humanism and new liberality
that Chaucer both advanced and dreaded. And in the end the new spirit,
among other things, would be the death of King Richard II.

Another poem perhaps written in the middle or late seventies, though
some parts are still later, is the multi-section work on the fall of the
proud which comes down to us as the *Monk's Tale* in the *Canterbury
Tales*. Some scholars have thought it possible that this was Chaucer's
Order of the Garter poem in 1374; but since the *Monk's Tale* is even
more obviously influenced by Italian poetry than is the *Parliament*, the
theory is not very persuasive. The poem of course contains no reference
to the Order of the Garter and, except for its general concern with
chivalry and Christian doctrine, contains no obvious relevance to St.
George's Day. True, such things, if once included, might have been

revised out for the Monk's presentation on the pilgrimage; and the people whose brief biographies are given might reasonably be viewed in Chaucer's day as chivalric figures, that is, good or bad knights—even Lucifer, who warred with Christ *miles,* Christ the Knight. But the poem's celebration of such an absolutist as Pedro of Castile, and its scorn of up-start commoners, would seem to link it with the period of parliament's increasing unruliness; and at least one of the poem's short biographies, that of Bernabò of Milan, whom Chaucer met on his Italian trip of 1378, "God of delit and scourge of Lombardye," must be very late, since Bernabò died in 1385.

When the poem first appeared it was undoubtedly much admired and must surely have enhanced Chaucer's reputation as a poet. Though Chaucer would return to French forms from time to time (in the *House of Fame,* for instance), he made no use here of those favorite genres the dream vision and complaint. To English aristocratic ears, the poem was in some respects a new kind of work, an original and fascinating creation. Englishmen had heard before moralistic rhymes on Lucifer, Adam, Cain, and the like. Such poems had been written back in Anglo-Saxon times and would continue to be written, mainly for schoolboys, down into the eighteenth century. Chaucer's audience had also heard before various poems (or short sections of larger poems, like the al-literative *Morte Arthure*) which combined short biographies from the Bible and Christian tradition with short biographies of certain later notables (Alexander, Julius Caesar, etc.)—poems, that is, telling of the so-called Nine Worthies, some biblical, some not, all of them ex-hibiting in their rise and fall the danger of trusting in Fortune. But Chaucer's visit to Italy had suggested to him a new way of dealing with these older poetic traditions, as well as providing him with new stories. There, where the spirit of humanism was awakening, Petrarch and Boc-caccio were writing short (and sometimes long) histories of great men, histories which focused as much on the character and deeds of the bio-graphical subject as on the moral to be drawn. That was of course a shift of emphasis already visible in Dante, in whose *Divine Comedy* characters like Farinata or the elder Cavalcanti emerge not simply as representative sinners but as people. In at least one palace Chaucer visited while in Tuscany he saw series-portraits of ancient and more recent great men. (Such portraits hung in Padua, where he may have met Petrarch.) In telling the stories not only of the traditional Nine Worthies or figures from Genesis but also of men as recent as Pedro, Bernabò, or Ugolino of Pisa, Chaucer gave English poetic expression to the new humanistic feeling: he extended old tradition in much the way Giotto had done in progressing from images of Paradise and the Fall of man to a series of pictures on the developing arts of humanity. Thus, in the eyes of his contemporaries, Chaucer proved his poetic mastery by writing well in a conventional way (greatly modifying even that) but also startled his listeners with something new to most of them, in all probability, humanism's at once intellectual and gossipy love of things current.

Modern readers have not found much to like in the *Monk's Tale* and have suggested that in his old age Chaucer himself found the poem wanting, since he gives it to the Monk as a sign of the man's prudishness, hypocritical sobriety (brought on by remarks of the Host), and intellectual shallowness, that is, his failure to see that Christian and Boethian standard doctrine on Fortune and free will might as readily support comedy (celebration) as tragedy. By standard doctrine—reflected in Chaucer's tale of Nebuchadnezzar—the enemy is not Fortune but man's inability to see beyond Fortune (or project his faith beyond Fortune) to the benevolence of God's plan, or Providence.

It can hardly be denied that the poem is one of Chaucer's less successful works, partly because it has no real principle of unity. But it is a subtler and more entertaining work than critics have generally noticed. Combining elements of the Nine Worthies tradition (the fall of the proud), the biblical-verse tradition, and humanistic biography, Chaucer moves between the broadly comic and the serious to develop a collection with more variety, more different kinds of interest, than the older forms allowed.

The poem begins casually, if not indifferently. Chaucer dismisses the Lucifer and Adam stories in a few lines each, simply making the orthodox point that one shouldn't "truste on blynde prosperitee" and bringing forward the age-old tradition that both fell for what might be called political reasons, Lucifer for disobedience, Adam for "mysgovernaunce." (They come, of course, to the same thing and reflect Chaucer's normal politics.) The Adam poem contains one curious oddity, though what we ought to do with it heaven only knows. Chaucer, whose later poetry contains innumerable obscene puns, writes here—unwittingly?—that Adam was begotten not "of mannës sperme unclenë" but by "Goddës owenë fynger." (Conceivably this reflects a late revision and has to do with the character of the self-righteous, slightly stupid monk.)

Chaucer dwells longer on the Sampson story. The key word "blyndë" in "blind prosperity" becomes in the retelling of the story comically literal. Consecrated (like a priest) to God Almighty, Sampson "stood in noblessë whil he myghtë see"; but in marrying a woman —that is, according to one strain in exegetical tradition, turning from the Supreme Good to a lower good, in other words becoming "blind"

—Sampson comes to be in fact blinded. He is imprisoned in a "cave," another stock exegetical emblem for the darkness of the spirit or, sometimes, hell; and there "they made hym at the queernë [mill or 'quern'] gryndë." Grinding, as we notice in the *Reeve's Tale* and in various remarks by the Wife of Bath, has the common fourteenth-century slang sense "copulate" (compare Bessie Smith's image, "coffee-grinder"); hence the cave where Sampson labors may also take on sexual meaning. Marriage, if we read allegorically, leads to dreary sexual slavery. The moral of the tale turns out to be that men should never tell their secrets to their wives. Thus the Sampson story becomes comically ferocious antifeminism, the same soft-headed streak in orthodox Christianity that Chaucer would later mock in the paired tales of the Man of Law and Wife of Bath (and in many another place), and the majestic idea of God's Providence comes to be equated with a husband's right to secrecy. The Sampson poem has, besides its comic misapplication of the allegorical method and its comically bellicose rant against women (a refrain throughout), some delightful visual imagery, for instance the sharp, economically rendered image of Sampson tearing up the city gates by night and carrying them on his back high onto a hill for all to see, or the image of Sampson imprisoned: "Now maystow wepen with thyne eyen blyndë!" Both the sharp imagery and the humor at the expense of pious antifeminists can hardly have failed to amuse the court of Edward III.

Later poems in the collection work in other ways. Some are quite serious, untouched by the old allegorical method or, so far as I can see, by ironic undercutting—for instance, the brief tragedy praising King Pedro as no other writer of the period chose to do, not even the chronicle-writer Ayala of Spain—but all have, in fact, poetic interest. Consider the image of Nebuchadnezzar in his madness, eating hay like an ox, lying in the rain: "And lik an egles fetherës wax his herës [hairs]; His naylës lyk a briddës clawës werë"; or the touching and shocking story Chaucer retells from Dante (missing the hint of cannibalism), the story of "Hugelyn of Pyze" (Ugolino), imprisoned and starved with his children, a story that gives Chaucer opportunity to try his hand at pathos and dramtaic irony: Hugelyn's youngest son, three years old, unaware that the family is condemned to starve, asks his father,

> "Fader, why do ye wepë?
> Whannë wol the gayler bryngen ourë potagë?   [*jailor*]
> Is ther no morsel breed that ye do kepë?
> I am so hungry that I may nat slepë . . ."

In their directness and simplicity, the poet's sure grasp of what people might really say and feel, such passages look forward to Chaucer's greater series, the *Legend of Good Women*.

Before leaving this chapter of Chaucer's life, that is to say, the period of his service under Edward III and his rise to high diplomatic status, it may be well to say a word more about some of his friends mentioned briefly already and add a few words about two or three other government servants who became his friends and, in a minor way, his fellow poets during this period. We've spoken already of the Oxford logician Ralph Strode, possibly an influence on Chaucer's inclination toward nominalism and perhaps the same "Rudolphi" celebrated for a long poem in Latin (probably), now lost. We've met too and need say no more of John Gower, the lawyer-poet familiar at court for his poetry readings both under Edward and, later, under Richard, until, toward the end, he lost his admiration for Richard.

Chaucer was well acquainted with brilliant, idealistic young Thomas Usk, who called Chaucer a "noble, philosophical poet" and followed him as a poetic disciple. From the admiration with which he speaks of Chaucer, one would not guess that he was not of Chaucer's party in politics, but unluckily he was not. He was ultimately hanged by parliament for the crime of espousing just but unsuccessful causes, that is, for daring to attack openly a grafter, Northampton, who had—whether Gaunt liked it or not—the protection of John of Gaunt. Chaucer had other poetic disciples: his student Thomas Hoccleve (or such is the relationship Hoccleve claims, and he probably told the truth); the monk John Lydgate, too garrulous for great art and too quick to flatter patrons, but an ingenious and talented follower of Chaucer's rhythmical innovations; and the widely admired French poet Deschamps, with whom Chaucer exchanged letters, poems, and flattering epithets, and from whom he got various poetic techniques and themes.

He also knew the wise old poet and diplomat Sir John Clanvowe,[12] author of at least one first-rate minor poem, "The Cuckoo and the Nightingale," written in (to some extent) the manner of Chaucer. Since Clanvowe and Chaucer shared missions and close friends, since both were staunch supporters of John of Gaunt (Clanvowe was one of the so-called Lollard knights), they undoubtedly knew each other—and each other's poetry—well. At any rate, they had in some respects similar minds and personalities. Both were poetic humorists and ironists, both were chosen to negotiate when matters were delicate if not downright embarrassing, and both took the usual medieval delight in pomp, display, and glorious deeds, as Clanvowe proved when he took his bold part in the famous tournament of Saint-Inglevert, in 1389 and 1390, in the march of Calais, the tournament begun when three French knights challenged all Christian men of arms to a splendid thirty-day fight in which they vowed they'd take on all comers. Many of Chaucer's friends were there, though Chaucer probably was not.

Another of Chaucer's friends was Sir Lewis Clifford. He was born around 1336 and, like Chaucer, was once taken prisoner by the French (in 1352, when Chaucer was a boy of about twelve). He was apparently attached to the court of the Black Prince and was, like Chaucer, a solid royalist and Lancastrian all his life. By 1389 he began to be mentioned repeatedly as present at meetings of the Privy Council, which means he was one of the trusted advisers in the braintrust of that keen intellectual King Richard. Froissart, mirror of royal opinion, speaks of him with great admiration. Clifford was frequently a diplomat on commissions in which Chaucer had a part. He negotiated truces on various occasions and worked on marriage treaties, notably toward the marriage of Richard II and Isabella, daughter of Charles VI of France. For all his intelligence and courage, he ended badly. Sick and frightened, he at last turned on the beliefs he and Gaunt had defended and gave the witch-hunting Archbishop of Canterbury a list of the tenets of those who had supported Wyclif, along with a list of people who secretly supported him. In his will, dated September 17, 1404, Lewis Clifford describes himself as "God's traitor" and directs that his "vile carrion" be buried in the furthermost corner of the churchyard of the parish in which he dies, and that no stone or other memorial mark the spot.

What that will really means is not clear, of course. But whether he believed he betrayed God in supporting Wyclif or in turning against him, pressed beyond an old man's endurance by the new religious and political régime, Clifford's tragedy is clear enough, and illuminating, like the tragedy of young Thomas Usk. In the late fourteenth century, survivors like Geoffrey Chaucer were remarkable men.

One might go on at length about Chaucer's friends and fellow poets,[13] but the point of these comments is merely this: In his main business, service to the crown, Chaucer was associated with men chiefly notable for chivalry, diplomacy, faith in intellectual inquiry, and what we might now call reactionary politics. They were solidly behind John of Gaunt or, when Gaunt's ideas and Richard's conflicted, ready to support (as did Gaunt) the king, and they were solidly against what historians have generally viewed as the liberal House of Commons. They backed Alice Perrers, all rushing to her aid when the Commons condemned her legitimate husband. In the court of Richard II, with its love of pageantry,

poetry, and painting, and its absolutist notions of what was right for
the crown and right for Commons, they were completely comfortable. For
better or worse, they were the fourteenth-century Establishment. They
could be critical, even angry—as Chaucer is in one of his poems to King
Richard, *Lack of Steadfastness*—but even in their worst moods they sat
like boulders on what history has judged the wrong side. What they desired of their world was law and order, firm and unchallenged monarchy,
or, in Dante's phrase, "The one will that resolves the many"; what they
saw all around them, and ardently hated, was instability, debased values,
endless struggle, a mad commingling of high and low, not Oneness but
Manyness—what Chaucer would describe, in his magnificent elaboration
of a poem by Boethius, as a cosmic fornication. In the Golden Age, he
says,

> Yit was not Jupiter the likerous,   [*lecherous*]
> That first was fader of delicacyë,   [*voluptuousness*]
> Come in this world; ne Nembrot, desirous   [*Nimrod (builder of*
> To regne, had nat maad his tourës hyë.   *the tower of Babel*)]
> Allas, allas! now may men wepe and cryë!
> For in ourë dayës nis but covetysë,
> Doublenesse, and tresoun, and envyë,
> Poyson, manslauhtre, and mordre in sondry wysë.

Seven: Life During the Minority of Richard ij~the Peasants' Revolt and Its Aftermath (1377~c. 1385), with More Scurrilous Gossip

CHAUCER WAS APPARENTLY AWAY ON some diplomatic mission when King Edward died—at any rate his name is missing from the list of courtiers given mourning clothes on June 21—and he may have been away again, or still, at the time of the coronation of young Richard. But while he worked abroad, probably still in desperate pursuit of more lasting treaties and of some marriage arrangement through which England might gain at least brief respite from war, and a chance to deal with her troubles at home, the poet must have listened eagerly to any snippet of news from across the Channel. The new king's policies, and England's complex problems, would have profound effects on Chaucer's life and poetry.

When Richard succeeded to the throne, he was a boy of ten. He was the nation's great hope, as was the boy-king Arthur in popular tales, or the New King Arthur, Edward III, Richard's grandfather, when he succeeded incompetent, indifferent Edward II; and in sign of their conviction that all would now be well, his people gave him, in the words of the chronicler now generally known as the monk of Evesham, a coronation "celebrated with great ceremony of a sort never seen anywhere before, in the presence of the archbishops, bishops, other prelates of the church, and all the magnates of his realm."[1] The pageantry and high ritual, universally applauded, were closely supervised and partly designed by Richard's uncle, the Steward of England, John of Gaunt, duke of Lancaster, who presided over the Court of Claims and later with his own hands delivered to the Chancery an exact record of the proceedings. It was all part of his high-minded plan to drag the nation back to unity, which is to say, to end the era of dissension and suspicion which Edward's long and costly wars had helped bring on and of which Gaunt himself was, in rude heads, the principal symbol.

Gaunt had regularly opposed the growing power of Commons, had sought to crush every possible threat to crown influence and had sought to extend that influence wherever possible, for instance by sponsoring speeches and sermons throughout the London area, wherein the learned John Wyclif might advance his arguments against Church control of secular offices. Wyclif was a bespectacled, soft-spoken scholar, a would-be Church reformer whose position on politics was honest enough: he was no toadie to Gaunt or any other man; and Gaunt's respect for Wyclif in the mid-seventies was not mere political opportunism. Gaunt had thought a good deal on political theory and, though he supported some clerics, was in general convinced that even the appearance of rule from Rome or, worse, from Avignon, in France, where the papacy was at present "captive," was dangerous. But Gaunt's open backing of an outspoken Church radical who opposed the sometimes greedy and self-interested rule of English or foreign bishops and proposed, instead, secular rule—rule by men like Gaunt—could not help looking suspicious. In any event, Gaunt's use of a churchman and of Church pulpits in his own political war against Church power threw the fat in the fire. Priests who disagreed with Wyclif answered him sharply, also from the pulpit, and a battle which might have been fought behind the scenes, as most great political battles are fought, became a people's battle, with the conservative local priest or bishop in the role of Christian hero, and Wyclif's apparent puppet master in the role of meddling outsider, even heretic. What Gaunt intended, it was felt, was to steal Church wealth—earthly succor of the sick and poor—to pay the bills of his own Savoy Palace and of his father's notoriously profligate court.

If the cries of "heresy" hurled at Wyclif (and Gaunt) were at first mostly rhetoric, the staff of the bishop of London soon realized the political usefulness of taking them seriously. Wyclif was vulnerable on numerous counts—for instance, his disapproval of the Eucharist—so that getting him condemned as a heretic should be easy, and his humiliation or even burning, if it came to that, would taint his political opinions and leave them too risky for future zealots to use against Church wealth. Wyclif was therefore accused and brought to trial before the bishop of London. Gaunt, feeling partly responsible for the position in which Wyclif found himself, and recognizing the ecclesiastical trial as at least to a large extent a cynical political move, a mockery of true religion, angrily broke up the hearings.

Invading that trial, asserting power by show of arms where he had none by law, Gaunt of course roused the angry indignation of all Londoners, men who jealously guarded their right to govern, inside London's walls, with nearly absolute authority. Gaunt's overreaching of his rightful authority did indeed have the look of an attempt to expand government power, if not his own direct power, and nothing in his subsequent pursuit of reconciliation with London did anything much to allay that suspicion. Nevertheless, he did, in his own haughty terms, work for reconciliation.

As Chaucer must have known well, to Londoners and other of his

enemies Gaunt seemed far more powerful and dangerous than he was. It
had been inevitable that, in 1377, with the Black Prince dead and King
Edward dying, Gaunt should be regarded as the real center of government and the man responsible for its mistakes. If he disagreed at times
with Alice Perrers and the hated London merchants with whom she
worked so closely—victuallers like Brembre, whose power Gaunt sought
to check by backing their political and economic enemies the mercers—
Gaunt's loyalty to the king precluded his publicizing his disagreement
with Alice and her cronies. If he had doubts about the policies of the new
force emerging in government, those former retainers of the Black
Prince who would become Richard's favorite servants and advisers, urging him toward a risky absolutist stance in defiance of the power of the
magnates, Gaunt's loyalty to Richard and to his own late brother kept
him from expressing those doubts in public. And so Gaunt led the administration, arguing positions not always his own, haughtily defending
even the king's right to give away millions to his mistress.

The chronicler Walsingham speaks of the ugly rumors in circulation
in the days of the Good Parliament of 1376 and afterward, how Gaunt
lived in open sin with his daughter's governess (that much was true),
how he'd poisoned the sister of his beloved first wife Blanche for her
inheritance and was seeking to poison his nephew Richard, how he was
plotting with England's enemy, France, to get a Papal bull declaring
Richard illegitimate, how Gaunt was in fact no prince at all but a Flemish
changeling smuggled into the abbey at Ghent in place of the daughter
who had been born to Queen Philippa. And the rumors won some credit.
Parliament's explicit recognition of Richard as heir to the throne encouraged the suspicion that Gaunt had personal designs on it—a suspicion useful to those magnates who believed, rightly, that Gaunt's influence in public affairs might threaten their own private interests or
limit their opportunities for self-advancement.

But for all the suspicions to the contrary, nothing could have been
farther from John of Gaunt's mind than raising old Norman or
Angevin precedents of setting aside the direct royal heir for an immediate member of the family more competent to rule, that is, someone
like himself. He loved his bright-eyed, eager nephew as he'd loved the
boy's father. Gaunt had been to the Black Prince not only a brother but
closest friend, and important elements of the plan Gaunt pursued—
among others, his reconciliation with the Londoners—originated not with
Gaunt himself, who detested the thought, but with the dying older
brother and gentle Princess Joan.

In short, from well before the death of King Edward in 1377, Gaunt
and those around him—including Geoffrey Chaucer, who would prove

himself the boy's brave and faithful friend—had based their hopes on no one but Richard.

Gaunt and his friends aimed at an ideal close to that of Edward I, a powerful monarchy responsive to the people, buttressed by a faithful and chivalric royal family with vast land holdings, kinship-bound barons, and vassals to support them in their support of the crown. Gaunt was, after all, not only a chivalrous knight but also an art collector and poetry reader; he fully understood the doctrine, especially popular with poets, of "courtesy"—mutual dependence and love up and down the feudal chain, a theme Chaucer would introduce years later into a poem (the *Legend of Good Women*) to be read at Richard's court, apparently because by that time Richard needed to be reminded. Gaunt needed no such lessons in courtesy. Like Steward Thomas of Lancaster before him, he took his duty to England seriously; unlike Thomas, he hated the faintest whiff of treason.

The great coronation ceremony for Richard was a part of Gaunt's plan, then, to bring the nation back to unity and focus all attention and loyalty on the king. In the Bad Parliament of 1377 Gaunt had made Prince Richard formal president of the proceedings, underscoring the legitimacy of his nephew's heir-apparency, and had engineered the peace-making general pardon for all civil and criminal offenses, in honor of what was called King Edward's "jubilee year"—Gaunt's invention. He worked diligently, as we've said, to patch up his quarrel with London, and when the Londoners repeatedly held back from parley with him, suspecting a trap, he forced the issue by a dramatic and highly calculated gesture: with Londoners present at the royal manor of Sheen, where Richard II, his mother, and his uncles were assembled to mourn King Edward, Gaunt fell at the young king's feet and begged him to take the matter into his own hands and pardon the citizens, as he himself was ready to pardon them. He showed no sign of awareness that he himself should require pardon from the Londoners, and his appeal for the king's pardon implicitly denied London's claim to virtual self-rule; but the gesture was effective. The Londoners, before they had time to think, were moved. Once again Gaunt had thrown the spotlight onto Richard, and to enhance his nephew's prestige still further, Gaunt "accepted" reconciliation through Richard with an old enemy, the bishop of Winchester, one of Wyclif's opponents. As May McKisack writes, "Walsingham's comment is just what [Gaunt] would have desired: 'O happy auspice that a boy so young should of his own accord (*nullo impellente*) show himself so solicitous for peace; that with no one to teach him he should know how to be a peacemaker!' "[2]

The same purpose is evident in the modifications in the coronation ceremony, probably also designed by Gaunt but perhaps by his friend Archbishop Sudbury. The archbishop's question to the people, whether they would give their will and consent to the new king, is for the first time placed *after* the coronation oath, transforming the people's role to consent and allegiance, obscuring the ancient English notion of election and heightening the real and symbolic power of the crown, source of national coherence. And a novel interpretation is given to the ritual moment when the magnates touch the new king's crown: the act binds the lords to service and support and to easing the burdens of the royal office. In a nation on fire with the private wars of magnates—a nation traditionally hypersensitive to symbol (as was Gaunt himself, not to mention King Richard)—it was a theatrical touch that could hardly fail to move the assembly to tears of joy and devotion.

And so the symbolic marriage of king and state was performed, and both the groom, "another Absalon," and the bride, England, seemed beautiful and young. The bankrupt government spared no expense, and neither did merchants or common people. The celebration was so filled with banners and noise and gorgeous dress, to say nothing of carts, tents, horses, jugglers, and bellowing drunks in the surrounding streets, that for the hundreds who got there late there was no place to stand. High hopes were evident everywhere, especially among the "lesser people." They thought of the king's splendid father and grandfather, then looked at Richard—handsome, like all Melusine's children, unquestionably intelligent, as firm, even obstinate, as any Plantagenet that had ever seen daylight, and yet, like Edward III, not unreasonable—and their spirits soared. As one contemporary poet put it,

> This stok is of the samë rotë;   [*stock . . . root*]
> An ympë beginnës for to growë,
> And yit I hopë schal ben ur botë!   [*be our salvation*]

The poet's paradox should have been right; Richard did have that salvation-bearing scion-of-Satan "imp" in him, and perhaps somewhere in Europe Geoffrey Chaucer and his diplomat friends, having heard that today was the day of coronation, toasted the faraway ten-year-old king with tears in their eyes, as there were tears in the eyes of their kinsmen at home, believing that now all was well, all was changed. But such optimism could not last.

England's situation was completely out of control, and even if Richard had been a seasoned warrior, a full-grown prince, for all his intelligence and courage and roaring popularity with the people, he might well have proved a straw in the whirlwind. As a mere child, he could do little beyond raising a few close friends to earlships—among others his young uncle Thomas of Woodstock, who would later betray him, to earl of Buckingham (afterward duke of Gloucester), and his beloved old tutor and guardian Guichard d'Angle to earl of Huntingdon. All real power lay with his formal counsellors and advisers.

The new king's first council, created largely in the patriotic and charitable spirit Gaunt had fostered, was a representative, even democratic council designed to block any one individual or clique, including Gaunt's, from gaining permanent control of policy. None of the king's uncles— Gaunt, Thomas of Woodstock, and Edmund Langley—had a seat, though they were made jointly responsible for preventing bribery or corruption. The government, and especially John of Gaunt, had dramatized its good faith, and the Commons had accepted it. But if 1377 was no time for tyrants, it was also no time for a fumbling democratic committee—and there was no third choice.

The Anglo-French war of 1369–89 was the most serious military challenge to the English government since the French invasion of 1216, and it was not only to Geoffrey Chaucer, still struggling in vain to win some marriage alliance, that Richard's first year on the throne seemed a disaster. "In this year," the monk of Evesham writes,

> there was a complete collapse of the peace negotiations. . . . During this same period, the Scots burnt the town of Roxburgh at the instigation of the earl of Dunbar. As a result lord Henry Percy, the new earl of Northumberland, entered the earl of Dunbar's land with ten thousand soldiers . . . burnt the towns subject to Dunbar, and plundered the area for three days.
>
> Afterwards the French landed on the Isle of Wight. . . . [W]hen they had looted and set fire to several places, they took a thousand marks as ransom for the island. Then they returned to the sea and sailed along the English coastline continuously until Michaelmas. They burnt many places and killed, especially in the southeastern areas, all the people they could find. As they met with little resistance they carried off animals and other goods as well as several prisoners. It is believed that at this time more evils were perpetrated than had been caused by enemy attacks on England during the previous forty years.
>
> In this same year, the French assaulted the town of Winchelsea. . . . While this battle was being fought, the French sent a group of their ships to burn the town of Hastings. In this same year, the French invaded England near the town of Rottingdean close to Lewes in Sussex. . . .[3]

And so it went. The English side fought bravely, from time to time. In Chaucer's circle people told the story of the French-born servant of the prior of Lewes, who "fought so stoutly, fiercely, and persistently against his fellow Frenchmen that his stomach was pierced by their swords and his bowels dropped to his feet. Disregarding this injury, he pursued the enemy, trailing his intestines far behind him."[4] But though brave enough at times, England was weakened and half torn apart, like the heroic Frenchman, by internal violence.

Chaucer never tells us directly what he thought of this period, though much of his *Canterbury Tales* reflects, in covert form, his perception of what was wrong: a lack, on every side, of trust and patience, a simplistic notion that force might prevail, as it does, at least for a time, in bad marriages. But probably much of what was wrong not even Chaucer understood until much later.

The nation's troubles had of course been building up for years, coming from all directions, insidiously growing, almost unnoticed or else stubbornly rejected as unthinkable. It had begun many years before the first of the plagues—in changing weather, in changing labor patterns, in changing attitudes toward law, religion, and intellectual inquiry—so that when it finally surfaced like a cancerous lump it was a cancer already metathesized, spread so universally that one could only make guesses at where it started. It was to surface most noticeably in the Peasants' Revolt of 1381, of which Oman wrote in his excellent though partly outdated study,

> To most contemporary writers the whole rising seemed an inexplicable phenomenon—a storm that arose out of a mere nothing, an ignorant riot against a harsh and unpopular tax, such as had often been seen before. But this storm assumed vast dimensions, spread over the whole horizon, swept down on the countryside with the violence of a typhoon, threatened universal destruction, and then suddenly passed away almost as inexplicably as it had arisen.[5]

Though the revolt was eventually crushed, what lay behind it remained basically unchanged—as no one knew better than Geoffrey Chaucer. Gradually, through the thirteenth and fourteenth centuries, a spirit more dangerous than even the plague—or so many people thought—had been growing in England, as in much of the world, a spirit Chaucer would dramatize for his courtly audience in a major section of his *Canterbury Tales,* the so-called marriage debate which, rightly understood, runs from the tale of the Man of Law to the *Franklin's Tale*: in the family, the state, even the Church, the old Anglo-Saxon idea of partial self-determination for all classes was reawakening.

In the eighth-century English epic *Beowulf*, lost and forgotten by Chaucer's time, the basic principle had been enunciated: a king's rights did not include violation of "the people's land or the lives of men." The French victory of 1066 had changed all that in England, replacing the direct relationship of the people and their king with what would become increasingly bureaucratic feudalism, which built walls of rank between the king and his subjects and meant, for the least of them, bondage. Edward's war, which gave the lesser people new significance, helped to stir up in the lower classes a wish to return to the old ways, to freedom— and the war was only one force among many that pushed men toward rebellion against the fourteenth-century status quo.

We observed earlier that the forces of radical change were already afoot in England well before the plagues, that the plagues, in fact, were as devastating as they were partly because, over the years, hordes of peasants had escaped from the country where the lowest of their group, the villeins, were bound to the land, and had come to what they imagined would be the freer, easier life of the big-city ghettos, that is (not in the modern sense), "suburbs." There, of course, they became odd-jobs laborers and often, since labor was overplentiful, thieves. If they were lucky— that is, if they managed not to starve, or die of sickness, or die by hanging or by some cutthroat's knife—they might happen to get passage to France or Scotland as foot soldiers. They could get rich in war, since Edward and his lesser commanders paid wages and even the lowborn were free to keep booty; and in Edward's time they could win their legitimate freedom from villeinage by noticeably courageous fighting. They returned to England professional killers, expert handlers of quarterstaffs, axes, knives, bows and arrows. Gangs grew up, both in town and in the country—numerous and fierce—gangs organized like battle units. Chaucer, in his old age, would be attacked by such outfits more than once. There can be no doubt, on the other hand, that labor was growing increasingly militant and dangerous, an ever-present threat to middle-class property and life, and that the villeinage system was already at this point weakened past repair. The same was happening all over Europe.

Ironically, the Good Parliament, for all its hatred of rebellious peasants, was itself a force that would ultimately spur the peasants to more violent rebellion. Brooding over memories of Crécy and Poitiers, Sluys and Espagnols-sur-Mer, both Lords and Commons were ruled by one dream, that of winning back provinces lost. No one seemed to understand that conditions had changed completely, that the circumstances which had given the Black Prince and Edward III their triumphs had vanished. France had learned how to deal with Edward's tactics and had won away many of England's allies, so that England was now too weak, and France too strong, for an English victory. Yet in 1376, years of unsuccessful expeditions and shrinking boundaries had not yet shown parliament what Gaunt and his marriage negotiators knew, that England's only hope was peace. To the Commons it seemed that the only explanation for the stream of disasters must be the corruption or imbecility of old Edward's (or later young Richard's) ministers, and so again and again they tried and imprisoned or (especially in Richard's time) beheaded them. The Lords, dependent on Commons for the necessary broadly based taxes, had no choice but to acquiesce.

Thus the power of what Geoffrey Chaucer saw as the bird-brained parliament grew by leaps and bounds in the seventies, and central government, repeatedly attacked and rebuked, began to totter. It seemed to the middle class a great leap forward when the widely representative Commons was able to impeach those financiers to the king (friends of Gaunt) whom they considered to be war profiteers. In most cases, if not in all, the government corruption they exposed was real. But one clear though unintended effect of the Commons witch-hunt was to undermine government credibility, so that when the peasantry burst into fiery rebellion in 1381, great numbers would believe that the king's ministers were again all corrupt (as now they were not) and that the peasants' best service to their king would be the murder of all his officials, starting with Gaunt.

As Commons grew stronger, extorting the aid of the king and magnates in its war on the peasants, the peasantry responded by organizing and by embracing more radical persuasions. We have no evidence, and there seems little likelihood, that there was ever any central committee of malcontents who coordinated strikes or issued orders for peasant uprisings; but there were bloody local strikes, as the Commons complained in 1377, and they were strikes not thought out by bumpkins. Yet though strikes took place all over England, and though some rebel peasants, especially in Norfolk, liked to speak of a "Great Society" (*Magna societas*), all who have studied the Peasants' Revolt agree that it was by no means the result of nationwide organization. It was the result, rather, of universally intolerable conditions (different conditions in different districts) and of the contagious idea that people had a right to resist unjust "auctoritee"—what Chaucer would call, speaking of the family but hinting at conditions in the nation as a whole, "the wo that is in mariage."

In towns the idea of revolt was largely spawned in what we may as well call manufacturing plants. In the old days the master of a trade did his work on a small scale, with two or three apprentices, each of whom aspired to become, eventually, a master. But England's increasing industrial activity—one more product of the war—had created by the late fourteenth century a class of great employers and a class of oppressed artisans with no hope of becoming masters. By false impediments and guild red tape, the employer deliberately made it difficult for his numerous employees to set up in business for themselves, so that apprentices who had completed their term of years must continue as poorly paid hirelings. These hirelings formed leagues and societies, usually disguised as religious orders, to work together for their rights.

One such person, of whom Chaucer must have heard numerous tales and whom he may have seen in action, since Chaucer had connections in that part of the country, was "the mad priest of Kent," John Ball, remembered today chiefly for his preaching a sermon on the rhyme,

> When Adam delved and Eve span,
> Who was then a gentleman?

He seems to have known little or nothing of Wyclif or of the Oxford rationalists; in fact, all of his ideas have been shown to be commonplace opinions among the peasant priests. But he apparently preached those opinions with extraordinary gusto. Part of Ball's program, his enemies claimed, was murder and the redistribution of land. The claim no doubt had some truth in it. He traveled up and down for twenty years, preaching discontent or, to put it another way, offering a vision that no one but the desperate or crazy would take seriously for centuries to come. What he offered, according to the hostile *Anonimal Chronicle,* was a kingdom of more or less equal peasants ruled by King Richard. At the time of the riots, the chronicler says, Ball advised the peasants "to get rid of all the lords, and of the archbishop and bishops, and abbots, and priors, and most of the monks and canons, saying that there should be no bishop in England save one archbishop only, and that he himself would be that prelate. . . . For which sayings he was esteemed among the commons as a prophet, and labored with them day by day to strengthen them in their malice—and a fit reward he got, when he was hanged, drawn, and quartered, and beheaded as a traitor."[6] Other leaders rose, fanatical and persuasive, in every part of England, a strange hodgepodge of dedicated visionaries, thugs, and opportunists.

Chaucer's England in the late 1370's had still other troubles. Second only to the magnates, the moneyed men—the merchant leaders, burgesses, and craftsmen, mainly concentrated in London—might have been the country's stabilizing power. But this group, like the magnates, could not overcome its private rivalries. And the Church, with its rich rents and lands, was just as bad. It was despised by Gaunt and all who stood behind him not only for its selfish misuse of power but also for its intellectual backwardness; it was insecure amid the discontents to which Wyclif was giving voice; and Church landowners, the most reactionary in England in terms of their demands of labor, services, and rents, had been the victims of riots by outraged villeins (for confinement in shackles, among other things) since before Chaucer's birth.

One more source of trouble in the first few years of Richard's reign was the presence, especially in London, of foreigners, particularly the Flemings. In those days the foreigners in England's larger towns were not only the desperate and destitute one sees now in, for instance, Spanish Harlem or London's East End. The fourteenth-century foreigner might be a fat, smiling merchant or manufacturer, and the destitute who skulked in their rags from street to street, peering around corners like alleycats, were as often as not native Englishmen, fugitive villeins, ne'er-do-wells willing to take any job, legal or illegal, since it seemed to them nothing could make their status any worse, not even hanging. The grievance of the impoverished Englishman against the foreigner, especially the rich one, was that, as it seemed to him, the foreigner was sucking the wealth out of the country and (as London merchants in fact claimed in parliament in 1381) secretly exporting England's gold and silver, for which he gave in return only useless luxuries. Since there was no cash in the realm, according to peasant reasoning, money was hard to come by and wages were low. This was the crime of the foreign merchant. That of the manufacturer, especially the manufacturer from Flanders, was that he was an unfair competitor who ruined the native artisan by using the cheap labor of his fellow aliens—also women and children. The argument against foreign workers and manufacturers was of course not all wrong. Ever since Edward III had first tempted the Flemings and Zeelanders to Norfolk, skilled artisans as well as common laborers had been coming from abroad in herds.

Such was the state of affairs in rural and urban England in the seventies and early eighties. The nation was sitting on a powder keg, though no one knew quite what to do about it, not even Chaucer's friend John Gower, who in his *Mirour de l'Omme* described the unrest and predicted social cataclysm but had no real advice to give on what might be done. Gower wrote,

> There are three things
> that bring merciless destruction
> when given the upper hand:
> a flood of water, a raging fire,
> and the lesser people;
> for the common multitude
> can never be stopped,
> neither by reason nor by discipline.
>   *Mirour de l'Omme,* ll. 26499–506)

Chaucer no doubt agreed. We find in his poetry some favorable portraits of members of the lower class: the stern, honest Parson on the Canterbury pilgrimage, or his brother the Plowman,

> That hadde ylad of dong ful many a fother;   *[carried . . . load]*
> A trewë swynkere and a good was he,   *[worker]*
> Lyvynge in pees and parfit charitee.
> God loved he best with al his hoole hertë
> At allë tymës, thogh him gamëd or smertë,   *[took pleasure]*
> And thanne his neighëbor right as hymselvë.
> He woldë thresshe, and therto dyke and delvë,   *[make dikes]*
> For Cristës sakë, for every povrë wight,   *[creature]*
> Withouten hire, if it lay in his myght.
> His tithës payde he ful faire and wel,
> Bothe of his propre swynk and his catel.   *[labor . . . possessions]*

And we find throughout the poetry a concern that the poor be treated fairly by those in authority over them. But for Chaucer (as for Shakespeare) the poor are, in general, amusing creatures, occasionally lovable, but sometimes foolish and always potentially dangerous. In the late 1370's they no doubt seemed mainly dangerous, especially to Chaucer, away from England much of the time on business for the king and thus unable to keep an eye on what was happening.

The Bad Parliament of 1377, not exactly packed but certainly manipulated by Gaunt, had been reactionary to the bone, devoted to undoing the measures of the previous Good Parliament. How a conservative body of this kind could concede the first poll tax in English history has sometimes been considered a wondrous puzzle, but the answer is fairly simple. Gaunt's purpose was to restore confidence in the monarchy, and that, he knew, must involve more than exonerating last year's public villains. He must balance the budget (or come somewhere near it), and he must in any way possible forestall the criticism and hostility of the Commons, presumably by easing their financial burden—at the same time bringing in more money than ever before to the royal Exchequer. Gaunt's solution was to switch from the usual subsidies on movable property (understandably unpopular with the merchants especially, whose large inventories were by such a tax their ruin) to a "tallage of groats," that is, "a groat, or four pence [$4], from each lay person of either sex older than fourteen years"—except for "notorious paupers who begged publicly"—and "from all members, male or female, of the religious orders, and all ecclesiastics promoted to a benefice, twelve pence."[7]

This strategy to some extent relieved the burden on merchants and manufacturers (though it stabbed Gaunt's old foe, the Church), and at the same time, at least in theory, it widened the tax base. It was a clever idea, but not fair to the poor. If Gaunt was indeed the engineer of the plan, and as the king's deputy he probably was, he deserved the hatred he received from the rebel peasants of 1381. Yet in Gaunt's defense it must be said that (1) the Commons' cooperation was desperately important to Gaunt's laudable goal of winning back confidence in central government, that is to say, the crown and what we would call civil service; (2) John of Gaunt and all those close to him, including Chaucer, were in later years increasingly sympathetic toward the downtrodden and deeply concerned about their general welfare, though most peasants never forgave "King John" for his supposed cruelty, a "haughty indifference" which, fairly judged, showed only that (3) to Gaunt, as to everyone else in politics, the peasants were an unknown quantity in 1377. No one knew how many peasants there were, how much they could afford, or even that the regulations they lived by were different from vill to vill.

The peasants were quick to point out the inequity of Gaunt's plan. They demonstrated, with the help of first-rate lawyers, that the plan was unfair, and, in rebellion against the unjust collection, they distorted the census, that is, lied about their numbers and thus paid a head tax on about one head out of ten. In 1379 Gaunt—or someone—responded with a new plan, a "sliding tax" in some ways comparable to our modern income tax, which acknowledged social differences. Historians have usually interpreted the graduated tax as a sign of the Commons' recognition of the principle of social justice, but that interpretation is doubtful. No one really believed in 1379 that the peasants would explode into widespread violence. The reason for the graduated tax was simply that by virtue of being more just, it would be more easily collectable. The plan almost certainly came from Gaunt, not the Commons.

In fact, the tax did prove collectable, more or less. But the administration of the tax was so crooked that the sum collected proved completely inadequate. In the January parliament of 1380 Lord Richard Scrope, Chancellor, revealed that the poll tax, "together with a similar subsidy granted . . . by the clergy," amounted to less than £22,000 at a time when the half-year's wages of English troops exceeded £50,000. Scrope's admission of failure resulted in his replacement by Simon Sudbury, archbishop of Canterbury. Sudbury brought back the "movables" tax, and he too failed. In a state of desperation, the government called another parliament to assemble at Northampton, deliberately avoiding Westminster because of the government's known unpopularity in London. Sudbury gave an accurate and depressing picture of how things stood, and the result was the flat three-groat poll tax of 1380.

It was an act of panic, as Gaunt must have known and as Chaucer must even more surely have known, back in England now, listening to the mutterings of common laborers at the customhouse, talking with seamen as their cargo was unloaded, or musing with thoughtful friends in his house over Aldgate. But Providence had given the government no choice. The graduated tax, though right in principle, had failed miserably, and the Commons was having no more of it. The "movables" tax was to the Commons' disadvantage, and they wouldn't accept that either. Gaunt, with his millions, couldn't understand that the three-groat tax was flatly beyond most peasants' means. Widespread tax evasion was inevitable, so that the government was forced to fierce measures for collection: an efficient program of evasion-hunting by inquiry commissioners empowered to punish offenders by imprisonment or any means "necessary." To England's detriment, the fierce measures worked. By the end of May over £37,000, approximately four-fifths of the total assessment, had reached the Exchequer. But the torch had been set to the powder keg. The shires visited by the king's commission of inquiry were the shires that exploded into violence. The first to rise were the home counties and East Anglia, partly because the peasants there were the most prosperous and class-conscious, and partly because the old manorial system was there least in force. The outbreaks began in Essex at the end of May 1381, and spread like wildfire over Kent, where Chaucer's family probably had holdings. There more than elsewhere the tactics of the rebels were those they'd learned as soldiers marauding in France: plunder, arson, and more or less selective murder.

A brother of Chaucer's friend and sometime fellow diplomat Sir John Burley—a man by the name of Sir Simon Burley, with whom Chaucer would later serve as justice of the peace and who was at this time beloved old magister of King Richard—is cited in the chronicles as one of the severest of the king's men. Since Sir Simon was a man with whom Chaucer would be closely involved in later years, one can't help but wonder what Chaucer thought when he heard of the man's behavior on this occasion. We're told:

> Afterwards, on Whit Monday [June 3] Sir Simon de Burley, a knight of the king's household, came to Gravesend in the company of two of the king's serjeants-at-arms and there he charged a man with being his own serf. The good men of the town came to Burley to arrange a settlement because of their respect for the king, but Sir Simon would not take less than £300 [$72,000] in silver, a sum which would have ruined the said man. On which the good men of Gravesend requested Burley to mitigate his demand, but they could not come to terms nor reduce the amount, although they told Sir Simon that the

man was a Christian and of good repute and so ought not to be
ruined forever. Wherefore the said Sir Simon grew angry and irritable,
much despising these good townsfolk; and out of the haughtiness of his
heart, he made the serjeants bind the said man and lead him to
Rochester castle for safekeeping. Great evil and mischief derived from
this action; and after his departure, the commons began to rise, wel-
coming within their ranks the men of many Kentish townships.[8]

In Chaucer's poetry all extreme positions, especially positions based on
self-righteousness, come in for humorous attack, and we may be sure
that Burley's obstinate insistence on what he believed he had coming
to him, however his former serf or all England might suffer, would be,
in Chaucer's mind, a piece of drunken stupidity. Though the peasants
might sometimes seem, to Chaucer, "a dirty and nasty people" (as
George Washington described his Yankee troops), he would have had
to say to Burley (if pressed to speak) what he wrote in his ballade *Gentilesse:*

> The firstë stok, fader of gentilessë—   [*i.e., Christ*]
> What man that claymeth gentil for to be
> Must folowe his trace, and alle his wittës dressë
> Vertu to sewe, and vyces for to flee.   [*follow*]
> For unto vertu longeth dignitee,   [*belongs*]
> And noght the revers, saufly dar I demë,   [*judge*]
> Al were he mytre, croune, or diademë.   [*Though wear he*]

Since Kent is not a large county and was much less populous in Chaucer's
day than now, Chaucer must have known, with his middle-class Kentish
connections, what Burley, coming in as a stranger, could not: the men of
Kent were a proud lot, loyal to the king but thoroughly fed up with his
high-handed ministers. If Burley imagined that any slightest sign of
capitulation on his part might open the floodgate to anarchy, he was mistaken. His intransigeance confirmed Kent's worst suspicions about men
of Burley's kind, and so the Kent war was on. Burley was dealing not
with ungrateful peasants but with men inspired, men with strong leaders
like Wat Tyler, Jack Straw, and John Ball. The peasants of Kent, Essex,
Sussex, and Bedfordshire tore down houses, burned barns and fields,
and, according to Froissart, marched on London in an army of sixty
thousand men to join the oppressed and angry journeymen of the city.

Chaucer, in his house over Aldgate, watched them come. What he
thought of it he does not say. He mentions the affair in the *Nun's Priest's
Tale,* comically comparing the outcry of an old widow, her two daughters, and all their farm animals (when their rooster is stolen by a wicked

fox) to the hideous noise of "Jakkë Straw and his meynée [retinue]" as
they rush to murder Flemings:

> This sely wydwe and eek hir doghtres two   [*humble*]
> Herden thise hennës crie and maken wo,
> And out at dorës stirten they anon,
> And syën the fox toward the grovë gon,   [*see*]
> And bar upon his bak the cok away,
> And cryden, "Out! harrow! and weylaway!
> Ha! ha! the fox!" and after hym they ran,
> And eek with stavës many another man.
> Ran Colle ourë dogge, and Talbot and Gerland,
> And Malkyn, with a dystaf in hir hand;
> Ran cow and calf, and eek the verray hoggës,
> So ferëd for the berkyng of the doggës
> And shoutyng of the men and wommen eekë,
> They ronnë so hem thoughte hir hertë breekë.
> They yolleden as feendës doon in hellë;
> The dokës cryden as men wolde hem quellë;
> The gees for feerë flowen over the treës;
> Out of the hyvë cam the swarm of beës.
> Sy hydous was the noyse, a, *benedicitée!*   [*bless ye*]
> Certës, he Jakkë Straw and his meynée
> Ne madë nevere shoutës half so shrillë
> Whan that they wolden any Flemyng killë,
> As thilkë day was maad upon the fox.   [*that*]
> Of bras they broghten bemës, and of box,
> Of horn, of boon, in whichë they blewe and powpëd,
> And therwithal they skrikëd and they howpëd—   [*shrieked*
> It semëd as that hevenë sholde fallë!   *and whooped*]

With all its mock-epic machinery, its rush of rhythms, the passage is
as full of merry turbulence as anything Chaucer ever wrote, but the allusion to the Peasants' Revolt is brief, and even the surrounding comic
allusions to the terrible yelling of fiends in hell and the final destruction
of all the world do not tell us much about Chaucer's real feelings. One
can guess them, probably. Philippa Chaucer was herself a Fleming,
and as the wife of a friend of John of Gaunt, "the most hated man in
England," at least by commoners, her danger, as well as Chaucer's,
was real enough.

    The peasants' success in 1381 resulted only in part from their violence,
though they were violent enough. The men they opposed, the king's

chief ministers, had the misfortune of being, on the whole, fair-minded men, not men like Simon Burley. Archbishop Sudbury, the king's chancellor, brought into government from his quiet life in Canterbury because of his reputation for wisdom and saintliness, was a reasonable and gentle man. As Professor Oman has written of him, "he would probably have been enrolled among the martyrs of the English calendar if only he had been more willing to make martyrs himself." He refused to crush Wyclif's supposed heresy because Wyclif's arguments encouraged reflection. He handled the king's affairs, including tax collection, without a trace of corruption, as did his colleague, the treasurer, Sir John Hales, "a magnanimous knight, though the Commons loved him not." Such men could not deal with the rise of the peasants because the peasants, they knew, had a partly valid point. They stalled and mused and struggled to do right, and by the time it was over the peasants, after loud, angry speeches, had chopped off their heads.

The failure of both the city of London and the royal government to crush the revolt in its early stages was a result of this same hesitancy and confusion. The time was the very pattern of the contemporary catastrophe Yeats describes: "The best lack all conviction, while the worst / Are filled with passionate intensity." The king's advisers were aware of the widespread sympathy the rebels had from the city's lower classes, and they undoubtedly disagreed fiercely among themselves about what should be done. Men influenced by Gaunt's ideas and patronage favored moderation (Gaunt himself was away in Scotland, working on peace negotiations which, because of the riots, came to nothing); men like the king's old mentor Simon Burley favored increasing sternness. In the end they apparently decided that their only hope must be a policy of conciliation. They began with an attempt to treat with the rebels, the king, his chancellor, treasurer, and personal retainers setting out by water from the Tower to meet with them. But the rebels looked wild and dangerous, pitchforks raised, longbows armed, battle rags flying—they had already demanded the heads of Gaunt and the chief officers of the state—and the royal barge turned back in alarm. Frustrated in his desire to speak with the king and knowing that his men were running short of supplies, Wat Tyler led his army up to Southwark, where they opened up the prison, destroyed one of the marshal's houses, then pushed on to Lambeth to burn the Chancery records, including their prime target, records of villeinage. They went from there to London Bridge and, with help from within, invaded the city; then on to Fleet Street, where they opened the prison, and on to the New Temple to burn lawyers' rolls and lawyers' houses and the houses of state officials. The Londoners, meanwhile, were destroying the most beautiful house in all England, where

Philippa had served and Chaucer had often been in attendance, John of Gaunt's palace of Savoy. Gaunt's splendid furnishings, stained glass, plate, jewels, and magnificent clothes were trampled under foot and burned or cast into the Thames. Gunpowder did the rest, leaving the palace black rubble. There was no looting, probably on Tyler's order. The rebels were not thieves or robbers, they said, but zealots for truth and justice. One man caught stealing a silver piece was hurled with his prize into the flames.

Young King Richard, in the Tower, watching the city catch fire around him, appealed in vain for advice from his advisers and at last, taking the reins in his own hands (if we believe contemporary chronicles), pardoned the rebels, promised them redress of their grievances, and commanded them to meet him the following morning at Mile End. He kept his word, and when he and his small party arrived there, the great crowd knelt, saying, "Welcome, King Richard! We wish for no other king but you." He promised, with sincerity, that he would gladly punish any "traitors to the realm"—by which the peasants meant people like Gaunt and customs controller Geoffrey Chaucer—if they could be proved such by law. But even as he spoke, it was too late for law. Another mob of peasants was now storming the Tower, where apparently by the policy of conciliation six hundred men-at-arms and six hundred archers stood back to let them through. They ransacked the privy wardrobe where the royal arms were stored and, unchecked by disciplinarians like Tyler, invaded the bedchambers and "attempted familiarities" with plump and terrified old Princess Joan, wife of the Black Prince and mother of the king, then found Sudbury, Hales, and others at their prayers and hurried them away to execution.

Yet Richard's moderation had done some good. Great crowds had left London, believing his Mile End promises, and those who remained —Wat Tyler's segment of the rabble army—Richard went out to meet the following day at Smithfield. Once again, King Richard was the hero of the hour. The story is beautifully told by Walsingham, but I must give a slightly altered version which is probably, all things considered, more nearly the truth.[9]

Wat (Walter) Tyler, a Kentish ex-soldier, was a fierce and intelligent revolutionary, though not in our modern sense, since what he sought was a return to the old days, the old ways, direct communication between commoner and king in a hierarchic universe, not "universal freedom" in our modern sense but the freedom of understanding and mutual respect between king and subject. In our time he would have wished to throw down the government entirely, perhaps, but he was a fourteenth-century man who believed with all his soul in the king, though he hated the king's ministers. Walsingham is therefore probably right that Tyler wanted (and thought the king wanted) "a commission for [Tyler] and his men to execute all lawyers, escheators and others who had been trained in the law or dealt in the law because of their office." It is probably true, as Walsingham says, that "He believed that once all those learned in the law had been killed, all things would henceforward be regulated by the decrees of the common people." He wanted, in other words, not tricky statutes and the deadly art of lawyerese, but law by "plain sense," common law as the peasants and men like the legendary Beowulf understood it.

When Tyler arrived at Smithfield to deal with the king, he was met not by the king, as promised, but by a knight, Sir John Newfield, who came up to him on an armed warhorse to hear what he might say. According to Walsingham, "Tyler grew indignant because the knight had approached him on horseback and not on foot, and furiously declared that it was more fitting to approach his presence on foot than by riding on a horse." Tyler drew his knife, and Newfield drew his sword. Not because he "could not bear to be so insulted before his rustics" but because he hated "gentlerymen" and had principle behind him, Tyler kept his ground, prepared to fight.

As King Richard saw Sir John's danger and wished to calm Wat Tyler's rage, he sternly ordered Sir John to descend from his horse and hand over the sword he had drawn on Wat. Newfield obeyed. But Tyler, Walsingham says, was still urgent to kill. Perhaps that is true; men do odd things when enraged; yet what follows is curiously slow, curiously deliberate, and, since it is the merchant class that dispatches Wat Tyler, head of the laborers' army, looks a little like plain murder.

> [T]he Mayor of London, William Walworth [fat, crooked Walworth, customs collector under Geoffrey Chaucer and close associate of collector Nick Brembre, who once hanged twenty-two of his enemies from one tree] and many royal knights and squires who were standing near came up to the king; for they believed it would have been shameful, unprecedented and intolerable if, in their presence, the king had allowed a noble knight to fall before him to so shameful a death. . . .
>
> On this the king, although a boy of tender age, took courage and ordered the mayor of London to arrest Tyler. The mayor, a man of incomparable spirit and bravery [!] arrested Tyler without question and struck him a blow on the head which hurt him sore. Tyler was soon surrounded by the other servants of the king and pierced by sword thrusts in several parts of his body.

From which he died. Wat Tyler had been misled by a kind of idealism. He believed he could talk to the king and win justice—as perhaps he might have if he'd found the king alone. His luck was bad, but then, so was Richard's, who by all accounts had no wish to see Tyler killed.

The peasants who stood watching the attempt at truce saw the murder and cried out, according to Walsingham: "Our captain is dead; our leader has been treacherously killed. Let us stay here together and die with him; let us fire our arrows and staunchly avenge his death!" If they had done so, the king might himself have been killed; and before it was all over, Richard would wonder if that might not have been better. However, the king, with marvelous presence of mind (Walsingham says), and with striking courage for so young a man, spurred his horse toward the peasants and rode amongst them, saying, "What is this, my men? What are you doing? Surely you do not wish to shoot your king? For I *will* be your king, your captain and your leader! Follow me!"

It was a trick, according to contemporary chronicles and according to most historians from that time to this. Richard's purpose, we are told, was to lead the rustics away from Smithfield where they might set fire to the houses. But that is surely a half-truth. Though worried about Smithfield, Richard was in earnest. Like the ancient King Alfred, to whom he looked as one of his models, Richard believed and would believe all his life that "the lesser people" were his strength and responsibility. In the end, in fact, he would die trying to raise among them an army to oppose his magnates.

Nevertheless, the bargains he struck with his rioting peasants were all undone by the magnates around him and by his wise old advisers, including Burley and London's Mayor Walworth. For their faith in the young king's promises, the peasants were rewarded by being hanged, drawn, and quartered, or beheaded—the punishment for treason. John of Gaunt, usually a force of moderation in the royal counsel, was still stranded up north and would remain there for months, and even had he been in London, he'd no doubt have been helpless. The king, in making his just and idealistic promises, had had no idea of the degree to which his government was indeed corrupt, or the extent to which those around him, men he loved (John of Gaunt, Simon Burley, or the court's star poet), were compromised. If the angelically beautiful, blue-eyed king had delivered on his promises, he would have found himself a man without family or friends, or no friends but such men as "the mad priest of Kent." More cynical yet ultimately more moderate counsel prevailed, to the good young king's bafflement and sorrowful indignation.

Within a year he had other things to think about. Those who had been seeking a marriage arrangement which might bolster England had a sudden change of luck. A proposal came, unsolicited, from Bohemia. Dark-eyed, wonderfully gentle Princess Anne was interested in alliance through marriage with (from the Czech point of view) mighty England. The negotiators—they may well have included Geoffrey Chaucer—studied the proposal with a touch of incredulity, and the more they studied it the better it looked: the Bohemians brought with them their own system of German and Slavic alliances. As for Richard, who married Anne in 1382, it was an incredible stroke of luck, considering the usual course of the marriage of convenience. He loved her and would continue to love her so devotedly that, years later, when she died, his grief would lead him to order the dismantling of a favorite palace on account of the memories that there assailed him.

It has seemed necessary to speak at some length about the conditions which led to the peasants' uprising and about the attitudes of Richard and his court advisers, since in important ways they illuminate both Chaucer's later poetry and his devoted though sometimes critical friendship with the king. But discussion of such general historical matters, though it may give us insight into Chaucer's prejudices and apprehensions, hurries us past the equally important specifics of Chaucer's life from Richard's coronation to the time of the revolt, so it will be worth while here to backtrack a little.

The period between 1377 and 1382 was not only a time of apprehension for Chaucer—not only a time when the peasants' enmity toward government officials directly threatened his safety and his family's—it was also a time of nearly continual nuisance, frustration, and annoyance. He put up, almost constantly, with the inconvenience of medieval travel. After his first work as negotiator on the ultimately abortive marriage treaty for the hand of Marie of France (1376), he had traveled during late February and most of March 1377 to Flanders and parts of France, including Paris and Montreuil, probably still partly on the same mission (if Marie died in May).[10] In any event, he traveled abroad "on the king's secret business" and was probably in company, for at least part of the time, with the famous general and veteran peace negotiator Sir Thomas Percy, who was away at the same time and, according to crown records, went to some of the same places. During the spring of 1377 Chaucer made various other voyages to divers parts overseas, presumably difficult and important missions, since in April Chaucer received £20 ($4,800) for his work; and apparently he was off again in May, when he was given a deputy at the port of London, Thomas Evesham—a "citizen of London" and moneylender to the king, for years associated with customs collection—to cover Chaucer's absence while he traveled to "remote parts." Riding mile after mile on his horse, or jouncing along in his medieval carriage through bandit-filled forests, or standing unsteadily on the deck of some ship as it plowed through French- and pirate-infested seas, his mind running back to England where thieves ran the customhouse putting his reputation and even life in jeopardy, the poet must have found it took all his famous good humor to keep his heart up. He was off again on June 22 (or so), 1377, this time to negotiate a marriage between some second princess of France and King Richard —a mission for which the government did not get around to paying him until March 6, 1381.

Nor was that the last of it. Between May 28 and September 19, 1378, Chaucer was given another deputy, Richard Barrett, associated with the London customhouse for some fourteen years. During this period Chaucer made what is usually called his second (but possibly his third) trip to Italy, this time (as we've said in another connection) to Lombardy, to deal with Bernabò Visconti, lord of Milan, concerning a possible marriage alliance with Caterina. The negotiations may also have had to do with Sir John Hawkwood, Bernabò's son-in-law, on war-related matters (Chaucer was paid out of the war account), and may have had to do with England's tangled relationships with Galeazzo Visconti, the Pope.

Chaucer apparently traveled to Italy as head of a party of five persons beside himself, sailing from Dover to Calais, and then making, once again, the dreary journey overland, covering at best about fifty miles a day through the beautiful though scarred summer scenery of France, then up into the lonely, terrifying Alps, making poorer time now, travailing on to the music of waterfalls—horses sweating and straining, pushing back against the load as the road sloped downward, and our hero sweating too, perhaps, because the traveling party was small, this time, more vulnerable to the mountains' wild-man bandits, unless, possibly, his party had by now been joined by that of Sir Edward Berkeley, ten men and ten horses probably traveling on the same mission.[11] While in Lombardy, the poet must certainly have seen and spent time in the Visconti Libraries, of which the Visconti were rightly proud and which contained at this time one of the most beautiful books ever made, the Visconti *Hours*. Chaucer apparently admired Bernabò, as did Richard II. Bernabò's love of food, art, women, and fine horses made him, in Chaucer's book, a "God of delit."

To protect him from lawsuits while he was away in Italy, Chaucer appointed two attorneys, John Gower the poet, and Richard Forester (or Forster), probably the man who was his fellow esquire in 1369 and his successor as tenant of the mansion over Aldgate. Why Chaucer needed lawyers no one knows for sure. It may well be that he was merely being cautious. It was standard procedure to get "letters of protection" when one left for abroad, that is, letters of protection against suits in one's absence. But these may not have seemed to him enough just now. They covered a man against litigious aggression, but they could not provide him with legal means of suing others for gain or self-defense. The general hostility against government officials may have led him to feel it would be well to take every precaution.

The discomfort of the endless journey to Italy was not its only inconvenience. It seems not to have been very profitable for Chaucer. Moreover, back in England again the poet was immediately annoyed by trifling debts to the crown from the year before, among others two red-tape fees (for the sealing of letters patent—fees a little like the heavy charge made in present-day England for a notary's seal) and a London sheriff's charge from 1377 that Chaucer must return an overpayment made him by the crown. Chaucer got both of these annoyances waived, along with others later, and in November won from the Exchequer the arrears on his wife's annuity since Richard's confirmation of the grant. Almost certainly John of Gaunt had a hand in getting the payments made up.[12]

As all this suggests, and as much of Chaucer's later experience confirms, working for government in the fourteenth century, whatever its advantage in the way of prestige, was a great deal of trouble. Chaucer's troubles with the Exchequer in the late seventies were only the beginning. Though at times he and Philippa received full and prompt payment—for instance, when he was in personal attendance at the wool quay, and thus in close relations with Exchequer personnel (he generally did better at collecting his wages than almost anyone else among English civil servants of the fourteenth century)—he as often as not had to win what was owed him by getting his own debts to the crown excused (as when he was robbed of crown money while serving as clerk of the king's works), by appealing for patronage gifts, by borrowing from the Exchequer and then asking to have the debt forgiven (Alice Perrers's old trick), or—probably as last resort—by dropping a word in the ear of John of Gaunt. For his French negotiations in 1376–7 he received no pay until 1381, and that in the form of a "gift" from the king (£22, or $5,280), and for his Lombardy trip he was not paid until the end of November 1380. His troubles, of course, were not with Richard or the regents but with the crown's officious—and rightly officious—employees. The unwritten rule of the debt-hounded government was, "Never pay anything till your creditor threatens to kill you."

Though collecting from the crown was always difficult, that is not to say that Chaucer was at this time in financial straits. Besides his annuity he had his customhouse wages of £10 ($2,400) yearly plus his annual "reward" (or *regardum*) of 10 marks ($1,600), plus bonuses of various kinds; and the work may have brought him considerably more. As controller of customs he had taken an oath never to receive any "gift" for performing his duties, but that oath was not always strictly honored; indeed it was probably broken far more often than not, as in the case of one John Bell, who was shown in court to have accepted tips—and Chaucer may have done the same. He also received wages—no one knows how much—for his second office, controller of petty customs,[13] and, beyond that, for his work as controller of the wool custom and subsidy. Besides these wages and rewards, it should be added, Chaucer had received for some time benefits from wardships granted him by the king. When Edmund Staplegate of Kent died in 1375, leaving as his heir a son by the same name, still a minor, Chaucer was granted wardship of the child, which meant he was responsible for maintaining the heir in a manner appropriate to his estate and keeping his property from deterioration, all for a price; and meant, further, that when the heir married it was by the warden's sufferance, for which the warden, Chaucer, was to receive payment—in this case £104 ($24,960). Chaucer was also given custody over William, son of John Soles, also of Kent, and over William's feudal lord, another minor, Richard Lord Poyning—both of which custodies brought Chaucer handsome income.

When we begin to put together all of Chaucer's activities in the late seventies and early eighties—repeated trips for the king to remote parts, repeated battles with the Exchequer to get payment for his work, trips down into Kent to inspect the properties of his wards, meetings with Gaunt and other officials on foreign policy, that is, the government position on the treaties he and his fellow commissioners must negotiate, record keeping for the customhouse (when he was not replaced by a deputy), and, despite all that, the writing of at least one long and difficult poem (the *Parliament*), the fruit of much study and thought—we begin to get the full richness of Chaucer's little dig at the Man of Law in the *Canterbury Tales:* "Nowher so bisy a man as he ther nas, / And yet he semed bisier than he was." For all his easygoing ways, his willingness to stop and look at a young man's poetic effort, or to chat with strangers about this and that (as he shows himself doing in various poems), Chaucer knew as well as any man in England what it was to be busy.

It seems possible, if not downright likely, that into his busy schedule of 1379 or '80 Chaucer managed to fit at least one pretty wench. On May 1, 1380 (Chaucer must have relished the symbolism), he was released by Cecily Champain, or Cecilia Chaumpaigne, daughter of William Champain, baker (he had died in 1360), and his wife Agnes, from a charge of *raptus*. A study of court records involving *raptus*, or *rapere*, shows that the word covered a multitude of sins in fourteenth-century law, and that in the case against Chaucer the poet may have been either a principal or an accessory. Most Chaucerians, on the general principle that a man is innocent until proven guilty—and in this case we will probably never get proof—have inclined to think Chaucer was more or less innocent, that is, that at worst he was somehow involved in an attempted abduction of some young person, perhaps to make an advantageous marriage. His father, they remind us, was the victim, while a young man, in a similar case. But there are reasons for taking a darker—or perhaps more cheerful—view. In the opinion of one eminent legal historian, Professor Plunkett of the University of London, in Chaucer's case *raptus* can only be interpreted as either "rape" or, more probably, "seduction"; for "if only abduction had been involved, then the release would have proceeded from the injured party, viz., the feudal lord, parent, husband, or employer of Cecilia," rather than from Cecilia herself. Plunkett continues, "There is really no evidence [for the charge of rape]. That Chaucer seduced Cecily we may well believe. But there is nothing to suggest that she could have convicted him of a felony" [which rape would be, whereas seduction would not].[14]

It is difficult to believe on other grounds as well that the case involved only abduction or that Chaucer was only an accessory. As witnesses to Cecily Champain's release, Chaucer called in some of his most powerful friends, busy, enormously important men he would hardly have called in to help with some mere trifle. He called Sir William Beauchamp, Lord Abergavenny, chamberlain of the king's household, captain of Calais, diplomatic envoy under whom Chaucer served on various occasions and whom the king made custodian of Pembroke Castle for the minority of the heir of the late earl of Pembroke in 1378. He called in Sir John Philipot, wealthy merchant, collector of the customs (whose doubtful records Geoffrey Chaucer approved), moneylender to the crown (enormous sums, which brought enormous interest), and lord mayor of the city of London. He called in William Neville, knight of the king's chamber and Admiral of the Fleet from the Thames northward; called in the gracious old poet and veteran diplomat Sir John Clanvowe, another of Richard's own household knights; and, finally, called in Richard Morel, who lived near Chaucer in the Aldgate ward and was a member of the huge and powerful Grocers' Company.[15] Against such firepower, Cecilia brought forward one cutler and one armorer, citizens of London known to court records only for debt suits, small business transactions, and the sale of used arms and artillery from the petty wardrobe of the Tower of London to raise money for the king. The baker's daughter, it seems, had no real chance. Just possibly (though improbably), since the coincidence of dates is notable, Cecily got for all her trouble the quick-witted "little son Lewis" whom Geoffrey Chaucer dearly loved and for whom he wrote the book of the *Astrolabe* and perhaps two other astronomical books. It should be mentioned that Lewis did, apparently, grow up with Chaucer's name, which makes it unlikely that he was the child of anyone but Philippa. In 1403 both he and Thomas Chaucer received payment as men-at-arms at Camarthen royal castle. But the fact that Lewis was almost certainly not Cecily's son is no proof that Chaucer, now forty years old, rich and powerful, more often away from his wife on business for the king than not, never slipped into bed with a pretty and soft baker's daughter.

Critics have sometimes been annoyed by Chaucer's failure to make more of such matters as the Peasants' Revolt and have often declared him a moral trimmer. Aldous Huxley complains that "Where Langland cries aloud in anger, threatening the world with hell-fire, Chaucer looks on and smiles," and G. G. Coulton objects, in exactly the same vein, that "Where Gower sees an England more hopelessly given over to the Devil than even in Carlyle's most dyspeptic nightmares—where the robuster Langland sees an impending religious Armageddon . . . there Chaucer, with incurable optimism, sees chiefly a Merry England."[16] Such objections are nonsense. When we study his opinions as embodied in his poetry, we find that, as Professor Howard Patch once put it, "considering the chief interest of the polite literature of his day, it is remarkable, after all, what democratic sympathy Chaucer shows—how little he has confined his material to people of high station, and what a wealth of knowledge he has of the lower classes."[17] In fact, in all his later poetry and especially the *Canterbury Tales,* Chaucer actively argues for a balanced view of all estates, a social program of mutual concern and "commune profit," a willingness to forgive, bargain, take responsibility, understand. All Chaucer's poetry carries sentiments like that expressed in the *Parson's Tale* with regard to pride in riches:

> . . . of swich seed as cherles spryngeth, of swich seed sprygen lordes. As wel may the cherl be saved as the lord. . . . I rede [counsel] thee, certes [certainly] that thou, lord, werke in swiche wise with thy cherles that they rather love thee than drede. I woot [understand] wel ther is degree above degree, as reson is, and skile [sensible] it is that men do hir devoir [duty] ther as it is due; but certes, extorcions and despit of youre underlynges is dampnable.

With this compare the Wife of Bath's ideas on "gentilesse," presented as a kind of joke in context, but serious just the same, since Chaucer will

again and again work them into his poetry and prose (as he does in his
entirely serious short poem, *Gentilesse*), as if in an attempt to make the
lords in his courtly audience wake up to the truth. Or compare the
Clerk's celebration of the patient peasant girl, Griselda, married to a
lord whose whimsical and willful tyranny—and whose failure to understand the proper feudal interdependence and love of lord and vassal—
hint at problems visible in England. The Wife has just insisted that
women cannot stand being tyrannized, and where tyranny appears wives,
that is, in effect, the subjugated, will rebel. The Clerk presents a wife
who does not rebel and, in asides to the pilgrims, points out repeatedly
the painfulness of her situation and the oddity of her husband's behavior.
For instance, he says of Griselda's tyrannical husband,

> He hadde assayëd hire ynogh biforë   [*tested*]
> And foond hire everë good; what neded it
> Hirë for to tempte, and alwey moore and morë,
> Though som men preise it for a subtil wit?
> But as for me, I seye that yvele it sit
> To assaye a wyf whan that it is no nedë,
> And putten hire in angwyssh and in dredë.

In calling attention to Griselda's position as vassal to her husband, and
in emphasizing the relationship of Griselda and other tyrannized vassals,
Chaucer makes as explicit as possible the political implications of his
tale. And he makes equally clear his political warning. Griselda is a
model of patient submission, but let no husband or king imagine that
those subject to him will behave as did Griselda. This story is not told,
he tells the pilgrims, in order that other wives should follow Griselda
in humility, "For it were importable, though they woldë—it cannot be
done. Chaucer will appeal even more directly for justice and reason in
his ballade addressed to King Richard, *Lack of Steadfastness:*

> O prince, desyrë to be honourable,
> Cherish thy folk and hate extorcioun!
> Suffre nothing that may be reprevable
> To thyn estat don in thy regioun.
> Shew forth thy swerd of castigacioun,
> Dred God, do law, lovë trouthe and worthinessë,
> And wed thy folk agein to stedfastnessë.

Or one might mention Chaucer's complaint against tyranny in the
Legend of Good Women, apparently introduced for the sole reason that
the work was to be read at the royal palace at Eltham or Sheen.[18]

In short, Professor Patch's defense of Chaucer's concern about social justice, his observation that Chaucer knows a good deal about the lower classes, goes nowhere near far enough. Whereas Langland rants at the evils of the age, threatening that soon God will take things into His own hands, and whereas Gower warns that society is sick and appeals to Richard to take some action—just what action he cannot say, except that the lower classes need "discipline"—Chaucer writes careful, philosophical poems in which, very often, a central concern is political theory. In early and middle-period poems like *The Former Age,* written sometime in the late seventies or early eighties, he takes positions not far from those of men like John Ball (except that Chaucer is never rabid), namely, that originally men were all made equal in Adam's day and during the Golden Age, and that pride has wrecked order. In the late, so-called marriage group of the *Canterbury Tales,* he deals far more subtly and cautiously with the problem of rights against order and degree. Against the authoritarian position of the Man of Law, whose tale urges that the subject be "constant" in any adversity, women willingly submitting to men, vassals willingly submitting to lords, and so on, whatever the anguish they endure, he sets the tale of the Wife of Bath, who knows by personal experience the "wo that is in mariage" if the husband is a tyrant.

The debate which follows, down through and including the *Franklin's Tale,* is much too complex to be fairly summed up by any brief discussion (the subject is one we'll be forced to return to), but one can say without much oversimplification that the dim-witted but goodhearted Franklin comes to what is close to Chaucer's own position: all classes must be ruled by "patience." To both lords and vassals, husbands and wives, the Franklin's advice is, "Lerneth [learn] to suffre [put up with things], or ellës, so moot I goon [loosely, "sure as day"], / Ye shul it lernë, wher so ye wole or noon."

Chaucer of course hated the Peasants' Revolt. He believed in degree, acceptance of duties, submission to authority, convinced to the soles of his feet that if authority became corrupt—as he knew it was during most of his life—it was not the business of peasants to correct things but the business of authority to correct itself. He hated peasants when they forgot what seemed to him their proper place, but in all other situations he liked them: he watched their antics, their sorrows and pleasures, with a perspicacious eye, and some while after their ferocious revolt, when his heart had calmed, he blamed not just the peasants but also, and even more strongly, the burgesses and lords for their tragic violation of what he saw as God's right and proper system.

In fact, even in 1381 Chaucer may have had personal reasons for finding as much fault with lords as with peasants. Professor Williams has pointed out some curious facts about Chaucer's fortunes in 1381–2. Gaunt's power in government was badly shaken during the Peasants' Revolt and in the months immediately following, and it remained shaky during his long absence in the north. His protector's weaknesses may also have affected Chaucer. On June 19, 1381, just after the revolt, Chaucer sold his family home in London. On August 1, he asked for and received an advance of 6s.8d. ($80) on his annuity from the government. And he asked for and received a similar advance on November 16. In a record dated September 29, 1382, Chaucer and one John Hyde were paid for acting *successively* as controllers of the customs during the preceding year. Perhaps Chaucer was ill or incapacitated for a while in 1381, but that seems doubtful, since his absence on other occasions had never required the appointment of a new controller (he was usually given a deputy). It might be, again, that with John of Gaunt in political shadow, Chaucer voluntarily relinquished an office where, as a friend of Gaunt and as a man not closely allied with the faction of the collectors he supervised, he might be unsafe. Or it might be that Chaucer was removed by Gaunt's enemies from an office that was not only lucrative to the controller but also an observation post from which a check could be made on where customs fees were going. Williams writes:

> If Chaucer was removed because he was a friend of Gaunt's, the enemies of Gaunt acted prematurely. Late in the year the Duke's power seemed greater than ever. Not only was his candidate for Lord Mayor of London, John of Northampton, elected in the beginning of November, 1381, but the session of Parliament beginning about the same time saw Gaunt's most powerful enemies forced to eat crow and beg his pardon for deserting him in the dark days of the Revolt. The following year, with Northampton as Mayor and Gaunt restored to his accustomed influence, Chaucer was *reappointed* to his controllerships (April 20 and May 8).[19]

Granted, we have no reason to believe that Brembre and company were Chaucer's deadly enemies. But we may well believe that Chaucer was at this time as closely allied with Gaunt's circle as with the circle of Richard's most trusted advisers, and that Chaucer was affected by Gaunt's eclipse. He may well have been glad to remove himself from what might easily turn out to be crossfire.

For a few years after Gaunt's return to influence, Chaucer remained in London, living quietly up over Aldgate with his wife, for whom he frequently went down to the Exchequer to pick up her annuity check, and tended to his business at the customhouse. Richard was now happily married to Anne of Bohemia, so that Chaucer was no longer needed to work on marriage negotiations, and the peasants were temporarily quieted, so Chaucer was free to write poetry and pursue his studies. He translated Boethius' *Consolation* and some of the short poems that work inspired, and he wrote and then endlessly tinkered over his tragicomic masterpiece *Troilus and Criseyde,* a poem in which one minor concern is the struggle of chivalric princes (Hector and Troilus) against parliament's self-interest and ultimately tragic shortsightedness (in trading Criseyde for the traitor-to-be, Antenor).

During this period he wrote, besides, the *House of Fame*—his great burlesque of Dante and almost everything else, especially the idiotic self-importance of people who think reputation or place-in-history to be valuable (the magnates and Richard were now jockeying for power, as were all the courtiers in Richard's court)—and he perhaps began thinking about the *Legend of Good Women.*[20] When not writing he went over his collectors' accounts, keeping the cheating to a minimum, let us hope, and possibly forcing the collectors to ingenious stratagems for fear of Gaunt, who might ask Chaucer for reports.

It was for the most part a peaceful time for Chaucer, or so it seems from this distance. Though the work was drudgery, he need not go to the office every day. Theoretically at least, he could put off his audits until a few weeks before the time he was required to turn them in, and if he was forced to work day and night sometimes to meet his deadlines, that was his own affair. As for any problems that might arise at the wharf, he could arrange to have someone like Richard Barrett cover for him. Barrett was an old-timer at the customhouse and a man in whom Chaucer had sufficient faith that he would later recommend him and promise to be responsible for him as his deputy.

When he did work at the office, he might sometimes step out to talk with loafing sailors waiting for their cargo to be unloaded and weighed, or he might watch and listen to the wool-quay carpenters at work. When he'd first taken office—by now that was nearly ten years ago—there had been three large houses down the length of the wharf, one for the wool custom (in the keeping of Barrett since October 1377), the second for the petty custom, the third used for storage and perhaps sometimes, lately, for the petty subsidy. The first house, and possibly the second as well, had a great dark tronage hall for the weighing of goods, its heavy wooden walls lined with incoming woolsacks, each as hefty as a man, and bulky handtrucks and wagons—handles shiny from wear, wooden wheels worn crooked—and beside the iron scales, the large, shaped stones used for weighing. But in 1382-3 John Churchman had begun work on a new house on the quay, for the accommodation of merchants.

It was originally planned as a tronage hall above cellars, with a count-inghouse and small chamber for a latrine in the upper storey, but in 1383 the plan was expanded to include another storey with two chambers and a garret. That building was barely finished when in 1385 John Church-man began work restoring or replacing the house for the petty custom.

As we've said, Chaucer may have been the government official in charge of this work. He would later be sued by a John Churchman for debt—Churchman's only recourse if the government refused to pay him. And besides his knowledge of the fourteenth-century building boom in Tuscany, Chaucer had seen, in his years as a servant to the crown, a fair amount of government construction. While the poet was in his household, Edward III had been constantly engaged in building—for instance, the round tower at Windsor, one of Edward's triumphs, and the beautiful castle of Queensborough on the island of Sheppey, begun in 1361 as a gift for Queen Philippa. (There was a great deal more.) Chaucer must have watched with some attention, both then and now in the early eighties, since he would later be thought qualified to serve as clerk of the king's works.

During this period, after 1382, Chaucer had more time for writing poetry—and for social climbing—than he had ever had before. Some-times, in all probabilty, he would leave London for a few days, traveling north with Philippa to visit her sister Katherine or putting in an appear-ance at one of the king's palaces, perhaps to read a poem. He was still associated with the royal court, as well as being a familiar presence in the court of Gaunt. In the last years of Edward III, after his appointment to the controllership, he continued to be styled Edward's "esquire" in official papers, though he was not in regular attendance. And though we have no record of his having been called "esquire" during this period in Richard's court—the records of the period are sketchy, however—we do have a record from 1380 about the Lombardy trip, in which Richard calls him "nostre bien ame Geffrey Chaucer," and a record from 1385 in which his name is listed among the names of the king's servants.

For all its tricky politics, Richard's court was one in which Chaucer was at ease. Though his rank was not of the highest, he was a favorite there. Gentle Queen Anne, whom Chaucer had in all probability helped toward her happy marriage, had a great love of poetry, especially Chaucer's, extraordinary at the time for its intelligent and sympathetic treatment of women; and there was no strong reason for an urbane, amusing poet to run foul of the court politicians surrounding the queen. Simon Burley, white-bearded and sagging of eye, was an old reactionary whose absolutist, divine-right theories and belief in stern discipline were probably a major influence on Richard's policy,[21] but Chaucer and

Burley could get along and did so, well, for many years. They served on
legal commissions together and had, of course, common acquaintances
and interests. Burley was a great lover of books, and not just the saints'
lives which all knights read or anyway stared at for mortification, but
poetry as well; and even if Burley's opinions about books were narrow-
minded and sometimes boringly pedantic, Chaucer was a man willing to
listen to anybody, old or young, brilliant or dull, as the surviving comments of his friends and poetic disciples all show. There were perhaps
some men in Richard's court whom Chaucer must pretend to like more
than he really did. There was—easily the worst of the lot—Richard's
young favorite Robert de Vere, earl of Oxford, a stupid fop whom
Richard advanced and coddled as Edward II had advanced and coddled
Gaveston. De Vere hated Chaucer's friend Gaunt and saw no reason
to disguise his feelings. But all situations have disadvantages, and Oxford could be viewed as too inept to be really dangerous, even though
he was undeniably difficult, forever plotting the murder of one great
magnate or another (one of the magnates he repeatedly plotted to kill
was John of Gaunt). Chaucer no doubt treated Oxford coolly, but he
was in no position to make an enemy of a man so powerful.

As for Richard, whatever his faults he was the king. A handsome
man with golden hair, overbearing at times (like an Oriental monarch,
he liked men to grovel on the floor before him) but a generous patron,
a man Geoffrey Chaucer could easily understand and sympathize with,
even if he could not entirely agree with Richard's policies. Admittedly,
King Richard had not exactly fulfilled his early promise. No one knows
precisely where he got his ideas on what kingship should be—perhaps
before 1380 from old Guichard d'Angle, an unreconstructed admirer
of Pedro the Cruel and of the Black Prince's annihilation of Limoges
(but no one held Guichard's opinions against him; he had suffered much,
and a man whose house has been struck by lightning is not a good judge
of thunderstorms). Or the king may have received some of his ideas
from Simon Burley, or Richard Abberbury, another apologist for tyrannical firmness. Or perhaps he got them from books on Roman law, or
from one or more of the scholarly friars King Richard admired and had
always at hand, as his father the Black Prince had done before him.
(Chaucer's ferocious though comic attacks on well-to-do friars in the
Canterbury Tales had considerably more bite for his original audience
than they have for us. When one recalls the jokes at the expense of friars
by the democratic Wife of Bath, one wonders at Chaucer's daring. He
must have had in Richard's court something of the immunity granted
the traditional court Fool.)

But wherever he got his absolutist notions, Richard's ideas on kingship were far from those of Gaunt, who favored a balance of the estates, and far from those Chaucer's characters defend in the *Wife of Bath's Tale,* the *Clerk's Tale,* and elsewhere. Given Richard's genius—not as a military leader but as a plotter, political theorist, chess player, and manipulator—the king may have worked out much of his theory entirely by himself. His views had, of course, firm emotional grounding. May McKisack writes:

> The effects of the coronation ceremony on an impressionable child of ten may well have been profound; and the king's customary appearances at the opening of each parliament would have served to keep alive memories of a drama in which his had been a leading part. No doubt his mentors [Princess Joan, John of Gaunt, and others] tried to teach him that kingship implied responsibilities as well as privileges; but his whole environment in childhood and adolescence was such as to foster notions of himself as a unique personage; and such notions must have been strongly reinforced in 1381. Richard's courage in the face of the rebel hosts is sufficient refutation of the calumny that he was by nature a coward or a weakling; but their astonishing readiness to follow him was heady flattery for his self-esteem. He alone, it seemed, could control them and it was for him alone to determine their fate.[22]

At Mile End, he'd watched the crowd of peasants go down on its knees, saying, "Welcome, King Richard! We wish for no other king but you." He gave his pardon, as he would do again at Smithfield, saving the day when his advisers were helpless. Then, as if he were no king at all but some disobedient small boy, he was forced by those advisers to watch the humiliating betrayal of his promises—trials and executions of men to whom he had given his word. Never again would he be so open. More humiliations followed: councils controlling his every significant decision, parliament judging and frequently denying his every political suggestion. His grandfather, at fifteen, was running his own war; his father, at twenty, was hailed as the most brilliant soldier in all Europe. Richard became a solitary schemer, though one who could collect and make brilliant use of the best available advisers. He became a chess fanatic, a discerning art critic (one more mark of his independent mind), and a bearer of grudges whose most remarkable quality was that when he finally took his vengeance that vengeance was surprisingly moderate and controlled. He developed, in the first years Chaucer knew him as king, the tendencies of a classical neurotic—not of the psychopath most historians have thought him. His neurotic tendency showed up in his compulsive, almost furious study of history, poring over old books, weighing, considering, theorizing, and in his intense veneration of his murdered great-grandfather, Edward II. Like his hero, Richard would be a pacifist—in which he was politically right, of course. With friends' advice, he would choose as his wife Anne of Bohemia, aligning himself with the Pope and European peace. He would emulate Edward II in his scorn of parliament's interference with his household, his favoritism, and his love of athletics; and he would see in his great-grandfather's blunders a cunning and purpose old Edward II would have found amazing or, more likely, bewildering. Much of all this was not temperament but policy, which brought even Chaucer around at last. A supremely powerful king might well prove the only hope against the jockeying magnates, and the exoneration of Edward II might strengthen the position of the crown henceforth.

But the wise, balanced Chaucer cannot help having seen that Richard did have a tendency toward what was called in that day "melancholy." It showed most plainly in the king's occasional violent fits of temper and in emotionalism all but unexplainable except on a hypothesis that the king was drunk. The stories are probably exaggerations and in some cases have been shown to be lies, part of a plot by the usurper Henry IV and his fellow revolutionaries to make Richard seem, like Edward II, a homosexual and an incompetent, and like Queen Isabella, hopelessly insane. But the stories have probably at least a grain of truth in them, which is merely to say that Richard was capable of inexplicable behavior and terrifying rages. When Archbishop Courtenay ventured to remonstrate with the king on his choice of counsellors, Richard drew his sword and leaped forward to stab him through the heart, and when his faithful attendant Michael de la Pole, "the brains of the court party," as McKisack says, intervened in Richard's madness, Richard was prepared to fight Pole. Another time, when he heard the news that the English were about to take Gravelines, the king went galloping through the night from Daventry to Westminster, pausing only to change horses at St. Albans, and then, when he'd recovered from his ride, lost interest and did nothing. (There was nothing to be done.)

His temper proved disastrous, as much to himself as to anyone else, in 1385 when he was in Scotland on his first military campaign. In a brawl near York, his half brother John Holland killed the heir of the earl of Stafford, and Richard, in a paroxysm of rage and grief, swore he would deal with his brother as a common murderer. The bitterness of the quarrel apparently brought on the death of their mother, Princess Joan. Chaucer made no direct comment, or at any rate left none in his poetry. But he was writing at the time *Troilus and Criseyde,* and there, in the fifth book, he brooded at length on the melancholy of a prince who, feeling betrayed in love, abandons the Venus in his character for Mars. Revenge is all young Troilus can think about, and in his melancholy rage, he futilely strikes out at his enemies until, in effect, he kills himself on the sword of "fierce Achilles." The poem is in no way a political allegory, but its central concern, the effect of a man's putting faith in love —in the broadest sense, charity—as opposed to the effect of his putting all his faith in power (the warring inclinations of Troilus' character), was a concern Richard's court could understand.

Chaucer, despite reservations, was firmly committed to Richard's court and was accepted there as one of Richard's own. In a writ issuing liveries of mourning for the funeral of Princess Joan, Chaucer was given three and a half ells of black cloth, and he is classed with Richard's esquires and sergeants. With a heavy heart, the poet took his part in the nation's mourning for his late friend and patron. The princess died at Wallingford Castle on August 7, 1385, the day Richard's army crossed the border into Scotland. Her body was wrapped in swathings of waxed cloth and borne to Stamford in Lincolnshire, on the main road north, to be buried beside her first husband, Thomas Holland. Richard postponed the funeral, as he would later postpone Queen Anne's, in order that it might be performed with due pomp, and she was finally buried in the Stamford church of the Gray Friars, after the king's return from Scotland, probably in January 1386 when the judges in the Scrope-Grosvenor case (in which Chaucer was, as we've seen, a witness) adjourned for the trip north and the ceremony.

When Chaucer and Philippa attended the funeral, their grief no doubt encompassed more than the death of the gentle, plump old princess. Chaucer was now a man of forty-six, dignified and graying, and knew these people around him well, including young Richard. Kneeling by his mother's elevated catafalque, twelve great towering candles around it— in the background darkness archbishops, bishops, other prelates of the Church, and all the important magnates of his realm—Richard was no longer the hope of England. He was her danger. Gaunt watched, uneasy but reserved, and Chaucer must have looked on sadly. The king's uncle Thomas of Woodstock, soon to be duke of Gloucester, moody and remote in that large, solemn crowd (snowlight coming in through the high stained-glass windows), was beginning to think things over, incline toward treason.

Eight: the Rise of Gloucester and Chaucer's Fortunes as a Royalist in Evil Times (c.1385-1389)

AS EARLY AS NOVEMBER 1381, parliament was complaining about Richard's vast retinue and colossal expenses, as earlier parliaments had complained about the retinue and expenses of the young king's hero, Edward II; but despite various efforts by parliament and by Richard's uncles, including John of Gaunt, the king's extravagance continued —huge gifts and lucrative appointments for such favorites as Michael de la Pole, who helped to arrange Richard's marriage to Anne of Bohemia, for Simon Burley and his relatives, and for many, many others, including Geoffrey Chaucer. Edward III's war debts were still unpaid (those not reneged on earlier), and new debts were mounting. The crown itself and most of the crown jewels were in pawn to the city of London, and when Lancaster's chancellor, Richard Scrope, tried to break the spiral, Richard and his courtiers dismissed him.

In such times war was the traditional solution: new lands, rents, and ransoms for the upper class, occupation and booty (and a slash in population) for the lower. Though John of Gaunt was against the ruinous war with France, he had been pushing since Queen Anne's coronation for renewed war in Spain for a variety of reasons, chief of which, perhaps, was the fact that Castilian galleys were continually raiding the English coast but could be stopped, or better yet, turned against France, if Henry the Bastard were knocked from his throne, or rather, Gaunt's throne. Moreover, these were the days of the great Papal schism, when two Popes, Pope Urban VI and his French rival, Clement VII, each with his own political backing, claimed exclusive rule of the Church. If directed against the Clementists of Portugal, the war Gaunt proposed could be counted as a holy crusade—at least by those Christians who backed Urban.

This is no place for discussion of the great schism; suffice it to say that the time was a dark one for Christianity, and the cynicism shown by the contention of two men for the position as spiritual father of

Christendom was as deep in England as elsewhere. Gaunt's plan of an anti-Clementist crusade lost to another plan, the bishop of Norwich's "glorious crusade" in Europe, opposed by the English Lords but favored by Commons and by the king's advisers, partly because it would be led by bishops, not secular magnates like John of Gaunt, whose ever-growing power they meant to keep in check, but chiefly because it would be financed by the selling of plenary remissions from the Pope—indulgences capable, according to the Pope, of remitting the sins'of both the living and the dead. "Angels from heaven, the pardoners were saying, would descend at their bidding to bring souls out of purgatory and waft them to the skies."[1] Gaunt fumed in indignation, as did his friend John Wyclif, who scoffed at such pardons. So did Chaucer, of course. He listened in amazement to the preposterous claims of the pardoners, and he would later immortalize the whole scoundrel lot in his "gentil Pardoner of Rouncivale" with his wallet full of pardons "comen from Rome al hoot." He writes in the *General Prologue,*

> But of his craft, fro Berwyk into Warë,
> Ne was ther swich another pardoner.
> For in his male he haddë a pilwe-beer   [*pillow-case*]
> Which that he seydë was Ourë Lady veyl;
> He seyde he haddë a gobet of the seyl
> That Seint Peter haddë, whan that he wentë
> Upon the see, til Jhesu Crist hym hentë.   [*called*]
> He had a croys of latoun ful of stonës,   [*false gold*]
> And in a glas he haddë piggës bonës.
> But with thisë relikës, whan that he fond
> A povre person dwellynge upon lond,   [*person (parson?)*]
> Upon a day he gat hym moore moneyë
> Than that the person gat in monthës tweyë. . . .

The "glorious crusade" was a disaster. It harmed rather than helped England's military and political position, and it converted not one soul to the English choice of Popes.

These days things were generally going badly for Gaunt and therefore, to some extent, for Chaucer. The king was now eighteen, full of strong opinions about what monarchy should be: its quasi-magical and divinely appointed power and magnificence, its dependence on no one. He had become a young man impossible for even Gaunt to keep in line, partly because his ideas were well thought out and, though opposed both to Gaunt's ideas and to his self-interest as a magnate, hard for a loyal Steward of England to answer. Though Gaunt did not hesitate to speak sternly of Richard's evil counsellors, and to urge their dismissal, especially that of the king's fatuous young hawking friend Robert de Vere, earl of Oxford, Richard more and more went his own stubborn way, giving out crown possessions and favors, proving his divine right and his people's obligation to support his munificence whatever he might spend. Complaints grew louder; Gaunt's attempts to restrain the king grew fiercer (his failure lost him his brief popularity); and Richard's resentment of his uncle's interference smoldered.

At the Salisbury parliament of 1384, a Carmelite friar by the name of John Latimer told Richard that his eldest uncle was plotting his murder. Perhaps because of his extraordinary faith in the decency of friars—a faith like that which Chaucer mocks in his "lord of the village" in the *Summoner's Tale*—or perhaps because the whole thing was a plot engineered by Oxford, and Richard was in on it, or perhaps because Gaunt seemed to Richard more hostile than he was, Richard believed the friar's charge against Gaunt. Gaunt, it should be mentioned, could stage some pretty masterful scoldings, as when he posted his men at every door of Richard's palace, letting no one in or out, then went himself to the king to give one of those cold-blooded steely-eyed tongue lashings that made Gaunt the terror of all enemies. At any rate, hearing the friar's accusation against Gaunt, Richard was ready to have his uncle hanged at once. Gaunt defended himself with stern dignity—he could in those days still match the golden-haired, hotheaded young man who was always so certain he must be right—and the lords present for the parliament persuaded the king to hold the friar in prison while the charge against Gaunt was investigated. On his way to the prison the friar was intercepted by a band of Lancastrians, including the king's half brother John Holland, was brutally tortured, and finally killed. If Geoffrey Chaucer, when he heard the news, was sorry for the friar, it did not temper his hatred of the mendicant brood Richard and his courtiers coddled. From behind the mask of the ferocious Summoner he would write, a short while later,

> ye han oftë tyme herd tellë
> How that a frerë ravysshëd was to hellë
> In spirit onës by a visioun;
> And as an angel ladde hym up and doun,
> To shewen hym the peynës that ther werë,
> In al the placë saugh he nat a frerë;
> Of oother folk he saugh ynowe in wo.
> Unto this angel spak the frerë tho:
> "Now, sirë," quod he, "han frerës swich a gracë
> That noon of hem shal comë to this placë?"

"Yis," quod this angel, "many a millioun!"
And unto Sathanas he ladde hym doun.   [*Satan*]
"And now hath Sathanas," seith he, "a tayl
Brodder than of a carryk is the sayl.   [*barge*]
Hold up thy tayl, thou Sathanas!" quod he;
"Shewë forth thyn ers, and lat the frerë se
Where is the nest of frerës in this placë!"
And er that half a furlong wey of spacë,
Right so as beës out swarmen from an hyvë,
Out of the develës ers ther gonnë dryvë
Twenty thousand frerës on a routë . . .

If the earl of Oxford was behind this plot against Gaunt's life, no
evidence was found. While Gaunt's friends were torturing the friar
to make him talk, the king's second uncle, Thomas of Woodstock, later
earl of Gloucester, burst into the royal chambers in a rage and swore he'd
cut down anyone, including the king, who tried to impute treason to his
brother the duke of Lancaster. Richard and his courtiers were cowed, for
the moment, but they were determined sooner or later to rule without
a trace of interference. As the struggle between the king and his magnates grew more fierce, Thomas of Woodstock would resist more and
more recklessly. As for Gaunt, recognizing the direction of events, he
demanded and received backing for a new expedition to Spain, got
Richard's formal recognition of his claim as king of Castile, put his son
and heir Henry Bolingbroke in charge of his affairs at home, and sailed
out of Plymouth harbor, July 9, 1386, to put Richard out of mind and
fight for his own crown.

With Gaunt out of England, Thomas of Woodstock's power would
increase by leaps and bounds, and Chaucer, loyal to the king, would
find himself dangerously involved in the struggle. In 1385, when Gaunt
was seeking ways to avoid confrontation with Richard and his court, and
Thomas of Woodstock was becoming the main voice of opposition,
Chaucer seems to have sought, probably with Gaunt's help, a government
position less dangerous and controversial than the office of controller of
customs. He gave up his house over Aldgate and the customhouse work
that apparently went with it, partly, no doubt, because there was no longer
much profit in customs collection, and any collector or controller who
had profited by customs collection in the past would be sure to come
under the scrutiny of parliament and its leader Woodstock, now duke of
Gloucester. (Under Gloucester's tight-fisted régime, the crown even
charged Queen Anne for bed and board.) And it may be that Chaucer
had reason to feel threatened by Gloucester's rise. Three years later, in

May 1388, while Gloucester was in full control of government, Chaucer saw fit (or, more likely, was forced) to "surrender at his own request" his pensions to John Scalby. He won them back only after 1389, when Richard was back in power. Most Chaucerians have doubted that the poet really did surrender his annuities at his own request; but he may well have done so, as a voluntary proof that he meant to be no trouble, whatever his loyalties. It was apparently not necessary in any other case for Gloucester to seize an annuity from an enemy and claim the enemy had volunteered it as a gift.

In any event, if Gloucester's ascendancy hurt Chaucer's fortunes, the king took care of them despite his uncle's wishes. No records survive to give positive proof, but in 1941 Margaret Galway convincingly argued that when Chaucer left his work as controller of customs (1385) he already had at hand a much better job as "clerk," or general custodian and steward, of the king and queen's favorite palaces, Eltham and Sheen (perhaps one or two others as well), and that in place of Aldgate, he probably had as his personal residence nothing less than the small royal manor at West Greenwich, on the crown estate called Rotherhithe.[2] It will be enough here merely to summarize the evidence.

The palaces of Eltham in Kent and Sheen in Surrey were respectively about seven and eight miles from London. The Greenwich royal manor, occasionally used in the time of Edward III but not sufficiently ostentatious for Richard, lay midway between them; thus one man could conveniently take charge of the upkeep and repair of all three. Around 1370 Robert Sibthorp had done just this as "clerk of the great works at Eltham, Shene and Retherhythe," and soon afterward became (as Chaucer would become in 1389) chief clerk of the king's works. As chief clerk, Sibthorp had an assistant who covered Eltham, Sheen, Rotherhithe, and Banstead (near Sheen).[3] Another man, one Arnold Brocas, became chief clerk of the king's works in 1381 after serving as clerk of the works at Eltham, Havering, and Hadleigh (in Essex). These and other records show that normally before becoming chief clerk of the king's works a man had to prove himself as clerk of three or four estates; and they show, too, that the clerkship of Eltham and nearby manors was a usual stepping stone.

We have clear evidence in Chaucer's poetry that he at some time lived in Greenwich and had dealings with Eltham and Sheen. In early manuscripts, including the best, the Ellismere, a scant allusion to Chaucer's place of residence in the *Envoy to Scogan* has the marginal gloss "Greenwich"; and a line in one prologue to the *Legend of Good Women* speaks of delivering a poem at Eltham or Sheen. Chaucer's name appears as a member of a Greenwich board of freeholders in 1396, which proves he lived there at that time if not earlier; and in the "Reeve's Prologue" (c. 1385) there appears what might be a joking allusion to Chaucer's habitat, when the Host speaks of "Greenwich, ther [that] many a shrewe [crook] is inne." There is other evidence as well, all tending to the conclusion that Chaucer's great editor Skeat was right in his educated guess that "It is highly probable that Chaucer's residence at Greenwich extended from 1385 to the end of 1399, when he took a new house at Westminster."[4] It was surely because John Churchman knew about Chaucer's responsibilities at Eltham and Sheen that, in suing the poet for unpaid bills, he had sheriffs search for Chaucer, to no avail—thanks undoubtedly to graft or influence—in both the counties of Kent and Surrey.

In 1385 when Richard was preparing to fight the Scots and French in the north, he felt it necessary to arrange for the care of his estates and family in his absence. He officially assigned three of Chaucer's friends, Sir Lewis Clifford, Sir Richard Stury, and Sir Philip Vache, with other knights and squires, to see to "the comfort and security of his mother [Princess Joan] wherever she shall abide within the realm, rendering other services befitting the estate of so great a lady." Presumably he did the same for his queen, and apparently Chaucer had a part in the king's provisions. On April 6, 1385, Richard granted Chaucer £10 ($2,400), a sort of loan or retainer unrelated to his stipend from the customs or his annuities, which Chaucer received "into his own hands" at Eltham. Other records show that the poet was out of London in April, June, and again in October, by which time he was certainly living in Kent or he could not have been appointed (October 12) as justice of the peace to replace the deceased Thomas of Shardelowe.

Chaucer's position in connection with Eltham, Sheen, and Rotherhithe involved various kinds of work, including supervision of whatever building was being done on the king's estates, the upkeep and repair of the large dwelling houses, outbuildings (barns, mews, lodges, gatehouses, and so on), gardens and garden walls, park fences, lakes and fishponds, bridges and walkways. The clerk had to provide building materials and arrange for their cartage, had to pay the workmen's wages and the wages of regular custodians, foresters, and gardeners, and keep detailed accounts. It was obviously a job that meant considerable hard work; but though Chaucer's supervision of upkeep and repairs was by no means a sinecure, it was abundantly rewarding. The king's estates were magnificently beautiful places. Froissart speaks of Eltham's long vine-covered walkways, and various poems and paintings from the period give us clues to the beauty of such settings—the forests and deer parks, manicured paths that might open unexpectedly on a still lake with lilypads, a valley full of flowers, a memorial shrine half hidden in ivy, or the grotto of some ancient hermit.

Chaucer's delight in this country life comes through trumpet-clear in the poetry he wrote from Greenwich. Though his sprightly Prologue to the *Legend of Good Women* is partly a joke making fun of sentimental nature lovers, it is full of nature fondly observed, observed not merely for the allegorical use that can be made of it. When he praises the little red and white English daisy, much employed in fourteenth-century poetry for allegorical reasons, Chaucer mentions details which make his tramp through the meadow early in the morning seem a walk he has really taken, and more than once; he speaks of how daisies fill the whole meadow, embroidering it, how the daisy "upryseth erly by the morwe [in the morning]" and spreads itself "ayein the sonne," and of how it closes again at dusk. And he tells how

> . . . doun on knes anoon-ryght I me settë,   [*knees*]
> And, as I koudë, this fresshë flour I grettë,   [*greet*]
> Knelyng alwey, til it unclosëd was,
> Upon the smalë, softë, swotë gras,   [*sweet grass*]
> That was with flourës swote enbrouded al,
> Of swich swetnesse and swich odour overal,
> That, for to speke of gomme, or herbe, or tree,
> Comparisoun may noon ymakëd bee. . . .

We find of course the same love of nature in the opening lines of the *General Prologue to the Canterbury Tales,* or in the country life passages in the *Knight's Tale, Miller's Tale,* and *Reeve's Tale,* all written at about this time.

It was probably during this period, too, that he came to know well those country types he would immortalize in the *Canterbury Tales.* Every reader can see at a glance how superbly Chaucer characterizes old "gnofs" like the Reeve or Miller or delightful wenches like the old carpenter's young wife Alisoun. But it is easy to miss the subtlety with which he sets down such minor characters as, for example, the "povre widwe" in the *Nun's Priest's Tale.* The old widow is the perfect "humble peasant" and is meant to contrast with her proud rooster, Chauntecleer; but Chaucer's sly, ironic wit refuses to sentimentalize even the ideal type of Christian humility. He writes:

> This wydwe, of which I tellë you my talë,
> Syn thilkë day that she was last a wyf,   [*that same*]
> In paciencë ladde a ful symple lyf,

For litel was hir catel and hir rentë.   [*property*]
By housbondrie of swich as God hirë sentë
She foond hirself and eek hir doghtren two.   [*provided for*]
Thre largë sowës haddë she, and namo,
Three keen, and eek a sheep that hightë Mallë.   [*cows*]
Ful sooty was hirë bour and eek hir hallë,
In which she eet ful many a sklendre meel.
Of poynaunt sauce hir neded never a deel.   [*a great deal*]
No deyntee morsel passed thurgh hir throtë;
Hir dietë was accordant to hir cotë.   [*cottage (produce)*]
Repleccioun ne made hirë neverë sik;
Attempree dietë was al hir phisik,   [*moderate*]
And exercise, and hertës suffisauncë.   [*sufficiency*]
The goutë lette hirë nothyng for to dauncë,   [*prevented*]
N'apoplexië shentë nat hir heed.   [*hurt*]
No wyn ne drank she, neither whit ne reed;
Hir bord was servëd moost with whit and blak—
Milk and broun breed, in which she found no lak,
Seynd bacoun, and somtyme an ey or tweyë;   [*Broiled bacon; egg*]
For she was, as it were, a maner deyë.   [*dairywoman*]

If the good old woman puts the proud to shame, the life of the proud
also casts ironic light on the life of the old woman. Patience and the
simple life are good, but she has no real choice, "For litel was hir catel
and hir rentë." She has no need of "poynaunt sauce," an extravagance
hard on the digestion; but then she has none of those delicate meats
spicy sauces improve. Not that the rich really fare better than the poor
widow. No "dainty morsel" passes through her lips, but then, as Chaucer
wittily points out by altering the expected word, a morsel is no longer
"dainty" when it passes through the "throat." And so the portrait continues, slyly poking fun at both the humble and the proud, yet respectful
for all that. Whereas courtiers in Chaucer's day were beginning to make a
fuss about when one ought to drink red wine and when one ought to
drink white, the old widow sensibly drinks no wine at all—because she
has none. And whereas the rich life of the wealthy can lead to gout and
an end of all dancing, simple and devout peasants did not develop gout
—not that it helped their dancing: they thought dancing sinful. We find
this same affection, humor, and deft, sure touch in all Chaucer's country
portraits from the late eighties or the nineties. Clearly, one of the rewards
of life in Kent was that it gave Chaucer rich new material.

For Chaucer the work at Greenwich was rewarding in another way as
well. Though he was a king's man, he was all his life more funda-

mentally a queen's man—in the service of the countess of Ulster, Queen Philippa, Blanche of Lancaster, and to some extent Alice Perrers. Now, in the mid-eighties, he was in fairly regular attendance on Queen Anne, to whom he had affectionately alluded at least once—probably twice—in *Troilus and Criseyde* (in Book I, ll. 171-3, and in Book V, l. 1778, where "Penelopeës trouth" is usually taken as a reference to faithful Anne), and for whose amusement he now wrote the *Legend* and began the *Canterbury Tales.* He probably read for Anne more or less regularly, as he is shown doing in the frontispiece of one of the *Troilus* manuscripts, and probably traveled with her to Wallingford Castle in July and August 1385, to visit Princess Joan. The two ladies felt great affection for one another, and Joan was now too ill to travel, as she'd done in the past, to visit Anne. Both ladies, according to a fairly standard reading, are complimented in Chaucer's Prologue to the *Legend.*

When Chaucer moved to Greenwich, he probably took all his family with him except for Elizabeth, who was now in a convent, generously helped by John of Gaunt. Thomas Chaucer was now twelve or so, away at school at least much of the time, probably in London; before long he would be placed in the retinue of some great lord, probably Gaunt, for training as a squire, after which he would become Gaunt's regular retainer. Lewis was four or five, still in the care of his nurse, presumably. Though Chaucer's work for the king kept him busy, we can be sure he spent as much time as he could with his children, and perhaps with Lewis especially. In families like Chaucer's, it was not unusual to get a child started on his reading early, and we know from Chaucer's remarks in the *Astrolabe* that Lewis was quick, especially at mathematics. Sometime before Lewis was ten Chaucer may have written for him his book on the *Sphere,* that is, the planet Earth, which his treatise on the use of the astrolabe would follow. It may be that Lewis, and sometimes Thomas, went along with their father when he inspected the work of his carpenters and masons, or visited tenants on the royal estates; he may have taken them boating with him on the royal lakes and ponds, partly for pleasure, partly for a look at dike walls and bridges. He was no doubt, as his own father had been, ambitious for his children. They could hardly have managed as well as they did in later life, even granting Gaunt's friendship, without the security and confidence that comes with parental love and encouragement. We know that Thomas's main work in later life—and it was probably the same with Lewis—was taking care of such royal holdings as Petherton Forest. It was probably in Greenwich, tagging along after their father, watching and listening, joking with him on the way home, that they got their first taste of stewardship over crown lands.

Philippa Chaucer was probably there too, and possibly not well. She was now in her mid-forties—old age for a woman of the Middle Ages, worn down by childbearing and, even more, by living indoors in a time when houses, whatever their elegance, were drafty, damp, and cold. (If Philippa had more than three children, no record survives; but the odds are that, like other women of her class, she had more than three children and that some or all of those others died in infancy.) It may possibly have been Philippa's health that persuaded Chaucer and his courtly patrons that the family should move to the country. All this is of course pure speculation, but it is apparently the case that Philippa had now given up all work as a lady-in-waiting and that she no longer collected her annuities in person. Within three years she would be dead.

If Philippa was ill, Chaucer's life was hectic indeed at this period. Besides all his work as steward for the king, seeing to the upkeep of his two favorite residences, he was writing harder and better than ever before, dashing off rough copies for his scrivener Adam, a boy with long, curly locks, Chaucer tells us, and sometimes a careless copying hand, so that the poet was once tormented into writing—sharply but affectionately (as the comic "scallë" shows)—

> Adam scriveyn, if ever it thee bifallë
> Boece or Troylus for to wryten newë,   [*Boethius*]
> Under thy long lokkës thou most have the scallë   [*scabby disease*]
> But after my makyng thou wrytë morë trewë;
> So ofte a-daye I mot thy werk renewë,   [*must*]
> It to correcte and eek to rubbe and scrapë,
> And al is thorugh thy negligence and rapë!

Though Chaucer was writing for Queen Anne the final draft of the *Troilus* (perhaps), the whole *Legend of Good Women,* and parts of the *Canterbury Tales,* he had other demanding work besides, work that kept the bills paid and heightened his prestige but also, obviously, kept him from Philippa and the children. As we've said, he was made, in 1385, a justice of the peace, and he would soon be elected to parliament to fight battles of the greatest importance to the king.

Though the patent of Chaucer's justiceship is dated October 12, 1385, he may have begun his work as JP, filling out the term of Thomas Shardelowe, as early as February of that year, the date of his petition for a deputy to look after the customs. He remained a justice, with one brief interruption, through 1388. During Chaucer's time, until the last year he served, the job brought in no stipend or wages; in 1388 justices were authorized to receive a strictly nominal 4s. ($48) per diem up to twelve days a year; but this was apparently never paid. Some justices nevertheless grew rich, none more conspicuously than Sir Simon Burley. Margaret Galway points out that complaints about the justices were repeatedly lodged by the House of Commons, claiming that these powerful officials "by reason of outrageous fines and other grievances, had worked more to the destruction of the king's subjects than to the reformation of abuses."[5] Among other things, justices were accused of accepting bribes and extorting ransom from prisoners. Between £200 ($48,000) and £300 ($72,000) passed through the justices' hands at a single session, and those who wished to could easily help themselves. Probably Chaucer was one of those who profited, though his natural prudence, the virtue he mocks and celebrates in the *Tale of Melibeus,* may have kept his profit within reasonable bounds. (Burley's lack of that virtue was to cost him his head.)

During Richard's reign, the justices held sessions four times a year for about three days each, meeting at various places in the county, including Greenwich, as the justices decided among themselves. Sessions began early in October, early in January, and about mid-March and mid-June, depending on the date of Easter. Special or petty sessions might be held at any time, at the justices' convenience. All the resident justices were supposed to attend every session held, but later statutes demanding attendance suggest that this requirement was not always met by every justice. The resident's business was

> . . . to see to the enforcement of statutes concerning the regulation of wages, prices, labor and other matters, a task which often involved judicial as well as administrative business. He was also expected, among other things, to see that the inhabitants of his district did not go about armed, practice terrorism, hold unlawful meetings, brawl at inns, or damage property not their own. He was empowered to arrest "suspects" and to take sureties from anyone who threatened injury to another. His jurisdiction covered "all manner of felonies and trespasses" short of treason. These headings included murder, arson, abduction, extortion, abuse of weights and measures, coining of false money, and every variety of theft from petty larceny to the misappropriation of land. The punishments justices could impose were loss of life or limb, imprisonment, fines, forfeiture of chattels to the crown and of lands to the lord.[6]

In addition to the four regular sessions there were special sessions, like that which Chaucer attended at Chislehurst, concerning the abduction of one Isabella Hall in 1387. In these special sessions the business of a justice of Chaucer's rank was to arrest offenders, examine them under oath, and draw up an indictment for the professional justices who were to hear and determine the cases. In trivial cases, the resident justice no doubt acted as judge. No record of any Kent peace session held before Chaucer has been discovered, but several records illustrating typical Kent offenses of a more serious nature—mainly felonies—are summarized in the *Life-Records*:[7] two murders, one felonious assault and threat of murder, and one murder in self-defense.

The office of JP was a minor one for Chaucer (assuming he did not take large bribes), and very little need be said of it. Since the commissioners met only four times a year, discounting special sessions, cases came thick and fast when the regular sessions met. Chaucer had ample, though fleeting, opportunity to study the rascal mind, possibly including the mind of the false coiner or alchemist which he celebrates in the *Canon's Yeoman's Tale*. He must also, from time to time, have been responsible for imprisonments and possibly the severing of a robber's hand or the branding of a fleeing laborer. What he thought of such cruelties—this poet whose work everywhere bespeaks his fundamental gentleness and talent for understanding both sides of every question—we can only guess. If he was sorry to do what he was forced to do, what law enforcement took for granted in those days, he made it up, in a way, with brilliant, sympathetic portraits of scoundrels like the Pardoner.

It was not entirely accidental that by 1386 the county of Kent was largely in the hands of King Richard's friends, from the great, like Burley, to the relatively small, like Chaucer. In 1386 the showdown between Richard and Gloucester came. Though we have no evidence that King Richard or any other interest made any attempt to pack this particular parliament, Kent was clearly a pro-royalist county, and one MP from Kent was Geoffrey Chaucer. Unlike most fourteenth-century MP's, he served only once. He and his Kentish colleague, William Betenham, received two shillings a day for sixty-one days, so Chaucer must have attended the whole stormy session, at the same time fitting in certain other minor business—testifying at the reconvened Scrope-Grosvenor trial on October 15, picking up his annuity and Philippa's on October 20, attending the great hall in the Court of Common Pleas to main-prise his brother-in-law (husband of Chaucer's sister Catherine) Simon Mannington, summoned for debt, on November 13, and on November 28, the day of parliament's dissolution, drawing his reward as controller of the London wool customs. He would surrender that controllership within the week, and ten days later he would surrender his controllership of the petty customs. We can only guess that Chaucer was shaken by what he saw in that session of parliament and thought it a good idea to get out of Gloucester's way.

Chaucer knew before he set out from Greenwich as MP from Kent that Gloucester was the enemy. Gloucester—or rather Thomas of Woodstock, since it was during this parliament that he would receive the more elevated title, duke of Gloucester—was an impressive man, in some ways like his brother John of Gaunt. Gaunt was cool, inclined to seem haughty with enemies or strangers; when he lost his temper it was usually by design, one more brilliant act. Woodstock's temper, on the other hand, was as real as it was terrible, and would eventually prove his ruin. Both had extraordinary will power: they could hold wrangling factions together for years and swing weaker men to positions those men must themselves have found astonishing. Like Gaunt, Woodstock attached great importance to the code and values of chivalry. As a young man he formed a "company of May," apparently writers of poems and carols, whom he remembered fondly in later life.[8] He was a great general, a redoubtable jouster, a man much admired by his enemies the French, who said of him that he spoke like a true king's son. He was fond of music: kept a blind harper in attendance, had an organ in the hall of his great London house, and had tapestries showing angels playing musical instruments. He was fond of literature: kept one of the largest libraries of the time, and had in it not only saints' lives and prayer books but histories, romances, and poems in several languages, including poems by Chaucer. His piety was legendary, more noticeable than Gaunt's because he kept no mistresses, more generously and publicly supported convents, churches, and religious schools, and dressed as somberly as a country priest.

As long as Gaunt had supported Richard, Woodstock had done the same; but now Gaunt was away, and France was gathering an enormous invasion force. The only question for England was, who was to lead the fighting, Richard's courtiers or war-tested magnates chosen by assent of parliament? Chaucer looked on as Richard's chancellor, Michael de la Pole, with young Richard seated on the dais behind him, presented to parliament the king's request for an army of defense. Then Richard coolly retired to his palace at Eltham to await parliament's decision. Word came, during the deliberations, that the despised Robert de Vere, earl of Oxford and marquis of Dublin, had now been exalted to duke of Ireland, and, as a political sop, Thomas of Woodstock had been named duke of Gloucester, and the king's third uncle, Edmund Langley, to duke of York—titles trivial by comparison with de Vere's.

Parliament, no doubt influenced by Gloucester's rage, sent word that it demanded the removal of the king's chancellor and also removal of his treasurer. Richard, in answer, ordered them to be silent, and asserted that he would not at their request remove "a scullion from his kitchen." More messages passed, among others Richard's declaration that he would be willing to meet with a small number of the most important members of the Commons—a group in which the king's man Chaucer would be prominent—but at Gloucester's insistence the proposal was rejected; and so, eventually, came the famous meeting of the king and his uncle, the duke of Gloucester, and Gloucester's friend, Thomas Arundel, bishop of Ely. Both had good reason to hate and fear the king's favorites, especially the scheming would-be murderous de Vere, now duke of Ireland. In a speech bristling with the understandable rage of chivalry against Richard's unmilitant, deer-hunting court, Gloucester demanded that the crown be responsive to the people's needs and ominously warned that, should the king refuse, then "by ancient statute and recent precedent," the people had a remedy. The thinly veiled allusion to the fate of Edward II forced Richard's capitulation.

At parliament he accepted with seeming meekness the impeachment, fining, and imprisonment of Pole, the removal of certain others, and the formation of a "great and continual council" to manage his affairs. Parliament dissolved and Chaucer hurriedly fled home, resigning those customhouse positions that might put him in Gloucester's line of fire. As for the king, he soon showed his scorn of the proceedings. He remitted Pole's fine and sent him to Windsor, where Simon Burley was his jailer and where the king himself went for Christmas. While the council began its work, sealing writs on its own authority, Richard and his favorites slipped away to roam England, Ireland, and Wales, gathering an army and, more important, gathering up legal opinions.

First at Shrewsbury and then at Nottingham, the king met with the highest law officers in the realm and set before them carefully stated questions concerning the legality of the parliament of 1386. Gloucester learned of the meeting with the judges from the archbishop of Dublin, who was present at the meeting at Nottingham. Professor R. H. Jones writes,

> The anxiety of Gloucester and his associates when they heard the archbishop's tale is easy to imagine, for Richard's questions and the replies of the justices amounted to more than a preparation for war against the commission [the council]. They raised ghosts which had been dormant for more than half a century. The awesome word *treason,* with all that it implied of forfeiture, hanging, quartering, disemboweling, and attainted blood had been introduced into the controversy. Taken as a whole, furthermore, the questions constituted a more explicit

and elaborate statement of certain aspects of the royal theory of prerogative right than any which had yet appeared.[9]

The judges' unanimous and inescapable decision—they answered under oath and, despite their later claim, without constraint[10]—was that actions like those of Gloucester and his friends were treasonable. What Richard was after, it needs to be observed, was not an appearance of legality, when the time might come for him to take his revenge, but true legality—defense and clear definition for all time of an English king's rights and privileges.

Armed with his judgments but not, unfortunately, with horsemen and swordsmen, since he imagined his enemies would be bound by the rule of law, the king returned to London and called his lordly enemies to meet him. They excused themselves on the grounds that the king had surrounded himself with men eager to kill them. Richard issued a royal proclamation—a weapon he would use as a substitute for gunpowder much of his life—that no one in the city was to sell anything to the earl of Arundel. Immediately Gloucester, Arundel, and doddering but shrewd old Warwick began to muster forces in Harringway Park, north of London. They withdrew then to Waltham Cross and from there sent out cunning propaganda circulars explaining their opposition to the favorites and calling for support. The propaganda worked, rousing the citizens, and Richard was forced to compromise. Gloucester insisted that he and his companions had never meant harm to the king himself but only meant to save him from evil counsellors. Gloucester demanded trial of the counsellors and demanded that the king imprison them until parliament could assemble. Richard ceremoniously agreed and ordered the meeting of parliament in eleven weeks. His agreement to imprison his favorites slipped his mind, however, and all except Nicholas Brembre—who bravely stayed in London, trying to raise troops—escaped to England's forests.

Parliament, when it met, was furious. (Chaucer, apparently by choice, was not there.) According to the Westminster chronicler, some of the lords wished to depose the king and replace him with Gloucester, who was not unwilling, but old Warwick persuaded them to a course more prudent: gather up an army and hunt down Robert de Vere, duke of Ireland. The army, commanded by, among others, Gaunt's son Henry Bolingbroke, trapped de Vere's army, but failed to catch de Vere, who escaped into fog and whom the king managed to hide and smuggle overseas. Richard retreated for safety to the Tower and apparently began plotting to get help from France against his upstart barons. He sent word to, among others, Geoffrey Chaucer, who sighed, no doubt—this was no work for a born survivor—but immediately dropped everything and took out papers for travel to Europe. For some reason Chaucer never made the trip, though others did. Meanwhile, a solemn parley was arranged at the Tower. Some years earlier, in 1385, when Richard, nineteen and childless, was about to go to war in Scotland, parliament had appointed Mortimer as his heir, and Richard had assented. Now the lords spoke sternly to the king, reminding him that his heir was of an age to rule, "whereupon Richard, *stupefactus,* promised to be governed by them, saving his crown and his royal dignity."[11] The lords appealing to him—the "lords appellant" (Gloucester; Richard Arundel; Thomas Beauchamp, earl of Warwick; Thomas Mowbray, earl of Nottingham; and Gaunt's son Henry Bolingbroke)—took the promise seriously and intended, by God, to govern.

On February 3, 1388, the "Merciless Parliament" convened at Westminster Hall. On February 14, Michael de la Pole, de Vere (earl of Oxford, duke of Ireland), the king's chief justice Robert Tresilian (who'd drawn up the shrewdly phrased questions for the judges), and the archbishop of York were pronounced guilty of treason and, except for the archbishop, saved by his cloth, condemned to its gruesome penalties. Three days later Chaucer's associate, enormously fat Nick Brembre, was charged. When he protested his innocence and offered to defend himself in battle, the king tried to intervene in his behalf, but the five appellants threw their gauntlets clanging at Brembre's feet, and other gauntlets followed "like a fall of snow." On technical grounds, trial by combat was denied. There was debate and struggle and great doubt on all sides that Brembre was guilty of any capital offense, but after three more days of thoroughly crooked and cynical justice he was condemned. Meanwhile Tresilian was caught—already condemned *in absentia.* He was dragged on a hurdle to Tyburn and brutally executed, and Brembre was given the same punishment the following day.

More trials, condemnations, and executions followed. Tyburn ran shoetop-deep in blood. Never before in English history had so many men of gentle birth been executed on such flimsy pretexts. Though it is undoubtedly true that many of Richard's courtiers were greedy, irresponsible, and wrongheaded, none of them was ever proved a criminal and none, certainly, was deserving of murder by the machinery of law and order. In some cases—that of Simon Burley, for instance—the appellants themselves were in fierce disagreement, Henry Bolingbroke staunchly defending Burley, and Edward III's timid, poetry-writing youngest son, Edmund Langley, duke of York, offering to champion Burley in battle against his own brother, the duke of Gloucester. But Gloucester won, his passion not tempered by Gaunt, and he settled down to control of the throne he was half-inclined to believe he ought to occupy. Yet it is probably true to say that it was indeed the king's advisers, not the king, that he hated, and probably true, too, that had he not destroyed the king's beloved friends, the king, when his turn came, would have spared him.

Gloucester's triumph was brief. On May 3, 1389, at a meeting of the great council, Richard asked mildly what his age was. When he was answered—"twenty-two"—he announced his intention, since he was now of full age, of ruling the kingdom in person. It was impossible to object. Moreover, the council's more important enemies were all dead or driven into hiding. In November of that year the last possibility of Gloucester's return to power collapsed when, with all his opponents around Richard destroyed and his hopes in Spain voided, John of Gaunt arrived in England.

The period of Gloucester's supremacy (1386–88) was a grim time for Chaucer, and England's political situation was probably the least of it. It was probably during the summer of 1387 that Philippa Chaucer died. Chaucer drew her last annuity payment on June 18 of that year, and on November 7 he drew his own but not his wife's. Strange to say, for all the facts we have about Chaucer's life, we know nothing of what may have been the most intimate part of it. We may speculate that it was Philippa's final illness or death that spared Chaucer the trip to France when Richard was ensconced in the Tower and in need of help from abroad; but however that may be, Chaucer was with her, or at any rate nearby, when Philippa died, and in all probability so were the children, home from school for the summer. Except for his poem, much earlier, on the death of Blanche of Lancaster, he writes nowhere of the death of a beloved wife—writes only, and often, of the pleasures of love and marriage; and that may be our best clue to what he felt. He speaks often of what women desire of men and men of women—exactly what William Blake meant, in the highest physical and spiritual sense, "The lineaments of satisfied desire." And he makes comedy of men and women who cannot understand that simple truth. It seems impossible that he can have been one of the incompetent husbands his comedies present. He must then have loved his wife and been loved by her, and as for her death, for all his sorrow, he had no faintest doubt—not even his worst villains have the faintest doubt—of the possibility of heaven and the reunion of loved ones. Like other good medieval men, he wept and buried her and walked in the fields with his sons.

Nevertheless, after her death he had no easy time keeping his spirits up. Because he was on the wrong side—that is, the king's side—he was harried and harassed. In 1388, the year of the Merciless Parliament, his Exchequer annuities were transferred—at "his own request," whatever that means—to John Scalby, one of Gloucester's men. It was also in

1388 that Chaucer first began to be sued for debt by John Churchman, by Henry Atwood (or atteWood), hostler, William Venour, grocer and former mayor of London, John Layer (or Leyre), another grocer, and by Isabella Buckholt, administratrix of the goods of Walter Buckholt. No one knows exactly what Chaucer's debts involved, but it seems certain that at least one of the men who sued him, William Venour, was a moneylender. Another, Walter Buckholt, had business connections with Chaucer when the poet became chief clerk of the king's works. During and after Chaucer's clerkship, Buckholt acted as deputy parker for the king's park at Clarendon and he may later have been deputy parker at Charing Cross as well. Thus some of Chaucer's debts may have been personal, and then again some or all may have come about because of his work for the king. In the end, of course, it all comes to the same thing. While Gloucester ran the government, Chaucer had unusual difficulty collecting what was due him; and even after Richard took on his kingship in 1389, the government continued to pay Chaucer irregularly, forcing him to stratagems that may well have filled him with weariness and depression of a kind he had described in another connection long ago, in the *Book of the Duchess:*

> Al is ylychë good to me—   [*alike*]
> Joye or sorowë, wherso hyt be—   [*whatsoever*]
> For I have felynge in nothyng,
> But, as yt were, a masëd thyng,   [*dazed*]
> Alway in poynt to falle a-doun. . . .

The amounts of the debts for which his creditors harass him are all relatively small—£3 6s. 8d. ($800) to John Churchman, £7 13s. 4d. ($1,840) to Henry Atwood, £3 6s. 8d. ($800) to William Venour, and so on. Considering the amounts of money Chaucer handled after 1389, when Richard made him chief clerk of the king's works, these debts, still up for collection, must have been mere matters of nuisance; in fact, he regularly failed to appear when summoned and then settled out of court. But though the debts do not tell us, as earlier biographers imagined, that Chaucer was a spendthrift who in his later years suffered for his prodigality, they do reveal that as clerk of the king's works, riding back and forth all over England, a widower now and sometimes discouraged about his poetry, Chaucer was a harried and at times downright unhappy man.

Richard asked for and received the right to govern in May 1389, and immediately began restoring his friends—those who survived—to office.

Chaucer was made chief clerk of the king's works on July 12, an office he would hold until June 1391, by which time he was already connected, probably, with Petherton Forest. He was also given back, in 1389, his Exchequer annuity.

No doubt the office of chief clerk of the king's works seemed at the time Chaucer received it a splendid promotion; but it would soon prove drudgery perhaps beyond anything he'd imagined before. As clerk, he was responsible, according to the writ that gave him his appointment, for

> . . . our works at our Palace of Westminster, our Tower of London, our Castle of Berkhamstead, our Manors of Hennington, Eltham, Clerendon, Shene, Byfleet, Chiltern, Langley, and Feckenham, our Lodges of Hathebergh in our New Forest, and at our other parks, and our Mews for falcons at Charing Cross; likewise our gardens, fish-ponds, mills and park enclosures pertaining to the said Palace, Tower, Castles, Manors, Lodges, and Mews, with power (by self or deputy) to choose and take masons, carpenters and all sundry other workmen and laborers who are needful for our works, wheresoever they can be found, within or without all liberties (Church fee alone excepted); and to set the same to labour at the said works, at our wages.[12]

In taking the job he replaced one Roger Elmham, who had been clerk in all the places named in Chaucer's patent and also for Windsor Castle, including the Windsor manor and lodge, Hadleigh Castle in Essex, and various other manors and lodges. While Chaucer was in office, Windsor remained in control of the constable of the castle; but on the same day as Chaucer's appointment as chief clerk he was also made clerk of the works for St. George's Chapel at Windsor, apparently because construction was in progress there, and the king wished to relieve the financial burden on the Windsor account by throwing the work on the Exchequer.

The drudgery of the work was at least to some extent offset, of course, by the fact that it had a certain importance, even aesthetic importance, and by the fact that the work required talent and experience, even a touch of vision, so that a man could take pride in it—could even consider him-self, if he liked, one of the government's more important officials. He and his assistants would at any rate have a more lasting effect on the appearance of England than would most of their contemporaries. Richard's reign was notable for lavish construction, though the building program was not yet in full swing when Chaucer took the clerkship. Chaucer spent approximately what clerks before him had spent; his im-mediate successor and all who followed during Richard's reign spent vastly more. Even so, an occasional record gives a hint of the consider-able size of Chaucer's undertaking. He employed some of the same master craftsmen used by later clerks and paid some of them extraordinary wages—among others Hugh Swayne, or Hugh Purveyor, a London tiler, and the master mason (and architect) Henry Yeaveley, "the Wren of the fourteenth century," designer of the nave of Westminster Abbey. Choosing such men, helping to revitalize English architecture—rebuilding sections of the Tower and wharf, constructing or repairing lakes, ponds, canals, reshaping the English landscape—must have been for Chaucer at least a little like writing poetry.

He withdrew from or was removed from the clerkship June 17, 1391 —he was now fifty-one or so—transferring his accounts, materials, etc., to one John Gedney, such materials as 101 tons of Stapleton stone and 200 cartloads of Reigate stone for repair of St. George's Chapel, Windsor Castle. Various conjectures have been advanced on why Chaucer left or lost his clerkship, including theories "that he was dilatory" and "that he was unsuccessful as a man of business."[13] Such theories express a charming Romantic prejudice about the poetic life, the idea that poets love adventure and are temperamentally unsuited to being shackled (as Wallace Stevens was so happily) to account books. Chaucer would undoubtedly have smiled at such notions. It's a wonderful thing, he would have said, to be solidly established, to live in a fine house with an army of servants and assistants, to have a hand in things. "Money is a kind of poetry," Wallace Stevens wrote. Chaucer might have argued that 200 cartloads of Reigate stone, gleaming white in the sun, soon to be shaped by human toil into architecture, is an impressive sight. In short, his reasons for leaving the clerkship were probably mundane. The chief work done during Chaucer's time in office was construction he was especially well suited to supervise, the continuing repair and further rebuilding of the wool wharf near the Tower and the houses near the Tower for weighing wool—a project for which Chaucer was paid or assigned over £654 ($156,960), more than half his total expenditure as clerk of the works. (His next largest expenditure was £100 [$24,000] for the work on St. George's Chapel, still unfinished when he left office.) The project was of course an important one for the king, since it involved customs collection, and it may well have been an important one for Chaucer—he may even have had some part in getting it authorized —since as controller of customs he had had first-hand experience with the program's inefficiency. It should be mentioned here that Chaucer was also involved, in 1390, along with his friend Sir Richard Stury and others, in another waterways project, survey and repair of the walls, ditches, etc., on the Thames between Woolwich and Greenwich. A violent freak storm had struck before dawn on March 5, 1390, terrifying the populace and smashing in houses, barns, and hedges. It had blown down more than a hundred oaks at Eltham, just south of Greenwich, and caused extensive flooding and damage to bridges, walls, and drains. The business of Chaucer's commission was to determine what landholders were responsible for repairs and to bring judgment against any whose careless upkeep of their waterways had contributed to the damage. Chaucer's appointment to this job of inspecting damaged waterworks, determining such matters as which ruined watergates were rotten before the storm struck, shows plainly that he was considered an authority on these things. Since his clerkship ended just when his work on the wharf and weighing house ended, the obvious explanation of his leaving the clerkship would seem to be that he was hired as clerk of the king's works because of his special knowledge of the mechanics of wharf construction and customs, and when that special knowledge was no longer needed he was awarded a different, equally desirable but less arduous job.

During his stint as clerk, Chaucer did of course oversee work other than that on the wharf and St. George's Chapel. For instance, he erected the huge scaffolds for jousts at Smithfield in May and October of 1390, as well as scaffolds and barriers for judicial duels whenever an accused man sought to prove his innocence in trial by combat—standard procedure when there were no witnesses to a crime. Such jousting grounds had to be solidly built. For one judicial duel in 1380, the crowd was said to be greater than at Richard's coronation. Chaucer and his assistants had hundreds of other minor construction jobs in hand, but the great work of the period was, as we've said, the Tower and wharf project.

Chaucer's clerkship was, all in all, one of the most difficult offices he ever held. The accounting alone might well have been considered full-time work, yet the office involved far more than that. We have no evidence that a clerk had to be an architect, though at least one great builder, William of Wykeham, did hold the post before Chaucer's time; but the records show that the clerk did in fact, not just in theory, arrange for the buying, hauling, and care of a great variety of building materials, tools, implements, containers, machines, and so on; that if any of these materials were stolen, it was the clerk's business to get them back; and that when the work was finished, he was responsible for selling off leftovers. He was responsible for sitting in judgment on recalcitrant workers, and responsible for finding laborers, skilled and unskilled, and for seeing that laborers, carters, and so on got their pay.

Chaucer was thus on the road a good deal between 1389 and 1391. It was not only a tiresome and arduous business but dangerous as well. Even the best fourteenth-century English roads were crooked and narrow, closed in by high walls, overhung by the huge old beams of trees, and oftentimes darkened (as they are in some parts of England today) by rain or fog or, in the winter, drifting snow. After dark there were no lights along the way: medieval houses in the countryside had shutters, not windows of glass, so that even a relatively populous town could be as silent and dark as a present-day mountain village in, say, Crete. English villages were farther apart then than now; it took days to ride from one major center to another—for instance, for Chaucer to reach the king's works in York; and there were fewer travelers on the walled, rut-filled roads. It was a good time for gangs of highwaymen, and England was full of them.

On September 3, 1390, near the notorious "foul oak" in Kent, a huge, morose old tree where both hangings and robberies frequently took place—according to the parliament of 1387, Nicholas Brembre one dark night hanged twenty-two felons there without bothering about a trial—a newly formed, professional Kentish gang took position in the limbs and shadows to wait for its prey. They were no country bumpkins: two could plead their clerical knowledge of Latin to escape the penalties of civil law; two were old hands at escaping jail; all the gang's members had probably had war experience, and they had all been operating for a long time with one gang or another and had never been taken as highway-men.

But they miscalculated when they decided to rob the portly, graying servant of the king coming under them now, right on schedule, on his horse. Chaucer's horse whinnied and violently shied toward the center of the road as the gang dropped suddenly on every side, swords drawn, and shouted (if we may trust old folksongs), "Stand!" Chaucer, as a man of sense, obeyed. The highwaymen took his horse and other property, probably including the property of the one or two guards riding with him, then perhaps beat him up (since the word used in the indictment against them is *depredare,* take by force, rather than the weaker word *furari,* steal), took from him £20 ($4,800) belonging to the king, and fled.

It was of course Chaucer's business to have contacts all over central England and especially in Kent, and it was the law's special business to see that the king, above all, should never be robbed with impunity. Even if the gang had not been so foolhardy as to rob Chaucer a second and third time at Westminster and then at Hatcham (both on September 6), the crown might well have tracked them down. The man who seemed such easy pickings was the gang's undoing.

The records are confusing, or at any rate inconsistent, and have been variously interpreted. Chaucer may, some think, have been robbed only once, not three times. If we take the records literally, he lost £20 6s. 8d. ($4,880) at the foul oak on September 3, and on September 6 at Westminster £10 ($2,400), and at Hatcham in Surrey approximately the same. The robbers were identified and brought to trial—or to a series of trials—before an unusually powerful commission of judges, with many of whom Chaucer had been acquainted as JP. One of the robbers, Richard Brierly, a member of a gang that worked in various counties, pleaded not guilty then later changed his mind and turned state's evidence (in effect), naming as his associates an Irishman, Thomas Talbot *alias* Broad, Talbot's clerk Gilbert, and William Huntingfield, previously a member of a famous Surrey gang. Later Brierly accused one Adam Clerk of helping him in another robbery in Hertfordshire. Adam pleaded not guilty and challenged Brierly to judicial combat, which took place on May 3, 1391. Brierly was defeated and hanged. Adam was hanged a year later for another crime, a robbery in Tottenham. William Huntingfield, who had a special fondness for stealing horses and who had such charm that Richard Manston of Lancashire was willing to risk being hanged himself to help Huntingfield escape, was brought to trial June 17, 1391, on charges of having robbed Chaucer at Westminster and Hatcham. He was found guilty of the Westminster robbery and pleaded his clergy, that is, proved he could read Latin and thus claimed the right to be judged by a Church court. The Hatcham robbery required a Surrey jury, which was summoned for October 6, by which time Huntingfield had escaped from jail. He was recaptured and tried for prison breaking, to which he confessed. What became of him after that is uncertain. Since his plea of clergy is canceled on the Controlment Rolls, the likelihood is that, for all his Latin, he was hanged. As for Thomas Talbot, he too pleaded clergy and was handed over to the archdeacon of York in 1396 as a clerk convict, at which point he vanishes out of history. His clerk Gilbert was outlawed for failure to surrender himself but was apparently never caught and tried. On January 6, 1391, Chaucer's concern in the matter ended when he was excused from having to repay the stolen £20. Five months later he was out of the clerkship altogether, though not yet paid all that was owed him by the government. He would go on trying to collect from the crown, and would go on being harassed for small debts, until the end of his life. But he would receive, at the same time—both from Richard and from Gaunt's son, Henry IV—the honors due him as the greatest living poet in Europe. He would visit Oxford often, where he had various old friends and where his "little son Lewis" was studying, and until Gaunt's death he would be a frequent guest of John of Gaunt, where Thomas Chaucer was a favorite retainer and where many of Chaucer's old friends and their numerous children were either retainers or regular visitors.

Nine: the Deaths of Gloucester, John of Gaunt, and the Hero of this Book

 WE HEAR OFTEN OF POETS WHO AT SOME point lose their creative power, as Wordsworth and Coleridge both believed they did; and it has often been suggested—at least twice by Chaucer himself—that Chaucer was such a man. It is of course true that he came nowhere near finishing his enormous project the *Canterbury Tales;* but we may perhaps be mistaken in taking too much to heart his statement that "elde [old age], that in my spirit dulleth me, / Hath of endyting all the subtilte / Wel nygh bereft out of my remembraunce." Those lines, from the Envoy to the *Complaint of Venus,* do sound, I think, like the serious lament of an old man annoyed at his inability, of late, to write poetry as he once did, and they may also suggest, since they appear in a poem addressed to some "princesse" or, perhaps, to certain "prynces" (the manuscripts differ), that at the time he wrote them he was not presenting much poetry at court, or that the poetry he did present was not as favorably received as were his earlier works—such masterpieces from the middle or late eighties as *Troilus and Criseyde,* the *Legend of Good Women,* and some of the earlier Canterbury tales.

But we should remember, in trying to understand what these lines mean (or in considering the more obviously joking lines about his sleeping muse in the *Envoy a Scogan*), that even when Chaucer is most serious, the strain of ironic self-mockery runs deep. In poem after poem he jokes about his mental or physical deficiencies, and while the joking reflects a perfectly serious self-critical habit of mind, it also comically exaggerates what the poet sees as his actual defects. His lines to Henry Scogan make clear that he was not, in his last years, as prolific as he had once been, but they do not really say much more than that. In the poem to Scogan he gives joking advice, then imagines Scogan refusing to take him seriously and exclaiming, "Lo, olde Grisel [Gray-head] lyst [loves] to ryme and playe!" To this imagined exclamation Chaucer protests:

> Nay, Scogan, say not so, for I m'excusë—
> God helpë me so!—in no rym, dowteles,
> Ne thynke I never of slep to wakë my musë,
> That rusteth in my shethë stille in pees.
> While I was yong, I put hir forth in press;   [urgency, press]
> But al shal passë that men prose or rymë;
> Take every man hys turn, as for his tymë.

286

His muse has been sleeping soundly for years and not even for this poem, Chaucer says, will he awaken her. Yet the envoy to Scogan shows anything but a decline in poetic power. Thus Chaucer's claim that he has forgotten the art of poetry may have meant to Chaucer not at all what it would mean to the rest of us.

We have fairly good evidence that what actually happened is that in his last years Chaucer did *not* write less brilliantly than he'd written before (though he was now writing less), but, rather, wrote in a quirky new way. He became less interested in poetry as mimesis, or the imitation of character and action, and increasingly interested in poetry as an exalted and significant form of—in the most literal sense—clowning. Though he may have had his doubts about the odd new direction in which his art had moved, he was in fact discovering an approach to art that would come into general favor among artists only in the twentieth century. How, one asks, did this remarkable shift of direction come about?

In the early nineties King Richard was doing well; and so, of course, was Chaucer. The poet was relieved of his arduous job as clerk of the king's works (in 1391) and given employment less demanding, apparently two brief stints as subforester of Petherton Forest but for the most part no work but stewardship over the royal estate at Greenwich, if it is true that he lived there until 1397 or even 1399, when he retreated to a smaller but still fine house protected by sanctuary, where his creditors or (perhaps) the government's creditors could not trouble him. In other words, for several years—between 1391 and 1397 or so, with only brief interruptions, as we'll see—Chaucer was, for the first time in his life, his own man, "wel at ease," reaping the benefits of a life of strenuous public service. He was often in London, where he picked up his annuities and an occasional royal gift, settled out of court, from time to time, with creditors, and visited old friends. He probably gave readings at the royal court—he'd been doing so, off and on, for years, and Richard's esteem for the poet had not diminished; when the king's fortune takes a dangerous turn, shortly before his death, Chaucer will be one of the first he will call upon for help.

Chaucer was now a widower, his sons were away, one in the service of Gaunt's court, one at school, so he had ample time to write. Philippa's death was receding in time, and the emotions which must have attended that wound in the flow of Chaucer's life were gradually being calmed and ritualized in the accepted medieval way, by the regular singing of requiem masses, the lighting of candles, and, perhaps, by annual memorials. He had company when he liked. His sister Kate and her family lived nearby; Gaunt was back in England; students came to visit and work with him. And the mansion he lived in, with its various servants, its wide lawns and parks, was all any poet in his right mind could desire. Old as in some moods he thought himself, he had not lost all interest in beautiful women or in the royal court's gossip about ladies and their gentlemen. We have, from the late nineties, one broadly comic invitation to love, which the poet wrote for "Rosemounde," and two delightful verse-letters on love and marriage, the one to Scogan on the occasion of his renunciation of a lady he'd been pursuing, and one to Bukton, whose approaching marriage seems to have struck Chaucer as not a good idea. The common interpretation that the poem is an outright denunciation of marriage, it should be mentioned, is quite mistaken. Marriage *can* be bondage, Chaucer says. It can be the very "cheyne of Sathanas [Satan]." But if Bukton is sure of his love he need have no dread whatever, Chaucer adds, and he advises Bukton to look again at what Chaucer has written in the *Wife of Bath's Tale*.

In short, Chaucer had at last achieved what ought to have been an ideal situation for writing poetry. At least during the early nineties, he made good use of that opportunity, composing poetry not much different from the kind that had made him famous. He made during this period a sudden change in his grand plan for the *Canterbury Tales*. He had written by now, not necessarily in this order (since the *Prologue* is late), the *General Prologue*, the *Knight's Tale, Miller's Tale, Reeve's Tale*, fragmentary *Cook's Tale*, along with their prologues and introductions, and several others, including the present *Shipman's Tale*. Though the evidence is too intricate for presentation here,[1] we can be virtually certain that the original Man of Law's tale was the present *Tale of Melibeus*. (The Man of Law's introduction prepares for a tale in prose but is followed, surprisingly, by a tale in verse, obviously a late insert; and the *Melibeus* is full of legal jargon.) Watching court affairs from the quiet and seclusion of Greenwich, far from "the stremës hed," and talking with friends during his visits to London, Chaucer observed with increasing disappointment the growth of his beloved king's absolutist theory, and at last he was stirred to make his sentiments known in the most effective way available to him as an admired court poet. He began his great revision. He tore out the Man of Law's tale of Melibeus and inserted, instead, the Man of Law's tale of Custance, or Constancy, an intentionally overstated argument for blind submission to authority (to God, to king, to husband)—precisely what King Richard was demanding. The heroine's meek response to her father's order that she go marry a sultan far, far from home, is typical:

"Allas! unto the Barbre nacioun   [*barbarian*]
I moste anoon, syn that it is youre willë;
But Crist, that starf for our redempcioun   [*died*]
So yeve me grace his heestës to fulfillë!
I, wrecchë woman, no fors though I spillë!   [*die*]
Wommen are born to thraldom and penancë,
And to been under mannës governancë."

Even standing alone, this pious, carefully tongue-in-cheek tale—a work
not comic but ironic—must have struck the knowing in Chaucer's audience
as tactful criticism of some of King Richard's most cherished opinions.
But to remove all doubts, Chaucer followed the *Man of Law's Tale* with
a new tale for the Wife of Bath (she had been, in his earlier draft, the
teller of the *Shipman's Tale*). Whereas formerly the Wife was simply
the jovial revealer of women's wiles, she now becomes a bold advocate
of the rights of women, beginning her remarks with a frontal attack on
the lawyer's oppressive ideal, Constancy:

"Experiencë, though noon auctoritee
Were in this world, is right ynogh for me
To speke of wo that is in mariagë!"

Thus Chaucer's tactfully indirect series on right and wrong government,
that is, the "marriage group," was born.

He had never written more brilliantly. The colloquial lilt is as human
as ever, the imagery as luminous, the plotting as economical and sure.
And Chaucer's development of his overall theme is equally brilliant.
The Wife of Bath's argument is essentially a noble and selfless one, that a
wife (or subject) should be given control, whereupon she will inevitably
relinquish government to her lord out of love. But the argument she
offers has also its darker implications, for she claims that if a wife is *not*
freely granted control she will seize it and tyrannize her lord.

That argument sets the medieval hierarchy on its head, and the *Friar's
Tale*, which follows, lightheartedly develops that absurdity. The tale
begins:

Whilom ther was dwellynge in my contree
An erchedeken, a man of heigh degree,   [*archdeacon*]
That boldëly dide execucioun
In punysshynge of fornicacioun,
Of wicchëcraft, and eek of bawdëryë,
Of diffamacioun, and avowtryë. . . .   [*adultery*]

For smalë tithes and for smal offryngë
He madë the peple pitously to syngë.
For er the bisshop caughte hem with his hook,
They weren in the erchëdeknes book. . . .
He hadde a somonour redy to his hond;
A slyer boyë nas noon in Engëlond;   [*boy or devil*]
For subtilly he hadde his espiaillë   [*spy system*]
That taughte hym wel wher that hym myghte availlë.

It is of course the bishop's business to correct sinners (pull them back into the fold with his sheep crook), the archdeacon's business to serve the bishop, and the summoner's business to execute the orders of the archdeacon. In the *Friar's Tale* the summoner is chief agent, not servant, striking before the archdeacon has given him the order, as the archdeacon strikes before hearing from the bishop. In such a universe, the tale proves, only the lowest creature in the cosmic hierarchy, the Devil, can put things right.

Chaucer develops his debate on government down through the *Franklin's Tale,* where, as we said earlier, a balance of sorts is at last achieved. The husband in the tale works with full authority granted him by his wife and aimed at her benefit, exactly the arrangement recommended by the English political theorist Henry Bracton, who defines "the king's pleasure" (*quod principi placuit*) as not the king's private wish but the welfare of his bride the state. We need not trace here the argument of the tales or the functions, within the larger scheme, or the pilgrims' rivalries. The point is merely that in the early nineties, when Richard was in full control of the government and was beginning to act upon his theory of monarchy, Chaucer responded with magnificent stories of the mimetic sort, fitting them to his larger purpose.

We may doubt that he ever lost his ability to tell a dramatic story. The *Pardoner's Tale* is certainly late—that magnificent retelling of an ancient plague legend, thick with gloomy and mysterious atmosphere: the jangling guitars in the dark, smoky tavern, the eerie old man in black whom the three drunken revelers meet, an old man who may perhaps be Death, may perhaps be the Wandering Jew, or an ancient spirit from Welsh legendry, or nothing more than a frightened old man (the blurring of the image is of course intentional). And the *Nun's Priest's Tale* and *Canon's Yeoman's Tale,* stories as perfect as any ever written, are also certainly late works.

But though he had not forgotten how to write great stories, Chaucer became, in his last years, interested in another kind of art—an art rediscovered by important writers of our own time: the art of, so to speak, bad art. Perhaps the discovery was all but inevitable for a realist like Chaucer, once he had settled on the idea of a literary contest among the pilgrims. Someone, after all, had to lose miserably. Why not several?

He had toyed with bad art and unreliable narrators before. The *House of Fame* is, among other things, a clownish *Divine Comedy*. And though the poet's young friend John Lydgate admired it with monkish serious-ness, Chaucer's recent *Tale of Melibeus* was a parody of a popular bas-tard genre. A glance at how the *Melibeus* works will help us understand the comic impulse behind the later clowning poems.

From the coupling of the tale genre and the rhetoric book, with its lists of figures and quotations, came that blear-eyed prodigy the quotation collection tied to narrative. In this genre, typically, a character decides on so-and-so and quotes every possible authority on the subject; his friend objects and, in turn, quotes authorities; another friend points out dif-ficulties lodged in both points of view and, in *his* turn, quotes authori-ties . . . and so on. In the *Tale of Melibeus* Chaucer borrows an old and especially awkward quotation narrative and vastly expands it, making the absurdity more marked. Chaucer's character Melibeus is so violently angry that he is determined to kill his enemies. In such a situation a man is not likely to stop for thought, but Melibeus stops to give a long string of quotations justifying his impulsive and wrathful plan. His wife (Pru-dence) advises that he seek outside advice and gives justifying quotations. He decides she may be right and gives quotations proving it, then seeks advice from his friends, who give him advice with innumerable quota-tions. Prudence disagrees with the friend's advice and proves with quo-tations that Melibeus should listen to her instead. And so on.

Here, obviously, Chaucer is creating intentionally bad art, originally no doubt a prank on the courtly audience that had assembled to hear him, expecting, as always, something vivid and delightful. Giving the *Melibeus* to his character "Chaucer" in the *Canterbury Tales,* and prefacing it with that character's actually sly but seemingly pitiful appeal that the Host not once more interrupt him, Chaucer achieves a similar effect, this time a prank on the pilgrims.

But though Chaucer had earlier played, on occasion, with intentional bad art, during his last years—living in virtual retirement, free to write, if he wished, for his own satisfaction—he began to work more earnestly with this curious new form he'd discovered, what I should like to call the "clown poem," a work of art designed as inept imitation not of life but of art, a work which achieves the ends of art by indirection or— gleefully—not at all! Now and then he took poems he'd written long ago and no longer liked, such as the *Monk's Tale,* and fitted them to his new purpose. More often he wrote magnificent new atrocities, such as the

Physician's Tale, the *Tale of Sir Thopas,* the *Prioress's Tale,* or the *Manciple's Tale.*

Chaucer had been impressed for years by the questions posed by philosophical nominalism, especially the notion that no man can really understand or communicate with another. He may not have agreed with the nominalist's solipsistic view, but the question was difficult and serious. He had worked with it, years ago, in the *House of Fame.* The symbolic superstructure of that poem—implied (as various critics have shown) by biblical allusions, quotations from the classics and the *Divine Comedy,* and so on—had been calculated to remind the reader of God's vast and orderly plan of the universe; but "Geffrey," the poem's narrator, had been characterized as a dimwit incapable of even glimpsing that plan, though he benefited from it all the same. Later, in the first three tales of the Canterbury collection, Chaucer had dealt again with the problem, limited human intelligence and man's tendency to impose his own character on the universe. The *Knight's Tale* presents what we should probably take as Chaucer's opinion on how the universe works: Divine Providence is just and merciful. But the drunken Miller immediately rises to "requite" the Knight, and gives a vision of the universe as *he* understands it, and then the Reeve tells a tale which presents a third opinion. For the Miller, people get exactly what they deserve, not more than they deserve, through the mercy of God, as the Knight would insist. And for the Reeve, whose chief motivation is spite (as he tells us), revenge is everything, so that the truth about the world is that people get the worst their enemies can do to them. Who is right, the Knight, the Miller, or the Reeve? And if an answer is possible, how do we convince the drunken Miller or the irascible old Reeve? That is precisely the nominalist argument: there is no common ground of humanity, no "human nature" as celebrated by Aquinas; no understanding. Then how can there be justice in the world, fair government, ordered society? That is the theme of the *Canterbury Tales.*

No fourteenth-century nominalist used the word "relativism," but every nominalist understood at least something of that queasy feeling we get while we laugh at a play by Samuel Beckett. The shock set off by the fourteenth century's study of optics was not much different from the shock set off by men like Einstein in our own age. If there is no norm for human vision—or, in our own age, if time and space slither—what can we be sure of, what absolutes survive? For a devout Christian artist, the only absolutes, finally, are (1) God's love and (2) man's art, that is, the trustworthy emotion and perception of a man who carefully sets down what he sees. But nominalism teaches that all vision, even the artist's vision, is mere opinion. One *feels* there are truths that can be discovered, not just affirmed (as we affirm, on scant evidence, God's justice and love). But how can one defend them? All serious artists today, I think, face what nominalists faced: the impossibility of saying anything, though one knows, or at certain times briefly imagines, that there is something profoundly true that, somehow, one might say.

Christian and optimistic to the soles of his feet, Chaucer could look with serenity on his own artistic helplessness. Even in the more conventional of his latest tales—the *Nun's Priest's Tale,* for instance—he could not present any noble value without sharp ironic undercutting, a kind of undercutting he hadn't felt he needed, some years earlier, when he was writing of the ennobling effects of love on Troilus (Book III, ll. 1799 ff.). But in the late clown poetry, the act of writing *itself* is mocked as absurd.

Chaucer's Physician in the *Canterbury Tales* is a more or less decent, intensely serious man—as is any artist—yet the "work of art" he creates, the *Physician's Tale,* is a catastrophe. Trying to present a lifelike character (he will later tell the pilgrims how to raise little girls as virtuous as this Virginia), he chooses exactly the wrong poetic devices, all of which make her a figure of art, not life. The Physician imagines Dame Nature —an allegorical abstraction—speaking of having created Virginia:

> "Lo! I, Nature,
> Thus kan I *forme* and *peynte* a creature,
> Whan that me list; who kan me *countrefete?*
> Pigmalion noght, though he ay *forge* and *bete,*
> Or *grave,* or *peynte;* for I dar wel seyn,
> Apelles, Zanzis, sholde werche in veyn   [*work*]
> Outher to *grave,* or *peynte,* or *forge,* or *bete,*
> If they presumed me to *countrefete. . . ."*

This sort of thing goes on for several more lines; and when the tale itself comes, it is equally unconvincing: Chaucer carefully removes every feature of motivation in his source (a great work by Livy), introduces confusion and plot inconsistency, ghastly padding to fill out lines, and so on. When the *Physician's Tale* was read—Chaucer performed it presumably in the priggish Physician's voice and manner—his courtly audience must have been left in stitches. The Pardoner, who tells the following tale, is not, like the Physician, essentially upright (though rigidly moralistic); instead he is a self-confessed scoundrel, a homosexual and probably a eunuch who brazenly flaunts his abnormality and makes obscene advances to Harry Bailey himself, Host of the pilgrimage, stirring the innkeeper to rage. Yet base and offensive as he is, the work of art he presents is a masterpiece.

In other late works, Chaucer explores the problem of art's unreliability in other ways. In the *Second Nun's Tale* he imitates an antique genre, in fact an antique set of religious emotions, those proper to the long-outmoded saint's legend, and for textural richness superimposes on this ancient music an alchemistical allegory. If the poem had been written in, say, the ninth century, its subject would have been the life of St. Cecilia, and its central emotion would have been humble Christian devotion. Written near the close of the fourteenth century, the ancient genre itself, and the simple religious emotion that informed it, become the object of the poet's exploration. In the *Tale of Sir Thopas* Chaucer parodies the most popular doggerel form of his day, the metrical romance, at once satirizing the form and (as Lewis Carroll would do with Robert Southey's rhythms later) showing what kinds of material its rhythms cried out for. Again, in his most ambitious clown poem, the *Manciple's Tale,* he bloats a simple fable about how the Crow became black into a comic masterpiece of pretentious nonsense. The poem closes with what might stand as Chaucer's comment on the nominalist conflict—the urge to speak and the doubt that anything can be said. For sixty-two lines (in outrageous parody of some lines by John Gower), the Manciple speaks of the importance of not speaking (lest one bring evil on one's head, as did the crow in the fable), babbling lines that might serve as a model of art so bad that, finally, it's good.

> Lordyngës, by this ensample I yow preyë,
> Beth war, and taketh kep what that I seyë:
> Ne telleth neverë no man in youre lyf
> How that another man hath dight his wyf;   [*lain with*]
> He wol yow haten mortally, certeyn.
> Daun Salomon, as wisë clerkes seyn,
> Techeth a man to kepen his tongë weel.
> But, as I seyde, I am noght textueel.
> But nathelees, thus taughtë me my damë:
> "My sonë, thenk on the crowe, a Goddës namë!
> My sonë, keep wel thy tonge, and keep thy freend.
> A wikked tonge is worsë than a feend;
> My sonë, from a feend men may hem blessë.
> My sonë, God of his endelees goodnessë
> Walled a tongë with teeth and lippës ekë,   [*also*]
> For man sholde hym avysë what he speekë.
> My sonë, ful oftë, for to muchë spechë
> Hath many a man been split, as clerkës techë;   [*killed*]
> But for litel speche avysely
> Is no man shent, to spekë generally.   [*hurt*]
> My sonë, thy tongë sholdestow restreynë

At allë tymes, but whan thou doost thy peynë
To speke of God, in honour and preyerë.
The firstë vertu, sone, if thou wolt leerë,
Is to restreyne and kepë wel thy tongë;
Thus lernë children whan that they been yongë.
My son, of muchel spekyng yvele avysed,
Ther lassë spekyng haddë ynough suffisëd,
Comth muchel harm; thus was me toold and taught.   [much]
In muchel spechë synnë wanteth naught.
Wostow whereof a rakel tongë serveth?   [Knowest thou . . . rash]
Right as a swerd forkutteth and forkerveth
An arm a-two, my deerë sone, right so
A tongë kutteth freendshipe al a-two.
A jangler is to God abhomynable.
Reed Salomon, so wys and honurable;
Reed David in his psalmës, reed Senekkë.
My sonë, spek nat, but with thyn heed thou bekkë.   [nod]
Dissimule as thou were deef, if that thou heerë
A janglerë speke of perilous mateerë.
The Flemyng seith, and lerne it if thee lestë,   [please]
That litel janglyng causeth muchel restë.
My sone, if thou no wikked word hast seyd,
Thee thar nat drede for to be biwreyd;   [betrayed]
But he that hath mysseyd, I dar wel sayn,
He may by no wey clepe his word agayn.   [call back]
Thyng that is seyd is seyd, and forth it gooth,
Though hym repente, or be hym neverë so looth.
He is his thral to whom that he hath sayd
A tale of which he is now yvele apayd.
My sonë, be war, and be noon auctour newë
Of tidyngës, wheither they been false or trewë.
Whereso thou come, amongës hye or lowë,
Kepë wel thy tonge, and thenk upon the crowë."

This late, intentionally clumsy poetry has not been much admired until recently. Perhaps it was not much admired in Chaucer's day; we will probably never know. But whatever his friends and patrons may have thought of it, writing such poetry, and chuckling over its awfulness, was one of the pleasures of the poet's peaceful old age.

Though his moment of success was destined to be brief, by the mid-nineties Richard had made himself a popular king—if one criticized for arrogance—and seemed, with Gaunt's help, to have patched up relations with his magnates. Scotland was quiet; Gaunt and Gloucester, along with Thomas Percy and Chaucer's friend (God's traitor) Sir Lewis Clifford, had brought off a four-year truce with France (a truce that would later be extended); Richard's pacifist policy had brought in a boom of prosperity, though most lords seemed not to understand at the time that peace and the new prosperity were related; and Richard himself had achieved peace in Ireland, almost without bloodshed, honoring and knighting those barbaric wildmen, as the chronicle writers of England called them, and pardoning the malcontents who'd risen against him, even offering to admit native Irish kings and chiefs to full legal status under the crown. Though some Englishmen were horrified, no one could deny the effectiveness of Richard's strategy. The former appellants seemed, in general, to be reconciled now to Richard's rule, partly because, in the economic boom, they prospered by it—or all were reconciled but Arundel, still defiant and suspicious, and rumored to be secretly in support of local rebellions against Lancaster and Gloucester in 1394. Arundel openly attacked John of Gaunt in parliament for his undue access to the king (that age-old and, of course, legitimate complaint), his overbearing manners in council and parliament, his overly self-enriching acquisition of the duchy of Aquitaine, his costly and self-serving Spanish mission, and the peace treaty he was at the time engineering with France. Richard ferociously defended his uncle and his own pacific policy against Arundel's old-fashioned and suicidal blood lust, forcing Arundel to groveling apology and frightening him into requesting, a short while later, a special charter of pardon for his earlier misdeeds. Despite the charter, all was not forgiven and forgotten on either side. When Queen Anne died that summer— throwing the king into a paroxysm of grief—old Arundel failed to join the funeral procession from Sheen (the greatest funeral ever seen in England) and appeared late at Westminster Abbey with a request, outrageous under the circumstances, that he be permitted to withdraw from the service. Richard struck him to the ground in a fury, "polluting the sanctuary with Arundel's blood," ordered him jailed in the Tower for weeks, and later forced him to take an oath of good behavior with bond set, if Arundel should break that oath, at an incredible £40,000 ($9,600,-000).

But Arundel was, for a time, the exception. Nottingham (Thomas Mowbray) had been brought around long since and, by Richard's policy of conciliation, made warden of the east march of Scotland and captain of Calais; Warwick had retired from politics; and Gaunt's troublesome son Henry—one of the lords appellant who had worked against Richard and arranged what Gaunt, among others, saw as the murder of Richard's friends—was no longer active, being frequently abroad, fighting with great success and joy in whatever small battles broke out on land or sea, building up a glorious reputation. Though the king's pacifist policy (frequently blamed on Gloucester and Gaunt by contemporaries) was not itself popular, no one could find strong grounds for denying the advantage of peace under a crown buttressed—as it was expressed in that original coronation rite—by family solidarity and the lords' consent. As for Gaunt, his natural inclination to loyalty was powerfully reinforced now by need. Constance of Castile had died in March 1394; he could hope for no better than the role of an English baron. He played that role carefully and wisely, as well as theatrically, making himself chief advocate of Richard's policy—and was duly rewarded. In January 1396, he married Katherine Swynford; parliament granted legitimacy to their children, and Gaunt's holdings and liberties were greatly enlarged. Except in Gaunt's own heart, the misdeeds of his heir, Henry Bolingbroke, as one of the appellants, appeared to have been forgotten. Richard's position was further strengthened in that he also, by grants and favors, made at least some friends among the lesser territorial aristocracy, the class which furnished parliament's knights of the shire.

On March 9, 1396, Richard achieved his twenty-eight-year truce with France and the marriage alliance which served as its symbol and support. The pale, pretty child-queen Isabella was formally delivered to him at Calais in October, with the spectacular pageantry that was Richard's special art. It seemed the greatest achievement to date of Richard's policy, and those who were there were struck by Richard's obvious—indeed, extraordinary—delight in his tiny queen; but the achievement would prove to be in fact the beginning of serious troubles. The treaty's first draft had contained a clause pledging the French royal house to support King Richard "against all manner of people who owe him any obedience and to aid and sustain him with all their power against any of his subjects." This ominous-sounding clause, dropped later, was probably intended to refer to English Gascony or, possibly, to rebellions of English peasants, but it filled the English aristocracy with uneasiness. And there were other problems. Richard's marriage to a child raised succession doubts, and his seemingly fantastic hope of winning the crown as Holy Roman Emperor—a hope he was actively pursuing at this time—stirred up doubts, or strengthened doubts, of the king's mental balance. Weird rumors began to circulate. It was said that when the body of his former favorite, Robert de Vere, was returned to England, the king had ordered that the coffin be opened and "had gazed long and earnestly upon the face of the embalmed corpse, clasping the jewel-laden fingers."[2] King Richard's disturbed behavior in the late nineties gave color to such stories. He began to talk as if obsessed, in public and private, about his murdered forbear, Edward II, whom he had come to see—as a matter of policy, but also as a matter of intense personal emotion—as a martyred saint. He had for years been imitating what he considered Edward's style: the favoritism, the extravagant gifts, the piety, the pageantry, the hawking, the lordly disdain of parliamentary interference with his personal affairs. It was a ploy which his enemies were glad to use against him. His intelligent and frequently explained pacifist policy became laziness and ineptitude like Edward's. Richard's love of the arts, his marriage to a sexually unthreatening child, his use of the new French handkerchief, became to hostile rumormongers proofs that, like Edward II, he was homosexual. Richard scorned the rumors, insisted on what he saw as the legitimate parallels, and bullied his way on. It was a dangerous idea, and the king was too much the conscious artist not to be fully aware himself of the possible conclusions of the course of imitation he'd set himself: either he would justify absolutism, reversing history's judgment of Edward II and changing the end of Edward's life story in his own life story, or Edward's tragedy must happen twice. He played the strange game courageously, perhaps partly because only toward the end did he come to the full realization that he could lose.

Richard was still in firm control in 1397, when the Commons complained about the extravagance of his court and, with typical arrogance, the king not only forced them to abject apology but demanded and got from the Lords a resolution that exciting the Commons or anyone else to reform of the royal household was treasonable. His success in bullying parliament led him further, to carefully designed attack and the ultimate destruction of the whole work of Gloucester's Merciless Parliament of 1388. Gloucester inevitably began moving now toward his sometime friend, sometime enemy, the thoroughly unreconstructed earl of Arundel. He made furious attacks on the king's French policy and quietly split with his moderate older brother, Gaunt. Rumors reached Richard that Gloucester was hatching a plot to kill him—the rumors were almost certainly true—and, brooding on the fate of Edward II, Richard decided to strike.

He managed the thing with his usual flair. He issued invitations to a splendid banquet. Gloucester pleaded illness; Arundel stayed home in his fortified castle at Reigate. Old Warwick, who accepted, was received with great cordiality, taken by the hand and royally comforted, and only after the typically Ricardian magnificent dinner clapped in irons and conducted to the Tower. A little later the king took Arundel by treachery, exactly as his enemies would later take Richard. (Like the earlier battle of Edward II and his barons, it was all to be a chess game of mirror moves.) Richard swore a solemn oath before Arundel's brother, the archbishop, that Arundel would suffer no bodily harm if he agreed to come to Richard; when Arundel appeared, the king seized him and locked him up in Carisbrooke Castle. Then he went after Gloucester. With a small army of household troops, Londoners and friends, he rode to Pleshey by night, and when Gloucester, like the king's son he was, came to meet him, in procession with the clerks and priests of his newly founded collegiate church, Richard told him that since Gloucester had refused to heed his invitation he'd come down here to fetch him. With dignity, Gloucester asked for mercy, that quality Geoffrey Chaucer had always insisted "renneth soone in gentil herte." The king replied that Gloucester would be shown just so much mercy as Gloucester himself had shown Sir Simon Burley.

When parliament met, September 17, 1397, it was publicly proclaimed that the three lords were being held on a charge of treason. Soon afterward Arundel's brother Thomas, archbishop of Canterbury, was added to the list. It was a strange parliament for an enlightened place like England. Armed men were everywhere, since the king had invited magnates friendly to himself to bring their armed retinues for his protection, and he'd ordered out his own retainers and yeomen, including the famous Cheshire archers. Westminster Hall was not available, so the estates gathered in a temporary building in the palace yard. Inside it a throne of unusual height had been erected, with space on each side for the appellants and the accused, and space in front for the estates. The archbishop of Canterbury was impeached for his part in the proceedings of 1386–88, found guilty "by notoriety," and sentenced to forfeiture of his temporalities and to perpetual banishment. Then Gaunt, as Steward of England, began the crown's appeal against the three magnates.

He informed Arundel of the charges against him and added, according to one chronicler, "Since parliament has accused you, you deserve according to your own idea of law to be condemned without answer." Arundel's attempts at self-defense were overwhelmed when, in imitation of the action of the Gloucester parliament in its condemnation of Nicholas Brembre, the present appellants threw their gauntlets at Arundel's feet. By command of the king, the lords temporal, and the spokesman for the clergy, Lancaster declared him guilty of treason and pronounced the usual sentence, which the king immediately mitigated by substituting the ax for hanging, drawing, and quartering. Arundel was escorted by the king's Cheshire archers to Tower Hill, and there, in the presence of the two Hollands and his own son-in-law, the earl of Nottingham, beheaded.

Gloucester's case, from the king's point of view, was a touchy one. He had always had support in parliament and was famous for his ability to swing men's opinions; moreover, though he was certainly guilty, in

Gaunt's mind, of treason, he was Gaunt's beloved younger brother. The odds that parliament would convict him were high, but perhaps not as high as the king might have wished; and the king's purpose, which was partly, of course, personal revenge for the lawless murder of his closest friends in 1388, but also partly, and just basically, an impersonal, visibly legal demonstration of the power of the crown (power Gloucester more than anyone else in 1388 had sought to diminish), would be a purpose unfulfilled if Gloucester escaped conviction. Thus it was that when Gloucester was ordered to appear, word came that he was dead already. He was probably murdered, conceivably without Richard's knowledge, perhaps by his former ally Nottingham, now a staunch member of the royalist party. In eccentric but technically legal proceedings he was posthumously convicted of treason and condemned to forfeiture of his estates.

Then old Warwick was brought in. He offered no defense, but, according to the chronicler Adam of Usk, "like a wretched old woman, he made confession of all contained [in the appeal], wailing and weeping and whining that he had done all, traitor that he was, submitting himself in all things to the king's grace." He was sentenced to the full penalty of treason, which the king commuted to perpetual banishment on the Isle of Man. According to Walsingham, Warwick's confession was dearer to King Richard than all the lands of Arundel and Gloucester.

Within the next few months the king managed, again with great show of legality, to rid himself of lesser enemies by banishing them and, in some cases, seizing their property, which he redistributed among his supporters or attached to the crown. Among others of his lesser former enemies, he found it necessary to deal with the duke of Norfolk and Gaunt's son, Henry, who was by now duke of Hereford and a famous naval hero, a handsome young man nearly as popular with ordinary Englishmen as Richard's father the Black Prince had been. It was, for Richard, a difficult situation. Henry, on his father's advice, had repeated to parliament a conversation between Norfolk and himself, in which Norfolk had urged him to strike at the king, telling him that Richard was out to take revenge on them as he'd taken revenge on Arundel and the rest. Norfolk insisted that the treasonous suggestion came from Henry.

Richard hesitated, racking his wits for a reasonable and politically safe solution. He formed a committee to study the matter and work for a compromise, but both Hereford and Norfolk were stubborn, each insisting that the other was a traitor and a liar. Richard ordered a judicial battle between them, then realized that that was no good either, since if Norfolk won, the victory might be construed as giving credit to his charges against the king, and if Henry won, the victory would give further honor to a magnate popular with the people and potentially threatening to Richard. And so as soon as the two arrived for battle, Richard, almost certainly on Gaunt's advice, abruptly canceled the combat and banished Gaunt's son for ten years, Norfolk for life. Richard had of course merely postponed his ugly problem.

Nevertheless, it seemed that at least for the moment the king had won his fight for power, had done it legally, reinforcing traditional Anglo-Saxon respect for rule by law, and had done it, considering the temper of the times, with remarkable moderation. If he'd been able to use that power well, English history might have followed a very different course. But while Richard was a better man than most historians have allowed, fate was against him.

Though a remarkable number of kings and Popes of the fourteenth century were clinically madmen, it is probably not true, as I've said, that Richard was one, though he was certainly disturbed. Walsingham is a hostile chronicler, but we may perhaps believe of a man like Richard— an idealist and political visionary, hypersensitive aesthetic, violently emotional, secretive, treacherous when necessary, but also deeply religious— that his sleep was broken by Arundel's ghost, so that he was afraid to go to bed without a guard of Cheshire archers, though not, as Walsingham claims, three hundred of them; most people in the Middle Ages seem to have believed, at least tentatively, in ghosts. And it is probably true, though no evidence of insanity, that for fear that the people might venerate Arundel as a martyr, just as Thomas of Lancaster had been venerated in the time of Edward II, Richard had Arundel's tomb removed.

But Richard's streak of paranoia was probably no more than fear of real enemies and betrayal-prone friends—like his beloved cousin the duke of Aumerele, who would later trick him into dawdling in Ireland, giving Henry time to snuff out resistance to the revolution. As for his alleged megalomania, Richard made magnificence one strong element of his policy. As Professor Jones has shown, Richard's absolutist theory, like that of Henry VIII (or that of Pedro the Cruel), required that the king be held a virtual god. The peace of the kingdom depended on the king's absolute control of the magnates with their huge private armies. That in turn required that the king have the greatest court and army in the land, and that his person be respected as holy, even magical—hence Richard's emphasis on symbolism, pageantry, ceremony; his elevated throne; his claim to have rediscovered a sacred relic in Canterbury with which he could cure illness. It was policy, not megalomania, that led him to attach his crown firmly to religious awe and to the power of the arts. But having said all that, we may as well admit that he did have some inclination toward megalomania.

But whether one calls it policy or madness, it is a fact that Richard's seeming megalomania kept pace with his seeming gloomy paranoia. Having established that it was treason to demand reform of the royal household, he increased his retinue to vast proportions, spent more than any earlier English king on pomp and pageantry—tournaments, masques, banquets, and new construction of palaces, castles, and other crown works, including Westminster Abbey. According to Adam Usk, King Richard would on feast days sit on a lofty throne from dinner time to vespers, speaking to no one but watching his courtiers like an eagle. Anyone who caught his eye was to genuflect at once. And Walsingham tells of the king's dependence on soothsayers and other psychics who told him (and, through him, the people) that he would one day be the greatest of all princes in the world. It's disconcerting, to say the least, to imagine Geoffrey Chaucer giving readings at such a court, the proud, glaring king on his high throne, friars and soothsayers in obsequious attendance. What was the king's reaction, or the reaction of the audience, to the poet's humorous, glancing attacks on psychic mumbo jumbo or the chicanery of astrologers—in the *Franklin's Tale,* for instance:

> He hym remembred that, upon a day,
> At Orliens in studie a book he say   [*saw*]
> Of magyk natureel, which his felawë,
> That was that tyme a bacheler of lawë,
> Al were he ther to lerne another craft,
> Haddë prively upon his desk ylaft;   [*left*]
> Which book spak muchel of the operaciouns
> Touchyngë the eighte and twenty mansiouns
> That longen to the moone, and swich folyë
> As in ourë dayës is nat worth a flyë,—
> For hooly chirches feith in ourë bilevë
> Ne suffreth noon illusioun us to grevë.

How personally did the king take the forthright criticism, in the *Clerk's Tale,* of the fictitious young marquis who thinks of nothing but hunting and hawking (always a major complaint against Richard) and refuses to worry about engendering an heir, to his people's great sorrow and distress?

Now, in the late nineties, Richard's arrogance was all but intolerable as, despite growing opposition, he sought to make himself the absolute law of England. He called Geoffrey Chaucer out of retirement to travel throughout the land, probably to muster support for Richard, and Richard himself began to move through England with his army, terrorizing his enemies to prove to them his strength. Soon the Cheshire guard was no paranoic precaution: he had come to be hated.

On February 3, 1399, Richard lost the protection of John of Gaunt. The catastrophe was not merely that with Gaunt's death, at fifty-eight, Richard had lost his chief supporter and apologist. Gaunt's holdings in rents and lands were enormous, and added to those of his son and heir, the king's old enemy, Henry Bolingbroke, duke of Hereford, they would outweigh the power of the crown. Given Richard's theory of monarchy, the problem was flatly unsolvable. In desperation he changed Bolingbroke's banishment to life and blocked his inheritance of his father's lands, but kept the Lancaster holdings intact for Henry or his heir to sue for later. It was the most moderate course available. Henry returned to England with an invasion force, and headed toward his ancestral castle Pontefract, where huge numbers of the common people joined him, along with the greatest magnates of the north.

Richard, away in Ireland, as convinced as ever of his divine authority, may well have felt confident even now. He had spoken so long and so emphatically of his absolute rights and protection by heaven, he had prayed so ardently, like Edward II before him, and he had so often witnessed his own saintly ability to cure the sick (or so he and others of his time were persuaded), that he may well have felt himself invulnerable, as Shakespeare would later picture him, and may have said something in substance not much different from the words Shakespeare gives him in his famous speech to Bolingbroke's supporter the earl of Northumberland:

> If we be not [king], show us the hand of God
> That hath dismiss'd us from our stewardship;
> For well we know, no hand of blood and bone
> Can grip the sacred handle of our sceptre
> Unless he do profane, steal, or usurp.
> And though you think that all, as you have done,
> Have torn their souls by turning them from us,
> And we are barren and bereft of friends,
> Yet know, my master, God omnipotent,
> Is mustering in his clouds on our behalf
> Armies of pestilence; and they shall strike
> Your children yet unborn and unbegot,
> That lift your vassal hands against my head
> And threat the glory of my precious crown.
> Tell Bolingbroke—for yon methinks he stands—
> That every stride he makes upon my land
> Is dangerous treason: he is come to open
> The purple testament of bleeding war;
> But ere the crown he looks for live in peace,

> Ten thousand bloody crowns of mothers' sons
> Shall ill become the flower of England's face,
> Change the complexion of her maid-pale peace
> To scarlet indignation, and bedew
> Her pastures' grass with faithful English blood.

But Bolingbroke did indeed stride on, God averted His eyes, and Richard, cut off, betrayed by friends, was soon beaten.

In the official legend concocted by Henry, the king "with cheerful countenance" volunteered to resign and expressed a desire that Henry succeed him. He was, according to that legend, a creature of "incalculable moods"—as indeed he was. It was said that he alternately wept and joked while his kingdom slipped from his fingers. In fact, it was his overconfidence rather than vacillation or weakness that destroyed him. When the earl of Northumberland swore on the Host that the king's majesty and power should not be disturbed if he went inland to treat with the rebels, the king believed him and said, pale with rage, "Some of them I will flay alive."[3] (He had earlier threatened to put Henry to death in such a manner that it would be talked about even in Turkey.) Richard met Henry at Flint and learned he was the rebel army's prisoner. From there he was taken to London, where Henry was applauded as a conquering hero and Richard was hooted through the streets as he was hauled to the Tower. Soon afterward, inevitably, since a jailed king means ceaseless plotting and bloodshed, he was put to death in the dungeons of Pontefract Castle.

Chaucer had no comment, or at any rate none that has come down to us; but what he thought was no doubt what he had written years earlier to another friend, Sir Philip la Vache, when his fortune darkened:

> Flee fro the prees, and dwellë with sothfastnessë,
> Suffyce unto thy good, though it be smal;
> For hord hath hate, and climbing tikelnessë,   [instability]
> Prees hath envye, and welë blent overal;   [weal blinded]
> Savour no more than thee bihovë shal;
> Reulë wel thyself, that other folk canst redë;   [counsel]
> And trouthë thee shal delivere, it is no dredë.

He bowed to the new king, son of his long-time friend and patron, now dead, and returned to his house, his retirement.

Though we have spoken of Chaucer's last years of writing, it remains for us to treat—briefly, of necessity, since not much is known—his whereabouts and everyday activities. As we've said, for two brief periods he was apparently the deputized virtual ruler of North Petherton Forest in Somerset. In the eighteenth century, Thomas Palmer of Fairfield Park, grandson-in-law of Sir Thomas Worth, of Petherton Park, wrote, apparently on the basis of Petherton Park roles he had himself examined, that the foresters of the family of Mortimer appointed substituting foresters; that in the fourteenth year of the reign of Richard II (1390–91), Richard Britte and Geoffrey Chaucer served as subforesters; and that Chaucer was again subforester, by appointment of "Alianor countess of March," in the twenty-first year of Richard's reign. Palmer's historical notes contain minor inaccuracies, as we know by checking against other sources on one or two entries, but they may be treated as evidence—the only evidence we have—that Chaucer did hold some office or offices in connection with North Petherton. He may have been appointed the first time by Sir Peter Courtenay, who was then the "farmer" in actual possession of the bailiwick of the Somerset forests; he may have been appointed by the Mortimers themselves or at their suggestion; or he may have been appointed by someone close to the king himself, since the property was the king's concern during the minority of the heir to it. Chaucer had dealings with both the family and Courtenay, who were at the time involved in what would turn out to be an eight-year court fight over whether Courtenay, as farmer, was in trespass. If Chaucer was appointed the second time by Eleanor, countess of March, it must have been after March 16, 1399, when the bailiwick was first assigned to her, and not, as Palmer's notes say, in 1397–98.

What Chaucer's duties and rewards were, during those brief periods as subforester, no one knows. Essentially, no doubt, he was the man who judged and delegated responsibility for upkeep and repairs, ordered the arrest of offenders of all kinds, and in general did the work of a man part governor, part lawyer, part superintendent of custodians—work of a kind he'd been doing for the king for years. Though his job was in effect that of a deputy, which usually meant residence, it seems highly unlikely that he in fact moved to Petherton. In 1390 and 1391 he was still clerk of the king's works. In 1398 he was probably traveling to various parts of England to win support for the king (protection papers were issued to him in May 1398 on grounds that he was "engaged upon the king's business")[4] and though for some time he had been regularly receiving his annuity payments in person, usually in cash, the payment for June 4, 1398, was received by William Waxcombe, who was that year an agent of the king and probably forwarded the money to Chaucer.[5] In 1399 he was living in London. During his first stint as subforester, then, Chaucer must have ridden back and forth from his house in Greenwich—

a long, hard trip—and during his second he must have commuted from either Greenwich or London.

The job had, no doubt, its rewards. It offered opportunities for financial gain even greater than the opportunities available to an unscrupulous JP. Chaucer, we may assume, was discreet in taking advantage of those opportunities—he can hardly have been like his own outrageous Reeve—but he probably did not treat the work as charity to the crown. At any rate, his position as subforester was one often sought by the bourgeois rich, not the least of whom, a short while later, would be the poet's son (or whatever), Thomas Chaucer. Thomas was connected with Petherton Forest not in Chaucer's capacity but in one more exalted, as keeper of the Somerset Forests and the park of Petherton during the minority of the heir, Edmund Mortimer, at a rent of £40 ($9,600). After Edmund Mortimer came of age, Thomas leased the property for £50 ($12,000) annually, apparently right up to the time of his death in 1434. Since Thomas paid rent and was himself the "farmer," he had the right to collect rents and services, which together came to vastly more than £40 or, later, £50. Geoffrey, as a deputy, received only a stipend and whatever he saw fit to skim.

He probably continued to live at least most of the time in Greenwich up until 1397 or even later. An Exchequer debt of 20s. ($240) was passed from the London and Middlesex sheriffs to the sheriff of Kent in 1391, implying that Chaucer was believed to be living there at the time. From 1393 to 1397 the Kent sheriff reported that he could find no goods to distrain and was unable to seize Chaucer, which means, almost certainly, that Chaucer was in Kent—quite prominently so—and the sheriff, since the debt was trifling and the debtor important, preferred not to notice. In 1397 the still uncollected debt was returned to the bailiwick of London and Middlesex, so Chaucer was probably back in London, though he was soon to be away again, traveling throughout England in 1398.

Despite the joking complaint in his verse-letter to his poet friend Henry Scogan, that Scogan is "at the stremës hed" and Chaucer forgotten in the backwoods, Chaucer was never in fact far from London throughout most of the nineties, and never far from the bounty of his patrons or the applause of his audience. The annuity he'd surrendered to John Scalby during Gloucester's accroachment was never taken away from Scalby, but a new and larger annuity (£20) was granted to Chaucer, "beloved esquire," in February 1394, "because of our special grace and for good service," and on October 13, 1398, Richard added the grant of a tun of wine yearly. Chaucer's access to court and city life is shown by, among other things, the fact that he regularly collected his money in person from the London Exchequer (with only three exceptions). The city was not, after all, too far from his quiet house in Greenwich. His fortune did not change, unless for the better, when King Richard fell. Henry of Lancaster, on the day of his coronation, not only confirmed Richard's £20 annuity but gave an additional 40 marks yearly ($6,400) to Chaucer for life (perhaps a replacement of the grant from John of Gaunt)—all this, by the way, not at Chaucer's petition, apparently, but because it suited the new king's pleasure, and not as routine business (like the privy-seal confirmation of the annuity of Thomas Chaucer, later that month), but by "exemplification" and "confirmation tested by the king,"[6] which is to say, as a sign of extraordinary favor. A few days afterward, Henry confirmed Richard's grant of an annual tun of wine.

If Chaucer was out stirring up support for King Richard in 1398, it may at first seem odd that the poet should be so prized by Henry IV. Part of the explanation, no doubt, is that he was viewed as a typical public servant, loyal to "the crown," not to some particular king; and part may be that Chaucer's work for Richard was essentially symbolic, therefore harmless. He was a famous and widely respected reader, or "lecteur," who in troubled times could make an audience forget its anger at injustices and laugh at rapscallions, or rise above politics to a broader, more philosophical perspective on lordship and vassalage, rights and obligations, secular power and the demands of God. If Chaucer's entertainments could distract men's minds from political evils, the usurper Henry IV had as much need of Chaucer's talents as had Richard II. But probably Henry valued Chaucer anyway. He was a family familiar, a relative of sorts, husband to the sister of Henry's father's third wife. In 1395, when Richard was at the peak of his popularity and England was semi-euphoric with wealth after years of scraping by, Henry had provided Chaucer with fur for a floor-length scarlet gown—a gift as special and symbolic as the gift from Richard, a few years later, of a tun of wine.[7] Henry's gift was obviously a mark of respect—respect all the court was meant to notice and join in (the fur and the color made the robe like a king's)—and so Geoffrey Chaucer and the court understood it. Whatever doubts Gaunt may have had about his heir, and whatever partisanship Chaucer may have felt for the children of Katherine Swynford, his nephews, Chaucer was neither Henry Bolingbroke's political enemy nor his supporter, but a poet glad to serve if his talents, uncensored, undistorted, were of use. He accepted the young lord for what he was, focusing on his virtues—as we are told he accepted even the most execrable efforts of poets who came for help with their work, which he always read with interest and in which he always found some good. He was, whatever else, a man of peace, compassion, and understanding, a man who, in all important things, was a paragon of virtue, a "true poet" in Milton's moralistic sense. He gave tone to whatever court he served, making that court seem worthy of trust and, indeed, helping to make it so. It was, in short, not for his politics but for the ambiance he gave politics by his eminence as a poet, and for his ability as a man and as a diplomat to keep poetic detachment without loss of empathy—his gift, like Shakespeare's, for comprehending pain from a snail's point of view, or the point of view of pagans dead centuries ago —that Chaucer was admired from Northumberland to Florence, and rewarded by kings and barons.

He expected such rewards. When none came, fortunately for us, he wrote comic begging poems. Several of the last poems he wrote are of this kind, for instance the outrageous love poem to his empty purse:

> To yow, my purse, and to noon other wight
> Complayne I, for ye be my lady derë!
> I am so sory, now that ye been lyght;
> For certës, but ye makë me hevy cherë,
> Me were as leef be layd upon my berë;   [bier]
> For which unto your mercy thus I cryë:
> Beth hevy ageyn, or ellës mot I dyë!
>
> Now voucheth sauf this day, or yt be nyght,   [vouchsafe]
> That I of yow the blisful soun may herë,
> Or see your colour lyk the sonnë bryght,
> That of yelownesse hadde never perë.   [peer]
> Ye be my lyf, ye be myn hertës sterë,   [steering oar]
> Quene of comfort and of good companyë:
> Beth hevy ageyn, or ellës moote I dyë!
>
> Now pursë, that ben to me my lyvës lyght
> And saveour, as doun in this world herë,
> Out of this tounë helpë me thurgh your myght,
> Syn that ye wolë nat ben my tresorerë;
> For I am shave as nye as any frerë.
> But yet I pray unto your curtesyë:
> Beth hevy agen, or ellës moote I dyë.
>
> *Envoy*
> O conquerour of Brutës Albyon,
> Which that by lyne and free eleccion
> Been verray kyng, this song to yow I sendë;
> And ye, that mowen alle oure harmës amendë,
> Havë mynde upon by supplicacion!

The poem is typical of Chaucer's late witty style, with its punning and its delight in the outrageous. The idea in the first stanza is amusing though not startling: the lightness of the empty purse is compared to the lightness (fickleness) of a lady; but by the third stanza, all decorum has been abandoned: as a noble lady like Dante's Beatrice may act as a kind of saviour to her lover, leading him out of "this tounë"— a common medieval expression for "the Old Jerusalem," or the physical world[8]— into the New Jerusalem, Paradise, so, Chaucer claims, his beloved purse can save him. Since the poem is addressed to King Henry ("conquerour . . . / Which that by lyne and free eleccion / Been verray kyng"), we know that "old Grisel" was still clowning, right up to the end. His reference to "this tounë" probably means, on the literal level, not "town" in our modern sense (though that was one available sense in the fourteenth century) but "town" in the sense of "walled enclosure," that is, a house or group of buildings surrounded by a wall. The reference is, then, to Chaucer's house next to the Lady Chapel within the walled grounds of Westminster Abbey, where he'd sought sanctuary, presumably, from his creditors. Though King Henry was generous, he apparently never gave Chaucer enough to free him of the need for sanctuary.

Chaucer moved into his smaller house, next to Westminster Abbey, in the garden of the now-long-gone Lady Chapel, or Chapel of Our Lady, December 24, 1399, and remained there until sometime in 1400. He leased the house, probably filling out the unexpired portion of an earlier lease, for fifty-three years, and some while after his death the lease went to Thomas Chaucer, who held it, as the poet had probably done, rent-free or, rather, by courtesy of the crown. Though it was not the royal manor at Greenwich, it was hardly a house to be ashamed of. It was thought fit, immediately after Chaucer's death, for King Henry's personal clerk and physician, Master Paul de la Monte, on whom Richard II, toward the end of his reign, had piled extravagant favors; a house fit, after de la Monte's tenancy, for William Horscroft, chief skinner to the crown, from whom Richard had bought quantities of furs, cloaks, and hoods; and fit, as I've said, for Thomas Chaucer, distinguished member of John of Gaunt's retinue, later chief butler (under Henry) to the crown, and financial equivalent of the modern multi-millionaire.

Chaucer's occupation of the house attached to Westminster Abbey— together with the portrait and numerous copies which show the poet, grown old, meekly holding his rosary—has sometimes been taken as evidence that he became, toward the end of his life, fanatically religious, losing all perspective on the necessities of man and the demands of God, much as his friend Sir Lewis Clifford did. Such a view finds support, in some people's minds, in the "Retraction" at the end of the *Canterbury Tales,* and in the story told by Thomas Gascoigne, chancellor at Oxford in the middle of the fifteenth century. Talking about people who repented too late, Gascoigne mentions, among others, Judas Iscariot and the poet Geoffrey Chaucer.

It is true that many men in the Age of Faith suffered violent pangs of remorse and fear as they felt death creeping in; but it is unlikely that Chaucer was one of them. He was religious not only in his palsied age but all his life: from his first long poem on he shows his deep and comfortable Christianity—his firm belief in God's love and mercy, and his doubt (like Dante's) that acquisitive real-life friars and Popes have much to do with a sinner's reaching heaven. From the beginning to the end of his poetic career, Chaucer's position is clear and unvarying. He defends one virtue, *charity:* the good man's willingness to give the benefit of the doubt, to find some nobility in even the most wretched and deplorable of men; and though he treats many vices, there is only one that he attacks ferociously, again and again: self-righteousness. Chaucer's specific interests change—from thoughtful exploration of sex and love, in the early poems, to the fascination he shows in his very latest work with parody and calculated ugliness—but the theme never changes: God is love, and so is man at his best, whether he proves it in bed or singing at the altar; and evil is non-love, the fear, pride, concupiscence, bigotry, or high doctrine that lead a man to think about no one but himself, forgetting the cornerstone of Christian faith.

It is impossible to believe that after arguing all his life God's goodness and mercy, and accommodating a conviction much like Gaunt's and Wyclif's that the spirit of the law is more important than the letter, Chaucer in the end reversed himself; impossible to believe that after long nurturing in his own character an ability to forgive, understand, and celebrate (a talent that in all men blessed by its possession extends ultimately to humble acceptance and forgiveness of oneself), Chaucer in the last fifteen minutes of his life changed his mind about God's abundant mercy, cried out in abject terror, and wrote the Retraction.

It may be, as some critics have argued, that the Retraction is an artistic device for closing the *Canterbury Tales.* That point of view seems more than reasonable in the light if Chaucer's late experiments with unreliable art, his concern with nominalist claims that all vision, even that of the great artist, is mere opinion and impossible to communicate. As the Manciple speaks to deny the value of speech, Chaucer spends a lifetime making art and in the end, half-joking, half-serious, retracts his life.

But Chaucer's Retraction speaks of all his work, not just the poems in the *Canterbury Tales,* and so the suspicion remains that it has more to do with real emotion in Chaucer's life than with the structure of the *Canterbury Tales.* If so, how did this comfortable and secure Christian come to write the Retraction? We can only guess. Let me offer my own guess—my own fictional reconstruction.

It's true that Chaucer was religious, though never morbidly so. Most men were in some sense religious in his day, and Chaucer was helped toward reflection on heaven by the fact that his life, like the lives of most people in the fourteenth century, was not overly happy. He'd lost friends and relatives to war, plague, accident, old age, and the rough-jawed machinery of justice: his wife, fellow diplomats, and court entertainers, now lately John of Gaunt and King Richard. He was delighted to get his lease on the high-chimneyed, window-filled house beside the Abbey, but not merely because it had the church in view. It also had a view of gardens where sometimes young, middle-aged, or old lovers walked (which is what gardens are for) and where sometimes cats jumped careless birds and murderous toads sat motionless for hours, praying to the Virgin for a fly. "Yes, good," said Chaucer, gazing out the window like the dreaming child he still was, in a way, like all of us; then the rhyme he'd been looking for suddenly came, from nowhere, as rhymes always come, transmuting the idea as a soldier is transformed by the sword that dubs him knight, and more words followed in a miraculous flood, so that his scrivener, Adam, whom he'd immortalized once in a fond, scolding poem, looked at all those words in dismay, shook his head, and sighed.

He had a great deal to do and, he was beginning to suspect, not much time left to do it. He had potched a bit at law, this past few years, increasing his winnings by moderate but not meager attorney's fees; but he'd given that up now, to devote all his time to settling his finances, watching the leaves change, and, above all, straightening out the clutter of his manuscripts, laboring to make of them one finished book, his polished *Complete Works.* He was alone in the house now, except for the servants and the endless stream of visitors—Thomas and Lewis, who were now in the retinue of King Henry; sometimes an eager young poet like Hoccleve; or sometimes a fellow public servant from the days under Edward or Richard—some gouty, blear-eyed courtier put out to pasture, like himself, still much honored but half-forgotten—with whom Chaucer would sit up till after dark, playing chess on occasion, or recounting old stories till both their wits were dim and their tongues were half stone from pure weariness.

He talked with priests, occasionally with professors; kept abreast of court gossip; kept writing and revising. First drafts came harder now than formerly, as he'd complained to Scogan. He kept losing the thread,

the images that came were less spontaneous, less alive; he was all technique, all irony and self-mockery, fatally drawn not to beauty and truth
and the comic light touch, as he'd been when he was young, but to the
poem as aesthetic disaster—the poem as written by the most execrable of
poets, or the narrative recounted by the confused and unreliable narrator.
(At times he secretly believed these things were among the best he'd ever
done.) He kept writing, frantically, racing the hourglass, now and then
a new piece, but mostly revisions.

He'd fixed already (well, more or less) his Prologue to the *Legend
of Good Women,* discreetly removing the late Queen Anne. But he had
much more to do—above all, make sense of his great work, the *Canterbury Tales.* He'd changed horses midstream (as he'd privately admitted
to John of Gaunt one night). He must get the thing in order, get rid of
the inconsistencies, all those changes he'd introduced, and fill in, if possible, the missing tales. It was a mountainous project for a man of his
years, and in some ways perhaps a foolish one, or so he sometimes
thought when he was tired. "An owtlandish thyng of pride," he said, half
in jest, in the confession box. His confessor leaped at it, naturally, and
Chaucer, ruefully smiling, let the young fool rail. It was a confessor's
business, after all (he thought), to berate a man, lead him from his
wickedness. Who was Geoffrey Chaucer to deprive a gentle priest of his
niche in life, his "part in the great universal hymn," as he'd written one
time—or something to that effect. What poem was it? he wondered.
He pursed his lips, tapped his forehead with two fingers, but memory
failed him. "Welaway," he thought, "I grow old, I grow old." Line for a
poem. He breathed deeply, closed his eyes; the confessor talked on. There
was much he disapproved of in Chaucer's work . . . as was natural,
natural. Hardly more than a boy, this priest—inexperienced, idealistic
. . . He thought of King Richard and sighed again. The priest was no
doubt right, from a certain point of view. Any action, however well intended, could cause some man harm; any poem, however noble, on the
pleasures of this world could cause sorrow if it reached the wrong eyes, a
dim, unsophisticated wit . . . The priest was delivering absolution now.
Chaucer crossed himself, got up off his knees. He felt once more that
curious, light pain, like a mouse peeking cautiously past the edge of his
heart. "No time for illness!" he thought in mild alarm.

But a few weeks later, work or no work, the poet saw that he must die.
On the night of Chaucer's death, the confessor and the rest were more insistent than usual, as was right, of course, though tiresome and stupid—
like all life, the old poet was tempted to think, mourning the huge book
unfinished on his desk, parchments out of order, some of the best parts
missing altogether, lent out and not returned—but he carefully resisted

the inclination toward despair and prayed for greater strength. Every breath was like flame, and from time to time he could feel himself sliding sickeningly, entering a swoon. He was in no condition to argue theology—and in any case, what difference?—"Whatevere the sooth ys, I wol lerne yt ryght soone," he thought. He sank into darkness, an ominous rumble like wind or waves or some ancient prayer in Celtic. He remembered, for some reason, a huge sunlit tree. To his surprise, it spoke. Then there was light again, painfully bright, and noise from the street: iron horseshoes, clanging bells. Weakly—they'd bled him again, it seemed, made him weak as a baby—Chaucer raised his head from the bolster, then feebly moved his hand. Blurry faces; voices. No one understood. "Bring my book," he said. The priests showed nothing, so far as he could see. One offered him—stupid fool—a prayer book. It was Thomas, or perhaps Adam Scrivener who brought him the great thick collection and laid it, heavy as a boulder, on his knees. "Laste page," he whispered. They eventually understood and took from him all but the final page. There was writing on it, but his eyes refused to focus. "Quill and ink," he said. Some blurred shape brought them.

Then tortuously, painfully, feeling slightly foxy (though for no clear reason), he gave them their desire, and understood that of course they were right in a way: now that he was dying, following the shadowy, fog-shrouded road of Philippa and Gaunt, poor huffing, bug-eyed Brembre, and that tragic fool Gloucester, it was easy to see that he might have done more for expiring humanity. No one living or ever to be born would escape this painful, slightly frightening, but above all humiliating thing that was happening even to him, Geoffrey Chaucer, his body wasted, his eyes half blind, his voice like an adder's, old grim Grisel Death shaming him like an old smell of catshit in the house (yes, yes, he should have written poetry to ease men through this, should have written holy saints' lives, fine, moving songs about the gentleness of Jesus, the foolishness of thinking all one's life about the world): Letter by letter, he scratched out his message to whomever it might concern:

Now preye I to hem alle that herkne this litel tretys or rede, that if ther be any thyng in it thatliketh hem, that therof they thanken oure Lord Jhesu Crist, of whom procedeth al wit and al goodnesse. And if ther by any thyng that displese hem, I preye hem also that they arrette it to the defaute of myn unkonnynge, and nat to my wyl, that wolde ful fayn have seyd bettre if I hadde had konnynge. For oure book seith, "Al that is writen is writen for oure doctrine," and that is myn entente. Wherfore I biseke yow mekely, for the mercy of God, that ye preye for me that Crist have mercy on me and foryeve me my giltes; and namely of my translacions and enditynges of worldly vanitees, the whiche I revoke in my retracciouns: as of the book of Troilus; the book also of Fame; the book of the xxv. Ladies; the book of the Duchesse; the book of Seint Valentynes day of the Parlement of Briddes; the tales of Caunterbury, thilke that sownen into synne; the book of the Leoun; and many another book, if they were in my remembrance, and many a song and many a leccherous lay; that Crist for his grete mercy foryeve me the synne. But of the translacion of Boece de Consolacione, and othere bookes of legendes of seintes, and omelies, and moralitee, devocioun, that thanke I oure Lord Jhesu Crist and his blisful Mooder, and alle the seintes of hevene, bisekynge hem that they from hennes forth unto my lyves ende sende me grace to biwayle my giltes, and to studie to the salvacioun of my soule, and graunte me grace of verray penitence, confessioun and satisfaccioun to doon in this present lyf, thurgh the benigne grace of hym that is kyng of kynges and preest over alle preestes, that boghte us with the precious blood of his herte; so that I may been oon of hem at the day of doom that shulle be saved.

When he finished he handed the quill to Lewis. He could see the boy's features clearly now, could see everything clearly, his "whole soul in his eyes"—another line out of some old poem, he thought sadly, and then, ironically, more sadly yet, "Farewel my bok and my devocioun!" Then in panic he realized, but only for an instant, that he was dead, falling violently toward Christ.[9]

Appendix: the Pronunciation of Chaucer's Middle English

ENGLISH HAS NEVER HAD A PRETTIER SOUND than it had—apparently—in Chaucer's day, and every serious student of Chaucer's poetry will eventually want to master the fine details of its phonology. There are various readily available books which treat, among other things, pronunciation of Chaucer's dialect. For introductory purposes, the best are (for American readers) the standard American editions of Chaucer's work, that is, especially, the editions by F. N. Robinson, D. W. Robertson, Jr., and Albert C. Baugh. Another excellent, very brief introduction is that of E. Talbot Donaldson in the *Norton Anthology of English Literature*.

In all such introductions one repeatedly encounters such phrases as "It is important to maintain the distinction between such-and-such and so-and-so," for instance between "open *o*," as in *broth* (or *aw*, shucks), and "close *o*," as in *note*. Nothing could be truer, but when one listens to distinguished Chaucerians deliver scholarly papers at medieval conventions, or when one listens to the records made by great Chaucerians past and present, one discovers surprising differences of opinion about how things ought to be pronounced. For instance, some specialists make consonants sound much like consonants in modern English, except clearer, more precise, while other specialists speak consonants as they would in Danish or, God help us, German. For the beginner there's a valuable lesson in this: Chaucer's Middle English is relatively easy to fake. What follows here are some notes on how to fake it convincingly, so that one gets pretty clearly the sound of Chaucer's verse, making people who know the correct pronunciation believe momentarily that perhaps they've learned it wrong.

1. Read aloud or recite with authority, exactly as when speaking Hungarian—if you know no Hungarian—you speak with conviction and easy familiarity. (This, I'm told by Hungarians, is what Hungarians themselves do.) This easy authority, however fake, gets the tone of the language, its warmth and, loosely, outgoing character—not pushy, like low-class German, not jaundiced or intimate-but-weary, like modern French, and not, above all, slurred to a mumble, like modern American. Make Middle English open-hearted, like Mark Twain's jokes.

2. Pronounce vowels like vowels in modern European languages, especially French, German, or Italian (but resist the temptation to drag

in the consonant sounds of those languages). Thus *a* is *ah,* as in *"Ah,* so there you are!"; *e* is *ay,* as in *"Say* there!"; *i* is *ee,* as in *"Gee,* it's Marie!"; *o* is *oh* as in *"O!";* and *u* is, for the most part, *oo,* as in *"Who?"* That is, the vowels *a e i o u* are, basically, *ah ay eee oh ooh.* Make them long or short exactly as you would in modern English. To be extra impressive, add the following complications:

3. Distinguish between "close *e"* (*e* with the throat closed, like the sound of an oboe) and "open *e"* (*e* wide-throated, like the sound of a clarinet); that is, distinguish between the tight *e* of *eek!* or *meet,* and the easy, breathy *e* of *there* when *there* is pronounced with a touch of Irish, to rhyme with *air.* (In Middle English, any *e* followed by *r* rhymes with *air.*) For purposes of faking it is fair to say that if a word is spelled *ea* in modern English (as in *sea* or *beast*), it had an open *e* in Middle English; if spelled *ee* in modern English (as in *see* or *sleet*), it was a close *e* for Chaucer. And the same goes for close and open *o:* words now pronounced like *note* or *stone* were open for Chaucer, like the *o* in our word *cloth;* words now pronounced like *mood* or *good* (modern *oo* either long or short) were close *o* for Chaucer, like the *o* in our *so.* If this is too confusing, try to follow, in general, the pronunciation of the Cisco Kid: "Boot hombray, thees ees nut yoor peesstol." For the sound *al,* very common in Chaucer, say *ahl,* as in "Ah'll be seeing you."

4. Final *e:* Many words in Chaucer have a pronounced final *e,* as in *knowe, fewe,* etc. (In this book, final *e*'s which are pronounced are marked with two superior points: *ë.*) Pronounce the *e* like the *a* in *sofa.* In a line of verse, this *e* is silent if the word which follows it begins with a vowel but pronounced if the word which follows it begins with a consonant (except *h* and sometimes *w* or *y*). So that in the line, "That, by my trouthe, I take no kepe," the final *e* in *trouthe* is silent, the final *e* in *take* pronounced.

5. Diphthongs (that is, two vowels together, as in *cause*) can be a problem for the faker. For instance, for Chaucer *fewe* and *newe* are not quite rhymes. Short of learning Anglo-Saxon (which is behind the annoyance) or picking up the sounds by ear through listening to recordings, the faker can only depend on these two principles: (a) that *au* and *aw* are always *ow,* as in *cow* so that *cause = cowzuh, drawe = drowwuh, daunger = downjer;* and (b) when pronouncing any other diphthong, take the Middle English sounds of the vowels taken separately and squeeze them togeher, so that *iu* becomes *ee + oo = yew.* This works about half the time, which is good odds.

6. As for consonants, the rule is simple, pronounce every one of them except when you're positive the word is French (one can swallow the *g* in *sign,* for instance) or when the consonant is an initial *h.* With

g or *gg*, pronounce as you'd pronounce the same word in modern English (e.g., *juggen*, modern *judge*, has the sound *dj*, but *frogges*, modern *frogs*, has the sound *gg*).

7. For consonant clusters like *th* or *gh*, all you really need is this: Like any consonant or consonant cluster that can be either voiced or unvoiced (*z* is voiced, *sss* is unvoiced), *th* tends to be unvoiced at the beginnings and ends of words but voiced in the middle (between vowels). (*F* in Middle English is always unvoiced, *v* always voiced.) Thus *that* is unvoiced (like the *th* in *thin*) but *bathed* is voiced (like the *th* in *then*). Similarly, *s* is unvoiced (or hissed) in *saw* and *was* but voiced in *resoun* (ray-zoon). The *gh* sound is slightly but not excessively German, as in *ich* or *nach;* and *ch*, even in French words like *chivalrie*, is almost always pronounced as in *church*.

8. Some words in Middle English are accented in peculiar places—for example, *coráge* or *solémpnely*—and some can be accented as the poet pleases, as in *náture* and *natúre*. Take the pronunciation that makes the rhythm feel right, not, of course, that every line has to be rigidly iambic. In most doubtful cases, no one can really prove you wrong. For instance, one may read either, "For thére is phisícién but oón," or, "For there is phisícién but oón," or even, "For thére is phîsicién but oón" (slightly hovering over the first two syllables of *phisicien*) and the solemnest phonologist can only muse that he himself would read it somewhat differently. There are of course downright ridiculous readings, but it's comforting to notice that most of them have been urged, from time to time, by reputable scholars.

9. One last word about *e*'s. Don't say *nay* for *nuh* (as in "I ne have," that is, "I haven't"), or *thay* for *thuh* (as in "the cat"). Say *thay* when Middle English *the* means the pronoun *thee* (as in "thee, thou cat"). And watch for occasional long *e*'s at the ends of words, as in *beaute* (*bay-oh-tay*, i.e., "beauty").

If you do all this, or some of it, and at the same time put across the *sense* of the lines you read, only pedants and people of mean spirit will notice your errors. You will, of course, make errors. Practice, both alone and with sympathetic friends; listen to records; if you feel desperate, take a good course and, thereafter, blame your teacher.

Notes

INTRODUCTION

1 For modern English versions of the *Morte Arthure* and other poems treated
here, and for more extensive critical comment, see John Gardner, *The Alliterative Morte Arthure, The Owl and the Nightingale, and Five Other
Middle English Poems in a Modernized Version with Comments on Poems
and Notes* (Southern Illinois University Press, Carbondale, Illinois, 1971)
and *The Complete Works of the Gawain-Poet* (University of Chicago Press,
Chicago, Illinois, 1965). Some useful earlier critical discussions of the *Morte
Arthure* are William Matthews's *The Tragedy of Arthur: A Study of the
Alliterative Morte Arthure* (University of California Press, Berkeley and Los
Angeles, California, 1960), and the reviews of this by John Finlayson in
Medium Aevum 32 (1963) 74–7, and J. L. N. O'Loughlin in *Reviews of
English Studies*, n.s. 14 (1963) 179–82.

For the general notion that Chaucer's poetry is soberly Christian, see the
work of D. W. Robertson, Jr., especially *A Preface to Chaucer: Studies in
Medieval Perspectives* (Princeton University Press, Princeton, New Jersey,
1961); and for criticism of the Robertsonian method, see, for example, Jean
Misrahi, "Symbolism and Allegory in Arthurian Romance," *Romance Philology*
17 (1964) 555–69, Francis Lee Utley, "Robertsonianism Redivivus," *Romance
Philology* 19 (1965) 250–60, Donald R. Howard, *The Three Temptations:
Medieval Man in Search of the World* (Princeton University Press, Princeton,
New Jersey, 1966), and R. E. Kaske's review, "Chaucer and Medieval Al-
legory," *English Literary History* 30.2 (1963) 175–92. At this writing, the
standard work on John Gower (somewhat outdated) is that of John H. Fisher,
John Gower, Moral Philosopher and Friend of Chaucer (New York University
Press, New York, 1964). More modern studies of Gower are in preparation
by Russell D. Peck and Thomas J. Hatton.

2 See Barbara Nolan and David Farley-Hills, "The Authorship of *Pearl:* Two
Notes," *Review of English Studies* 22 (1971) 295–302.

3 This book is not the place for detailed argument that Chaucer understood the
Neoplatonic point of view easily available to any man of his time and place
or that he understood the Neoplatonic love doctrine reflected in his poems.
All Chaucerian scholars know well the poet's familiarity with such versions
of Neoplatonic thought as those of Macrobius and Boethius; and his understanding of the implications of Plato's *Timaeus*—nearly all the Plato that was
available in his day—has recently been argued by Robert M. Jordan in *Chaucer
and the Shape of Creation: The Aesthetic Possibilities of Inorganic Structure*
(Harvard University Press, Cambridge, Massachusetts, 1967), pp. 10–43. His
detailed knowledge of conventional love doctrine has long been recognized.
See, for instance, E. E. Slaughter, *Virtue According to Love in Chaucer* (Book-
man Associates, New York, 1957). Rather than replow that ground here, I
simply mention, when necessary, the available studies, occasionally pointing out
supporting evidence—since the whole concept of courtly love has lately come
under fire—and hurry on to the applicability in particular poems of the materials
others have collected. Though my analysis at times finds Chaucer a trifle

heretical, if it is true that courtly love or any other involvement in the world
is heresy, I do not make much of that either but merely note here that my
findings lend support to the judgment of, among others, Mary Edith Thomas,
presented in her study, *Medieval Skepticism and Chaucer: An Evaluation of
the Skepticism of the 13th and 14th Centuries of Geoffrey Chaucer and His
Immediate Predecessors—An Era that Looked Back on an Age of Faith and
Forward to an Age of Reason* (William Frederick Press, New York, 1950).

CHAPTER ONE

1 George Williams, *A New View of Chaucer* (Duke University Press, Durham,
North Carolina, 1965) pp. 10–16. Various scholars, including J. M. Manly,
have argued for a later date—1345 or 1346—mainly on the grounds that
Chaucer's poem the *Book of the Duchess,* composed not before 1369, is too
immature for a poet of almost thirty; but all recent critics of the poem agree
that it is in fact one of Chaucer's minor masterpieces, by no means crude and
immature, and some have argued for a date of composition later than 1369,
perhaps even 1377 (a bad idea suggested by Michael D. Cherniss in "The
Boethian Dialogue in Chaucer's *Book of the Duchess,*" *Journal of English
and Germanic Philology* 68.4 [October 1969] 655–65).
    Another argument for dating Chaucer's birth later than 1345 is the fact
that, in 1399, he leased a house for fifty-three years at a rental of 53s. 4d.
(see Hazel Allison Stevenson, "A Possible Relation Between Chaucer's Long
Lease and the Date of His Birth," *Modern Language Notes* 50 [1935] 318–
22). By this theory, Chaucer was fifty-three in 1399 and whimsically made use
of his age in making up the lease. Williams points out that 53s. 4d. is exactly
four marks, and Manly viewed the fifty-three years as the unexpired part of
an earlier lease.
    Still another argument for a birth date around 1345 is the once standard
notion that Chaucer was a page in the household of the countess of Ulster
in 1357. Williams' analysis of this notion is too complex to summarize here,
but his conclusion is, rightly, "that the Countess' household records do not
prove, or even lend support to the hypothesis that Chaucer was a page, and
therefore a boy under sixteen years of age, in 1357. What the records really
show is that he was a minor employee in 1357, and probably *not* a page"
(p. 13).
    At a trial in 1386, Chaucer is reported in the official register as having
"borne arms for twenty-seven years," that is, since 1359. Since the king's
levies called up all able-bodied men between the ages of sixteen and sixty,
the court record has been taken as proof that Chaucer *first* took up arms in
1359 and must therefore have been sixteen. Williams confutes that theory as
follows: "As a matter of fact . . . there had been no military expedition for
Chaucer to join (except that Black Prince's private raid [with his private army]
in 1356) since 1355. That is to say, he would have had no occasion to become
'armeez' in the king's service before the autumn of 1359—unless he had been
born before the autumn of 1339. What this part of the record shows, therefore, is that Chaucer was at least sixteen years old in the autumn of 1359—but
whether just sixteen or several years older, is not indicated" (pp. 13–14).
Williams' argument is not really weakened, it seems to me, by the fact that
Englishmen did sometimes slip into the army at fifteen, as the poet's father

seems to have done. Williams concludes: "All that the records permit us to say is that Chaucer was born before 1346. But in view of the fact that he had a responsible position as Prince Lionel's courier in 1360, and that this position would certainly not have gone to a mere stripling, we must believe that Chaucer was at least twenty years old in 1360. In other words he was born no later than 1340, or possibly early in 1341, and he may have been born a little earlier than 1340" (p. 16).

Manly, Rickert, *et al.* (*Chaucer Life-Records,* edited by Martin M. Crow and Clair C. Olson from materials compiled by John M. Manly and Edith Rickert, with the assistance of Lilian J. Redstone and others [Oxford University Press, London, 1966], hereafter cited as *Life-Records*), in arguments published before Williams' analysis, would date Chaucer's birth at "probably nearer 1345 than 1340" (p. 9, *n.* 1). For their argument, answered above, see *Life-Records*, pp. 372–4. In 1328, by the way (Speght's date for the birth of Chaucer), John Chaucer, the poet's father, was not yet married.

2 John Matthews Manly, *Some New Light on Chaucer: Lectures Delivered at the Lowell Institute* (Henry Holt and Company, New York, 1926; reprinted by Peter Smith, Gloucester, Mass., 1959), pp. 74–5.

3 *Life-Records*, p. 10.

4 F. J. Furnivall, *Life-Records of Chaucer,* Part II (Kegan Paul, Trench Trubner & Co., London, 1900), p. vii.

5 Williams, pp. 11–13.

6 G. G. Coulton, in *Chaucer and His England* (Russell & Russell, New York, 1957), p. 12, follows Mr. V. B. Redstone in taking it as certain that "the poet's ancestors were *chaussiers,* or makers of long hose. . . ."

7 For further details on Chaucer's early ancestors, see *Life-Records,* pp. 2–3 and p. 2, *n.* 2.

8 In giving modern equivalents for medieval sums, I assumed at the time of this writing (mid-July 1974), 1*s.* = $12.00, £1 = c. $240.00. Even without the added inconvenience of the present inflationary spiral, such estimates are necessarily very rough, since some things cost more in the Middle Ages than now, for instance "buttons" (they were then jewelry), while other things cost much less, for instance timber. George Williams, writing in the mid-sixties, conservatively estimated 1*s.* = $10.00 (p. 12). The editors of Edith Rickert's *Chaucer's World* (Columbia University Press, New York, 1948), p. 175, *n.* 57, estimated that the minimum value of a shilling in 1376 was $7.50. Another group of writers calculates that the fourteenth-century pound is now £60.

9 Manly, p. 22.

10 Manly *et al.,* in *Life-Records,* suggest—unconvincingly, I think—that John Chaucer's trip may have been a military expedition and that the "John Chaucer" meant in this record may have been that "John de Northwell, son of Agnes Chaucer of London, to whom William de Northwell deeded certain properties in Northamptonshire and Bedfordshire" (p. 4). I think John de Northwell (Chaucer's half brother) was too young, and the nature of the company with whom "John Chaucer" traveled, mostly rich merchants, suggests that the mission was diplomatic, as I argue later.

11 *Life-Records of Chaucer,* Part 2, pp. 47–8.

12 See Coulton, *Chaucer and His England,* p. 16.

13 Coulton, pp. 16–17.

14 Coulton, p. 17.

15 Coulton, pp. 19–20.

16 Cf. Manly, *Some New Light on Chaucer,* p. 25, and *Life-Records,* p. 4, *n.* 10.

17 Manly, pp. 47–8.

18 *Life-Records,* p. 5.

19 Even in the Middle Ages, "chivalry" meant different things to different people or in different contexts. In its narrow legal context it meant, in England, the tenure of land by knights' service, and had nothing to do with morality. In a slightly broader sense it meant, simply, "cavalry"—cf. "chevalier"—and in a still broader sense, the expected behavior of a *chevalier* or knight. The court of chivalry, created by King Edward III, had jurisdiction in cases of legal and moral offenses by knights in times of war or peace, and apparently made the tacit assumption that a knight's behavior should at least approach that proposed in the various thirteenth-century French books on chivalry and exemplary biographies of knights. After Edward's time the court of chivalry dealt mainly with precedence, coats of arms, and so forth. It can be argued that "chivalry" was a word so broad in the fourteenth century that it meant nothing at all; nevertheless, when a knight told a lady, "I is thyn awen knyght," she was meant to believe him.

20 An Anglo-Norman lament ascribed to Edward II has been discovered and edited by P. Studer, who accepts the ascription (*Modern Language Review* 16 [1921] 34–46). V. H. Galbraith doubts that the poem is Edward's ("The Literacy of the Medieval English Knights," *Proceedings of the British Academy* 21 [1935] 231, *n.* 6).

21 May McKisack, *The Fourteenth Century, 1307–1399* (Oxford University Press, London, 1959), pp. 95–6.

22 See McKisack, p. 63.

23 McKisack, p. 21.

24 Though the Church regarded moneylending at interest as a grave sin, it was common throughout Europe. "Cahorsins" from southern France and "Lombards" from north Italian towns, though ostensibly Christians, openly loaned at interest, sometimes doubling as pawnbrokers loaning on collateral. Jews had done the same until they were expelled from most parts of western Europe in the late thirteenth and early fourteenth centuries. German Jews remained in business until the fourteenth-century exterminations. Interest rates were from 20 to 40 per cent, and even so the rate of failure of moneylenders was astronomical, partly because the code of chivalry did not, in general, extend to businessmen. Evasions of the letter of the law were common: money loaned not for interest but for special favor, the taking of deposits to be repaid on demand and which might be invested in the meantime, and life-insurance gambling, whereby the man who borrowed need pay nothing back if he was lucky enough to die within a specified period of time—a game still popular. See David Nicholas, *The Medieval West, 400–1450: A Preindustrial Civilization* (The Dorsey Press, Homewood, Illinois, 1973), pp. 137–68, *et passim.*

CHAPTER TWO

1 See Edith Rickert, *Chaucer's World,* edited by Clair C. Olson and Martin M. Crow (Columbia University Press, New York, 1948), pp. 4–7, and for further detail on Vintry Ward tenements, *Life-Records,* pp. 10–12.

2 Derek Brewer, *Chaucer in His Time* (Thomas Nelson and Sons, London, 1963), p. 101.
3 See H. S. Lucas, "The Great European Famine of 1315, 1316, and 1317," *Speculum* 5 (1930) 343–77.
4 See Rickert, *Chaucer's World*, pp. 15–25.
5 From G. G. Coulton, *Life in the Middle Ages* (Macmillan Company, New York, 1930), pp. 120–1. The translation is Coulton's.
6 See those collected by Rickert, pp. 13–19, *et passim*, and in Coulton's *Life in the Middle Ages*.
7 Rickert, pp. 95–6.
8 Rickert, p. 97.
9 Rickert, p. 98.
10 G. G. Coulton, *Medieval Panorama: The English Scene from Conquest to Reformation* (Macmillan Company, New York, 1938), pp. 105–6.
11 Coulton, *Life in the Middle Ages*, v. 4, p. 210.
12 Coulton, *Medieval Panorama*, p. 115.
13 Rickert, pp. 101–2.
14 Rickert, p. 119.
15 Rickert, p. 119.
16 See Coulton, *Medieval Panorama*, pp. 392–3.
17 David Nicholas, *The Medieval West, 400–1450: A Preindustrial Civilization* (The Dorsey Press, Homewood, Illinois, 1973), p. 217, *et passim*.
18 Coulton, *Medieval Panorama*, p. 493.
19 From the *Chronicron Henrici Knighton,* quoted by R. B. Dobson, ed., *The Peasants' Revolt of 1381* (Macmillan and Company, London, 1970), pp. 59–63.
20 See Rickert, p. 121, *n.* 33.
21 Brewer, p. 127.
22 For the list of books, see Rickert, pp. 121–2.
23 C. F. Spurgeon, *Five Hundred Years of Chaucer Criticism and Allusion* (Cambridge University Press, Cambridge, 1925), v.1, p. 114.

CHAPTER THREE

1 Marchette Chute, *Geoffrey Chaucer of England* (E. P. Dutton, New York, 1946), p. 42.
2 These arguments were first offered by George Williams, *A New View of Chaucer* (Duke University Press, Durham, North Carolina, 1965), pp. 12–13.
3 G. G. Coulton gives glimpses behind the scenes at a mystery play in *Life in the Middle Ages* (Macmillan Company, New York, 1930), v. 2, pp. 138–42. From fragmentary lists of props, costumes, and so forth, it is possible to calculate the cost of these pageants. A complete set (there would be twenty or more pageants in one day's playing) could cost considerably more than a modern Broadway play.
4 Froissart tells of a wonderful dream Charles VI had of a "cerf volant"— flying horse. See Haldeen Braddy, *Geoffrey Chaucer, Literary and Historical Studies* (Kennikat Press, Port Washington, New York, 1971), pp. 71–5.
5 Adapted from Froissart by Edith Rickert, *Chaucer's World* (New York, 1948), pp. 214–15.

324 *Notes to Pages 108–53*

6 F. George Kay, *Lady of the Sun: The Life and Times of Alice Perrers* (Barnes & Noble, New York, 1966), 63.

7 Bernard J. Manning, in *The Cambridge Medieval History,* planned by J. B. Bury and edited by J. R. Tanner, C. W. Previté-Orton, and Z. N. Brooke (Cambridge University Press, Cambridge, 1932), p. 63.

8 Williams, p. 19.

9 G. G. Coulton, *Chaucer and His England* (Russell & Russell, New York, 1957).

10 *Life-Records,* p. 17, *n.* 2.

11 *Life-Records,* p. 17.

12 Coulton, *Chaucer and His England,* pp. 22–3.

13 Coulton, *Life in the Middle Ages,* v. 2, p. 91. Cf. O. F. Emerson, *Chaucer Essays and Studies* (Western Reserve University Press, Cleveland, Ohio, 1929), pp. 182–246.

14 Emerson, pp. 245–6.

15 See T. R. Lounsbury, *Studies in Chaucer* (Harper and Brothers, New York, 1892), v. 1, pp. 56–7.

16 Emerson, p. 246.

17 See *Life-Records,* p. 20.

CHAPTER FOUR

1 J. M. Manly, *Some New Light on Chaucer* (Henry Holt and Company, New York, 1926; reprinted by Peter Smith, Gloucester, Mass., 1959), p. 13.

2 Manly, p. 13.

3 Quotations of Fortescue, here and below, are drawn from Manly, pp. 15–18.

4 For fuller elaboration of these arguments, see George Williams, *A New View of Chaucer* (Duke University Press, Durham, North Carolina, 1965), pp. 20–157, and Manly, pp. 29–30.

5 For more detailed discussion of the Oxford question, see F. P. Magoun, Jr., "Chaucer's Great Britain," *Medieval Studies* 16 (1954) 146; A. Wigfall Green, "Chaucer's Clerk and the Medieval Scholarly Tradition as Represented by Ric. de Bury's *Philobiblion,*" *Journal of English Literature* (Johns Hopkins University Press, Baltimore, Maryland) 18 (1951) 1–6.

6 For an interesting contemporary holistic account of why acupuncture (and other things) works, see the transcribed lectures of Michio Kushi, e.g., "Acupuncture," *Ancient and Future Worlds,* transcribed by Joan Mansolilli (Tao Publications, 31 Farnsworth St., Boston, Massachusetts, n.d.).

7 Quoted by G. G. Coulton, *Medieval Panorama* (Cambridge University Press, London, 1938), p. 402.

8 Coulton, *Medieval Panorama,* p. 402.

9 For the story, from Adam of Usk's *Chronicon,* see Edith Rickert, *Chaucer's World* (Columbia University Press, New York, 1948), pp. 131–2.

10 *Chaucer in His Time* (Nelson, London, 1963).

11 It has occasionally been doubted that the "Philippa Chancy" of the annuity record was Chaucer's wife and, further, that Chaucer's wife was Sir Paon Roet's daughter. It has also been suggested, originally by gremlins, that the Philippa Chaucer who received the annuity was unmarried at the time but chanced to have the same name as the poet. For certain reasons, the argument requires that this lady later did (to end all the tiresome confusion, I suppose)

marry Geoffrey Chaucer. All reasonable doubts have been resolved on heraldic grounds by Russell Krauss in "Chaucerian Problems, Especially the Petherton Forestership and the Question of Thomas Chaucer," in *Three Chaucer Studies,* ed. Carleton Brown (Folcroft Press, Folcroft, Pennsylvania, 1932, reprinted 1969), pp. 36–7.

12 See Margaret Galway, "Phillipa Pan', Philippa Chaucer," *Modern Language Review* 55 (1960) 481–7, 483, *n.* 4.

13 Williams, p. 47.

14 *Chaucer's Official Life* (G. Banta Publishing Co., Menasha, Wis., 1912), p. 58. Cf. Williams, pp. 33–41. Against Hulbert's view, see G. G. Coulton, *Chaucer and His England* (Russell & Russell, London, 1927), p. 22; George H. Cowling, *Chaucer* (Methuen and Co., London, 1927), p. 13; G. K. Chesterton, *Chaucer* (Faber and Faber, London, 1932), p. 93; Nevill Coghill, *The Poet Chaucer* (Oxford University Press, London, 1949), p. 3; and Kemp Malone, *Chapters on Chaucer* (Johns Hopkins Press, Baltimore, Maryland, 1951), p. 22.

15 See Gareth W. Dunleavy, "The Wound and the Comforter: The Consolations of Geoffrey Chaucer," *Papers on Language and Literature* 3 (1967) 14–27.

16 Quoted by Krauss, p. 146.

17 Krauss, *loc. cit.*

18 Krauss, pp. 162–3.

19 Krauss, p. 163.

20 Williams, p. 50.

21 Williams, p. 48.

22 In an entry of May 15, 1372, of the *Lancaster Register* she receives a grant for "good and agreeable service" to Blanche of Lancaster, who died in 1369. See Krauss, p. 135, *n.* 11.

23 In a review of *Three Chaucer Studies, Speculum* 8 (1933) 535.

24 T. R. Lounsbury, *Studies in Chaucer, His Life and Writings* (Harper and Brothers, New York, 1892), v. 1, pp. 113–14.

CHAPTER FIVE

1 *Lady of the Sun: The Life and Times of Alice Perrers* (Barnes & Noble, New York, 1966).

2 *Geoffrey Chaucer, Literary and Historical Studies* (Kennikat Press, Port Washington, New York, 1971), p. 111.

3 The version I give is not standard. The standard version is that Alice, cunning and acquisitive to the bone, saw her chance in Windsor, and that Windsor saw a chance of advancement through Alice. The standard version does not fit any of the facts very well, certainly not the fact that Alice risked her neck to save Windsor when he was imprisoned in the Tower. At any rate, Chaucer admired William of Windsor, as did many in Chaucer's circle.

4 Kay, p. 12.

5 Kay, p. 22.

6 S. Luce (ed.), *Chroniques de J. Froissart* (Paris, 1888), VIII, 139, *n.* 3.

7 On this point and others below, see Haldeen Braddy, *Geoffrey Chaucer, Literary and Historical Studies,* pp. 107–15.

8 Braddy, p. 112.

9 See Manly, Rickert, *et al., Life-Records,* p. 40.

10 On this controversy see R. Davidson, *Forschungen zur Geschichte von Florenz,* 4 vols. (Berlin, 1896–1927), v. 1, p. 144, and v. 4, p. 461; and E. W. Anthony, *Early Florentine Architecture and Decoration* (Cambridge, Mass., 1927), *passim.* For brief summary, see Ferdinand Schevill, *History of Florence from the Founding of the City Through the Renaissance* (New York, 1936), p. 242.

11 Quoted by Edith Rickert, *Chaucer's World* (Columbia University Press, New York, 1948), pp. 278–9.

12 For details, see the correspondence between C. H. Bromby and St. Clair Baddeley in the *Athenaeum,* September 17–November 26, 1898.

13 See G. G. Coulton, *Chaucer and His England,* p. 45.

14 R. Ramat, "Indicazioni per una lettura del *Decamerone,*" in *Scritti su Giovanni Boccaccio* (Florence, 1964), pp. 7–19.

CHAPTER SIX

1 George Williams, *A New View of Chaucer* (Duke University Press, Durham, North Carolina, 1965), p. 26.

2 See Margaret Galway, "Geoffrey Chaucer, J.P. and M.P.," *Modern Language Review,* 36 (1941) 1–36.

3 See Haldeen Braddy, in *Three Chaucer Studies,* ed. Carleton Brown (Folcroft Press, Folcroft, Pa., 1932, reprinted 1969), 2, pp. 36–9.

4 For a summary of the theories, see R. M. Lumiansky, "Chaucer's *Parlement of Foules:* A Philosophical Interpretation," *Review of English Studies,* 24 (1948) 81–9. And see Williams, pp. 56–65, and Thomas Tyrwhitt (ed.), *The Canterbury Tales* (2nd ed., London, 1798), v. 2, p. 415.

5 Panel structure was a favorite form in Old English poetry. I discuss one example in *The Construction of Christian Poetry in Old English* (Southern Illinois University Press, Carbondale, Illinois, 1975), pp. 106–17. For comment on a late example of the form, see my *Complete Works of the Gawain-Poet* (University of Chicago Press, Chicago, Illinois, 1965), pp. 61–9.

6 See David Chamberlain, "The Music of the Spheres and the *Parliament of Foules,*" *Chaucer Review,* 5 (1970) 32–56.

7 Tyrwhitt, v. 2, p. 415; William Godwin, *The Life of Geoffrey Chaucer* (T. Davison for R. Phillips, London, 1804).

8 Braddy, part 2, pp. 1–101.

9 The theory originally brought forward by John Koch, in *Englische Studien,* 1, 287 ff., has been elaborated by O. F. Emerson, *Chaucer Essays and Studies* (Cleveland, Ohio, 1929), pp. 58–122.

10 "A New Interpretation of *The Parlement of the Foules,*" *Modern Philology,* 18 (1920) 5.

11 Braddy, p. 81.

12 On Sir John Clanvowe and Sir Lewis Clifford, see G. L. Kittredge, "Chaucer and Some of His Friends," *Modern Philology,* 1 (1903) 1–18.

13 On Chaucer's friends, see Manly, pp. 70–234, *passim.*

CHAPTER SEVEN

1 Quoted in R. B. Dobson's collection, *The Peasants' Revolt of 1381* (Macmillan, London, 1970), p. 92.

2 May McKisack, *The Fourteenth Century, 1307–1399* (Oxford University Press, London, 1959), p. 398.

3 Dobson, pp. 92–3.

4 Dobson, p. 93.

5 Charles Oman, *The Great Revolt of 1381* (1906, reprinted by Haskell House, New York, 1968), p. 1.

6 Oman, p. 190.

7 Dobson, pp. 103–4.

8 Dobson, p. 126.

9 For Walsingham's version, which I follow except where it seems obviously wrong, see Dobson, pp. 168–81. My quotations are from Dobson's translation, slightly changed. Cf. McKisack, pp. 412–14.

10 For the debate see Haldeen Braddy, *Geoffrey Chaucer, Literary and Historical Studies* (Kennikat Press, Port Washington, New York, 1971), pp. 38–9.

11 *Life-Records*, pp. 60–1.

12 *Life-Records*, p. 83.

13 Chaucer probably received this earlier than 1382; the date of his official assignment as controller of petty customs. See *Life-Records*, pp. 150–1.

14 For the whole Plunkett-Watts reconstruction of the case against Chaucer, see P. R. Watts, "The Strange Case of Geoffrey Chaucer and Cecilia Chaumpaigne," *London Quarterly Review* 63 (1947) 491–515. In the Manly, Rickert, et al., *Life-Records*, p. 346, the Plunkett argument is quoted in a way which slightly distorts it to favor Chaucer's innocence. For other studies of the *raptus* case, see the works cited in *Life-Records*, p. 346, *n.* 1.

15 On Morel, see E. P. Kuhl, "Some Friends of Chaucer," *Publications of the Modern Language Association* 29 (1914) 270–2.

16 Aldous Huxley, *Essays New and Old* (Florence Press, London, 1926), p. 24, and G. G. Coulton, *Chaucer and His England* (Russell & Russell, New York, 1957), pp. 10–11.

17 "Chaucer and the Common People," n.p. (Southern Illinois University Library, Carbondale, Illinois), p. 3.

18 See *Legend of Good Women*, Prologue F, ll. 373–83, and Prologue G, ll. 353–88.

19 George Williams, *A New View of Chaucer* (Duke University Press, Durham, North Carolina, 1965), p. 36.

20 Not everyone agrees on this chronology. Cf. F. N. Robinson, p. xxix.

21 Richard H. Jones, *The Royal Policy of Richard II: Absolutism in the Middle Ages* (Barnes & Noble, New York, 1968), pp. 12–13.

22 McKisack, p. 425.

CHAPTER EIGHT

1 May McKisack, *The Fourteenth Century, 1307–1399* (Oxford University Press, London, 1959), p. 431.

2 Margaret Galway, "Geoffrey Chaucer, J.P. and M.P.," *Modern Language Review* 36 (1941) 1–36.

3 Galway, pp. 17–18.

4 W. W. Skeat, *The Oxford Chaucer*, Student's Edition (Oxford University Press, London, 1894), p. xiii.

5 Galway, p. 5.

6 As translated by Galway, p. 4.

7 *Life-Records,* pp. 356–8.

8 For more detail see Anthony Goodman, *The Loyal Conspiracy: The Lords Appellant Under Richard II* (Routledge & Kegan Paul, London, 1971), pp. 74–86.

9 Richard H. Jones, *The Royal Policy of Richard II: Absolutism in the Middle Ages* (Barnes & Noble, New York, 1968), p. 38.

10 See Jones, pp. 39–40.

11 McKisack, p. 454.

12 Galway, pp. 15–16.

13 See *Life-Records,* pp. 465–6.

CHAPTER NINE

1 I present this evidence in "The Case Against the 'Bradshaw Shift'; or, the Mystery of the Manuscript in the Trunk," *Papers on Language and Literature* 3 (1967) 80–106.

2 May McKisack, *The Fourteenth Century, 1307–1399* (Oxford University Press, London, 1959), p. 476, quoting Walsingham's account.

3 Richard H. Jones, *The Royal Policy of Richard II: Absolutism in the Later Middle Ages* (Barnes & Noble, New York, 1968), p. 104.

4 *Life-Records,* pp. 62–3.

5 *Life-Records,* p. 524.

6 At any rate, no petition has been found. See *Life-Records,* p. 527.

7 We have another record showing Henry's interest in Chaucer, but since I can make no particular sense of it, I ignore it. See *Life-Records,* p. 275.

8 On "this tounë," see John Gardner, *The Construction of the Wakefield Cycle* (Southern Illinois University Press, Carbondale, Illinois, 1974), p. 80.

9 He died, according to an old tradition, on October 25, 1400—a tradition based on the now illegible inscription on his tomb, which, according to John Stow, was erected by Nicholas Brigham in Westminster Abbey in 1556. See *Life-Records,* pp. 547–9.

Index

Abberbury, Richard, 259
ABC (Chaucer), 116–17, 128
Absalon (character), 96
absolutism, 168–9, 208, 227, 230, 234–5, 258, 264, 288–90, 298, 301, 303
accroachment, 43, 45
Adam Scrivener, 272, 313
Africa (Petrarch), 214
alchemy, 7, 35, 59, 82, 88, 141, 143–4
Alcuin, 10
Aldgate, 32, 33, 156, 188, 204, 209, 249, 266
Alfonso XI, king of Castile, 168
Alfred, king of Wessex, 37, 45, 77, 106, 138, 247
Alisoun (character), 188, 269
allegory, 81, 87, 128
analogy, argument by, 141–2
Anelida and Arcite (Chaucer), 105, 185, 213
Animadversions (Thynne), 130, 160
Anne of Bohemia, queen of England, 118, 174, 217–18, 247–8, 257, 258, 261, 263, 266, 271–2, 312; death, 296
Anonimal Chronicle, 237
Apocalypse, 87, 140, 144
Aquinas, St. Thomas, 18, 67, 75, 78, 145, 148, 292
architecture, 194–7, 281–2
Aristotle, 75, 77, 82, 138, 143, 214
Armitage-Smith, Sydney, 110
Arthur, King, 12, 15, 17, 98, 99, 205, 228
Arundel, Richard, earl of, 277–8, 296, 298–9, 301
Arundel, Thomas, archbishop of York, later of Canterbury, 276, 278, 298–9
astrology, 82, 143, 144
astronomy, 88, 253, 271
Attechapel, Bartholomew, 23, 153
Atwood, Henry, 280

Bach, Johann Sebastian, 4–5, 6
Bacon, Roger, 11, 18, 75, 82, 83 ,138, 143–4, 145, 215
Bad Parliament (1377), 219, 231, 239
Bale, Bishop, 136

Ball, John, 237, 242, 255
barons, 212; Edward II and, 43–50; Edward III and, 211; Richard II and, 50, 230, 274–7, 296, 298–301; *see also* Lords
Barrett, Richard, 249, 257
Bartholomew the Englishman, 62, 63–4
Beauchamp, Sir William, 252
Beaufort, Henry, 136 *n.*, 160
Beaufort, John, 155
Becket, Thomas à, 98
Beckett, Samuel, 292
Bedford, John, 27
Beethoven, Ludwig van, 4, 5
Beowulf, 81, 140, 234
Bergman, Ingmar, 72
Berkeley, Sir Edward, 249
Betenham, William, 274
Beverley, John de, 125
Bible, the, 80–1, 87, 142, 148–9
Black Death of 1347–51, 34, 70–1, 72–9
Black Knight, the (character), 139, 164, 165
Black Monday, 126
Black Prince (Edward, Prince of Wales), 5, 35, 105–7, 108, 111, 113, 114–15, 149, 171, 174, 182, 183–4, 217–18, 230, 259; death, 104, 172; in France, 105–7, 110, 123–5, 177; illness, 107, 176, 177; in Spain, 107, 152, 153, 168, 170; mentioned, 12, 30, 122, 131, 180, 189, 209, 213, 221, 226, 235
Blake, William, 82, 83, 279
Blanche of Richmond, duchess of Lancaster, 54, 107, 109, 113, 116–17, 118, 127, 129, 135, 136 *n.*, 139, 144, 174, 230, 271; death, 158, 175–6, 216, 279
Boccaccio, Giovanni, 185, 198–9, 202, 206, 214, 216, 221
Boethius, 17, 18, 77–8, 82, 83, 87, 89, 138, 141, 143, 144, 146, 212, 216, 217, 227, 257
Bolingbroke, Henry, *see* Henry IV, king of England
Book of Holy Medicines, The (Henry of Lancaster), 116

Book of the Duchess (Chaucer), 11, 14,
  16, 109, 111, 113, 116, 117, 118, 127,
  128–9, 139–40, 144, 160, 163, 164,
  176–7, 185, 205, 212, 213, 214, 216–
  18, 280; date of, 216
"Book of the Lion" (Chaucer), 205–6
Bracton, Henry, 141, 290
Braddy, Haldeen, 179, 188, 221
Brembre, Nicholas, 11, 207–9, 230, 246,
  256, 277, 278, 284, 299
Brétigny, Treaty of, 125
Brewer, Derek, 55, 79, 151
Brierly, Richard, 285
Britte, Richard, 305
Brocas, Arnold, 267
Buckholt, Walter and Isabella, 280
Buckley, Master William, 130
Bunyan, John, 9
Burley, Sir John, 209–10, 212, 241
Burley, Sir Simon, 208, 241–2, 244,
  247, 258–9, 263, 273, 274, 276, 278,
  299
Bury, Richard of, 138

Calais, 123, 226; siege of, 70, 98–9, 117
Calvin, John, 147, 148, 197
Cambridge, 88, 133
Canon's Yeoman (character), 215
Canon's Yeoman's Tale, 22, 35–6, 60,
  88, 143, 274, 290
Canterbury Tales (Chaucer), 11, 12, 14,
  16, 42, 50, 91, 115, 121, 131, 136,
  142, 149, 157, 186, 197, 200, 203,
  214, 216, 218, 221, 239, 251, 253,
  255, 259, 269, 271, 272, 286, 288–95;
  General Prologue to, 105, 111–12,
  131, 133, 136, 264, 269, 288; grand
  design, 288–92, 312; "marriage de-
  bate" on government, 234, 289–90;
  "Retraction," 121, 205, 310–11, 313–
  14; *see also* individual Tales
Canticle of Canticles, 144, 186, 212
Canzoniere (Petrarch), 202
carpenter, the (character), 68
Carroll, Lewis (C. Dodgson), 82–3, 294
Castile, 152, 168–70, 172, 183, 266
Cato, Dionysius, 80
Champain (Chaumpaigne), Cecily,
  251–2
Charles IV, king of France, 47
Charles V, king of France, 172, 175,
  210, 212; as dauphin, 122
Charles VI, king of France, 226

Charles the Bad, king of Navarre, 152
Chaucer, Agnes (mother), 23, 32–3,
  153
Chaucer, Catherine (sister), 30, 33,
  68, 274, 287
Chaucer, Elizabeth (daughter), 154,
  156, 158, 167, 271
Chaucer, Geoffrey: birth, 21, 51, 60;
  childhood, 23, 61–71; children of, 20,
  154, 158–61, 167, 271; death, 20,
  312–14; education, 23, 68–70, 77, 79–
  89, 92, 127–30, 133–45; faith of, 309–
  11; family background, 21, 22–3; income, 154–5, 156, 204, 207, 209, 248–9,
  250–1, 256, 267, 268, 273, 274, 279–
  81, 305–7; legal training, 129–30,
  133–7; marriage, 20, 117–18, 128,
  153–5, 161–7, 279; personality, 8, 11;
  travels, 190–203, 212, 248–9, 283–4
    POETRY: 128–9, 137, 139–45, 213–
  24, 253–5, 286–95, 308–12; forms,
  212–14, 222, 291–2; French influence,
  92, 128–9, 144, 205–6, 212, 216, 222;
  Italian influence, 82, 163, 198–203,
  206, 214, 215, 216, 221–3; realism
  v. nominalism in, 138–9, 146–7, 214–
  15, 216–17, 225, 292–3, 310; subject
  matter, 4, 10–11, 17, 120–1, 253–5,
  269–70, 292–5, 310; technique, 5, 6;
  translations, 127, 128–9, 140, 205,
  257
    PUBLIC SERVICE: 92, 127–8, 134–5,
  137, 155–6, 190–1, 194, 203, 204–12,
  248–51, 256–9, 266–76, 280–5, 287,
  302, 305–8; clerk of the king's works,
  92, 137, 194, 250, 258, 267, 280–3;
  controller of customs, 92, 156, 194,
  204, 206–7, 248, 250–1, 256, 257,
  266–7; court poet, 19, 92, 204–5,
  271–2, 287, 288–9, 307–8; diplomatic
  service, 8, 19, 20, 92, 122, 190–1,
  209–12, 226, 228, 248–51; justice of
  the peace, 33, 137, 208, 268, 272–4;
  in parliament, 33, 208, 274; subforester, 34, 137, 281, 287, 305; wardships, 251; war service, 122–6, 172,
  174; as yeoman, not page, 90–3
    RESIDENCES: 287, 305; Aldgate,
  156, 188, 204, 209, 266; Greenwich,
  267–9, 287–8, 305–6; Thames Street,
  22, 54; Westminster, 268, 309
Chaucer, John (father), 21, 22–4, 25,
  26–39, 43, 48, 49, 50, 54, 68, 132,
  153

Chaucer, Lewis (son), 88, 136, 167, 253, 271, 285, 311, 314

Chaucer, Mary (grandmother), 25–6

Chaucer, Philippa Roet (wife), 11, 20, 117, 135, 153–5, 156, 157, 159, 160–7, 173, 179, 209, 250, 272, 279

Chaucer, Richard (step-grandfather), 25, 26, 34, 73

Chaucer, Robert (grandfather), 24–6, 179

Chaucer, Thomas (son), 158–61, 167, 253, 271, 306, 307, 309, 311, 313

Chauntecleer (character), 40, 61, 269

chivalry, 37, 91, 103–4, 112, 154, 177–8

Christianity, 75–8; and Black Death, 72–3, 74–5, 76; and paganism, 67–8, 89, 185–6

Church, the, 237–8, 239, 263; v. state, 145, 148, 228–9

Churchman, John, 257–8, 268, 280

Cicero, 81

Clanvowe, Sir John, 225–6, 252

classics, translations of, 137–8

Clement VII, Pope, 263

clergy, 148, 149, 229, 237

Clerk of Oxford, the (character), 136, 198, 254

clerk of the king's works (title), 137, 194, 267, 281–3

clerks, the (Allan and John, characters), 119, 151–2

Clerk's Tale, 198, 260, 302

Clifford, Sir Lewis, 187, 226, 296, 310

Clinton, Robert de, 125

"clown poem," 291–2, 294, 308–9

Coleridge, Samuel Taylor, 286

Commentary on the Dream of Scipio (Macrobius), 11

Commons, House of, 20, 187, 207, 210, 212, 218–19, 220–1, 226–7, 228, 235–6, 239–41, 264, 273, 298; *see also* parliament

complaint poems, 212–13

Complaint of Mars (Chaucer), 213

Complaint of Venus (Chaucer), 286

Complaint to His Lady (Chaucer), 213

Complaint to His Purse (Chaucer), 308

Complaint unto Pity (Chaucer), 213

Confessio Amantis (Gower), 16

Confessions (St. Augustine), 10

Consolation of Philosophy (Boethius), 77, 138, 144, 257

Constance, Princess of Castile, 110, 135, 155, 170, 172, 297

Constancy (Custance, character), 288–9

Cook's Tale, 288

Copton, Hamo, 32, 33, 34, 73

Copton, John, 32

Copton, Nicholas, 32, 34, 65, 73

Coulton, G. G., 31, 66, 117, 151, 253

"counter parliaments," 46

Courtenay, Sir Peter, 305

Courtenay, Sir Philip, 187

Courtenay, William, archbishop, 148, 261

courtly love, 53, 112, 116–17, 178, 185, 217–18

Crécy, Battle of, 103, 104, 105, 106, 177

crime, 56–9; penalties, 52, 56

Criseyde (character), 120, 157

customs collection, 25, 29, 34, 49, 68, 156, 206

Dame Nature (character), 218, 220, 293

D'Angle, Sir Guichard, 171–2, 177, 187, 210, 211, 220, 233, 259

Dante, 53, 81, 87, 112, 159, 163, 176, 192, 193, 195, 197, 198–9, 200–3, 206, 212, 214, 216, 222, 224, 227, 257, 309, 310

Decameron (Boccaccio), 16, 198, 202

Defoe, Daniel, 40

De Musica (Boethius), 87, 217

Descartes, René, 142

Deschamps, Eustace, 128, 205, 225

Dispenser, Hugh, the elder, 44, 45, 46, 47, 48, 49

Dispenser, Hugh, the younger, 28, 44, 45, 46–7, 48, 49

Divine Comedy (Dante), 112, 163, 200, 222, 291, 292

Dominican Order, 72, 75, 145, 196

Donatus, Aelius, 80, 81

Donne, John, 7

dream-vision poems, 7, 8, 139–40, 212, 213, 216

Dugdale, Sir William, 130

Du Guesclin, Bertrand, 169, 170, 177

Duns Scotus, 145

eagle, the (in *House of Fame*), 6, 11, 83, 163

Easterling family, 31

Edmund Langley, duke of York, 158, 175, 190, 217–18, 233, 275, 278

education, 68–70, 79–89, 91, 92, 133–
    45; *see also* quadrivium; trivium
Edward I, king of England, 41, 49, 50,
    134, 231
Edward II, king of England, 28, 36,
    40–7, 48, 54, 56, 95, 228, 259, 260–1,
    298, 301, 303; murder of, 49, 52, 276
Edward III, king of England, 20, 27,
    28, 30–1, 47–8, 95, 97–9, 102–5, 107,
    108, 110, 111, 114, 134, 175, 179,
    180–1, 210–11, 225, 238, 258; and
    Alice Perrers, 35, 113, 180–9; Chaucer
    in service of, 92, 127–8, 134–5, 137,
    155–6, 190–1, 203, 204–9; claim to
    France, 51, 122, 126, 172; death, 212,
    221, 228, 230; and French war, 50–1,
    70, 98–9, 102–4, 105, 122–6, 168, 172,
    174, 177, 210–11, 235–36; marriage of,
    14, 47, 113–14, 173, 182; naval war-
    fare, 51, 70, 102–3; Order of the
    Garter founded by, 15, 70–1, 99, 114;
    Scottish campaign of 1327, 36–40,
    102, 103; sons of, 105–13, 114; suc-
    cession to throne, 47, 50, 228; men-
    tioned, 12, 21, 33, 91, 92, 155, 191,
    232, 235, 263
Edward IV, king of England, 134
Edward, prince of Wales, *see* Black
    Prince
Edward the Confessor, 98, 179, 183
Eight Parts of Speech (Donatus), 80
Eliot, T. S., 10, 129, 140, 141
Elizabeth of Burgh, countess of Ulster,
    23, 90–3, 95, 96, 97, 105, 108, 109,
    116, 118, 135, 271
Ellismere manuscript, 267
Elmham, Roger, 281
Eltham palace, 267–8
Emelye (character), 186
entertainment, court, 93–5, 96–7
Envoy to Bukton (Chaucer), 288
Envoy to Scogan (Chaucer), 267, 286–8
epistemology, 82–3
Equatory of the Planets (Chaucer), 88,
    143
Erasmus, 55
Eschenbach, Wolfram von, 178
Evesham, Thomas of, 233, 248

famine, 71–2, 174
Ferrers, Robert, 155
Flanders, 175; Chaucer in, 190, 248;
    Edward III in, 28, 30–1; trade, 34

Fleet Street, 131, 132, 244
Flemings, the, 238, 243
Florence, 191, 194–7, 198
Forester, Richard, 249
Former Age, The (Chaucer), 255
Fortescue, John, 133, 134, 137
France, 52; Chaucer as ambassador to,
    8, 190, 209–12, 248–9; English war
    with, 51, 70, 98–9, 102–4, 105–7,
    110, 122–6, 152, 168, 172, 174, 177,
    210–11, 233–4, 235–6, 263, 275;
    music, 193; pre-Chaucerian poetry,
    5, 144; Spanish war, 169–70; throne
    claimed by Edward III, 51, 122, 126,
    172; truce with, 296, 297
Franciscan Order, 75, 131, 145, 147, 196
Franklin, the (character), 255
Franklin's Tale, 94, 164, 234, 255, 290,
    302
Frescobaldi, Amerigo dei, 43
Friar, the (character), 131–2
Friar's Tale, 66, 289–90
Froissart, Jean, 36, 37, 64, 95, 98, 102,
    103, 113, 115, 122, 123, 128, 157,
    171, 173–4, 180, 191, 205, 210, 226,
    242, 268
Frost, Robert, 141
Fulke the Black, Count of Anjou, 97
Furnivall, F. J., 20, 23, 161

Galles, Owen de, 171
Galway, Margaret, 267, 273
games, 62–3, 99–102
Gascoigne, Thomas, 161, 310
Gascony, 105, 107, 108, 172, 297
Gasquet, F. A., 71
Gaunt, John of, *see* John of Gaunt
Gaveston, Piers, 42–4, 45, 47, 49, 259
Gawain-poet, the, *see* Massey, John
Gedney, John, 282
Geffrey (character), 6, 83, 87, 292
Genoa, 190–1, 192–3
Gentilesse (Chaucer), 242, 254
Giotto, 196–7, 222
Gisers, John, 31
glorious crusade, 264
Gloucester, duke of, *see* Thomas of
    Woodstock
Gloucester, earl of, 42, 44
Godwin, William, 20, 23, 217
Goethe, Johann Wolfgang von, 214
Good Parliament (1376), 187, 218–19,
    230, 235

Gothic Architecture (Morris), 55
Gower, John, 16–17, 18, 59, 117, 128, 130, 136, 164, 225, 238, 249, 253, 255, 294
grammar, study of, 79–88
Gray, Sir Thomas, 124
Great Pestilence, The (Gasquet), 71
Greenwich, royal manor at, 267–9, 270–1, 287–8, 305–6
Gregory XI, Pope, 184
Griselda (character), 254
Grosseteste, Robert, 18, 137–8, 143, 144–5
guilds, 56, 71, 236–7

Hainault, 36, 47, 113–14, 117, 159
Hales, Sir John, 244, 245
Hales, J. W., 163
Hanse, 31
Hatfield, 95
Hawkwood, Sir John, 249
Henry II Trastamara, king of Castile, 152, 153, 169–70, 171, 263
Henry IV, king of England (H. Bolingbroke, duke of Hereford), 136 *n.*, 155, 159, 160, 261, 266, 277–8, 285, 296–7, 300–1, 303–4, 307, 309, 311
Henry V, king of England, 136 *n.*, 160
Henry VIII, king of England, 301
Herbury, Henry, 23
Heyroun, Thomas, 25, 26, 31, 34, 36–9, 65, 73, 92
Hinton, John, 90, 91
Hoccleve, Thomas, 225, 311
Holinshed, Raphael, 88, 126
Holland, 47; *see also* Hainault
Holland, Sir John, 115, 213, 261, 265, 299
Holland, Thomas, 114, 262, 299
Homer, 11, 81, 87
homosexuality, 41, 42, 261, 293, 298
Horscroft, William, 309
Host, the (Harry Bailey, character), 11, 149, 223, 293
House of Fame (Chaucer), 6, 7, 11, 81–2, 83–4, 87, 96, 144, 146, 153, 162–3, 164, 197, 200, 206, 222, 257, 291, 292
housing, medieval, 54–6
Hulbert, J. R., 155
humanism, 197, 221, 222–3
Huntingfield, William, 285
Hus, Jan, 147, 197

Huxley, Aldous, 253
Hyde, John, 256

Inferno (Dante), 200
Inner Temple, 130–1, 133, 134, 136, 137
inns of chancery, 133
inns of court, 133–4
Introduction to the Categories of Aristotle (Porphyry), 146
Ipswich, 22, 24–5, 26
Ireland, 108, 126, 127, 180, 189–90, 296, 303
Isabella the Mad, queen of England (wife of Edward II), 5, 27, 36, 42, 43, 46–7, 48, 95, 113, 122, 261
Isabella, queen of England (wife of Richard II), 226, 297
Italy, 52; arts and literature, 5, 191–203, 205–6; Chaucer in, 8, 20, 156, 161, 190–203, 212, 216, 249

James, Henry, 193
January (character), 65
Jews, persecution of, 53 and *n.*, 73
Joan of Kent, princess of Wales, 114–15, 173, 183, 230, 245, 260, 261–2, 271
John the Good, king of France, 5, 30, 106, 111, 114, 116, 122, 125, 191
John of Gaunt, duke of Lancaster, 8, 24, 30, 35, 50, 60, 95, 107, 109–13, 115, 123, 211, 215, 216, 217–18, 225, 226, 262, 279, 296–7, 299–301, 310; alleged treason against Richard II, 158, 265–6; Chaucer's friendship with, 95, 109, 127–8, 135, 155–7, 161, 165, 188, 204, 208–9; death of, 119, 158, 303; in France, 123, 174–7; and Katherine Swynford, 109, 113, 157, 161–62, 297; marriages of, 36, 109, 110, 113, 116, 117, 156, 170, 172, 297; and parliament, 148, 187, 210, 219, 221, 228, 230, 231, 233, 239, 256; personality, 95, 109–11, 157–8, 275; relation to Chaucer's family, 153–62; and Spain, 110, 152, 153, 170, 172, 263–4, 266, 279; as Steward of England in Richard's early reign, 228–33, 236, 237, 239–41, 244–5, 247, 256, 260; and Wyclif, 147, 148, 149, 228–9; mentioned, 14, 20, 40, 54, 99, 171–2, 179, 189, 213, 250, 251, 257, 258, 259, 287–8, 307

John of Salisbury, 84
Johnson, Dr. Samuel, 67, 119
Jones, Richard H., 276, 301
jousting, 99–102
justices of the peace, 273–4

Kay, F. George, 181
Kent, county of, 241–2; Chaucer's con-
    nections with, 33, 137, 208, 209,
    267–8, 270–4, 284, 306
Kent, Thomas of, 209
Kilkenny, Statute of, 108
King Richard II (Shakespeare), 51, 99,
    119, 303
Knight, the (character), 50, 111, 178,
    186, 216, 292
Knighton, Henry, 72, 74
Knight's Tale, 78, 100, 102, 105, 167,
    178, 269, 288, 292
Knoll, Sir Robert, 190
Knyvet, Sir John, 218
Krauss, Russell, 158, 160, 161–2

Lack of Steadfastness (Chaucer), 227,
    254
"Lady Meed" (Langland), 13, 186–7
"Lady Philosophy" (Boethius), 87
"Lady White," 54, 116, 165, 176
Lancaster, duke of, *see* John of Gaunt
Lancaster, Henry, earl of ("blind
    Henry"), 27, 30, 36, 41, 42, 45–7,
    48, 54, 92, 116
Lancaster, Henry, earl of (the younger),
    45, 46, 48, 50, 62, 95, 98, 103, 105,
    107, 109, 116, 123–4, 125, 178
Lancaster, Thomas, earl of, 42, 43–6,
    47, 49, 50, 231, 301
Langland, William, 6, 13–14, 15, 56,
    73, 186, 253, 255
languages, study and use of, 70, 80,
    138, 145
Latimer, John, 265
Latimer, William, Lord, 188, 219
law, study of, 88, 129–30, 133–7
Layer, John, 280
Legend of Good Women (Chaucer),
    205, 225, 231, 254, 257, 267, 269, 271,
    272, 286, 312
Leibnitz, Gottfried Wilhelm von, 142
Leland, John, 135–6
Leon, Sir Harve of, 191
libraries, 79, 130, 136, 249

Limoges, siege of, 107, 177, 259
Lincoln's Inn, 131, 133, 134
Lionel, prince of England, 23, 90, 92,
    95, 96, 97, 105, 107–9, 123–5, 126,
    127, 135, 173, 180, 190
logic, study of, 79–80, 81, 82–3
Lollards, 115, 148–9, 150, 151, 189, 225
London, medieval, 21–2, 29–30, 31, 52,
    56–62, 67, 70, 71–2, 172, 183, 184,
    206, 229–30, 231, 306; Black Death
    of 1348–9, 71, 72–4; cathedral
    schools, 79; and Peasant's Revolt,
    244; population figure, 22
lords, 235–6, 264, 298; appellant, 278
Lounsbury, T. R., 125, 161, 163
Love Song of J. Alfred Prufrock, The
    (Eliot), 128
Luce, Simeon, 187
Luther, Martin, 147, 197
Lydgate, John, 56, 64, 158, 225, 291
Lyons, Richard, 35, 207, 219

Machault, Guillaume de, 92, 193–4,
    205, 212
Macrobius, 11, 18, 82, 143, 212
magic, 67–8, 144
Malory, Sir Thomas, 178
Malyn, Agnes, 26–7
Malyn, Robert, 24; *see also* Chaucer,
    Robert
Manciple, the (character), 133, 294,
    310
Manciple's Tale, 165, 292, 294–5
Manly, John Matthews, 22, 26, 118,
    130, 162, 189, 218
manners, medieval, 53–4, 69
Manning(ton), Simon, 33, 274
Man of Law (character), 224, 251, 255,
    288
Man of Law's Tale, 164, 205, 234, 288–9
Margaret of Flanders, 175, 190
Mari, John of, 191
Marie, princess of France, 210, 212,
    217, 218, 248
Mariolatry, 53
"marriage debate," 234, 289–90
Massey, Hugo, 14
Massey, John (the *Gawain*-poet), 14–
    15, 76, 93, 192, 214–15
mathematics, 7, 82, 88, 143
May (character), 65, 199
McKisack, May, 41, 49, 231, 260, 261
medicine, 88, 137, 142 and *n*.

Melibeus, *see Tale of Melibeus*
Melville, Herman, 215
Merchant's Tale, 65, 165, 199
Merciless Parliament (1388), 278, 298
Metamorphoses (Ovid), 80
metaphysics, 140–1, 143
Mile End, meeting at, 245, 260
Miller, the (character), 151, 269, 292
Miller's Tale, 67, 68, 96, 101, 119, 136, 151–2, 165, 188–9, 269, 288
Milton, John, 83, 307
Mirour de l'Omme (Gower), 17, 59, 238
misogyny, 53, 224
monarchy, 168–9, 208, 227, 230, 234–5, 258, 264, 288–90, 298, 301, 303; "marriage debate" on, 234, 289–90
Monk, the (character), 40
Monk's Tale, 202, 221–3, 291
Montagu, William, 99
Monte, Paul de la, 309
Morel, Richard, 252
Morris, William, 22, 55
Morte Arthure (anon.), 12, 13, 98, 99, 222
Mortimer, Sir Edmund, 95, 104
Mortimer, Sir Roger, 5, 27, 36, 40–1, 43, 45–6, 47–8, 50, 95, 98, 99, 104, 113, 114
Mortimer family, 45, 104, 278, 305, 306
music, 193–4; philosophy of, 82, 87, 88, 143, 144
mystery pageants, 96–7

Nájera, Battle of, 170, 171
naval warfare, 51, 70, 102–3
Navarre, 127, 152, 169
Neoplatonism, 18, 77, 144, 185
Neville, Sir John, 219
Neville, Sir William, 252
Newfield, Sir John, 246
Nicholas, David, 71
Nicholas (character), 101, 136, 152
nominalism, 75–6, 82, 138–9, 145–7, 214–15, 225, 292–3, 310
Norfolk, duke of, 300–1
Northampton, John of, 207, 209, 225, 256
Northampton, Treaty of, 48
North Petherton, *see* Petherton Forest
Northumberland, Henry Percy, earl of, 30, 233, 303–4
Northwell, Henry of, 32

Northwell, John of, 61, 65
Northwell, William of, 33
Norwich, bishop of, 264
Nottingham, Thomas Mowbray, earl of, 278, 296, 299, 300
numerology, 87, 143, 217
Nun's Priest, the (character), 215
Nun's Priest's Tale, 242–3, 269, 290, 293

Ockham, William, 18, 145–6, 147
Oman, Charles, 234, 244
L'Ordene de Chevalerie, 178
Order of the Garter, 15, 71, 99, 114, 204, 221
Ormond, earl of, 30
Ovid, 80, 81, 144
Owl and the Nightingale, The (de Guildford), 199
Oxford, 53, 88, 111, 127, 133, 138–9, 143–5, 149–51, 157, 197; Chaucer at, 135–7, 140, 149, 285; rationalists, 82, 193

Padua, 191, 198, 222
Palmer, Thomas, 305
Pan', Philippa, 91, 118; *see also* Chaucer, Philippa Roet
panel-structure poems, 213, 214, 216
papacy, 145, 148, 229, 261; schism, 263–4
Pardoner, the (character), 42, 264, 274, 293
Pardoner's Tale, 72, 172, 174, 193, 290
parliament, 105, 148, 218–22, 235–6, 239, 298–9; Chaucer in, 33, 208, 274; Edward II and, 43, 45–6, 263; Edward III and, 187, 210, 218–19; John of Gaunt and, 148, 187, 210, 219, 221, 228, 230, 231, 233, 239, 256; Richard II and, 260–1, 263, 275–6, 277–8, 298; *see also* Bad Parliament; Commons, House of; Good Parliament; Lords; Merciless Parliament
Parliament of Birds (Chaucer), 11, 153, 163, 200–1, 214–15, 216–21, 251
Parliament of the Three Ages (anon.), 13
Parson, the (character), 12, 216, 239
Parson's Tale, 121, 253
Parzival (Eschenbach), 178
Patch, Howard, 253, 255

Patience (Massey), 14–15, 214
Pearl (Massey), 14–15, 76, 214
peasantry, 210, 235, 236–8, 240–1
Peasants' Revolt of 1381, 16, 111, 148, 207, 234, 236, 240, 241–7, 253, 255–6
Pedro the Cruel, king of Castile, 24, 107, 152, 168–70, 171, 172, 177, 222, 224, 259, 301
Pembroke, earl of, 44, 252
Percy, Sir Thomas, 248, 296
Perrers, Alice, 33, 35, 113, 115, 155, 161, 173, 178–90, 206, 219, 226, 230, 250, 271
Peter IV, king of Aragon, 169
Petherton Forest, 34, 137, 189, 218, 271, 287, 305
Petrarch, Francesco, 81, 191, 202, 206, 214, 221, 222
Philip IV, king of France, 42
Philip VI, king of France, 103
Philip the Bold, Prince, 122, 175
Philipot, John, 207–8, 252
Philippa, queen of England, 47, 50, 60, 91–2, 95, 99, 109, 113–15, 117, 118, 153–5, 156, 157, 172–3, 179–81, 184, 230, 271
Philobiblion (Bury), 138
Physician, the (character), 136, 142, 293
Physician's Tale, 292, 293
physics, 7, 82, 143, 145
Picard, Henry, 30, 31, 32
Pierpont, Reginald, 91
Piers Plowman (Langland), 6, 10, 13–14
Pisano, Andrea, 196–7
Pits, John, 136
Plaghe, Simon de, 33
plague, 72, 172, 175, 177, 235; *see also* Black Death of 1347–51
Plantagenets, 97, 112–13, 221, 232
Plato, 6, 15, 17, 18, 75, 78, 112, 143, 146, 148, 189, 217
Plowman, the (character), 239
Plunkett, Professor, 252
Poe, Edgar Allan, 72, 215
poetry, art of, 87, 128, 137, 138–45, 212–24, 291–2
Poitiers, Battle of, 106, 110, 171
Pole, Michael de la, 261, 263, 275, 278
Pope, Alexander, 217
Poyning, Richard, Lord, 251
Prioress, the (character), 40, 53
Prioress's Tale, 68, 70, 292
Priscian, 80

Provan, Sir James of, 191
Prudence (character), 291
Purgatorio (Dante), 192, 197, 200
Purity (Massey), 14–15, 214
Pythagoras, 143, 217

quadrivium, 88, 137, 143
quotation narrative, 291

Rabelais, François, 20
Ravenstone, William, 79
realism, 216–17; v. nominalism, 146–8, 214–5
Reeve, the (character), 269, 292
Reeve's Tale, 119, 130, 151–2, 165, 224, 268, 269, 288
Regensburg, Berthold of, 67
Renaissance, 17, 193, 200, 213; *see also* humanism; Italy, arts and literature
Retieris (Rethel), battle near, 124
Rheims, siege of, 125
rhetoric (eloquence), study of, 79–80, 81–2, 84–7, 137, 140
Richard II, king of England, 8, 10, 16, 42, 43, 48, 54, 115, 159–60, 173, 210, 212, 221, 225, 226–7, 245–8, 254, 285, 295–304; birth, 115; Chaucer's service to, 20, 33, 34, 128, 156, 174, 208–9, 248–51, 256–9, 262, 267–8, 281–3, 287, 302, 305–7; Gaunt's alleged treason against, 158, 265–6; and Gloucester, 233, 266, 274–9, 298–300; and Ireland, 108, 296; marriages of, 217, 218, 226, 247–8, 256–7, 297–8; murder of, 168, 178, 304; a pacifist, 50, 110, 260–1, 296–7, 298; personality, 260–2, 297–8, 301–2; succession to throne, 221, 228, 230–3, 260; takes power, 279, 280; views on monarchy, 41, 110, 168, 258–60, 264, 288–9, 290, 298, 301–2, 303; and war with France, 236, 275, 296; mentioned, 12, 13, 40, 104, 172, 183, 188, 241, 309
Rickert, Edith, 220
Roet, Sir Paon of, 117, 118, 153
Roman de la Rose, 5, 112; Chaucer's translation of, 127, 128–9
Rose, Edmund, 90, 154
"Rosemounde" (Chaucer), 288
Rotherhithe, 267–8
Russell, Bertrand, 77

St. Augustine, 9–10, 16, 17, 77, 138, 147, 185
St. Bonaventura, 18
St. Cecile, 141
St. Erkenwald (Massey), 14
St. George, 204, 205
St. George's Chapel, Windsor, 281–3
St. Hilary, Marie, 113, 160
St. Jerome, 81
St. Paul, 11, 81, 138
St. Paul's Cathedral, 23, 60, 79
St. Peter, 10
Savoy Palace, 54, 111, 128, 183, 229, 245
Scalacronica (Gray), 124
Scalby, John, 267, 279, 306
Schopenhauer, Arthur, 146
sciences, 82, 88, 143–4
Scogan, Sir Henry, 286–7, 288, 306, 311
Scotland, 41, 42, 43, 45, 296; Black Death in, 73, 74; border raids, 37, 56, 233; 1327 campaign against, 36–40, 102, 103; 1385 campaign against, 261; Treaty of Northampton cessions to, 48
Scrope, Lord Richard, 240, 263
Scrope, Sir Thomas, 124
Scrope-Grosvenor trial, 122, 124–5, 274
Second Nun's Tale, 88, 141, 294
Second Shepherd's Play, 214
Seneca, 138
Shakespeare, William, 3, 4–5, 6, 8, 109, 215, 239, 308; quoted, 51, 99, 119, 303
Shardelowe, Thomas, 268, 272
Sheen palace, 267–8
Shipman, the (character), 149, 203
Shipman's Tale, 40, 288–9
Sibthorp, Robert, 267
Sir Gawain and the Green Knight (Massey), 10, 14, 15, 56, 93, 94, 192, 204, 214
Skeat, W. W., 268
Sluys, battle of, 51, 103
Smithfield, meeting at, 245–7, 260
Soles, William, 251
Some New Light on Chaucer (Manly), 218
Southampton, 32, 68, 70, 73, 102
Southey, Robert, 294
Spain, 110, 152–3, 168–70, 190, 263, 266
Speght, Thomas, 21, 130, 158, 190
Sphere (Chaucer), 88, 271
sports, 62–3, 99–102
Squire, the (character), 91, 111–12
Squire's Tale, 97, 214

Stace, Geoffrey, 26–7
Staplegate, Edmund, 251
sterling, origin of term, 31
Stevens, Wallace, 282
Steward of England (title), 46, 49, 176, 231
Stow, John, 30, 115
Straw, Jack, 242–3
Strode, Ralph, 88, 136, 225
Stub, Bishop, 157
Stury, Sir Richard, 174, 175, 177, 187–8, 208, 210, 211, 219, 220, 282
Sudbury, Simon, archbishop of Canterbury, 148, 226, 232, 240, 244, 245
Summa Theologica (Aquinas), 18
Summoner, the (character), 131, 265
Summoner's Tale, 265
superstitions, 59–60, 66–8
surnames, 24
Swift, Jonathan, 9
Swynford, Katherine Roet, 109, 113, 117, 136 *n.,* 153, 154, 155, 156, 157, 159, 160, 161–2, 213, 297, 307
Swynford, Thomas, 117, 155, 156, 159, 160
Symposium (Plato), 112

Talbot, Thomas, 285
Tale of Melibeus, 130, 273, 288, 291
Tale of Sir Thopas, 292, 294
taxation, 29, 31, 48–9, 185, 239–41; *see also* customs collection
Tempest, The (Shakespeare), 5
Thames River, 102, 211, 282
Thames Street, London, 22, 29–30, 31, 54, 60
theology, 75–8; study of, 88, 137
Theseus, Duke (character), 105
Thomas of Woodstock, duke of Gloucester, 113, 158, 173, 233, 262, 266–7, 274–8, 296–7, 298–300
Thomism, 75, 145, 200; *see also* Aquinas, St. Thomas
Thynne, Francis, 130, 160
Tolleshunt, William, 79
tournaments, 99–102, 226
Tower of London, 101, 137, 245, 281–3
translation, 137–8; exegetical, 8–12, 138, 205
transubstantiation, doctrine of, 148, 149
Trastamara, Henry, *see* Henry II Trastamara, king of Castile
travel, 190, 248–9, 283–4

Treatise on the Astrolabe (Chaucer), 88, 136, 253, 271

Tresilian, Robert, 278

trivium, 80–8, 137, 144

Troilus (character), 17, 121, 167, 195, 199–200, 201, 261–2, 293

Troilus and Criseyde (Chaucer), 11, 16, 18, 82, 97, 118, 120, 136, 157, 163, 166, 197, 199, 214, 215, 257, 261, 271, 272, 286

"Truth" (Chaucer), 13, 187

Twelve Conclusions (of Lollards), 148

Tyler, Wat, 5, 24, 207, 242, 244–7

Tyrwhitt, Thomas, 161, 217

Ugolino of Pisa, 222, 224

university education, 88, 133, 137–9, 143–5

Urban V, Pope, 171, 175

Urban VI, Pope, 263

Usk, Adam, 151, 300, 302

Usk, Thomas, 83, 208, 209, 225, 226

Vache, Sir Philip la, 187, 304

Venour, William, 280

Vere, Robert de, earl of Oxford, duke of Ireland, 259, 265–6, 275–6, 277, 278, 297

villeinage system, 235

Vinsauf, Geoffrey of, 138–9

Virgil, 10, 81, 82, 87, 186

Visconti, Bernabò, of Milan, 222, 249

Visconti, Galeazzo, 249

Visitation of Kent (Philpot), 33

Vox Clamantis (Gower), 16, 17

Walsingham, Thomas, 230, 231, 245–7, 300, 301, 302

Walworth, William, 207–8, 246, 247

Warenne, earl of, 44

warfare, 50, 70, 104, 210, 263; with France, 51, 70, 98–9, 102–6, 152, 172, 174, 177, 210–11, 233–4, 235–6; Scottish border, 36–40, 74, 102, 103, 233 261–2; in Spain, 152–3, 168–70, 263, 266; tactics, 39, 103–4, 106, 177

Warwick, Guy Beauchamp of, 44

Warwick, Thomas Beauchomp, earl of, 277–8, 296, 298, 300

Waxcombe, William, 305

Welshmen, 56

Wesenham, John, 26, 34

Westhale (Westhall) family, 25, 26

Westminster, 268, 309

Westminster Abbey, 282, 296, 302, 309

Westminster Palace, 137, 281

Whitehead, Alfred North, 141

Whiting, B. J., 162

widow, old (character), 40, 269–70

Wife of Bath (character), 51, 120, 166, 189–90, 215, 224, 253–4, 255, 259, 289

Wife of Bath's Tale, 127, 165, 189–90, 260, 288

William II, king of Hainault, 47, 113

Williams, George, 21, 23, 110, 137, 154–5, 156, 158, 161, 162, 207, 255–6

Windsor, Sir William, 180, 187, 219

Winner and Waster (anon.), 13, 204, 205

witchcraft, 67

Wittgenstein, Ludwig, 142

women's status, 25, 53

Worcester, earl of, 30

Wordsworth, William, 83, 286

Worth, Sir Thomas, 305

Wyclif, John, 5, 110, 111, 113, 115, 131, 136, 138–9, 147–9, 157, 162, 215, 226, 228–9, 231, 237, 244, 264, 310

Wykeham, William of, 148, 283

Yeats, William Butler, 244

Yeaveley, Henry, 282

York, duke of, *see* Edmund Langley

Zeeland(ers), 47, 238